Paths to a World-Class University

Lessons from Practices and Experiences

Edited by

Nian Cai Liu, Qi Wang and Ying Cheng
Shanghai Jiao Tong University, P.R. China

SENSE PUBLISHERS
ROTTERDAM/BOSTON/TAIPEI

A C.I.P. record for this book is available from the Library of Congress.

ISBN: 978-94-6091-353-2 (paperback)
ISBN: 978-94-6091-354-9 (hardback)
ISBN: 978-94-6091-355-6 (e-book)

Published by: Sense Publishers,
P.O. Box 21858,
3001 AW Rotterdam,
The Netherlands
https://www.sensepublishers.com

Printed on acid-free paper

TABLE OF CONTENTS

ACKNOWLEDGEMENTS

The editors wish to thank Mr. Peter de Liefde, Sense Publishers, for his support in the publication of this volume; Professor Philip G. Altbach, Monan University Professor and Director of the Center for International Higher Education, Boston College; Dr. Jan Sadlak, President of IREG - International Observatory on Ranking and Academic Excellence; Mr. Derek Maxwell Elli Harris and Mr. Peodair Leihy, for the linguistic editing of the manuscript; and Ms. Yun Miao, for her hard work on formatting the text.

JAMIL SALMI AND NIAN CAI LIU

PATHS TO A WORLD-CLASS UNIVERSITY[1]

The 1998/99 World Development Report: Knowledge for Development (World Bank, 1999) proposed an analytical framework emphasizing the complementary role of four key strategic dimensions to guide countries in the transition to a knowledge-based economy: an appropriate economic and institutional regime, a strong human capital base, a dynamic information infrastructure, and an efficient national innovation system. Higher education is central to all four pillars of this framework, but its role is particularly crucial in support of building a strong human capital base and contributing to an efficient national innovation system. Higher education helps countries build globally competitive economies by developing a skilled, productive, and flexible labour force and by creating, applying, and spreading new ideas and technologies.

Within the higher education system, world-class universities - regarded as research or elite universities - play a critical role in training the professionals, high-level specialists, scientists, and researchers needed by the economy and in generating new knowledge in support of national innovation systems (World Bank, 2002). In this context, an increasingly pressing priority of many governments is to make sure that their top universities are actually operating at the cutting edge of intellectual and scientific development.

WHAT DOES IT MEAN TO BE A WORLD-CLASS UNIVERSITY?

In the past decade, the term "world-class university" has become a catch phrase, not simply for improving the quality of learning and research in higher education, but also, more importantly, for developing the capacity to compete in the global higher education marketplace, through the acquisition, adaptation, and creation of advanced knowledge. With students looking to attend the best possible tertiary institutions that they can afford, often regardless of national borders, and with governments keen on returns on their investments in universities, global standing is becoming an increasingly important concern for institutions around the world (Williams and Van Dyke, 2007). The paradox of the world-class university, however, as Altbach has succinctly and accurately observed, is that "everyone wants one, no one knows what it is, and no one knows how to get one" (Altbach, 2004).

Becoming a member of the exclusive group of world-class universities is not achieved by self-declaration; rather, elite status is conferred by the outside world on the basis of international recognition. Until recently, the process involved a subjective qualification, mostly that of reputation. For example, Ivy League universities in the United States (U.S.), such as Harvard, Yale, or Columbia; the Universities of Oxford and Cambridge in the United Kingdom (U.K.); and the University of Tokyo, have traditionally been counted among the exclusive group of elite universities, but no direct and rigorous measure was available to substantiate their superior status in terms of outstanding results, such as training of graduates, research output, and technology transfer. Even the higher salaries captured by their graduates could be interpreted as a signalling proxy as much as the true value of their education.

With the proliferation of league tables in the past few years, however, more systematic ways of identifying and classifying world-class universities have appeared (IHEP, 2007). Although most of the best-known rankings purport to categorize universities within a given country, there have also been attempts to establish international rankings. The two most comprehensive international rankings, allowing for broad benchmark comparisons of institutions across national borders, are those prepared by the *Times Higher Education* (THE) and Shanghai Jiao Tong University (SJTU). Notwithstanding the serious methodological limitations of any ranking exercise (Salmi and Saroyan 2007), world-class universities are recognized in part for their superior outputs. They produce well-qualified graduates who are in high demand on the labour market; they conduct leading-edge research published in top scientific journals; and in the case of science-and-technology-oriented institutions, they contribute to technical innovations through patents and licences.

The few scholars who have attempted to define what world-class universities have that regular universities do not possess have identified a number of basic features, such as highly qualified faculty; excellence in research; quality teaching; high levels of government and nongovernment sources of funding; international and highly talented students; academic freedom; well-defined autonomous governance structures; and well-equipped facilities for teaching, research, administration, and student life (Altbach, 2004; Khoon et al., 2005; Niland, 2000, 2007). Recent collaborative research on this theme between UK and Chinese universities (Alden

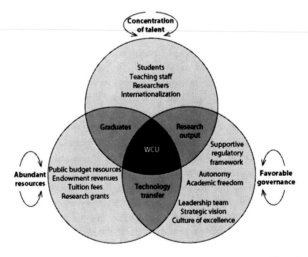

Figure 1. Characteristics of a world-class university: Alignment of key factors.

Source: Created by Jamil Salmi.

and Lin, 2004) has resulted in an even longer list of key attributes, ranging from the international reputation of the university to more abstract concepts, such as the university's contribution to society, both very difficult to measure in an objective manner.

In an attempt to propose a more manageable definition of world-class universities, this report makes the case that the superior results of these institutions (highly sought graduates, leading-edge research, and technology transfer) can essentially be attributed to three complementary sets of factors at play in top universities: (a) a high concentration of talent (faculty and students), (b) abundant resources to offer a rich learning environment and to conduct advanced research, and (c) favourable governance features that encourage strategic vision, innovation, and flexibility and that enable institutions to make decisions and to manage resources without being encumbered by bureaucracy (Figure 1).

PATHS TO TRANSFORMATION

Two complementary perspectives need to be considered in examining how to establish new world-class universities. The first dimension, of an external nature, concerns the role of government at the national, state, and provincial levels and the resources that can be made available to enhance the stature of institutions. The second dimension is internal. It has to do with the individual institutions themselves and the necessary evolution and steps that they need to take to transform themselves into world-class institutions.

In the past, the role of government in nurturing the growth of world-class universities was not a critical factor. In this regard, the history of the Ivy League universities in the United States reveals that, by and large, they grew to prominence as a result of incremental progress, rather than by deliberate government intervention. Similarly, the Universities of Oxford and Cambridge evolved over the centuries of their own volition, with variable levels of public funding, but with considerable autonomy in terms of governance, definition of mission, and direction. Today, how ever, it is unlikely that a world-class university can be rapidly created without a favourable policy environment and direct public initiative and support, if only because of the high costs involved in setting up advanced research facilities and capacities.

Recent international experience shows that three basic strategies can be followed to establish world-class universities:
- Governments could consider upgrading a small number of existing universities that have the potential for excelling (picking winners).
- Governments could encourage a number of existing institutions to merge and transform into a new university that would achieve the type of synergies corresponding to a world-class institution (hybrid formula).
- Governments could create new world-class universities from scratch (clean-slate approach).

Table 1 summarizes the pros and cons of each approach. It should be noted that these generic approaches are not mutually incompatible and that countries may pursue a combination of strategies based on these models.

*Table 1. Costs and benefits of strategic approaches for establishing
world-class universities*

Conditions	Approach		
	Upgrading existing institutions	*Merging existing institutions*	*Creating new institutions*
Ability to attract talent	Difficult to renew staff and change the brand to attract top students	Opportunity to change the leadership and to attract new staff; existing staff may resist	Opportunity to select the best (staff and students); difficulties in recruiting top students to "unknown" institution; need to build up research and teaching traditions
Costs	Less expensive	Neutral	More expensive
Governance	Difficult to change mode of operation within same regulatory framework	More likely to work with legal status different from that of existing institutions	Opportunity to create appropriate regulatory and incentives framework
Institutional culture	Difficult to transform from within	May be difficult to create a new identity out of distinct institutional cultures	Opportunity to create culture of excellence
Change management	Major consultation and communication campaign with all stakeholders	"Normative" approach to educate all stakeholders about expected norms and institutional culture	"Environmentally adaptive" approach to communicate and socially market the new institution

Source: Created by Jamil Salmi.

The establishment of a world-class university requires, above all, strong leadership, a bold vision of the institution's mission and goals, and a clearly articulated strategic plan to translate the vision into concrete targets and programmes. Universities that aspire to better results engage in an objective assessment of their strengths and areas for improvement, set new stretch goals, and design and implement a renewal plan that can lead to improved performance. By contrast, many institutions are complacent in their outlook, lack an ambitious vision of a better future, and continue to operate as they have in the past, ending up with a growing performance gap compared with that of their national or international competitors.

The following key questions need to be answered by governments and institutions to guide the quest toward establishing world-class universities:

- Why does the country need a world-class university? What is the economic rationale and the expected added value compared with the contribution of existing institutions?
- What is the vision for this university? What niche will it occupy?
- How many world-class universities are desirable and affordable as a public sector investment?

- What strategy would work best in the country context: upgrading existing institutions, merging existing institutions, or creating new institutions?
- What should be the selection process among existing institutions if the first or second approach is chosen?
- What will be the relationship and articulation between the new institution(s) and existing higher education institutions?
- How will the transformation be financed? What share should fall under the public budget? What share should be borne by the private sector? What incentives should be offered (for example, land grants and tax exemptions)?
- What are the governance arrangements that must be put in place to facilitate this transformation and support suitable management practices?
- What level of autonomy and forms of accountability will be appropriate?
- What will the government's role be in this process?
- How can the institution build the best leadership team?
- What are the vision and mission statements, and what are the specific goals that the university is seeking to achieve?
- In what niche(s) will it pursue excellence in teaching and research?
- What is the target student population?
- What are the internationalization goals that the university needs to achieve (with regard to faculty, students, programmes, and so forth)?
- What is the likely cost of the proposed qualitative leap, and how is it going to be funded?
- How will success be measured? What monitoring systems, outcome indicators, and accountability mechanisms will be used?

THE CHALLENGES OF ESTABLISHING WORLD-CLASS UNIVERSITIES

The highest-ranked universities are the ones that make significant contributions to the advancement of knowledge through research, teach with the most innovative curricula and pedagogical methods under the most conducive circumstances, make research an integral component of undergraduate teaching, and produce graduates who stand out because of their success in intensely competitive arenas during their education and (more importantly) after graduation.

There is no universal recipe or magic formula for making a world-class university. National contexts and institutional models vary widely. Therefore, each country must choose, from among the various possible pathways, a strategy that plays to its strengths and resources. International experience provides a few lessons regarding the key features of such universities—high concentrations of talent, abundance of resources, and flexible governance arrangements—and successful approaches to move in that direction, from upgrading or merging existing institutions to creating new institutions altogether.

Furthermore, the transformation of the university system cannot take place in isolation. A long-term vision for creating world-class universities - and its implementation - should be closely articulated with: (a) the country's overall economic and social development strategy, (b) ongoing changes and planned reforms at the lower levels of the education system, and (c) plans for the development of other types of higher education institutions to build an integrated system of teaching, research, and technology-oriented institutions.

Although world-class institutions are commonly equated with top research universities, there are also world-class higher education institutions that are neither research focused nor operate as universities in the strictest interpretation of the term. As countries embark on the task of establishing world-class institutions, they must also consider the need to create, besides research universities, excellent alternative institutions to meet the wide range of education and training needs that the higher education system is expected to satisfy. The growing debate on measuring learning outcomes at the higher education level is testimony to the recognition that excellence is not only about achieving outstanding results with outstanding students but ought, perhaps, to be also measured in terms of how much added value is given by institutions in addressing the specific learning needs of an increasingly diverse student population.

Finally, the building pressures and momentum behind the push for world-class universities must be examined within the proper context, so as to avoid over-dramatization of the value and importance of world-class institutions and distortions in resource allocation patterns within national higher education systems. Even in a global knowledge economy, where every nation, both developed and developing, is seeking to increase its share of the economic pie, the hype surrounding world-class institutions far exceeds the need and capacity for many systems to benefit from such advanced education and research opportunities, at least in the short term.

As with other service industries, not every nation needs comprehensive world-class universities, at least not while more fundamental higher education needs are not being met. World-class research institutions require huge financial commitments, a concentration of exceptional human capital, and governance policies that allow for top-notch teaching and research. Many nations would in all likelihood benefit from an initial focus on developing the best national universities possible, modelled perhaps on those developed as the land-grant institutions in the United States during the 19th century or the polytechnic universities of Germany and Canada. Such institutions would emphasize the diverse learning and training needs of the domestic student population and economy. Focusing efforts on the local community and economy, such institutions could lead to more effective and sustainable development than broader world-class aspirations. Regardless, institutions will inevitably, from here on out, be increasingly subject to comparisons and rankings, and those deemed to be the best in these rankings of research universities will continue be considered the very best in the world.

CONTRIBUTIONS TO THIS VOLUME

Reflecting the above points, the present volume provides insights into recent and ongoing experiences of building world-class universities, both at a national level and at an institutional level. It collects fifteen essays, most of which originated from papers presented at the "3rd International Conference on World-Class Universities (WCU-3)", held in November 2009 in Shanghai, China, and organized by the Centre for World-Class Universities at the Shanghai Jiao Tong University. The book is structured into two inter-related parts, that is, "the Role of World-Class Universities in National Systems" and "Institutional Practices of Building World-Class Universities".

The Role of World-Class Universities in National Systems

This section discusses the role of world-class universities in national education and research systems and addresses issues and concerns that governments need to take into account in making education policies. It also focuses on the nature of the elite research university in different socio-economic contexts, its contribution to the national higher education and research system, and its development in the current context of globalization and economic crisis.

In Marginson's chapter, the findings of ongoing research on global perspectives and strategies of Asia-Pacific research universities are presented. Marginson emphasizes that in spite of their varied strategic circumstances and resources according to national factors, the notion of world-class, such as global standing and institution effectiveness, has become the universal emphasis of research universities. As a result, strategies and actions of global, national as well as local dimensions need to be coordinated and integrated in universities' transformation.

Both Gallagher's and Yonezawa's chapters consider the policy tensions between developing world-class research universities and the quality and equity issues of research and education. Gallagher argues that a combination, that is, autonomous institutions operating in a market environment, with mission-based funding compacts as a means of safeguarding public good interests, allowing the universities the flexibility to be competitive and responsive. Drawing attention to the different contexts of world-class university policies among East Asian countries, in particular Japan's "Global 30" scheme, Yonezawa highlights the practical difficulty of internationalization of leading research universities without deteriorating research and education performance.

Next, in response to the point raised above, that is, transformation of higher education should be closely articulated with a range of social, economic and educational factors in relation to their country, Agachi, Moraru, Cucuruzan and Curaj argue that the possible route for Romania to develop universities of excellence is to build research intensive universities, whilst in the mean time turning a few universities into the world-class category. Ruiz-Rodgers shares the National University of Colombia's experience of building an internationally recognized centre of research and teaching within a different context of acute social strife, economic downturns and civil violence.

Van der Wende's contribution shows that the proposed European university ranking, a multi-dimensional university ranking, covering the various institution missions of education, research, innovation, internationalization, community outreach and employability. If this approach were adopted, it would have implications for national and institutional development, in terms of cooperation and competition, in that it would encourage and stimulate diversity of the European higher education system, whilst enhancing its convergence, and ultimately strengthen its position in global competition.

Institutional Practices of Building World-Class Universities

This section presents different strategies adopted by institutions around the world, in both developed and developing countries, in building universities and research centres of excellence. These practices can be mainly categorized into five main aspects, namely, building world-class universities requiring clear visions, strategic planning and strong management; high-quality research and teaching; effective human resources management; global/international partnership; and building a culture of quality.

Reflecting on the current world financial crisis, Casteen emphasizes the role of "Effective University Management in Difficult Times". In spite of the discrepancies among colleges and universities in the US, many institutions have experienced common challenges in recent decades. Universities, particularly public universities in the US, have been affected by massive reductions in state support with increasing demand for student enrolment at the same time. These pressures have forced the universities to seek greater operating autonomy from their respective state governments, to reform tuition policy while ensuring access, diversity and affordability issues, and have led to increased dependency on private support. Casteen also points out that the current economic downturn offers opportunities in the US to re-examine common practices in each area, re-think university governance, cut back on nonessential spending, and find less expensive ways of achieving goals, whilst sustaining excellence in teaching, research and service. The experience of Ecole Polytechnique Fédérale de Lausanne (EPFL) presented by Noukakis, Ricci and Vetterli reveals its own recipes to cope with academic challenges by asserting its mission, changing its structure and developing a new corporate culture. Specific strategies for other universities to draw on include designing clear positioning and action plans, improving quality of people at key managerial positions, encouraging competitive recruitment of senior and junior faculty, promoting interdisciplinary teaching and research, and diversifying funding resources. Zè Amvela's contribution shares the University of Yaoundé's experience of strategic planning and its concrete measures taken in the aspects of quality teaching and research, interdisciplinary research and international cooperation.

Building world-class universities requires high-quality research and teaching. Marlin draws the readers' attention to the tension between the desire of the university management to improve research performance and that of individual researchers to pursue their own research agenda. From Flinders University's experience, Marlin argues that identifying the sources of research support and engaging the university research community in the selection process are of great importance in conducting strategic research planning.

Making references to the National University of Singapore's experience, Ramakrishna and Krishna offer six factors for developing and supporting leading research intensive universities, namely, strong commitment for global recruitment of faculty, effective educational and research network with world leading institutions, solid support on building research infrastructure, attracting best talent including students and faculty, development of multi-disciplinary research to address national and global issues and challenges, and positive and harmonious partnership with the private sector and policy makers.

Following Ramakrishna and Krishna's point on educational and research network, Grant provides an account of the Global Partnership Network (GPN) established among five universities from different parts of the world in 2008. The GPN is a sustainable, research-led, tight multilateral network, emphasising professional education and curricular innovation. In spite of its initial success, Grant argues that the GPN needs to ensure its internationally limited membership, strong mobility for both students and faculty at all levels, international benchmarking for teaching and research excellence, multilateral research innovation and close co-operation among the members in its sustainable development. Maurer and Zheng review the University of Nebraska Medical Center's (UNMC) effort and policies to "Become a World-Renowned Health Sciences Centre in the Era of the Global Market", particularly in the aspect of promoting academic talent. Agreeing with Grant's argument, Maurer and Zheng propose that close international collaboration with prominent partners will enable their institution to achieve the goal of being world-class, as the strengths of each partner could be utilized towards a common goal, in this case that of meeting the healthcare needs of a whole population for our current global economy.

In his contribution, Lanarès argues that going towards excellence means not only creating and operating a rigorous quality assurance system, but also developing a culture of quality. The experience of the University of Lausanne implies three steps are needed to reach a broad convergence of ways of thinking and acting about quality and associated values, that is, to identify core values and the creation of an adhesion to these values, to translate the values into both concepts and practices of the quality system, and to influence collective and individual practices. The development of a culture of quality is a long term process and requires critical evaluation.

This book not only represents a contribution to the ongoing discussion on the topic of building world-class universities, but can be seen as being a continuation of the previous two volumes on this topic - "World-Class Universities and Ranking: Aiming beyond Status" and "The World-Class University as Part of a New Higher Education Paradigm: From Institutional Qualities to Systemic Excellence" (Sadlak and Liu, 2007 and 2009).

NOTES

[1] This introductory paper is based on the keynote speech of Jamil Salmi at the WCU-3 Conference. Part of the content is excerpted from Jamil Salmi's book entitled 'The Challenge of Establishing World-Class Universities' published by the World Bank in 2009, reproduced here with the World Bank's permission.

REFERENCES

Alden, J., & Lin, G. (2004). *Benchmarking the characteristics of a world-class university: Developing an international strategy at university level*. London: Leadership Foundation for Higher Education.

Altbach, P. G. (2004, January-February). The costs and benefits of world-class universities. *Academe 90*(1). Retrieved from http://www.aaup.org/AAUP/pubsres/academe/2004/JF/Feat/altb.htm

Institute for Higher Education Policy (IHEP). (2007). *College and university ranking systems: Global perspectives and American challenges*. Washington, DC: IHEP. Retrieved from http://www.ihep.org/assets/files/publications/a-f/CollegeRankingSystems.pdf

Khoon, K. A., Shuko, R., Hassan, O., Saleh, Z., Hamzah, A., Ismai R. L., et al. (2005, December). Hallmark of a world-class university. *College Student Journal*, Retrieved from http://findarticles.com/p/articles/mi_m0FCR/is_4_39/ai_n16123684.

Niland, J. (2000, February 3). The challenge of building world-class universities in the Asian region. *ON LINE Opinion*. Retrieved April 10, 2006 from http://www.onlineopinion.com.au/view.asp?article=997

Niland, J. (2007). The challenge of building world-class universities. In J. Sadlak & N. C. Liu (Eds.), *The world-class university and ranking: Aiming beyond status*. Bucharest: UNESCO-CEPES.

Sadlak, J., & Liu, N. C. (2007). *The world-class university and ranking: Aiming beyond status*. Bucharest: UNESCO-CEPES.

Sadlak, J., & Liu, N. C. (2009). *The world-class university as part of a new higher education paradigm: From institutional qualities to systemic excellence*. Bucharest: UNESCO-CEPES.

Salmi, J., & Saroyan, A. (2007). League tables as policy instruments: Uses and misuses. *Higher Education Management and Policy, 19*(2), 24–62.

Williams, R., & Van Dyke, N. (2007, June). Measuring the international standing of universities with an application to Australian Universities. *Higher Education, 53*(6), 819–841.

World Bank. (1999). World development report 1998/99: Knowledge for development. Washington, DC: World Bank. Retrieved from http://www.worldbank.org/wdr/wdr98/contents.htm

World Bank. (2002). *Constructing knowledge societies: New challenges for tertiary education*. Washington, DC: World Bank. Retrieved from http://go.worldbank.org/N2QADMBNI0

Yusuf, S., & Nabeshima, K. (2007). *How universities promote economic growth*. Washington DC: World Bank.

Jamil Salmi
The World Bank

Nian Cai Liu
Graduate School of Education
Shanghai Jiao Tong University, China

SECTION I:
THE ROLE OF WORLD-CLASS
UNIVERSITIES IN NATIONAL SYSTEMS

SIMON MARGINSON

1. GLOBAL PERSPECTIVES AND STRATEGIES OF ASIA-PACIFIC RESEARCH UNIVERSITIES

INTRODUCTION

Globalization is the tendency towards convergence and integration on the world scale (Held, et al., 1999). All research universities are now immersed in processes of globalization. This is directly apparent in the power of the global research system in local affairs. The drive to publish in journals with international standing is now universal to the science disciplines in research universities. Another global system is apparent in the impact of university comparisons and rankings on the local and national status of universities. A comparative survey by Ellen Hazelkorn (2008) for the OECD showed that comparative rankings and research output metrics have been quickly adopted in the visions, performance measurement systems and policy goals of both national governments and institutions. Furthermore, they enter the funding decisions of corporations and donors, and affect student choices. Globalization is also apparent in the growing mobility of students and faculty (Enders and De Weert, 2009). In this regard, between 2000 and 2007 the number of cross-border students increased by 59%, an annual rate of 7%, reaching a total three million a year (OECD, 2009, p. 312). Doctoral student mobility and the short-term movement of faculty are also growing although the trend in long-term academic migration is less clear (Marginson, 2009). Policy borrowing and the partial convergence in policy frameworks and organizational templates, albeit with national and local rhythms and variations (King, 2009), are other forms of globalization in higher education.

Individual universities, and individual national systems of higher education, do more than respond to globalization, as they are also primary drivers of global flows in knowledge, communications and people movement. Leading research universities are among the most internationalized and cosmopolitan of all human organizations and they constitute a world-wide network in which the Internet presence of each is visible to all the others. Rankings create the sense of a single common environment in education and research, such that all can be compared with each other. Meeting each other in conferences and on the web, in working together and through personnel exchange, research universities are continually reminded that they share essential attributes. Everywhere, university leaders instinctively understand - and tend to sympathize with - their counterparts across the world.

Universities and national systems of higher education are together creating a remarkable new dimension of activity, the global dimension of action, which is

N.C. Liu et al., (eds.), Paths to a World-Class University: Lessons from Practices and Experiences, 3–27.

positioned across and beyond the nation-state systems. In the last twenty years, especially the last ten, many cross-border initiatives and global strategies have emerged and Table 1 below provides a summary of these.

Table 1. Developmental strategies that are creating the global dimension of higher education and knowledge

	Strategy	Description/examples	Global spatial meanings
Strategies largely driven by national governments	Capacity building in research	Investment in research universities and institutes designed to lift the volume and quantity of research activity, with a view to strengthening national R&D-led innovation and/or the position of national universities in global rankings. There is now a global "arms race" in innovation spending in many countries. May be joined to policies of greater concentration of research in selected institutions, merger programmes, etc. *e.g. China, Korea, Germany, France*	A long-standing policy option for "national competition states" that has taken on a new urgency and greater importance in the more global era.
	Recreation of nation/city as a "global hub" for education and research activities	Building of the global role of local education and research institutions; together with investment in precinct, infrastructure and changes to policy and regulation, designed to attract: foreign education and research providers, students and investment capital. *e.g. Singapore, Qatar*	Designed to pull global flows of knowledge, people and capital towards a particular locality. May be joined to national capacity building in research, and educational exports.
	Negotiation of a global system of free trade in educational services, through WTO-GATS	Nations deregulate their education systems sufficiently to permit entry of foreign providers on the same terms as local providers, including subsidies etc.	The recreation of worldwide higher education as a single space for business and trade. (This has had little support among either national governments or universities and has not happened).

Table 1. (Continued)

Largely university-driven strategies	Partnerships between universities	Universities sign agreements with similar institutions in other countries; and carry out cooperative joint activities in: personnel and student exchange, curriculum, research, university organization, benchmarking, etc. *e.g. All research universities*	A longstanding strategy used much more in the last two decades. The effect is to create a lattice-like network around each university as the node. Some of these nodes are much thicker than others, indicating broader and more intensive global connectedness.
	University consortia	Formal networks consisting of a large number of university partners, typically 10-30. Sometimes more intensive micro-consortia are developed, with 3–5 partners. Activities are for university partnerships. *e.g. Universitas 21, Association of Pacific Rim Universities*	Consortia are also positioning devices with universities drawing status benefits from the strongest of their partners. The level of activity conducted through these large networks varies, but some universities drive a significant proportion of global work this way. Others maintain a broad set of connections and options.
	Transnational campuses	Universities establish branch campuses in another country, either in their own right (providing the premises themselves) or in alliance with a local partner that manages the site. Branch campuses are specifically permitted to operate by the local authorities. *e.g. University of Nottingham (UK) in Malaysia and China, RMIT University (Australia) in Vietnam*	Such foreign campuses can influence local educational developments over time, and also encourage more multiple or hybrid approaches and reciprocal flows of influence, with potential to leak back to the "mother" institution.
	Global "e-Universities"	Virtual delivery of programmes on the Internet, by either established universities or commercial providers specifically created for the purpose. Curriculum, student assessment, credentialing and administration are provided from one central location. Teaching intensity varies. *e.g. Cardean University, U21 Global, the University of Phoenix online*	Between the mid 1990s and the early 2000s there were significant investments in stand-alone e-U's, but they were unsuccessful in recruiting enough students. E-learning provided alongside or joined to face-to-face programmes, e.g. at the University of Phoenix, has been more successful.

Table 1. (Continued)

Strategies driven by both government and universities	Export of education on a fully commercial basis	Higher education in a national system deregulated as necessary to enable the provision of full fee places to international students, with provider institutions free to determine price and volume. e.g. the UK, Australia	Now a large scale trading industry; and the one established form of global educational capitalism. It has accelerated cross-border student mobility and positioned universities and students as entrepreneurs/consumers, though both also engage in non commercial global activities, for example, in relation to research.
	Knowledge city developments	Investment by universities, city authorities and governments in precinct and infrastructure, designed to attract foreign education and research providers, students and investment capital. A more modest version of the "hub" strategy that is often centred on promoting a small number of universities. e.g. numerous cities	Versions of this strategy are widely practiced among nations with advanced education and research systems. Some cities place much emphasis on this kind of mission in their develop-ment profiles. The balance between commercial international education and R&D varies.
	Regional developments in higher education and research	Agreed regional (pan-national) cooperation between national higher education systems, including: common research grant programmes; measures to align degree structures, curriculum contents and professional requirements; common systems for the recognition of institutions and qualifications, and quality assurance systems; comparison, ranking and evaluation of institutions on a regional basis. e.g. the formation of the European Higher Education and European Research Areas, via the Bologna reforms	Regional system building and partial convergence in higher education and research in Europe is creating a meso-level of activity between the national and global dimensions, and in the longer run is aimed at positioning Europe so as to be able to act as a unit on the global stage. It also encourages enhanced investments in higher education and research in Europe. There are also embryonic regional developments in South America and Southeast Asia.
Strategies pursued by multi-actors (universities, governments, publishing companies, etc.)	Data-based global comparisons of universities, and of research and publication/ citation	Comparisons of the number of leading researchers, publications and/or citations used to generate a vertical "league table" of university performance. e.g. Shanghai Jiao Tong University rankings, Leiden CWTS, Taiwan HEEACT	Outside the USA, global comparisons have been decisive in imposing on all universities overarching measures of performance and status, relativizing national performance measures,

Table 1. (Continued)

	outputs on a university-wide or field specific basis.	Comparisons of universities based on a range of elements combined into a single index and league table. *e.g. Times Higher Education Supplement*	which are now constantly referenced in debates about higher education and in investment decisions by: students, researchers, business and industry, and governments. More than any other method global rankings create an imagining of the global dimension of higher education.

The global dimension of higher education is being formed by three kinds of action. First, *acts of imagination*. As will be described below, leaders imagine the global dimension as a field of practical activity, and they imagine their institution's global activity prior to the attempt to create it. Second, the global dimension involves *acts of production* - global outputs such as research knowledge, messages, open courseware and other web postings, and global teaching programmes, like commercial degrees and e-U's. Third, the global dimension involves *acts of regulation*. Governments set many of the conditions of global activity, through the regulation of national systems, and via bilateral and multilateral negotiations.

Many universities in the Asia-Pacific region are involved in the formation of the global dimension of higher education (Marginson et al., forthcoming). However, some are more intensively involved than others owing to both their conditions and their choices. Moreover, the pattern of global inequalities means that the different national systems, individual institutions and individual university leaders are located differentially within the global dimension of action, whereby some have more global options. In this regard, some can work the global dimension as an extension of their local/national space, whereas for others it is a much more difficult terrain to navigate. Nevertheless, for all national research universities the global dimension is proving to be inevitable in its demands and transformational in its effects.

The chapter draws on a set of case studies of research universities in the Asia-Pacific region to review their global visions and strategies. Case studies were conducted in one leading national research university in each of 12 countries. The material drawn on in the paper is primarily taken from the interviews with the university head - the president, rector or vice-chancellor.

A Note on the Research

In this study, the Asia-Pacific region is broadly defined so as to include the Americas. The universities included are: Universitas Indonesia, the National University of Singapore, the University of Malaya in Malaysia, Chulalongkorn University in Thailand, the Vietnam National University in Hanoi, the University of Tokyo in Japan, the Australian National University, the University of Auckland in New Zealand, the University of Toronto in Canada, the University of Illinois (Urbana-Champaign) in the USA, the Universidad Nacional Autonoma de Mexico, and two contrasting Netherlands universities, Leiden University, and the University of Twente, which allows for a comparison with Asia-Pacific institutions. Leiden is a leading research-intensive university, whereas Twente is a newer technological university of less storied status.[1]

In each institution, between 12 and 20 interviews were conducted, however, this paper draws almost solely on the interviews with the respective university president/ rector/vice-chancellor. The interviews focused on the university leaders' imaginings of the global space, how they understand globalization; the tools they use to observe and interpret it; their perceptions of commonalities and differences between countries and universities; how globalization affects the imperatives confronting nation and university; the scope for initiative and response; the global/national/local interfaces, and whether and to what extent national policy helps or hinders the presidents; and their priorities for development of their own global operations.

The case study programme was conducted in institutions broadly similar within their nations: all are leading research universities, and nearly all are generally understood to be the number one or number two universities in the country. All are national and public sector institutions, and have been historically shaped by government. When compared with each other, from a global perspective, the individual universities are very different from each other in their levels of: resources, research performance and their rankings. Differing levels of funding and historically accumulated resources, and different languages of use, all affect the relative position. Because a common template of institutional type is used, these global variations are not so much due to differences in the missions or statuses of these universities within their respective national systems, but rather the global variations shown here are shaped by differences between the nations in terms of resources and also by local factors in each institution that can be identified by studying its history and organization. In this manner, the study helps to map the global dimension of action in higher education, by clarifying the place each national system has within the global setting and the same time eliciting local specific factors.

Local factors like history, organizational cultures, systems, policies and leadership closely affect institutions. For example the Universities of Tokyo and Indonesia, Vietnam National University and Chulalongkorn all train capital city elites, but only Tokyo was built by the nation into a global research powerhouse. UNAM plays the overwhelming role in Mexico; it conducts 30 per cent of all research and is closely affected by national politics. It is also less global in orientation than some other universities. Leiden in the Netherlands is very international in mission. Likewise the Australian National University has specialized in research and international networking since its foundation in 1946.

GLOBAL STRATEGIES OF UNIVERSITIES

In the emerging global dimension of higher education and research, some global strategies are led by governments, some by universities or their units, and others by publishing companies and other corporations. Often, a key initiating role is played by individual university executive leaders. Table 1 summarizes the strategies.

These global strategies have changed the possibilities, and the necessities, affecting all national systems and research universities. They are a mixture of old and new. There was always some international activity in higher education, but the global work has been greatly facilitated by synchronous electronic communication and one-world visualization enabled by the Internet. The global strategies employed today include: research concentrations; education hub strategies designed to pull global flows into the city or nation; cross-border collaborations, alliances and consortia; region-building in higher education, especially but not only in Europe; the commercial marketing of international education at home; the creation of transnational (offshore) campuses on a partner or stand-alone basis; and the creation of global "e-universities", designed to reach students everywhere. Some universities pursue a number of these strategies simultaneously.

At the same time, two other kinds of initiative have contributed to shaping and defining the global dimension of higher education and research. One is the process of multilateral trade liberalization through WTO-GATS, though the momentum for that development now seems to have slowed. The other is global comparisons, rankings and moves towards a world classification of the higher education sector.

The global strategies of universities and systems have been partly recession proof, thus indicating the universal creative momentum of globalization. In this regard, during the global financial crisis, with its downward pressure on budgets in most countries, much cross-border activity kept growing, for example, commercial exports and research collaborations. However, the fact that the financial capacity of some universities and national systems has been reduced must have inhibited some cross-border activity - after all the recession has inhibited activity in higher education as a whole, and cross-border work has to be subsidized from local and national resources. Nevertheless, cross-border activity has not been the first item jettisoned, which might have been expected a generation ago. This suggests that global activity is not longer considered ephemeral or at the margins of more substantial national and local functions, and that global activity has now become central and essential to the "Idea of a University".

WORLD-CLASS GLOBAL RESEARCH UNIVERSITIES (WCGRU)

At the institutional level the creation of global activity would appear to proceed through three phases, which are sometimes pushed together. First, the institution or nation concerned builds the *capacity* to operate globally, for example in research. Second, it focuses on improving global *connectivity*, not just electronically, but through partnerships, networks and the ongoing exchange of: personnel, staff and students. The third phase is global *activity*. University executives sometimes see building capacity and connectivity as ends in themselves, but capacity and connectivity are also conditions for global activity, in that once global capacity and global connectivity are established, the institution (or national system) has the freedom to act globally.

The global capacity of the individual university depends on its infrastructure: financial resources, physical resources such as communications and transport, facilities and specialist equipment, cultural/linguistic and intellectual resources, and organizational and regulatory mechanisms, including internal cultures and the rhetoric, systems and policies of the institutional and academic leaders. However, mission statements can be reinvented quicker than university resources, which are history-bound and practice dependant. Global capacity is also created and sustained in processes of institutionalization, the regularization of global relationships and interactions to embed them in the life of the institution (Held et al., 1999, p. 19). In this process, the university becomes not just self-referenced and nationally-referenced, but globally-referenced and this perspective is crucial, in that it needs to be able see its position in the global context if it is going to develop optimizing strategies. Moreover, global referencing is powerful in its effects on university thinking and in the present era of communicative globalization there has been the emergence of a new "Idea of a University", that of the "World-class Global Research University" or WCGRU.

The term "world-class university" (SJTUGSE, 2009) has been criticized, for being normative, thereby lacking an objective definition and thus immediately leads to the posing of the question: "What is world-class?" It has been lampooned by some scholars, particularly those in the United States, where all research institutions are secure in their global status, but the term is entirely meaningful for those nations and those universities who aspire to it. "World-class university" is an aspirational notion, one which reflects the desire to be globally effective and to be seen as such by the entire world.

In this context the term "Global Research University" (GRU) (Ma, 2008; Marginson, 2008) provides an objective descriptor that gives content to the notion of a "world-class university". A GRU must be globally networked, globally recognized and effective in local, national and global action. Moreover, it must house a global research capability and output in several fields, and maintain staff capable of inter-preting and applying findings in most fields of knowledge. Furthermore, it needs to have a viable local doctoral programme in some fields. Nowadays, owing to widening of aspirations, the research university functions of knowledge creation, dissemination, storage and transmission, and also research training, are now spreading from a limited group of nations to the majority of nations. In addition, a GRU must also pay academic faculty enough to attract and hold those staff with the potential to be globally mobile; or alternatively, inspire an affective commitment to university or nation that is strong enough to compensate for salaries below globally competitive levels, so as to be able to maintain stability in policy, funding and organization and to make the local setting acceptably habitable for staff and students.

Research capacity is central to the WCGRU for four reasons. First, knowledge is the common currency, the medium of exchange in which research universities deal and collaborate and in fact is often even more important to them than money, for it is already a global public good of economic value (Stiglitz, 1999). Further, in its natural state it flows freely across borders and is used everywhere without losing its value. Arguably, globalization has enhanced the universal character and intrinsic importance of knowledge. Second, the creation, interpretation and codification of knowledge, in the form of research, distinguishes such universities from other educational institutions, and almost all social organizations. Third, research capacity is closely associated with dominant notions of the "Idea of a University". Fourth, it is taken into nation-building strategies. This embedding of the university in research is grounded in the historical military and economic role of science and technology, which predates communicative globalization. Above all it was installed by the creation of the nuclear weapons that closed the Second World War. Thus research performance has long been the marker of university status, even in relation to first degree education where, strictly speaking, research is not in play.

In the interviews with Asia-Pacific presidents the aspiration to be a WCGRU was especially strongly felt in the universities most marginal to the global metropolis: Universitas Indonesia, Vietnam National University and the University of Malaya. It also concerned the University of Auckland, whose leaders nursed a sense of inadequacy in relation to the university's global position, even though Auckland was in the top 300 on research performance.

Our ambition is to meet international standards. To be in the top 200 universities in the world. Of course, this is the long-term vision. Not in one day… Our mission is to become a research university that meets international standards. We focus all our efforts to achieve that. (Mai Trong Nhuan, President, the Vietnam National University Hanoi)

The dividing line between being a WCGRU as opposed to not is a crucial distinction of each national system, for it demarcates the global sector from the rest. It is also expressed within institutions, in the distinction between on the one hand, research and graduate research or doctoral education, which are global activities, and on the other, first degree teaching and medium level graduate professional programmes (Horta, 2009). Several of the presidents emphasized that building global research activity in their institutions was central to their aspirations for WCGRU status. Moreover, they also expressed the view that English language publications have become more important than before:

Q. What impact has globalization had on a public research university like the University of Malaya?

A. We are now putting a lot of effort, money and resources and manpower into the research field… promotion to professor and associate professor now depends largely on publication. (Hashim Yaacob, Vice-Chancellor, University of Malaya)

Research development was touched upon in one way or another by all presidents. In this regard, the leaders of the Universities of Toronto, Illinois, Tokyo, Leiden and the Australian National University, all located in the Shanghai Jiao Tong University top 100, all expressed the view that they were secure about their standing as research universities, but took for granted the need to continually improve research outcomes.

ACTS OF IMAGINATION

Sources of the Imagination

In the study, interviewees were asked how they gathered information about global trends and developments on a continuing basis. For the most part, they emphasized networking with other presidents, consortia and other international meetings, and data gathered by their own personnel working on international matters. Moreover, person-to-person contact was seen as more effective than videoconferencing and the Tokyo executive vice-president, a member of the OECD committee for Science, Technology and Policy emphasized the importance of the regular OECD meetings: "That is a very big source". Only a small number were extensive readers, but all were regular and active users of email, and most used the Internet directly and frequently, for media and other sources.

> Now it is the era of information. We get lots of information from personal networking, and university organizations overseas, which always conduct workshops about the development of universities in the era of globalization. We also get information from the Internet, and journals of higher education, which can give us perspective. Next week I go to England for a meeting of Indonesian rectors on university management. We have been invited by the British Council. (Usman Chatib Warsa, Rector, Universitas Indonesia)

> The trick, of course, is to filter out what's good and useful. You have to be careful not to be too driven by your own prejudices. To some extent you talk to people with whom you're comfortable. So it's a matter of trying to step away from that and think about different ways of doing things. (Stuart McCutcheon, Vice-Chancellor, University of Auckland)

> It's absolutely astonishing how much one now draws information from all over the world in making any decision about any aspect of the university … I'm old enough to remember when travel was quite exotic, when colleagues would come back with slides from some remote place. In the small town where I grew up, you would have the high school auditorium filled with travelogue presentations, where some individual would present a speech and show slides. This was remarkable and highly entertaining, and would keep an audience spellbound. And now of course airplane travel is not a romantic or glamorous luxury, it's a nuisance, a necessary nuisance. Electronic communication occurs instantly, and you have information and embedded slideshows on every imaginable structure and institution. You can do a virtual tour of half the universities of the US. (David Naylor, President, University of Toronto)

The leaders saw it as being crucial to maintain an open outlook, imagining what was a potentially very heterogeneous set of strategic options, which created issues of monitoring and selection: "Our fundamental problem is that we try to do too much" (Stuart McCutcheon, Vice-Chancellor, University of Auckland). Several presidents emphasized strategic focus, but only the National University of Singapore (NUS), with its fully crafted global strategy, replete with active portfolios in each selected part of the world, seemed fully on top of this problem. Another problem mentioned by some presidents was the lack of discretionary time in which to imagine, speculate and explore the different strategic options.

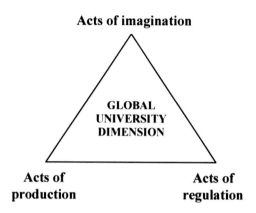

Acts of imagination

GLOBAL UNIVERSITY DIMENSION

Acts of production

Acts of regulation

Figure 1. Shaping of the global dimension by nations and institutions.

Understandings of Globalization

The most common definition of globalization used by the presidents referred to convergence and integration on a world-scale. In particular, the communicative aspect was emphasized:

> Globalization, to me in general terms, is the increasing convergence and inter-dependence of economies. In higher education globalization is the increasing convergence and interdependence of higher education systems. (Frans van Vught, Rector, University of Twente, Netherlands)

> The term "globalization" connotes an array of outcomes going far beyond the conventional view of closely linked world markets. In tandem, leaps of techno-logy and the Internet have shrunk time and space as well as levelled the global playing field. We live in a shrinking, flattening world. (Shih Choon Fong, President, National University of Singapore)

The president of the Vietnam National University noted that globalization could not be measured. "It is not scientific, not exact". It is a "feeling".

> Globalization makes the world more connected, more collaborative, more flat. That's my feeling about globalization. Reducing geographical boundaries. No geographical boundaries. Making the distance less. And you cannot live and work alone. Before you could. Now you cannot. You cannot do everything your own way. (Mai Trong Nhuan, President, Vietnam National University Hanoi)

A sense of "one-worldism" came through in several interviews. In both Mexico and at the University of Tokyo, globalization was discussed in terms of global ecology. The President of Chulalongkorn University in Thailand stated that:

> The world will become one. It's not that countries disappear or that the barriers between them will go away, no. But the system of the world will be more of a unified system. People can reach each other. (Khunying Suchada, President, Chulalongkorn University)

"Chula" graduates could be expected to work in many countries and should be prepared for that, she said. Graduate labour mobility was a key aspect of globalization for several presidents. Most stated that globalization created a more competitive, a more open and a more opportunistic environment for graduates and for universities. Half of the presidents noted that global competition in higher education had a downside. Some referred to the 1990s definition of globalization as world economic markets. One president said that while he was strongly in favour of "international-ization", which was central to the mission:

> I don't actually see globalization as a universal good. It has created more problems than it has given value in many instances. For us it means potentially hugely increased competition and a level of uncertainty that adds an un-necessarily difficult dimension to managing complex institutions.... I do see benefits from freeing markets from unnecessary constraints, but you can't make them totally free. For a university like this, I'm confident that we could survive in a much freer more competitive environment. But if it's totally de-regulated no Australian university would survive. (Ian Chubb, Vice-Chancellor, Australian National University)

Similarly the Provost at the University of Illinois, Linda Katehi, advocated "inter-nationalization" as learning from other countries and cultures, changing one's own outlook, and acquiring a sense of living in "a much larger world"; whereas global-ization was defined in imperial terms as "assimilating others to what we do rather than changing ourselves". Other nations saw the global expression of their own national cultures in positive terms and they wanted to be more globally influential. The Rector at the University of Indonesia and the President of Chulalongkorn in Thailand, both felt that the positive potential of globalization lay in the possibility of bringing distinctive attributes associated with their nations to the larger world setting.

> I think the Thai people are special in the way they behave... we are considerate of other people's feelings. I think that is a unique Thai way. We smile a lot, we are courteous, and we work very hard. Those that work offshore, they are mostly smart and they work hard, and at the same time they have these interpersonal skills that can work with other people. I would love to think that my students also have morals and good governance in their heads and the integrity of being a good citizen of the world. (Khunying Suchada, President, Chulalongkorn University)

At the University of Toronto there was a typical Canadian enthusiasm for cultural openness, mixing and cosmopolitanism. Within the case study group this attitude was shared, in more muted fashion, by the representatives from the ANU, Illinois and Leiden. "I think there is optimism about globalization in Canada that is probably greater than in any other nation" (David Naylor, President, University of Toronto). However, global openness was often seen as threatening for non English speaking cultures (see below).

The Global Higher Education Sector

The global dimension was imagined, above all, as a sphere of comparison. Perhaps the most important single influence in shaping the global sector was university rankings, except in the USA and Mexico. A bad global ranking hurt the university in the halls of national government, although a good ranking did not necessarily strengthen the university's position with government. At Chulalongkorn in Thailand a high ranking in the *Times Higher* table one year (121) might even have contributed to the university's continued funding problems.

> Yeah, that's what they said. Even though we don't give Chula lots of money they can still do well, they can survive. Don't worry about them. (Khunying Suchada, President, Chulalongkorn University)

In Malaysia, a declining ranking in the same *Times* collection generated public disquiet and may have contributed to the decision of the government not to reappoint the vice-chancellor, which the vice-chancellor himself felt was the case. Some presidents focused on the biases inherent in the rankings process, but regardless, they fed a strategic approach to rankings into their internal priorities and their incentive and reporting systems. Notwithstanding the methodological and political problems with rankings, it was generally accepted that they could not be ignored.

A few presidents emphasized the need for a greater steering capacity in relation to academic units and behaviour, so as to promote global activity. This was a particular concern for President Takeshi Sasaki at the University of Tokyo. However, most respondents seemed to be generally comfortable about their capacity to influence the international activities of the university.

When considering the global dimension of higher education as a whole, all the leaders emphasized the standing and influence of the American sector. When asked to name the institutions that most impressed them as models, they listed such institutions as Harvard, Stanford, MIT, Caltech, Berkeley and/or the University of California system as a whole, and sometimes large public research universities, such as Wisconsin. Cambridge in the UK was also mentioned several times. The major European universities were rarely acknowledged by name, except by the Rector at Leiden. In the non-English speaking countries in Asia there was a strong desire, albeit expressed in general terms, to source models of universities from Europe (especially Germany) as well as the USA/UK.

It was generally agreed across the whole study that the Chinese research universities would succeed in their ambition to develop as world-leading institutions. There was also general agreement that the NUS was particularly impressive, not just in its international work, but in all other aspects and nearly every other university had an active partnership with this institution. One university in the group that appeared to be highly internationalized, in terms of the volume and intensity of its global networking, was Illinois in the USA. Illinois had just negotiated a major agreement with the NUS and its leaders sang the praises of the Singapore institution.

The National University of Singapore was unique in the extent to which it had devised a detailed global strategy and was implementing it, and in the degree of emphasis placed on the global factors in university development. This advanced global orientation was a function of Singapore's own position as a nation:

> Singapore is a tiny island with some big neighbours, e.g. Australia, China, India, Indonesia and Japan. With no retreat or hinterland, globalization is not an option but a necessity for Singapore. We have no choice but to think "global", breathe "global" and to be "global". We constantly have to ask ourselves: "How can we build mutual respect?" "How can we be useful and relevant to the world?" … Singapore was global before the term "globalization" became fashionable…. In a global economy characterized by intense competition for talent, ideas and capital, Singapore's universities have also had to re-make themselves to stay relevant and thrive… the NUS has undergone a dramatic transformation, from a predominantly teaching institution training competent manpower for Singapore, to a research-intensive university respected in the global arena, and from a governance and management system closely aligned to the civil service to one based on performance and global best practice. (Shih Choon Fong, President, National University of Singapore)

The universities generally preferred to network actively with like-missioned institutions in other countries of roughly equivalent status to themselves, that is, with other universities of the type researched in the study - leading universities in the state/national/public sector. At the same time all the non-American universities were conscious on global inequalities, which had two vectors. One was linguistic and cultural, the other was understood in terms of political economy.

In relation to cultural aspects of globalization, the presidents from non English-speaking countries were concerned about the dominance of the Anglo-American world in higher education. Most stated that rankings criteria favoured the USA.

Q. What do you understand by the term globalization?

A. The unification of culture by the United States. It's a very bad aspect of the present phenomenon of globalization. The idea of globalization should mean that all people can access the Internet equally. Japan is an advanced, developed country. We have a completely different culture from the Western world. I think this is quite special. (Hiroshi Komiyama, Executive Vice-President, University of Tokyo)

Globalization has brought Indonesia into a big arena where the countries become borderless... globalization comes into all countries. The problems are different from country to country. Other countries may be more prepared than Indonesia in facing globalization. If Indonesia is not prepared, the country will become the consumer of developed countries... Western culture can now easily come into Indonesia. (Usman Chatib Warsa, Rector, Universitas Indonesia)

The President of the Vietnam National University made a similar point about the openness of Vietnam to American media and the potential for regressive cultural transformation, especially in the rural areas and among the uneducated. However, he was less worried about the potential dangers for the university, with its longer history of cross-border flows.

The economic form of inequality was stressed by the interviewees from each of Malaysia, Thailand, Indonesia, Vietnam and Mexico. In this regard, in Indonesia and Vietnam the universities could not afford subscriptions to basic journals. In Malaysia, which saw itself as an emerging economy, the financial firepower of Singapore was a constant reminder that the university was not yet a WCGRU:

Globalization [ideally] would be a world without borders. But we must always be aware that in the globalized world the field has not developed this way. The players are not the same size. What will be good for the bigger power may not be good for the smaller power.... What we are looking forward to in the globalized world is that things become freer and things become shared, but they must be shared... if it is rules of the jungle, best man wins, we are all dead. (Hashim Yaacob, Vice-Chancellor, University of Malaya)

Globalization affects differently each country and each group of countries. It has a completely different impact in the strongest economies, such as the United States and many of the European countries, and the newly developed Asian economies, than it has in countries such as Mexico, and the effect it may have in the least developed countries. It has an impact that really increases inequities. That has made it very difficult the dialogue at global and internal institutions, because the effects are perceived by government and society in one country as different from the effects that are perceived in another. (Juan Ramon de la Fuente, Rector, Universidad Nacional Autonoma de Mexico)

Relational Geographies

Nearly all presidents discussed the strategic significance of proximate neighbour countries. With respect to this, for the Dutch universities European developments were crucial. Leiden itself had initiated the League of European universities, a consortium of most of the strongest research-intensive institutions on that continent. At both Toronto and Universidad Nacional Autonoma de Mexico (UNAM) in Mexico, higher education in the USA exerted the main outside influence on faculty work. In the former, where there was always a choice in regionalization strategy between looking north and looking south, the rector felt that Latin America had been neglected, as very few UNAM students went to Spanish speaking countries, apart from Spain. He was hopeful that a small scale regional scholarship scheme might start to shift the field of vision. All of the Southeast Asian institutions networked within the ASEAN group. At Tokyo and at the Vietnam National University, the presidents noted regular meetings of East Asian presidents. At the ANU one of the four founding research and graduate schools had been the Research School of Pacific and Asian Studies.

> Internationalization is important for us because we're a small country stuck at
> the bottom of the world with many more populous neighbours around us and
> if we don't have good relationships with our region life it is problematic. (Ian
> Chubb, Vice-Chancellor, Australian National University)

Beyond proximity, globalization was associated with a broadening of international ties to include most world regions. Thus for example the University of Auckland in New Zealand had traditionally related primarily to the UK. In the 1980s it broadened to North America; in the 1990s it belatedly discovered Asia. However, all four English-speaking countries in the study acknowledged that their personnel and students were not sufficiently effective in working in studying in non English-speaking contexts because of language factors. The mono-lingualism of those countries prevented a more reciprocal pattern of people flows and retarded university collaboration. The spread of facility in Chinese national language, especially, was seen as a priority for development. However, no large-scale schemes to achieve this were underway.

ACTS OF PRODUCTION

All of the presidents discussed research collaboration, staff exchange, foreign student enrolment, local student exchange abroad, partnerships and networking. But the other universities' productive global activities were dwarfed by those of the NUS. This university had more than thirty joint degrees, with 19 partner universities around the world and 220 student exchange agreements in 38 countries, with over 1600 student places per annum. Moreover, the goal had been set to send 20% of undergraduates abroad for one semester each. There were also summer programmes or field trips in China, Indonesia, Belgium, USA and Australia. Furthermore, there were five joint research laboratories as well as numerous research collaborations.

People Mobility Issues

Most interviewees mentioned a recent growth in cross-border people traffic, which applied to both official visits, and ongoing faculty activity at discipline level.

> Individual level exchange has become much more intense and extensive.
> (Hiroshi Komiyama, Executive Vice-President, University of Tokyo)

A diverse student body was universally seen as positive and nearly all the presidents could name the number of countries from which their students had come. At Leiden, the rector, Douwe Breimer, talked of creating "a mini global environment" inside the university, which would expose the student to "different views and different opinions", thereby becoming "more of a global citizen". A similar concept was mentioned by Richard Herman, chancellor of the Urbana-Champaign campus of the University of Illinois. Sending local students abroad for part of their studies was considered to be much more difficult, except in the cases of Leiden and Twente in Europe and the NUS in Singapore, with NUS aiming to ensure that at least one fifth of all first degree students spent a semester abroad as part of their studies. Moreover, NUS had established a worldwide network of study centres and partners with WCGRU status. Elsewhere, the barriers to outward mobility were cost and in the English speaking nations, lack of student motivation and foreign language capacity.

Issues related to the global mobility of talent - how to stop researchers from leaving after graduation, how to draw high quality people from abroad, and how to keep them happy once inside the university - preoccupied all the presidents:

> In today's knowledge-driven global economy, talent, ideas and intellectual capital have taken centre stage.... The NUS has to compete in the global arena against universities with access to broader and deeper talent and resource pools. We believe that the quality of faculty is the single most important determinant of the quality of education and research. (Shih Choon Fong, President, National University of Singapore)

There were many unresolved issues in relation to people movement that affected global capacity. These issues absorbed a significant portion of the interviews. Lack of sufficient money for scholarships for international doctoral students was an issue cited by most presidents. Lack of student accommodation was mentioned at Tokyo and Leiden in the Netherlands. At Illinois there was concern about a recent slow-down in the supply of international graduate students from China - in engineering and the technologies foreign graduate students had become an indispensable component of the University's staffing. At a number of universities brain drain and unequal inward/outward flows were burning issues. In Mexico a large proportion of the best doctoral and post-doctoral personnel were lost to the USA every year. The rector at UNAM wanted the government to introduce a "brain gain" program that would bring in high quality academic labour to compensate for the outward movement. In New Zealand, Auckland was losing staff to better paid and more globally metropolitan locations. There was no apparent solution to brain drain at Vietnam National University and Universitas Indonesia given the rates of pay; though some world-class researchers and professors stayed in the country, or returned from working abroad, because of their commitment to the nation and its educational development.

A principal problem was the difficulty of attracting and/or employing foreign researchers. Inward mobility was often retarded by national regulation and in some countries this was joined to traditional academic protectionism. When pay rates were fixed centrally presidents had little discretion. In most countries it was difficult for foreigners to obtain permanent employment. The other issue was relative salaries. For example at Malaya faculty were locked into public service salary levels and it was impossible to offer foreigners a permanent position. The best they could obtain was a three-year contract. The salary level meant that Malaysian employment was attractive to staff from poorer nations such as Indonesia, and to some extent to staff from India, but has limited pulling power in the Middle East and none in Europe or the English-speaking world. Meanwhile neighbouring Singapore was paying US-level salaries, four times the level of Malaysia, and recruiting vigorously from everywhere including the University of Malaya. In Thailand pay rates were again too low to be globally competitive. In the Netherlands, there was political ambivalence about immigration. Visa delays were a key issue. In Japan the language factor inhibited potential recruits. This was an open concern at the University of Tokyo which wanted to grow foreign professors. Universities in the settler societies of Canada, the USA, Australia and New Zealand were more readily accessed by foreigners than were universities in low immigration countries, but the pulling power of the USA overshadowed the others.

Borrowing

However, global openness had an upside for Vietnam, and to some extent Thailand and Malaysia. It was seen to facilitate improvements in higher education quality. The National University of Vietnam sourced approaches to teaching, research and governance from across the world, particularly the USA.

> The College of Science has requested the University of Illinois to assist with the teaching of chemistry. We submit the curriculum and subject requirements [for consideration for the Illinois science faulty]. Physics uses the Brown University teaching program. Mathematics has gone to Wisconsin. The College of Economics draws on the Haas business school. We adapt the curricula of the best universities for implementation here. Of course we adapt it to suit our conditions. We also use their teaching technology, with modifications - that's very important. Also our staff go to the American universities to be trained and learn new ideas… every university has unique conditions and values/ it is not so easy to follow a whole university. But it is possible to learn from part of their activities. For example, in relation to the links between universities and industry, we have learned a lot from the Taiwan universities. For information technology I visit Carnegie Mellon. For social sciences and law, Harvard. For applied technology, MIT. So each university has very specific value. By adapting all of these examples we can make our own pathway. (Mai Trong Nhuan, President, Vietnam National University Hanoi)

Global linkages thus utilized could enhance the university, if it worked out as planned, provided local strategic and organizational coherence were maintained.

ACTS OF REGULATION

From the viewpoint of national authorities, the global dimension of higher education creates a dilemma. All national governments want "their" universities to be outstanding on the world scale. Most governments believe that strong research universities are essential to economic growth, because research powers innovation, and strong universities attract talent, build gravitational power of cities, and synchronize the nation with the global knowledge economy. But these economic payoffs are long-term and indirect. Further, good graduates and new research may leak offshore without being captured by local business. Most research becomes open global knowledge. It is impossible to target investment in universities for optimal national returns. Governments may feel that they can better achieve direct objectives by investing in schools or industry training. There is an ongoing tension between the national and global roles of universities.

In the interviews, relations between nation-state and university varied from case to case. The extreme case of close fit between government policy and institutional strategy was Singapore. NUS had been engineered as an instrument of national policy, with a principal role in shifting Singapore to a focus on knowledge-intensive products and services, which included the attraction of high skill global labour to the island. The national strategy was focused on global agendas, so that both parties shared an unusually strong focus on the global dimension.

I don't see a contradiction between the global mission and our national mission.... We call ourselves a global knowledge enterprise... We have to be global and national. I see that as the destiny. (Shih Choon Fong, President, National University of Singapore)

Elsewhere there was a weaker fit between government policy orientation and university global strategy orientation. A typical concern across all universities in the study, except the NUS, was that government was insufficiently focused on the global dimension of university activity, and its regulation of higher education was some way from the optimal form for global work. The view was commonly expressed that national governments expected universities to perform but provide insufficient support or interfere and cut across the institution's judgement about global priorities and strategies; or nation-centred regulatory requirements created barriers to global work, particularly in relation to foreign recruitment.

All of the presidents indicated a close knowledge of issues related to government politics, policy, funding and regulation. The national dimension was a natural home for them, one more closely defined and understood than was the global dimension because of their longer experience with it. But the problem was to reconcile and synergize the national and local dimensions of actions with action in the global dimension. This illustrates the point that universities are active at the same time in three dimensions, the local, national and global dimensions. We are in a glonacal era in higher education, in which imagining and production are global, national and local at the same time (Marginson and Rhoades, 2002; Marginson, 2007a) - even though regulation remains primarily national and local in form.

In the glonacal setting activity in one of the global, national or local dimensions creates conditions of activity in the others. Universities that effectively *coordinate* action in the three dimensions, so that each tends to produce the other, will benefit.

Figure 2. Dimensions of higher education.

Thus WCGRUs have to be strong enough in the global dimension to participate in its circuits or flows of activity. They must be embedded in a local setting that enables stable activity and adequate levels of support. And they must sustain investment from national government in a regulatory and policy setting that both enable global activity and maintain and develop reputation and custom at home.

There was variation across the study in the degree to which the university and its executive leaders were free to act globally on their own behalf.

> If the university has freedom it can develop knowledge without limit. (Usman Chatib Warsa, Rector Universitas Indonesia)

The capacity of the president (or rector or vice-chancellor) to act separately from the government was enhanced if the leader was not appointed directly by them, but was chosen by the university's governing body or community. This was true for the NUS in Singapore and the interviewees from Japan, the Netherlands the USA, Canada and Australia. In Thailand, government appointment was a formality after the main recommendation is made at university level, whereas in Malaysia government exercised direct control over the appointment and this affected leader behaviour. The term of office in Malaysia was three years and although there was provision for reappointment, vice-chancellors regarded by the government as being too independent were not appointed for a second term. In Vietnam President Mai Trong did not question the process of government appointment, but focused on the need for executive autonomy:

> When I met the president of Vietnam I said: "I do not ask you for more money. Give me more autonomy". More freedom. More responsibility. More transparency. More flexibility to meet the requirements of our society and globalization. More autonomy. We have full autonomy in teaching and research. But not in staffing and finance. (Mai Trong Nhuan, President, Vietnam National University Hanoi)

All of the universities had been touched to some degree or other by New Public Management (NPM) reforms instigated by government. In Indonesia, Malaysia and Japan the university had been newly modelled as entrepreneurial and encouraged to seek private funds. At the time of interview in Indonesia and Japan the process of change was incomplete and still seen as in doubt. At Chulalongkorn in Thailand a reform to enhance university autonomy had stalled. New Public Management systems were well established at NUS in Singapore and at Auckland and the ANU.

The global freedom of the university was greater if it could generate its own resources at scale and was not wholly dependent financially on government. In all universities in the group, there had been an increase in private income in recent years. But in most cases this trend had been accompanied by constraints or reductions in government spending, and continued controls over government funded activity. In Singapore government funding continued to increase but that case was unique in the group. Cuts to the state budget were hurting in Illinois though this was less of an issue in Toronto. ANU and Auckland were sharply constrained financially. On the whole, private income raising was more strongly established in Australia, New Zealand and the United States than elsewhere in the case study group; though ANU in Australia was not a major player in the commercial international market in which most Australian universities were very active. ANU received special research funding from government.

All of the case study universities were partly or wholly constrained in their capacity to vary tuition charges to domestic students, which set a limit on their capacity to be a quasi-private university as imagined in corporatization reforms.

Overall New Public Management reform had left all but Singapore worse off in financial terms, especially given the expansion of subsidized global activities. It is ironic that the National University of Singapore, the one institution with especially strong public financing, was also the institution where imaginings of higher education as a capitalist economic market were more pronounced than elsewhere.

Global Public Goods

One manifestation of the national/global tension was that the university presidents often had a different notion of the contribution of higher education to public goods, to that held by national government. Public goods produced in higher education are goods that (1) have a significant element of non-rivalry and/or non-excludability, and (2) are made broadly available across populations; and are inter-generational in that they meet needs in the present generation without jeopardising future generations. Goods without attributes (1) and (2) are private goods (Samuelson, 1954; Kaul et al., 1999; Marginson, 2007b). Some public goods take the form of "externalities" or "spill-overs", whereby an individualized good received by one person creates benefits for others who did not purchase the good in question. For example, the training of a technician can enhance the productivity and wages of other workers; the training is partly non-excludable. Other public goods include collective benefits, for example the joint value created by enhanced communication or knowledge systems, where the outcomes are non-rivalrous.[2]

Generally governments, influenced by the economic policy constructs of the role of higher education, tend to emphasize the competitive aspect of university work more than the cooperative aspect. This includes activity in the global dimension, where universities are mostly seen as an extension of the nation-state as a competition state. Where public good outcomes are noted by governments, the public goods are mostly understood in nation-bound terms, circumscribed by citizen identity and geography, for example, the role of higher education in providing equitable social opportunities, or contributing to employment creation in local areas. However, the presidents interviewed for this study were aware that universities contribute to more than the mix of public and private goods within the nation, and to more than the competitive position of the nation offshore. For active as they were in research and cross-border people flows, they thus had the potential to contribute to global public goods. Global public goods are goods that have a significant element of non-rivalry and/or non-excludability and are broadly available across populations on a global scale (Kaul et al., 1999, p. 2–3). Examples of such global public goods are disinterested research focused on worldwide problems in relation to the: environment, water and disease control.

Several universities in the study - Tokyo, Leiden, Toronto, Illinois and the ANU among others - were extensively involved in producing collective global public goods, with the central element being mostly knowledge, its production and dissemination. Illinois's contribution to capacity building in the National University of Vietnam, which was granted as being very helpful in Hanoi but generated few pay-offs for the American university, was another example of a global public good. More generally, research universities contribute to global relations and understanding by building bridges between nations and enhancing intercultural mixing, and several presidents referred to this.

Most presidents evidenced a strong normative commitment to their work in creating global public goods. For example, there was across-the-board support for research focused on monitoring and managing climate change, regardless of the level of resources of the university concerned. The presidents were personally attracted to the larger purpose embodied in the global role, and some were conscious that it helped to position their universities as players in the evolution of global civil society, thus moving beyond the limitations not only of their own nation-state and its priorities, but of the nation-state in general. But the question that arose was "how can global public goods be funded?", for national governments are generally reluctant to support extensive work on activities that primarily benefit people in other countries. This means that unless the research university can fund global public good activity from its own resources much of its potential contribution will be unrealized.

CONCLUSIONS

Worldwide higher education and research is a relational environment in which all research universities both contribute to the environment itself, and work within the positioning options possible in that environment. They can also develop new options. Global perspectives in higher education and research, which are shaped in the imaginations of university and system leaders, are continually evolving and further radical changes in global connectivity, capacity and activity are to be expected.

Global strategies have differing space-making effects and they create relationships of varying shape. Some open a new global zone of activity that anyone can enter, like open source publication (such as MIT's open courseware initiative). Others build more bounded spaces within the global dimension, but spaces that multiply, as in the commercial market in degrees. Some global activities involve the same institution moving across or between different country sites, as in transnational education. Some create world-spanning networks with no intrinsic centre; others are grounded, working outwards from a single national location, such as the hubs. Some work with a small slice or corner of the global dimension, such as student exchange with proximate neighbours. A few global moves have been set out to reconstitute the whole of global higher education as a single space, such as e-universities, the process of WTO-GATS negotiations, and global university rankings.

The global dimension of higher education is a collective work in progress and there is much freedom for action and innovation, especially where universities act by themselves without direct regulation by governments. If universities are to fulfil their potential in the creation of global public goods, such freedom is essential. However, across the world there is a notable inequality in each of the three elements of university capacity, freedom to act, and national capacity in higher education. Universities need a minimum threshold capacity in resources and ability to act in order to be significant global players. Those with advanced capacity, many in North America, have more strategic options than do others. A primary issue of global public good is the need to develop WCGRUs in developing countries.

This is a "glonacal" era (Marginson and Rhoades, 2002) in which universities are simultaneously active in the local, national and global dimensions. That is, action in one dimension can affect the potential for action in the others. For instance, doing well in global rankings may strengthen the position at home with government and local students or a local restructuring of the curriculum might make the university more attractive to global partners. National governments can build global capacity, or strangle it in red tape. Government funding enables local modernization and augments global research capacity. Universities that effectively coordinate action in all three dimensions tend to benefit. In this study those universities include NUS in Singapore, the University of Toronto in Canada, and Leiden in the Netherlands.

Some global strategies have been more successful, and will have longer lasting and deeper effects, than others. Much global activity is superficial. Of the global strategies in the table, national capacity building in research can only lifts the *relative* global position of when it is on a large scale, as has happened in China, Taiwan China, Korea and Singapore. Networks only have lasting effects when collaboration is embedded in longer-term arrangements such as combined degree structures. Of the three attempts to remake the whole global dimension, the WTO-GATS initiative to turn higher education into a world trading system has had only modest impact. Most nations retain policy control of their regulated and protected national systems, for these are expected to generate not just market (private) goods, but national public goods such as contributions to national economic capacity and social equity. The second attempt, the global e-universities, failed spectacularly. Most students find virtual degrees unattractive. But the third attempt to remake the global space, global ranking and research comparisons, has changed everything.

Some global strategies in higher education are brilliantly imaginative. When they first emerge they can be as creative as works in the arts and sciences; though their originality is soon hidden by all the imitators. Examples are Singapore's hub strategy, transnational education by Australia and the UK, the Shanghai Jiao Tong University ranking system which first appeared in 2003, the CHE web-based design-your-own university comparisons, and the Webometrics ranking. Leaders and organizations need certain skills for this kind of creativity, such as having imagination to see the "big picture" and reconcile the different trends, contexts and changes. They need to adopt a long-term view amid the short-term policy world and to hold onto their strategy without being distracted too much by knee-jerk markets. They need to be outstanding macro communicators and interpersonal networkers. They need a grasp of science, culture and business. They need to be cosmopolitan, whilst maintaining a strong sense of their own identity, agenda and goals. They need to be politically astute, because it is likely that national/global tensions will worsen. Good presidents need to be both dreamers and realists.

NOTES

[1]   Further studies are planned in the Philippines, Laos, Cambodia, Korea and one or two universities in China. A study in India is under consideration.

[2]   Goods are non-rivalrous when they can be consumed by any number of people without being depleted, for example knowledge of a mathematical theorem. Goods are non-excludable when the benefits cannot be confined to individual buyers, such as social tolerance, or law and order. Few goods are both fully non-rivalrous and fully non-excludable, but many have one or the other quality in part.

REFERENCES

Enders, J., & De Weert, E. (Eds.), (2009). *The academic profession and the modernization of higher education: Analytical and comparative perspectives.* Dordrecht: Springer.

Hazelkorn, E. (2008). Learning to live with league tables and ranking: The experience of institutional leaders. *Higher Education Policy, 21,* 193–215.

Horta, H. (2009). Global and international prominent universities: Internationalization, competitiveness and the role of the state. *Higher Education, 58,* 387–405.

Kaul, I., Grunberg, I., & Stern, M. (Eds.), (1999). *Global public goods: International cooperation in the 21st century.* New York: Oxford University Press.

King, R. (2009). *Governing universities globally: Organizations, regulation and rankings.* Cheltenham: Edward Elgar.

Ma, W. (2008). The University of California at Berkeley: An emerging global research university. *Higher Education Policy, 21,* 65–81.

Marginson, S. (2007a). The new higher education landscape: Public and private goods, in Global/National/Local Settings. In S. Marginson (Ed.), *Prospects of higher education.* Rotterdam: Sense Publishers.

Marginson, S. (2007b). The public/private division in higher education: A global revision. *Higher Education, 53,* 307–333.

Marginson, S. (2008). "Ideas of a University" for the global era. Paper for seminar on *"Positioning university in the globalized world: Changing governance and coping strategies in Asia"*. Centre of Asian Studies, The University of Hong Kong; Central Policy Unit, HKSAR Government; and The Hong Kong Institute of Education. 10–11 December 2008, The University of Hong Kong. Retrieved September 12, 2009 from: http://www.cshe.unimelb.edu.au/people/staff_pages/Marginson/Marginson.html

Marginson, S. (2009). The academic professions in the global era. In J. Enders, & E. de Weert (Eds.), *The academic profession and the modernization of higher education: Analytical and comparative perspectives*. Dordrecht: Springer.

Marginson, S., Kaur, S., & Sawir, E. (forthcoming). *Higher education in the Asia-Pacific: Strategic responses to globalization*. Dordrecht: Springer.

Marginson, S., & Rhoades, G. (2002). Beyond national states, markets, and systems of higher education: A Glonacal agency heuristic. *Higher Education, 43*(3), 281–309.

Organisation for Economic Cooperation and Development, OECD. (2009). *Education at a glance*. Paris: OECD.

Samuelson, P. (1954). The pure theory of public expenditure. *Review of Economics and Statistics, 36*(4), 387–389.

Shanghai Jiao Tong University Graduate School of Education (SJTUGSE). (2010). *Academic ranking of world universities*. Retrieved February 15, 2010, from http://ed.sjtu.edu.cn/ranking.htm

Stiglitz, J. (1999). Knowledge as a global public good. In I. Kaul, I. Grunberg, & M. Stern (Eds.), *Global public goods: International cooperation in the 21st century*. 308–325. New York: Oxford University Press.

Simon Marginson
Centre for the Study of Higher Education
University of Melbourne, Australia

MICHAEL GALLAGHER

2. THE ROLE OF ELITE UNIVERSITIES IN NATIONAL HIGHER EDUCATION AND RESEARCH SYSTEMS, AND THE CHALLENGES OF PROSECUTING THE CASE FOR CONCENTRATING PUBLIC INVESTMENT IN THEIR DEVELOPMENT IN AUSTRALIA[1]

INTRODUCTION

Around the world there is an interest on the part of governments in the capacity and performance of elite research universities within national higher education and innovation systems (Salmi, 2009). However, the level of interest and initiative varies, and for many countries, the motives are mixed and the measures vexed (Altbach and Balan, 2007).

Some countries (notably England and the United States) have well-established elite (talent rich, asset deep, prestigious) universities and research institutes, founded centuries ago in the origins of their higher education and research systems, currently performing at international heights. Other countries (e.g. China, Germany, Japan) are looking to promote some among their existing (including longstanding) institutions to become (again in some cases) world leaders. A few are appraising the international standing of their leading national universities, with some (e.g. Malaysia, India, Vietnam) building at the pinnacle of their national systems new institutions designed to become internationally reputable[2]. Elsewhere and mainly in second world economies (e.g. Australia, Canada, New Zealand, South Africa), a number of institutions are seeking to break out from national (or provincial) policy and financing frameworks that have levelled-down the performance peaks by distributing the available resources widely, in an effort to raise (or not let diminish in a period of participation growth) overall systemic quality, or for egalitarian objectives or, as in the case of South Africa, for historical redress of systemic dis-crimination. Another set of countries that have previously not participated at the forefront of knowledge advancement (e.g. in Latin America, and Africa) seek now to do so, alongside some former centres of intellectual and cultural distinction (and some newcomers) in the Middle East and former Eastern Bloc countries.

The divergent approaches being adopted between and within countries may reflect the interaction of several factors, including the economic strength and development position of nations, the balance of responsibilities between national and provincial jurisdictions, the general quality of their higher education systems

N.C. Liu et al., (eds.), Paths to a World-Class University: Lessons from Practices and Experiences, 29–66.

and the international standing of their leading universities, and the political trade-offs that are necessary within specific national contexts, particularly around issues of equity. Hence, in some countries the state may be seen to reinforce institutional positioning strategies, and in a few cases may push for strengthening, whereas in other countries the state plays a retarding role, dampening institutional differentiation and holding back the aspirations of the national elite, or adopting the stance that the elite will prosper irrespective of the national policy settings.

A major purpose of the concentrating countries is to step up their international economic competitiveness through increased national innovativeness - not only to adopt and adapt the product of innovations developed elsewhere, but also to generate the breakthroughs that provide the foundations of competitive advantage. At the core of the interest in the relative strength of nationally elite universities, is an understanding that the bar has been raised for participation internationally in the advancement of knowledge at a level sufficient to sustain "national" economic competitiveness, or at least boost the performance of enterprises or sectors within nations. That understanding is based on some real lifters of a higher bar including the increasing complexity of research problems being addressed across disciplines on large scales with the aid of sophisticated and powerful technologies, the associated rising threshold of input costs, and the intensifying competition for intellectual talent, particularly in the aggregations often needed for big scientific breakthroughs[3].

Often the issues associated with raising the performance peaks of the leading universities in a nation are being played out amid unsettled higher education policy and financing frameworks, including disputation over the sharing of costs and degrees of tuition pricing flexibility, alongside the accommodation of changes in the volume of student participation, whether to undertake expansion in some regions or contraction in others. And these contests are taking place in a broader context of rising claims for public expenditures in health, environment, security and other areas, recently complicated in several countries by the imperative to rein in aggregate government spending over the future medium term, as a means of moving back to fiscal balance following the economic stimulus measures introduced during the 2008–09 global financial crisis.

The issues can be hotly contested. In circumstances of expanding tertiary education participation, for instance, central funders have to make broad trade-offs between scale and quality. In this context, skewed distributions for research-related functions can be seen to divert available resources, without guaranteed or proportional returns, and reduce the scope for achieving reasonable education-related compromises. With regard to the allocation of public funds for university research, the trade-offs are more narrowly contested, and the apparent tendency is for competition in a more market-like, yet prestige-driven environment, so as to emulate research universities (Van Vught, 2008). On the one hand, given the inability of any nation to afford an entire system of "world-class research universities", emulation results in second rate imitation, where efforts are focused more on improving reputation than performance, and this diverts institutions from developing the programmatic diversity needed to accommodate varying student needs and circumstances (Meek, 2000).

On the other hand, the very suggestion of greater selectivity and concentration in the funding of university research meets with strong opposition from those institutions which do not see themselves as benefitting. Although this is chiefly a battle among contending higher education institutions, such opposition can be potent as, in real politics, the relative "losers" (in reputational relegation, even if they are not financially disadvantaged) are by definition more numerous than the probable "winners" and are likely to be located in politically sensitive electorates[4]. Regardless of the complaints of governments about the perils of provider capture in prestige-driven higher education markets, their own actions can be captured by political demands to protect weak providers.

Consequently, notwithstanding demand pulls, including expectations of local communities for universities to serve their needs, governments can be reluctant to promote or support the strengthening of universities already seen to be relatively strong in the national arena, even if by various comparisons they are not strong enough on the international stage. For their part, the universities that understand how much they need to increase their capacity and raise their performance in order to stay with the international pace-setters, also know they cannot stand by idly wishing for a government to gather courage, because elsewhere others are not waiting for them to catch up.

This paper considers the policy tensions for governments and explores options for research universities. First, the paper scans the changing context for higher education and university research. Second, it reviews the traditional roles of elite universities and outlines the main characteristics of contemporary elite universities and expectations about their contributions. Third, there is consideration of the arguments for and against the main policy drivers of elite outcomes: system diversification, institutional differentiation and investment concentration. Finally, the options for government policy relating to system structure and steering mechanisms, and for university positioning are outlined.

THE CHANGING CONTEXT FOR HIGHER EDUCATION AND UNIVERSITY RESEARCH

Figure 1 depicts the range of relations that universities might have within national contexts (Clark, 1983). This is to regard higher education institutions as embedded in common frameworks of societal expectations, regulatory frameworks, and co-operative or competitive linkages (Guri-Rosenblit, Sebkova and Teichler, 2007). Notionally, the locus of power can reside in any of the four corner forces. The academy is here understood loosely as the forums through which scholarly leadership is exercised. The interaction of the academy with the locus of power may shift according to political changes, including through the alliance of different forces, such as state-civil society alliances of the traditional European bent or state-market alliances of the neo-liberal school.

A key point is that the university cannot be self-referenced, not merely because it is not self-sufficient, in that it cannot sustain itself entirely without external support, but also because its core functions require it to be socially interactive in

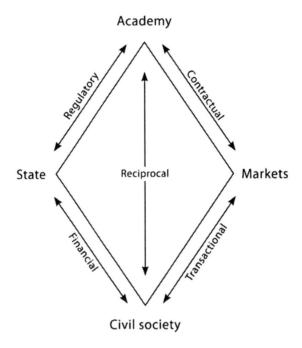

Academy

State   Reciprocal   Markets

Civil society

Figure 1. University relations in the national context.

its efforts to make sense of the world. Palfreyman and Tapper (2009) argue, for instance, in relation to Oxbridge that it's its "continuing ability to make itself indispensable to the dominant interests in state and society that accounts for its elevated status in the higher education hierarchy." This reciprocity can be seen from the origins of early western universities in church support[5]. The university has been a resilient institution, accommodating the shift from scholasticism to scientific method in the seventeenth and eighteenth centuries, embracing secular liberal education in the early nineteenth century, and accepting a responsibility to contribute to nation building in the aftermath of the Second World War. In contemporary terms, the relationships tend to be defined more pluralistically and include state-mediated expectations of university relevance to varying labour market and enterprise innovation needs, as a condition of continuing public support.

Various elements of civil society, including businesses and non-governmental organizations, are developing new and direct relations with universities, through joint identification and exploration of problems, community foundation funding of research, direct collaboration in research projects, and joint participation in matters relating to controversial areas of research, such as genetically modified organisms, stem cell research, climate change and research into aspects of terrorism.

Over recent decades, relations between universities and civil society have been mediated increasingly through markets for services, enabled by the state through regulatory and financial mechanisms. A preoccupation with economic contributions has reinforced transactional relations and controls and tended to diminish the role of universities as social and cultural institutions that discover, transmit and preserve knowledge of value beyond the limits of immediate utility or preference. At the same time, universities have developed enlarged roles through the accumulation of multiple functions from state directives, market opportunities and social expectations.

Instrumentalist purposes of the state and consumerist interests of students appear to have both widened and narrowed the social expectations of universities. In this regard, contemporary universities are expected to enrol and graduate a larger and more diverse student mix in an expanding range of fields of study, so as to meet an increasing variety of occupational requirements, undertake research directed towards "national priorities" and demonstrable "end-user benefits", with more exacting public accountability for the cost-effective use of resources, and satisfy larger expectations of tangible returns from investment in higher education - individual, regional and national returns.

Trends in public policy, including applications of "new public management" in a context of fiscal parsimony, prioritize competition as a driver of increased responsiveness of university supply to changing demand (student demand, labour market demand, and enterprise demand for applicable knowledge and know-how). Universities, however resilient they may be as institutional forms, necessarily shape themselves to survive in the conditions of their operating environment. But the political-economic environment for universities has not been evolutionary. Rather it has been subject to sudden shifts in sources of finance, alongside ambiguous policy intentions and inconsistent incentives. Indeed, the policy tendencies of governments present a set of challenges in themselves and several common contemporary tendencies can be identified, each of them cumulatively adding layers of homogenising pressure.

The first tendency is for governments to fund teaching and research at less than actual costs. As a consequence, there are risks to quality as evidenced by increasing student teacher ratios and class sizes, and pressures on institutions to diversify their sources of income. The greatest penalties are imposed on those institutions that win most of the competitive research funding. The result is that projects are pared back and infrastructure investments are deferred, including essential capital works to bring facilities up to standards required by health and safety regulators of scientific research. Moreover, internal cross subsidization of research from funds for teaching and infrastructure erodes the institution's fabric and reduces its attractiveness in the competition for talent.

The second policy tendency is associated with a shift from elite to mass to "post-mass" or "near-universal" tertiary education participation. Public concerns about the maintenance of academic standards are raised in the communications media by parents and others, and governments are obliged to respond. Governments tend to regard the tertiary education sphere much as they regard the secondary schooling sphere: accountability for results; efficiency and productivity; quality assurance of minimum standards; an inclination to homogenization with little concern for different provider purposes. Areas traditionally regarded as matters of university autonomy are seen to be open for governments to intervene.

The third tendency, which flows from the sound policy principle of transparency and openness in decision making about the allocation of resources, is that policies and procedures are and are seen to be even-handed and non-discriminatory. A one-size-fits-all approach can be seen in the use of normative financing, such as through formulaic schemes, where all institutions receive the same unit of resource for similar activities, such as for teaching in a particular field of study. Qualitative differences are not taken into account normally, partly because they are not readily measurable or their assessment is contestable, or there is a reluctance to expose poor performance. Hence, the policy approach creates incentives for sameness (Van Vught, 2008), whereas differentiation requires discrimination, which in turn requires good information and the exercise of judgement.

The boundaries of Figure 1 can be extended to international relations, such as academic research collaboration, competition for international students, intergovernmental agreements, and university contributions to solving global problems. For centuries, international scholarly interactions have been a function of universities. However, the nature of such interactions has changed over the last couple of decades, owing to major developments in transport, communications and technology, but also driven by new purposes, including the desire of national governments to form ties internationally through trade, investment and knowledge flows, and the desire of university leaders to build scholarly relations for institutional strategic positioning. In the latter case, where universities seek to fulfil their missions in the international (and in some respects global) context, they move outside the boundaries of their national policies and regulations, and may not feel bound by them.

Ambiguity is the dominant contemporary context for universities in most countries. The ambiguities derive in part from a "turbulent, volatile and contradictory" operating environment (Scott, 2005). Uncertainties range across several dimensions, including levels and forms of demand for higher education; kinds and types of supply of higher education; influences of innovations in technology and communications on teaching and learning and research; amounts and conditions of public funding; incentives and disincentives for private funding and supply of higher education; national regulatory regimens and their interactions with international developments; expectations of university contributions and impacts socially, economically and environmentally; and the relationships between higher education and university research.

Figure 2 retains the sets of national relations discussed above but situates them in the international context, identifying the major drivers that have implications beyond national boundaries. It is necessary to see national developments within this wider international context, not least because a nation may be making considerable progress against the circumstances of its past, yet falling further behind other countries, whose efforts are much greater. At the same time, the new international dynamics pose new challenges and opportunities. Nevertheless, the context is ambiguous in several respects, in that there are conflicting signals and significant information (and communication) gaps; contradictions in the apparent developments; and there are disagreements about their manifestations, directions and causes. Hence the following tendencies are tendered (tendentiously) for consideration.

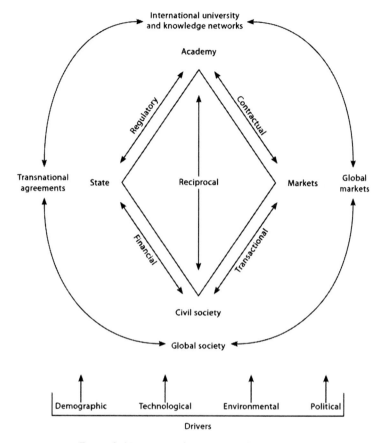

Figure 2. University relations in world context.

There is a Coincidence of Greater Community Needs, Greater Technical Capacities, and Greater Social Expectations (but not Necessarily Greater Resources)

Complex contemporary challenges require larger scale modelling and cross-disciplinary approaches to solving global problems, such as those relating to the world environment, the settlement and movement of people, pandemics, and terrorism. As the Association of Universities and Colleges of Canada has put it: "technological advances, which facilitate the development and exchange of knowledge and the generation and processing of research data, have created greater expectations that an increasingly wide range of problems can be researched and addressed in a more holistic fashion and at an accelerated pace" (Association of Universities and Colleges of Canada, 2008). As society becomes more knowledgeable, higher education comes under pressure to expand the kinds and types of knowledge it provides and to diversify the criteria by which it is judged (Bleiklie and Bvrkjeflot, 2002). The expectations are reciprocal, in that universities need to be resourced adequately

35

to develop the capabilities they need to play the roles expected. However, there are limits to the economic capacity of nations to meet the expectations of all universities, and priorities need to be established. No single university can meet all the expectations equally well, and it becomes necessary to promote institutional specialization in a flexible and complementary way within a national system.

Demographic Changes will Increase the Global Competition for Talent, Food, Water and Energy, while Requiring New Efficiencies in Education and Research in Developed and Developing Economies

The world's population is projected to grow from some 6.8 billion in 2009 to around 8 billion by 2025 (National Intelligence Council, 2008), with Asia and Africa accounting for the bulk of the growth. Population ageing in most of the advanced economies will coincide with youth bulges in less developed nations, predominantly in sub-Saharan Africa, the Middle East, the Caucasus and northern parts of South Asia. Through investments in education, the latter may be able to develop skilled worker bulges (*ibid*). However, the intensifying international competition for talent may lead to net drain from the poorer nations, exacerbating inequalities in development capacity. Given the population-driven growth in demand for food, water, energy and income in the third world, at a time of global environmental stress, the consequences could be disastrous. There arises a reciprocal responsibility on the part of elite institutions in advanced economies that grow stronger at the expense of weaker contributors, to assist in capacity building in the developing world.

Within developed economies where population ageing makes increasing claims on public and private resources, and where continuing investment in education, training and research is needed for underpinning the innovation necessary to sustain economic growth, there are likely to be rising expectations of improvements in learning productivity and the cost-effectiveness of research. Such expectations may give rise to incentives for specialization and collaboration, including through competitive and structural measures and performance-based funding.

Long-Term Research (both Basic and Applied) is Moving out of Enterprises and into Universities and Clusters of Universities with Enterprises.

In several industries, increasing pressure on companies to obtain revenue streams quickly, has led to declines or closures of research laboratories with capabilities for long-term research, with examples including Bell Labs, Lucent, Hitachi, HP, Exxon, IBM Research, RCA, GE Research, GM and Ford Scientific, and Westinghouse Research[6]. The short-term horizon of research in most of the remaining company labs effectively puts an end to their basic research (Natelson, 2007). At the same time, pharmaceutical corporations are maintaining significant in-house R&D capacity, whilst linking with universities and medical research institutes, globally. Leading pharmaceutical and biotech companies have undergone major R&D restructuring over the last five years, involving a consolidation of efforts through numerous acquisitions, both intra-pharmaceutical as well as purchases of biotechs by big pharmaceutical. Pharmaceutical companies are narrowing the focus of their research and development units through a more strategic concentration on key chronic illnesses. They are also adopting a focused, streamlined global approach, which is increasingly reliant on offshore strategic partnerships, academic collaboration and outsourcing to established networks of scientific expertise (Pharmaceuticals Asia Product News, 2009).

For universities to pick up the slack or participate in the new networks, it is necessary for them to invest in major facilities and equipment, and to fund inter-disciplinary research teams over blocks of time that exceed the normal 3–5 year terms of conventional national research funding schemes. In effect, there is competition between nations in making themselves attractive to the footloose R&D investment of corporations. Nations need to weigh up, prioritize and concentrate their own expenditures to achieve competitive scale and quality, without putting all their eggs in one basket. Moreover, it is prudent to allow some opportunistic investment in yet-to-be-realized areas.

Higher Education Graduates Need to be Prepared as Generalists and Specialists for National Labour Markets and Global Citizenship

The earlier functional specialization of higher education systems, involving a diversity of institutional types, can be seen to reflect the needs of occupationally segmented labour markets, particularly when skilled workers were required for clearly specialized roles (Bleiklie, 2007). Demand for specialized graduates continues in traditional professional fields (e.g. medicine, engineering), in new graduate occupations (e.g. paramedical, marketing), and in niche areas of specialization within parts of the services sector (e.g. sports, hospitality) (De Weert, 2009). However, developments in management and administration across various industries require a broad set of generic competencies including team work skills, communication and language skills, project management skills, adaptability, problem solving, and creativity. Academic competence interacts with these other competencies, through disciplinary and cross-disciplinary knowledge and understandings, reasoning, analytical and reflective abilities.

Future higher education graduates need to be able to deal with complex challenges facing the world and have the requisite skills and understandings to exercise global options for gaining employment anywhere they choose. Ramsden (2008) sees the need to improve the preparation of future graduates, including through curriculum overhaul: "we require curricula that are transdisciplinary, that extend students to their limits, that develop skills of inquiry and research, and that are imbued with inter-national perspectives" (Ramsden, 2008). Ramsden suggests that only such qualities will ensure graduates who are able to "embrace complexity, climate change, different forms of citizenship, and different ways of understanding individuality and co-operation".

Horizontal Differences among Higher Education Institutions are Blurring, and Vertical Differences are becoming more Stratified

More generic occupational competencies, greater upskilling of the workforce involving people re-entering education at varying points from different backgrounds, and cross-national mobility of students, are requiring more porous boundaries between institutional types and programmes in higher education. Increasing vertical divergences develop as the horizontal diversity reduces, giving rise to stratified systems, and "the realisation that success at the top of the system is determined in the international league of champions not the national league" (Teichler, 2006). However, concerns to provide equitable access require ladders enabling student mobility within a national system, through articulated programmes, credit transfer arrangements, and collaborative initiatives.

Higher Education Institutions are Becoming Overloaded with Multiple Missions

Universities are facing multiple expectations: producing knowledge and workforce for the needs of modern society, playing a central part in the innovation system, contributing to regional development, increasing social inclusion, and participating in the development of solutions to global problems. Governments tend to translate these expectations into roles and responsibilities, backed by specific-purpose funding or conditionality attaching to general grants. In the UK, for instance, the injection of "third stream funding" has given greater prominence to the development of university relations directly with civil society, through "engagement" as a reciprocal benefit, as distinct from "outreach" as a supply-driven "service" (Brink, 2009). Universities themselves take on wider activities, partly through societal pressure and partly in response to market opportunities. The accumulation of missions blurs strategic vision and can distract from core business and thus it becomes necessary to reassess and clarify mission goals and priorities.

Leading Performance Requires Group Capacity as Well as Individual Brilliance

In higher education and research, as in elite sports (whether golf, tennis, cycling or motor racing), individual excellence is necessary, but not sufficient, for success in the contemporary competitive environment. Aided by high technology and communications capacity, fields such as nanotechnology, biosciences, geosciences and environmental sciences, require major investments in interdisciplinary centres and related infrastructure. Concurrently with a need for highly creative individuals it is suggested that "big science of the "top-down" type (e.g. genomics and proteomics) is overshadowing individual research" (Arai, 2007). In the quest for innovation it is the ability to marshal resources, including intellectual capability, to achieve "significant advances" ahead of the competition that counts. In this regard, group productivity may be far more important than individual productivity: "scientific recognition is based on group output and the ability to capture significant attention based on quality and quantity of output, rather than output per researcher" (National Board of Employment, Education and Training, 1993).

Mass Higher Education Enables Customization

Enlargement of higher education participation increases the diversity of demand for services, in terms of curriculum content and orientation, study modes, places and times for learning, and trade-offs between convenience, quality and price. Sophisticated supply technologies, including powerful, ubiquitous computing and networking, allows for a university's teaching and research functions to be distributed in space, and possibly in time (Wulf, 2008). Markets for higher education services can provide a premium for niche services that reflect customer segmentation and the tailoring of programmes to meet the particular needs and circumstances of individual firms, public sector bodies, and groups of learners. The scale and diversity of demand, alongside the capacity of available technologies, allows for varying combinations of physical and virtual provision and, thereby, greater differentiation among providers in their value propositions. In mass higher education systems a significant differentiating feature is the quality of the student university experience that bonds graduates belonging locally, even when they are globally dispersed, especially the capacity of some institutions to provide learning intimacy.

In the Distributed Knowledge Society Universities are Permeable and Stable Organizations

The boundaries between universities and the external world are becoming more permeable, as knowledge is produced and disseminated by multiple players in diverse environments (Nowotny, Scott and Gibbons, 2001). One aspect of increasing porosity relates to education and training, and another relates to research and innovation. With regard to higher education, much depends on the breadth of view taken about purposes and expected outcomes. A broad view would include aptitudes, proficiencies, skills and understandings developed in workplaces and social as well as educational contexts. Issues arise regarding the extent to which education programmes build in or recognize relevant learning experiences outside the formal environment of the university. With regard to research and innovation, much depends on the breadth of view taken about purposes and expected impacts of research, there is increasing collaboration between universities and other public sector and community bodies and private firms, often involving a two-way flow of knowledge and know-how. Research problems may be defined in various contexts, and solved by participants working together in different places and from different perspectives.

Some suggest that this porosity in mass higher education makes a structured national "system" and solid hierarchies out of place, requiring "soft diversity" - more fluid structures, more flexible and adaptable institutional missions - rather than "hard differentiation" (stratification), in which institutions at different levels have different missions. In this view, "increasing research selectivity relates back to neat structured hierarchies in which the position of the elite universities is strengthened" (Scott, 2005). However, while complex interrelations with civil society and markets might make classification of institutions difficult, in terms of simple, unambiguous functional or hierarchical principles (Bleiklie and Byrkjeflot, 2002), the extent to which sources of knowledge within innovation systems have become more diverse need not imply any decline in the role of universities as fundamental research centres (Mowery and Sampat, 2005). Not only are more distributed modes of knowledge production and dissemination shifting functions out from universities to the wider society, universities also are absorbing (selectively or otherwise) the distributed capabilities and connections, thereby functioning on a wider scope. The university must remain relatively stable to continue producing the next generation of researchers and the reproduction of cultural norms (Henkel, 2002). The new challenge is in the global context where the world's leading universities "operate in an environment in which traditional political, linguistic and access boundaries are increasingly porous" (Mohrman, Ma and Baker, 2008). In that environment top universities seek out partners that have distinguishing sets of complementary capabilities.

Competitive Success Requires Strategic Collaboration

Very few institutions have sufficient capacity to compete alone in the contemporary environment in any industry. The most successful organizations collaborate with others, including their competitors, at different points along the supply chain, where they do not have distinctive competitive advantages, and can share common costs or work together to expand the scale of the market (Brandenburger and Nalebuff, 1996). The alliances within the airlines industry illustrate the advantages that accrue to the companies and their customers, through cross-travel and shared services. Advances in communications and technology offer new possibilities for university specializations and course-sharing in cyberspace - global hubs & spokes - along with cross-national institutional alliances. Partner selection involves consideration of multiple factors, including complementary capacities, reputation for reliability, and prestige.

Local Support Sustains Global Standing and Global Connections Advantage Local Communities

Simultaneously, research universities must keep up with the global pace-setters in knowledge advancement, attend to the quality of the student experience, and engage with their local supporting communities. It is the strength of local support that ultimately sustains a university, and it is a responsibility of the university to flow through to the benefit of local communities its advantage of global access to the world's knowledge networks. The means of transfer are numerous and include contributions to public policy consideration, evidence and argument; translation of research to application in practical settings; continuing development of practising professionals; and awareness raising through public communications.

ELITE UNIVERSITIES PAST AND PRESENT

In exploring the role of elite universities in the contemporary context, it is worthwhile to reflect on prior understandings of their roles and on the changing relations between them and the state, markets and civil society.

The predominant Western notion of a university derives from the nineteenth century writings of John Henry Newman in England and Wilhelm von Humboldt in Germany. In his 1852 essay *The Idea of a University*, Newman saw the university as "a place... in which the intellect may safely range and speculate... where inquiry is pushed forward...discoveries verified and perfected, and...error exposed by the collision of mind with mind" (Newman, 1852). Humboldt envisaged learning as a mutual process between students and teachers within institutional environments, whose characteristic was that "they always treat learning in terms of incompletely-solved problems. They are engaged in a process of continuous inquiry" (Humboldt, 1810). Contemporary research universities have evolved more along the lines of the Humboldtian model of education embedded in research, following the American research university, pioneered by the University of Michigan and Johns Hopkins University in the late nineteenth century, through the incorporation of graduate education and research along with liberal education in a single institution. In Australia and elsewhere, the research function of universities did not develop until the mid twentieth century on the base of elite undergraduate education.

The second half of the twentieth century, at least for developed economies, radically redefined formerly understood roles of universities and their external relations. These redefinitions reflected the imperatives of the times, ranging from a broad nation-building agenda in the immediate post-Second World War period, through an extensive period of accommodation to demographically driven growth in demand for higher education, involving increased reliance on private financing, alongside more deliberate investment in human capital and R&D, as a perceived source of productivity growth and enhanced economic competiteness.

When we look back at conceptions of university roles around fifty years ago, we get some sense of the extent of shift and the limits of the current discourse. In 1956, the Committee on Australian Universities, chaired by Sir Keith Murray, assessed the condition of a then elite university sector, whose primary role was seen to be the education of "the able young", with a secondary but connected role for research. The committee observed in its 1957 report that "when the student enters the university he should be entering a community with an intellectual and social climate of its own...universities have not only to teach subjects; they have also to be equipped to give young human beings an opportunity to stretch their mental powers and to learn something of their fellow human beings" (Parliament of the Commonwealth of Australia, 1957). In contrast, a current review of the Australian Qualifications Framework starts from the narrow premise that the purpose of a Bachelor degree is "to prepare individuals for professional work who apply a body of knowledge in a range of contexts and/or as a pathway for further learning." (Australian Qualifications Framework Council, 2009)

With regard to research in universities, the Murray committee understood the role of "patient capital", in terms of practical benefits arising from discoveries from research that was not necessarily undertaken for practical purposes, and the stimulation for learning that it affords:

> Advances in knowledge have come because free inquirers have been pursuing their own ideas and insights, devotedly and with great persistence, in pursuit of enlightenment for its own sake...Such men have double value. In the first place, they are necessary to keep the march of human knowledge on the move;

and in the second place they are the men from whom ambitious and energetic students wish to learn, and from whom they should be given the opportunity to learn. Without them human discovery of basic truth would grind to a stand-still, and the teaching of the able young would become stale and unprofitable.

This view echoed the advice of Vanevaar Bush in his report, *Science the Endless Frontier*, to the President of the United States in 1945:

Scientific progress on a broad front results from the free play of free intellects, working on subjects of their own choice, in the manner dictated by their curiosity for exploration of the unknown. Freedom of inquiry must be preserved under any plan for Government support of science. (Bush, 1945)

The Menzies government, which introduced federal funding for universities, accepting the advice of the Murray committee, effectively entered into a social compact with the then established group of universities. The rationale was one of mutual dependency and responsibility, expressed in the following terms:

No independent nation in the modern age can maintain a civilized way of life unless it is well served by its universities; and no university nowadays can succeed in its double aim of high education and the pursuit of knowledge without the good-will and support of the government and the country. Govern-ments are therefore bound to give to universities what assistance they need to perform their proper functions; but in their turn universities are bound to be vigilant to see that they give the services to the community that are required by the necessities of the age. (Parliament of the Commonwealth of Australia, 1957)

The Murray committee also recognized that universities require a high level of independence and flexibility to fulfil their role, including where necessary revealing errors and deceits, and being critical of taken-for-granted views and policy assump-tions. At the same time, the committee was clear that the public recognition and support that enables universities to prosper thrusts on them a heavy responsibility to play their part in meeting the nation's legitimate needs.

This appreciation of mutual dependency and responsibility remains valid today, but its rationale and expression are necessarily different from that of fifty years ago. On the one hand, mutual responsibility is even weightier in the contemporary era of complex global challenges. That is, contemporary universities need to draw upon their various strengths and connections in creative and vigorous ways, to help build the capacity of communities to tackle unprecedented challenges. On the other hand, there have been two major changes affecting the two core functions of universities. The first is that student participation in higher education has expanded beyond the elite "able young", and the employment destinations of graduates have extended into a wide range of areas. Consequently, society needs to find ways of accommodating the diverse growth in the best possible ways, and higher education institutions have to provide education and training appropriate to diverse student and labour market needs. The second change involves the orientation and funding of research, with a focus on ways and means of promoting direct industry access to scientific knowledge, know-how and instrumentation and an emphasis on research commercialisation and national research priorities. This more comprehensive view than that of Vanevaar Bush recognizes that the course of scientific progress is driven not only by basic research, and that elite research universities are only one source of new knowledge. Problems set outside the university also define the research agenda, and they can be no less challenging or fundamental or important than those of intellectual interest to a university professor. Hence, the notion of a national compact between government and universities, as a group, can no longer be predicated only on the roles of the elite research universities; it must be broader or it must be replaced by a range of compacts related to varying institutional roles.

A particular difficulty is that in accommodating the enlargement of higher education, and in seeking more direct access to the tacit knowledge of researchers to solve commercial and community problems, a narrowly instrumentalist view of the contributions of universities has crowded out other views, including appreciating the need for a balance of plural capabilities to meet diverse needs. In particular, there has been an over-correction with an anti-elite sentiment, because the apparent assumption is that an elite role is no longer appropriate or useful and therefore it should be replaced or absorbed. The redefinition of the purpose of a bachelor degree in Australia is a case in point, in that if the degree is seen to be solely for the purpose of preparing individuals for professional work, where does a generalist arts degree fit? What is the worth of a degree in literature or history or philosophy under such a limited view? In a similar vein, the predecessor to the current Australian government refused funding for several research projects which had been recommended through peer review, on the grounds that they served no demonstrably useful purpose, following a campaign by a section of the media against alleged academic indulgence.

Relevance may well serve as a guiding principle for a large part of contemporary higher education and university research - whether through curriculum orientations to graduate "employability" or immediate commercial applications of research. However, relevance in the sense of demonstrable utility has swamped the policy discourse in a dangerously reductionist way. It would be an intellectually impoverished country, and one that risks limiting its capability to sustain itself, that places no value on the pursuit of knowledge in areas that have no obvious immediate usefulness. There has to be a place for the exploration of curiosity and uncomfortable thoughts, not everywhere but at least somewhere and even there not exclusively. Public policy needs to comprehend the less obvious, subtle and indirect ways and means by which some universities make their social contributions. Australia's Productivity Commission in its 2007 report on Public Support for Science and Innovation showed some understanding[7]. Similarly, in Canada a broad view has been taken about research, including basic research which is seen to serve as "a national strategic reserve" - making available the expertise needed to address unexpected events when they occur. The Canadian view is a balanced one, analogous to a financial investment portfolio[8].

In their reflective essay of 2008, *What are universities for?*, published by the League of European Research Universities, Geoffrey Boulton and Colin Lucas offer a corrective to the narrow and immediate instrumentalism of government policies in many countries. They note a "growing tendency to see universities as sources of highly specific benefits... particularly marketable commodities for their customers, be they students, business or the state." They suggest that research universities are able to make such contributions, because they deal with the universality of knowledge:

> They seek to understand that which we do not understand; they seek to explain complexity; they seek to discover that which is hidden from us. They seek to establish what is common to all of us and what distinguishes us each from another or each group from another. These things are common to the whole of university endeavour whatever the discipline. They are not "academic" in the pejorative sense of the word, but are of profound, practical utility. They are the foundation upon which the university enterprise rests and upon which its significance for society is built. (Boulton and Lucas, 2008)

Hence they argue that governments should respect the essential core of the research university and not act to erode or circumscribe it. This is not a novel reminder, for as Derek Bok observed in 1990, universities "help in but do not determine" outcomes such as effective corporate governance, sound financial regulation, competent government, effective schools, improved health or reduced poverty. He cautioned that "we will debase our academic institutions and the work they do if we think of them merely or even primarily as means rather than ends." (Bok, 1990)

The capacity of universities to undertake long-term research is fundamental to their direct and indirect contributions to national innovation. The research literature indicates that basic research is an important source of (i) the skills (particularly those based on tacit knowledge) required to translate knowledge into practice (Salter and Martin, 2001), (ii) an enhanced ability to solve complex technological problems, and (iii) the "entry ticket" to the world's stock of knowledge, providing the ability to participate effectively in networks and absorb and exploit the resulting knowledge and skills (Martin and Tang, 2007). Additionally and importantly, basic research, or long-term research whether "curiosity-driven" or "use-inspired" which explores underlying issues, underpins disciplinary advancement.

To sustain economic competitiveness, countries like Australia must be able to generate new knowledge and understand and interpret that generated elsewhere; they cannot rely on a strategy of passive absorption of foreign technology. To benefit from the public good of world knowledge, nations have to be actively engaged in cutting edge research. Free riding on the rest of the world's research is not a realistic option - because the links between researchers are personal and they are based on informal trading in ideas, techniques and devices. To access and make sense of basic research you have to be a contributing insider to the community of international researchers in a field. Moreover, the capacity to understand and use the results of basic research performed elsewhere requires a considerable investment in institutions, skills, equipment and networks (Pavitt, 2001).

Characteristics of Contemporary Elite Universities

Today we might define a research university, in its ideal type, as a community of intelligent people, new and experienced, together searching for knowledge in a culture of discovery and in systematic ways that are open to scrutiny and contest. Elite research universities are structured to enable intellectual conversations across the generations and across various academic disciplines (Shapiro, 2001). They are places where "the able young" can and do challenge orthodoxy and complacency, and where they learn not only content knowledge and technique, but also how to think analytically and independently. They are actively engaged with their communities, and have a special capacity to connect expert and lay views in tackling problems (Kerr, Cunningham and Tutton, 2007).

Input characteristics. Elite universities may be distinguished by five sets of inputs, that is, the quality of the students they attract; the expertise of academic faculty and administrative staff; the depth of research capability; institutional asset strength and revenue diversity; and high-cost needs.

Generally, elite universities attract concentrations of young talent through student admissions, typically the top attaining cohorts of recent school leavers, most-promising doctoral students and top tier post-doctorates. Within national systems, Moodie (2009) distinguishes between "selecting" and "recruiting" universities, noting that recruiting universities operate in a buyers' market, whilst selecting universities operate in a sellers' market (Moodie, 2009). However, within the global environment, nationally selecting universities face stiffer competition and become recruiters, needing to offer inducements to attract talent, especially graduate research students.

It is in these universities that the leading professors in their fields are typically found. These institutions also attract high-quality academic and administrative staff, through recruitment processes that are open to national and international competition.

Within nations, elite institutions are the key nodes of research capability (infrastructure + expertise). They are typically the most successful in winning competitive research grants and industry research sponsorships, and they have greater diversity than others in their sources of income through donor support and returns from research commercialization. Nevertheless, they have higher cost needs arising from the complexity of their undertakings, including interdisciplinary centres, integration of research elements in student education, and greater technological infrastructure for discovery and translation.

Activity and output characteristics. Elite research universities may be distinguished also by the nature of their activities, notably the ground-breaking work they do; their role in underpinning basic research; their leadership in the development of disciplinary knowledge; their contributions to educational innovation; their public policy inputs, analysis and critical commentary; and the conduits they provide for international scholarly dialogue.

Within the Australian higher education system, Group of Eight (Go8) universities are characterized by the emphasis they give to research and research training performed with reference to leading international standards; substantial time devoted to advanced hands-on undergraduate and graduate training in scientific theory and research methods linked to cutting-edge research; hosting of major research infrastructure and instrumentation; and strategic efforts to commercialize useful knowledge and intellectual property.

In terms of outputs, elite universities produce highly regarded outcomes, including graduates who take up leadership roles in the professions, business and public service. They supply the bulk of the nation's future academic workforce. Elite universities are home to the major producers of high quality research publications, exhibitions and performances. Moreover, they source the major contributors to policy debates and the formation of solutions to national and global problems.

How Valid is it to Treat the University as a Whole Institution for Evaluation or Comparison?

Many universities in Australia, as in Europe and other parts of the world, are characterized by a coexistence of departments of different quality in their teaching and research. Some may claim broad parity across institutions, notwithstanding differences in specific areas, but that is a questionable view based on several assumptions, including the perspective that weaknesses in one area are offset by strengths in others. The evaluative criteria applied to "professional" fields, such as engineering, law, accounting and medicine, are specific to those fields; they differ from one another, and from those, also varied, criteria applied to the humanities and natural sciences. One university may be regarded highly for its philosophy and physics but not well regarded for its psychology. Moreover, a university may be highly regarded for the quality of its research in a particular field, say mathematics, but score poorly on measures of student satisfaction with teaching in the same field. Conversely, student satisfaction with teaching may be reasonably high in a university whose research performance in that area is relatively low.

However, acceptance of scattered mediocrity is a complacent view, and a dangerous one in a highly competitive international environment, which no longer suffices, especially where major problems call for contributions across multiple disciplines, all of which need to be strong. In universities with large shares of strongly performing areas, through the institutional culture of expectations, especially when performance is subject to rigorous evaluation against international benchmarks, there is possibly greater pressure on weaker areas to improve or be bolstered or removed. Clearly, there are many institutions with some strong areas of expertise. The distinguishing feature of elite research universities is the concentration of their expertise and the institutional culture that drives and derives from the quest to excel. One of their functions in national systems of higher education is to increase the pressure on other institutions to raise their performance, including by opening up their facilities to others and working in collaboration with them.

Thus, it is both valid and invalid to compare universities on a whole of institution basis and a mix of university-wide and field-related indicators is likely to be most informative.

THE NEED TO CONCENTRATE RESEARCH CAPABILITIES IN ELITE UNIVERSITIES

Among the various motives attributed to the movement for building up elite universities is that associated with national pride. It is argued, for instance, that relatively low rankings on global league ladders have induced some governments to skew their investments in favour of "nation positioning institutions" (Hazelkorn, 2008). Moreover, the rankings are seen not merely as a reflection of actual drivers but as drivers themselves, defining what quality means and shaping university mission and balance of activity (Marginson, 2007), inflating the "academic arms race", inducing universities to chase ever more resources (Ehrenberg, 2004), intensifying competitive pressures, establishing as a worldwide norm the science-strong research university of the Anglo-American tradition, and giving emphasis to institutional stratification and research concentration (Marginson, 2007).

More purposefully, the movement can be understood to be driven by concerns to (a) strengthen and integrate capabilities, in order to address complex and pressing national problems; (b) increase the international visibility of national strengths for attracting talent and inwards investment; (c) open up opportunities for collaboration with universities in other countries that have a similar reputation for excellence; (d) and ensure sufficient capacity for cutting-edge research for the nation through access to world knowledge developments. These motives reflect a view of contemporary universities as engines of innovation and economic development and sources of solutions to social and environmental problems. One of the drivers of innovation is the clustering of talent and the production of new knowledge. In this regard, large research-intensive universities are among the most effective aggregators of highly qualified personnel (Usher, 2009).

In many fields of research in the natural sciences there is a "critical mass" or threshold effect, and "large, well-funded and well-led research groups produce more publications, of higher impact, and receive much higher international recognition than do smaller groups." (National Board of employment, Education and Training, 1993) There are several advantages of scale in research, as noted in a HEFCE (2000) review of research funding policy:

> A larger group of researchers adds to overall vitality, through peer stimulus, the opportunity to exchange and develop ideas, and to be spurred by visible achievement. Second, the per capita marginal costs of research (administration, clerical support, etc) are reduced when a larger group contributes to infrastructure. This factor is significantly accentuated by the high cost of major equipment and facilities in the experimental sciences. Third, larger groups make possible the simultaneous and parallel development of research themes, leading to an overall acceleration. Fourth, group size contributes to diversity of thought and of sub-discipline, increasing the likelihood of cross-fertilisation and fruitful development. Fifth, larger groups of research students provide a more supportive atmosphere for research training. (Higher Education Funding Council for England, 2000)

Concentration involves targeting new funding to build the capacity to sustain new heights of excellence. Typically, new funding is allocated on the basis of proven performance judged against international benchmarks, wherever it is to be found, and where there is genuine potential to scale-up. Additionally, concentration is one dimension of a differentiated system, and differentiation is necessary to create the diversity needed to accommodate, cost-effectively, an enlarged population of learners and to support a wide spectrum of innovation, whether in hi-tech manufacturing, mining, agriculture, or services, including the public sector. However, achieving diversity through differentiation in higher education is a difficult challenge.

The Difficulties of Differentiation

One can consider differences among higher education institutions - what van Vught calls "external diversity" (Van Vught, 2008) and Teichler calls "horizontal diversity (different types of institutions with different functions)" (Teichler, 2004) and differences within higher education institutions - "internal diversity" and "vertical diversity (different levels of quality of inputs, processes and outputs)". When a higher education system is structured on the basis of functional specialization (e.g. nurse education colleges, teacher education colleges, institutes of technology, research universities), there is a wider variety of institutional types but the variety of activities (e.g. range of educational offerings) within an institution is more limited than in the system of more comprehensive institutions (e.g. polytechnics or universities). Hence, "internal" or "vertical" diversity involves activity differences (what is done and how much), as well as qualitative differences (how well it is done). It does not necessarily follow that a wider range of internal functions result in a greater variety of ways and means of conducting those functions within a system, nor does it follow that the quality of particular functions is either raised or lowered. The apparent trade-offs between structural specialization and comprehensiveness, have been perceived differently in those countries that have opted for distinctive institutional types and those adopting unitary systems. However, it is not clear to what extent higher education systems are becoming more integrated or dispersed, convergent or divergent, homogeneous or heterogeneous.

As a useful guide to policy options, Frans van Vught and others have pointed to the range of drivers of sameness and difference in higher education systems (Van Vught, 2008). The strong drivers of homogenization include the power of academic norms that place most value on research-based prestige, reinforced by rewards in the academic labour market (Fairweather, 2009); normative policy settings of governments, financial incentives and regulations (including at the international level); and "market mechanisms" encouraging competition for similar rewards. However, some see greater competition in mass higher contexts creating opportunities for new institutions to enter the market with new products and services, and for established institutions to take up niche positions, and the growth of various private providers around the world gives this view support.

Some suggest a reduced need for functional specialization and the concurrent development of "more hierarchical and horizontally permeable systems" (Scott, 2009). The case for greater hierarchy arises from the intensification of international competition at the top, which represents recognition of the high costs of research, and an acceptance of prestige drivers. The case for horizontal porosity arises from a number of the changes discussed earlier, including changes in labour market requirements affecting the nature of graduate supply and the need for further learning, growth in international student mobility, changes in knowledge production affecting the conduct of research, and the multiplication of the missions of higher education institutions.

However, there are countervailing pressures suggesting the need for greater heterogeneity of higher education providers, to accommodate growth in participation of people of diverse, such as backgrounds, talents, motivations and job expectations, and to do so cost-effectively. Some contend that we are witnessing "more and more vertical and horizontal specialization, far beyond the classical divide, between teaching only and research universities" (Laredo, 2007). This development is seen to be driven by the growth of private providers, developments in educational technologies, and the integration or non-integration of new missions with teaching and research. Mission multiplication involves some over-loading of institutional responsibilities, with risk to quality and efficiency, indicating some scope for separation or at least redefinition of roles.

In structural terms, there are several options, including unitary systems of comprehensive institutions, although this is a very expensive option in view of the high costs associated with quality research; articulated links across functionally specialized institutions; or institutional federations or alliances of institutions with complementary capabilities. In strategic terms, whatever the structural composition, there is a need for mission clarity and renegotiation of resources for activities linked to missions, with the flexibility to adapt to change.

Frans van Vught (2008) defines differentiation as the process by which higher education systems diversify through the emergence of new entities (Van Vught, 2008). However, it is useful to distinguish between diversification as creating and accommodating variety, and differentiation as enabling and declaring divergence. In business terms, a company may diversify its customer mix and its product range, such as by offering high-cost and low-cost options, but differentiates itself when it offers a unique value proposition (Feldman, 2009); when it does what others don't or can't, and when it makes itself unlike the rest of its type. Differentiation as an institutional strategy that allows for price premiums above those of institutions adopting a low-cost strategy, may derive from brand image, customer service, product uniqueness, technology, facilities or accessibility (Porter, 1985). A higher education system may be highly diversified in its student mix and educational offerings, but relatively undifferentiated in terms of institutional types and distinguishable characteristics of institutions within each type, including recognition of differences in the quality of degrees.

Australia, for example, has a diverse but largely undifferentiated university system. There is great diversity in the student body, whether domestic or international, preparatory, undergraduate or graduate, in terms of age, ethnicity, prior knowledge and experience, motivations and aptitudes and mode of participation (full-time, part-time, external, virtual or mixed). There are areas where efforts can be seen as being made by these universities to differentiate themselves from one another, which include diverse criteria for student admission, differences in degree structures and requirements, and in curriculum, pedagogy and means of assessment. Moreover, there are differences in institutional research capability and orientation, the integration of research and education, the extent and nature of engagement with communities, the operation of commercial enterprises, and levels of international-ization. For instance, the University of Melbourne with its "Melbourne Model" has departed from the Australian practice of professional specialization for the bachelor degree, and moved to a general bachelor's degree with professional preparation for the master's degree. A number of technological universities have developed graduate capabilities that align with the employability expectations of employers. The University of Western Sydney has an extensive programme of community engagement functions. Swinburne University has deliberately focused on a niche set of research fields. Monash University has a global strategy involving offshore campuses and internationalized curricula. Greater flexibility for universities to develop these various differences, according to the missions they have set for themselves, including the flexibility to offer special services at price premiums, would help achieve a more diverse and differentiated higher education system that would be more responsive and efficient than the current arrangement.

Nevertheless, Australia, like the German and Scandinavian systems, has a formal framework of "parity of esteem" in the equivalence of qualifications, and government policy and financing frameworks treat all universities on the same basis. This approach can be seen to reflect a former period of horizontal specialization of higher education institutions, before the closure of the binary divide, when the advanced education sector was presented as "equal but different" in comparison with the university sector.

Australia, in 1986, set out on the Dawkins' agenda to collapse the binary divide and create an undifferentiated "unified national system" of universities. Subsequent allocations of public funding for teaching and research have been premised on the basis of a "fair-go": an Australian virtue of unimpeded opportunity for new players who are willing to make an effort, alongside even-handedness and transparency in the rules of the game. The Dawkins approach led to an evening-out and eventual normalization of funding rates per student place by field of study, across old and new universities. It provided targeted funds to encourage teaching staff to obtain higher degrees and, through a "clawback" from established universities, provided funds to promote research in the newer institutions.

The outcome has been flat. More specifically, the 19 pre-Dawkins universities, which together accounted for 90.26% of total research income in 1995, had a reduction in their share to 87.35% in 2005, a loss of 2.91 percentage points. This 2.91% shift went to the 11 smallest research performers of the post-Dawkins' institutions, which together gained 1.91 percentage points, taking their combined share to 3.8%. Four of the previous institutes of technology increased their share, with the net rise for the five new technology universities being 1.11 percentage points, and bringing that group to a combined share of 7.5%. The Go8 share stayed at around 70%, notwithstanding some shifts within the group. The biggest declines were among the pre-Dawkins post-1950s universities. This policy of spawning tadpoles, while forgetting to feed the frogs, has bogged down the nation's capacity for making great leaps forward.

Subsequent policy implementation, across party-political boundaries through the 1990s to the present, including the formulation of national protocols for university status, has seen the continuation of an even-handed, non-discriminating approach. In the provision of government funds for scholarships, for instance, a "base" grant is made automatically to all universities, with additional numbers typically scaled to enrolment size. Where performance-related measures have been included in funding formulae, they have often been implemented with buffers and caps, in order to smooth the distribution of gains and losses. This was the case with the former block schemes for research infrastructure (IGS) and research training (RTS). Moreover, the smoothing approach has been continued with their replacement schemes: the SRE (formerly RIBG) provides a higher indirect cost rate for competitive research grants, but the JRE (formerly IGS) has removed competitive grants from the income metric in the allocation formula. Hence, the institutional shares of total SRE +JRE funds in 2010 are unchanged from the shares of total IGS +RIBG in 2009. With all boats rising this is perceived to be a clever domestic outcome politically.

Governments have difficulty in formally marking institutional differences and treating institutions differentially. Further, there are no readily acceptable ways for institutions to describe what they are if they are not a research university, that is, are they teaching-intensive, business-facing, regionally engaged, equity-dedicated, technological, innovative and/or regional? With respect to this, there should be status in teaching well, developing professionals, translating research, and contributing to regional community development and policy and financing ought to permit some institutions to do a few things very well rather than having to do a lot of things reasonably well.

Martin Trow identified, some time ago, that it is unreasonable, unfair and inefficient to place expectations on institutions to become what they are not set up to be:

A central problem for higher education policy in every modern society is how to sustain the diversity of institutions, including many of which are primarily teaching institutions without a significant research capacity, against the pressure for institutional drift toward a common model of the research university - the effort alone shapes the character of an institution to be something other than what it is - a prescription for frustration and discontent. (Trow, 2003)

The US and Japan have higher education systems, which are hierarchically differentiated, (e.g. within research institutions there are clear differences in prestige and quality). Interestingly, the German Excellence Initiative is seen to represent, in policy terms, "a termination of the longstanding fiction of a qualitatively homogeneous higher education system supported by de facto legal homogeneity" (Kehm and Pasternack, 2009). The question arises as to whether, or to what extent, non-structural and non-formal understandings of qualitative differences among institutions might promote differentiation.

Arguments against Special Treatment for Elite Institutions

Within national contexts, claims favouring elite universities can be contentious because their acceptance implies and may produce institutional differentiation within national systems. Several lines of counter argument can be identified.

The first institutionalist rejection of concentration is quibbling and it is that the advocates of concentration are simply self-interested in the promotion of their institutions, as if the opponents are indifferent.

A second line of argument, and one that is able to be tested to some extent against evidence, is that concentration is inherently unfair - it favours those institutions that have accrued advantage; if others were to be given equivalent treatment over time they would achieve (eventually) at least commensurately; and balanced investment should have regard to future potential as well as past performance.

At the time of debate about the closure of the binary divide in Australian higher education in the late 1980s, the then central institutes of technology argued that they were undertaking research of community value that was neither properly recognised nor funded, and that elevation to university status would enable them to develop their potential for the benefit of the nation. As it turned out, some twenty years later, the share of research performed by that set of institutions has increased only marginally, notwithstanding a major shift of government funding towards application-oriented research. However, the combined effect of a large number of small gains on the part of the many newcomer institutions has resulted in no change in the share of the top performing eight universities. They have much increased amounts of research funding, in absolute terms, but have not moved ahead in relative terms, whereas in many other countries the performance gap has been widening between the top universities and the system average.

Selectivity (supporting the best wherever they are found) and concentration (targeted funding to strengthen capability), were expressed in 1987 as the dual principles to guide the funding of higher education research in Australia. However, the subsequent course of policy development has been driven by selectivity alone. Some argue that concentration is an outcome of selectivity[9], but that is not the apparent outcome in Australia. A continuing reliance on a policy of selectivity alone would effectively hold back the leading universities, just as a reliance on concentration alone would thwart the emergence of new research areas. The combination of selectivity and concentration allows for a balance of opportunities.

Some will assert that provision needs to be made for new and emerging areas, and that institutions with the potential to build up strengths should be aided to do so. Moreover, some will add that a failure to enable new areas to develop effectively entrenches the privilege of institutions that were given assistance many years ago when they were at the fledgling stage. Without doubt, emerging strengths should be fostered, particularly in areas (both in fields of inquiry and in institutions) that promise national benefits. However, potential is more than promise and it does not grow without roots. That is, disciplinary and cross-disciplinary breakthroughs are normally not made by novices and new areas of strength have emerged in Australia, historically, on the back of a track record of performance validated by academic peers.

A third line of argument is that preferential treatment of internationally-referenced elite institutions undermines the dynamism of the system as a whole, leading to complacency, ossification and diminution of research of national, regional and local relevance that is highly valued by users[10]. On the one hand, notwithstanding the benefits of agglomeration, there are off-setting benefits for a society through having competition among talented researchers from different locations. In this regard, where resources and talents are too concentrated, inquiry can be subject to too much "group think" (Litan and Mitchell, 2008). On the other hand, there are inefficiencies associated with encouraging all flowers to bloom:

We are creating congestion in the pipelines of knowledge, and this has become a liability. It gets in the way of scientific advance. We have to become more selective about true knowledge creation. In fact, we need to devise a system of incentives that will promote self-selection and specialization, so that those with a comparative advantage in knowledge creation will not be crowded out by those with a comparative advantage in preservation and transmission (including, but not limited to, teaching), and vice versa. (Trajtenberg, 2008)

A fourth line of argument is that support of the elite is anti-egalitarian; it reduces equity of opportunity for students and reproduces inequality. This argument is sometimes put in the context of equating elite (best) with elitist (privileged), with all its connotations of snobbery and anti-democratic sentiment. Nevertheless, the problem of the reproduction of social disadvantage must be addressed, for it is both inequitable and inefficient to deny individual access to opportunity and bar society from the benefits of broader contributing capacity. Rothblatt (2009) has observed with regard to advanced western economies, the tendency to invest discriminatingly in elite universities stands somewhat at odds with "the long recent history of government efforts to promote more egalitarian educational opportunities and, with such actions, to mitigate the effects of social and historical privilege". Moreover, the entrenchment of highly selective access to the top universities can mean that "the screening value of admission is likely to increase more than the intrinsic educational value", with the perceived advantage of elite institutions becoming more exaggerated, with negative implications for democratic societies (Geiger, 2009).

Taking a long view, elite universities around the world have moved beyond places of passage for the privileged to the more academically talented. Contemporary elite universities are academically elite; they are no longer socio-cultural finishing schools for the modest performer, even if demonstration of merit reflects socio-economic background and opportunity (Palfreyman and Tapper, 2009). In this regard, Palfreyman and Tapper (2009) note the shift towards merit-based selection on the part of Oxford and Cambridge, and Geiger (2009) reports similar shifts for the US Ivy League, along with the shift from teaching to research, in determining institutional reputation. This is neither to accept that the status quo is sustainable nor Trow's assumption that massification would lead to expansion and diversification of the system, thereby providing an automatic protection for elite institutions, resulting in them not having to change their values (Trow, 1973). Elite institutions have continuous responsibilities to seek ways of widening access, a matter that is considered further below.

Importantly, as Morhman et al. (2009) have noted, the predominant theme of policy discourse in recent decades has been the transition from domestic elite to mass participation in higher education. Less noted has been the imperative to participate internationally in the formation of research-based universities that provide knowledge for all, not just for elites (Mohrman, Ma and Baker, 2009). The global community benefits through the public good contributions of high-end research that improves understandings and makes breakthrough discoveries. Individual nations also benefit from the ability of their leading universities to participate in this global advancement of knowledge.

Finally, it is argued that concentration of research capability relegates some institutions to "second-class" or inferior status, with resultant disservice to their communities. This concern is heightened by the prospect that elite institutions might only cooperate with one another, nationally and internationally, in such matters as research, student exchange, and recognition of qualifications. That is, in this line of advocacy there can be a conflation of institutional interests with student and social interests.

Nevertheless, a difficult issue that needs to be addressed is that of the mission and position of those higher education institutions that are not in the elite club. As noted earlier, academic norms and the structure of incentives prioritize research, and horizontally different institutional types are inevitably seen in vertical relationship to one another, at least by the academic community, even if not by the lay. Strengthening of the top implies that institutions elsewhere in the system will have to carve out what will be perceived as middle and lower positions, being defined as teaching-intensive, regionally-engaged, and variously contributing to expanding opportunity, second-chance learning, professional education, innovation take-up, or modification of existing knowledge solutions. This matter is also considered further below.

These various counter arguments may be rebutted in part, for instance, by reference to international imperatives, with other countries intensifying investment in their leading institutions, in the context of increasing international competition for talent and the need for scale for contemporary research into complex problems. That is, countries needing a step-change in their research competitiveness cannot afford a step-by-step dilution of their research investment. However, the counter arguments cannot be dismissed entirely and the question is not whether to sustain elite strength, but how to balance that purpose against other aspects of the national interest.

The elite institutions themselves have to be sensitive to that requirement. Indeed, they are by definition in the minority, and governments are bound to their political constituencies to have regard to the mainstream majority of institutional needs and aspirations, without being captured by them. Most important is the mutual responsibility that flows from the support the community gives to elite institutions. Sheldon Rothblatt, following Martin Trow, observes that elite legitimacy derives from the viability of other types of institutions serving important needs, and that they have an obligation to serve inclusively:

> The world-class research university is underpinned by a great variety of other types of tertiary educational institutions upon which its legitimacy, indeed its very success, depends. They serve an immense variety of public needs and provide the opportunities for upward mobility that any generous-minded and decent nation requires. Those institutions possess talent - talent very often

originating within the famous universities. They are engaged in the noble task of uncovering student ability where it might otherwise be neglected. Universities that have scaled the heights in a new environment of fierce rivalries retain an obligation to give creative thought as to how an entire national system can thrive without being partitioned into haves and have-nots, and riven by ruinous jealousies (Rothblatt, 2009).

OPTIONS FOR GOVERNMENT POLICY

The policy challenge is to cater cost-effectively at an acceptable level of quality for education of the general population, while ensuring sufficient capability to participate at the forefront of knowledge formation. The policy objective is to achieve coherence within the national higher education system through a balance of complementary capabilities that work together, not apart, in meeting society's needs. It may well be the case that the bulk of resources need to be dedicated to those institutions which serve the bulk of the demand, and that they should be resourced sufficiently to be good at what they do and build up distinctive strengths. Concurrently, without "cementing-in" any institution or accepting without evidence its claims for special treatment, it is necessary to achieve system-wide development of acceptable quality, without diminishing the outcomes of the elite performers.

What strategies and tactics might be adopted to ensure that countries can sustain and benefit from their elite institutions? In relation to governmental strategies for higher education expansion and university research concentration, ten broad options may be identified, ranging from soft to hard, or from "hands-off", through "hands-hovering" to "hands-on" interventions. Some options can be combined; the magic option is the right combination.

Drift Option

Drift options involve letting concentration or dilution happen. They can be lazy, through avoiding the hard decisions, or they can be deliberate, without declaring any explicit intention or preferred outcome, in the context of other policies and incentives. Such deliberate approaches may be more or less overt (e.g. selectivity in research funding or open competitive funding for centres of excellence, or preferential funding for certain institutions as part of broader initiatives, such as in energy or health policy) in the expectation that things will sort themselves out eventually on the merits or otherwise. This "muddling through" (Lindblom, 1959) rather than "grand plan" approach. has the advantage of being low-risk politically and of leaving developmental options open rather than closed off, but has the disadvantage of low predictability of outcomes.

Increased Autonomy and Operational Flexibility for Institutions

In systems with high levels of central control, or where degrees of autonomy differ among institutional types, university responsiveness and adaptability may be improved through greater devolution of responsibilities. The assumption is that the increased institutional flexibility will give rise to diversity of institutional ways and means, if not missions, given a relaxation of the state controls that produce conformity. However, as indicated earlier, autonomous institutions are free to mimic others, and in a culture of prestige-driven norms can be expected to pursue an emulation strategy. Hence, some boundaries need to be set and incentives established to encourage diversification. Nevertheless, without institutional autonomy, there can be no differentiation, because this is a strategy uniquely determined by each institution; autonomy is essential to any combination of policy options.

Specific-purpose Programme

In order to provide incentives for different institutions to focus on different areas and develop different strengths, governments may provide specific funds, such as for widening participation, regional engagement, translation of research, teaching excellence, collaboration or other activities. This approach is more likely to produce differential outcomes when the allocations (or, in a harder variant the eligibility to participate) for different funding streams, whether reward-based or improvement-based, are limited to a few rather than shared among all institutions. However, pressure typically mounts for such programmes to be systemic, and institutions can be creative in playing to the rules of the game, so the differentiating impacts of the measures are reduced. Nevertheless, there need to be incentives, other than research-related ones, to encourage higher education institutions to play to their strengths.

Competitive Funding

Competition for major grants (such as for centres of excellence, major equipment, research clusters) or tenders for the provision of services (such as contracts for professional development programs, or regional delivery of educational services) can help to promote diversification and differentiation. Competitive schemes have the advantage of being open to multiple contenders against transparent criteria. However, they can tie up institutional resources unproductively in bidding processes. The tiered competition approach of the German Excellence Initiative, alongside its openness, has several attractions - everyone knows the criterion standards; no institution is arbitrarily excluded; many can win something; but only a few can clear the height of the bar necessary for top-up funding for excellence. However, the bigger the competitive stakes the more attention needs to be given to options for the unsuccessful bidders (and non-bidders).

Performance-based Funding

Performance-based funding approaches reflect a view that institutions should be funded, not for what they are, but for what they do. They are typically related to a set of quantitative indicators measured over intervals of time, and funding flows in accordance with improvements in the measures. They may be used to encourage some institutions to expand their level of activity in particular areas, whether in terms of student mix, types of community engagement or contributions to innovation. Their effectiveness in promoting differentiation depends on clarity of purpose and the selection of indicators.

Quality Assessment

Distinct from "quality assurance" - a process that encourages tick-a-box compliance and which itself promotes standardization - quality assessment is concerned with outcomes and how good they are. In terms of educational quality, assessments may affect accreditation to offer programmes, or funding for institutions and programmes. In terms of research, assessments may affect eligibility for funding of doctoral students or participation in particular programmes. Referencing qualitative assessments to international benchmarks can be difficult, and given the limits to available international metrics (relating predominantly to research), it becomes necessary to rely on peer judgements or other subjective indicators of esteem, about which there are predictable challenges, relating to cultural differences in respect of education, and perceived conflicts of interest through associations in respect of research.

Classificatory and Reporting Schema

Governments may seek to provide more nuanced signals to the community about the relative strengths of institutions (within a nation or group of nations) than those conveyed by rankings, against a single metric or limited set of variables. Such information might include comparative descriptors and ratings against multiple criteria, at the institution-wide and field of scholarship levels (e.g. student mix, progress and satisfaction, curriculum breadth and depth, amenities and services, graduate destinations, research performance). Nevertheless, too great a number of descriptors add to costs and confusion. Harder variants of this approach include placement of institutions into typological categories and rankings within typologies. The advantages of typologies are that they enable understanding of institutional orientations and characteristics, improve the information available to guide student choice, provide pointers for businesses seeking to collaborate with institutions, help identify possible partners, and assist the process of policy formulation. However, limits on the availability of comparable data sets, especially across nations, can reduce the meaningfulness of comparisons. Moreover, classificatory approaches need to be fluid rather than fixed, and revised periodically to reflect changes in institutional positioning. However, as with the US Carnegie classification, the modifications build extra complexity with implications for their usefulness to students and others. Point unclear Furthermore, typologies may expose similarities and differences but they do not reveal qualitative performance differences.

Structural Designation

Governments may create or designate institutions to function at different places in the structure of higher education systems. There is a range of possibilities, according to level of educational qualification awarded; breadth by field of scholarship;

balance between teaching and research; extent of research concentration; regional catchment and service; orientation of educational programmes; mode of educational delivery and provision for certain categories of learners. Many institutions cross several such categories, and should be permitted some flexibility to adapt to changing demands and opportunities. Rigid and static structural forms, as discussed earlier, can lead to ossification. It can be difficult to obtain the consent of established institutions to limit their scope and coercive use of accreditation and funding mechanisms, especially to force mergers or takeovers, can create strong resistance. Moreover, designation by government bodies carries a heavy political risk, particularly where institutions that feel they are relegated seek to exert leverage through political influence to advance their position.

Market Mechanisms

Governments may move the higher education industry, including public institutions, into a more demand-driven, competitive environment. This might involve funding (government subsidies and loans) that follows student choice, in respect of teaching, along with institutional tuition pricing flexibility. This approach assumes that competition will stimulate differentiation and innovation in product range and service. It has the advantage that structural outcomes are seen to be the result of market drivers rather than government decisions, although that does not mean that government will be exonerated and thus saved from claims for compensation. As discussed earlier, competition in status markets may not result in significant institutional differentiation, but can lead to loss of diversity through closure of offerings in areas of low student demand. Further, deregulated approaches, particularly involving tuition prices, typically meet with organized community opposition.

Mission-based Funding Negotiations

Market failure may be mitigated and institutional differentiation promoted through mission-based funding compacts between government and individual institutions, and perhaps involving other community interests. Such compacts could extend beyond performance-based funding agreements and cover mission diversity, educational profiles, research focus and linkage, community engagement, collaboration with business and industry, differential funding rates and pricing flexibility, regulation proportional to risk, and performance levels related to standards. An advantage of the compacts approach and its focus on mission is that it can act as a complementary mechanism to aligning institutional goals with the incentives provided through the use of some combination of the other options above. In contrast to the option of structural designation by government, or the use of principal-agent models of service purchasing, the compacts approach allows for mutual agreements. However, much depends on the authority and flexibility of the negotiators.

In contemporary circumstances, the most coherent combination of options for public universities are autonomous institutions operating in a market environment, with mission-based funding compacts as a means of safeguarding public good interests. This combination allows the universities the flexibility they need to be competitive and responsive, noting that the competition nationally and internationally involves private institutions and public-private partnerships.

POSITIONING OPTIONS FOR ELITE UNIVERSITIES

Today, there are great expectations that research universities will help the community address many complex economic, social and environmental problems, whether on a local, national, regional or global scale. It is crucial that universities contribute actively, and it is essential that they preserve the conditions that enable them to do so. Elite universities are unlikely to gain the support they need to that end, if they do not demonstrate their benefits to the communities that sustain them and contribute visibly to broad national objectives.

The foregoing considerations suggest seven imperatives for the sustainability of elite research universities:

Integrity

The first relates to the essence of being a research university, and involves safeguarding the things that matter to a culture of free inquiry. In the continuous search for sources of revenue, and the too frequent tendency of funders to attach compromising conditions on their contributions, the important thing is for a university to be true to itself, to know what it stands for and to stand up for truth. To some this may sound old-fashioned, and it is, but no less relevant today than in the past.

Intensity

The second requirement relates to the combination of focus, persistence and scale that enables knowledge advances in the contemporary research environment. This involves concentrating on those things a university can do best, dedicating sufficient resources to build and sustain strength (critical mass of expertise and high-capacity technology as required by the field), and being able to devote time to task (capacity for long-term research).

Contributing to Inclusiveness

Elite universities have the responsibility to play their part and pull their weight in the social inclusiveness agenda of a nation. For instance, the Group of Eight universities recognize they have a distinctive role to play in ensuring Australia's higher education system meets broad community goals and needs, and provides opportunities for all those with academic potential. The universities aim to reflect in the student and staff bodies the different educational and cultural backgrounds of Australian society. Based on the key capabilities of Go8 universities, the main ways in which they can contribute to a more socially inclusive higher education system are to:
– Increase aspirations and readiness for those with the capacity to succeed in higher education;

- Provide multiple pathways for access, including through structured arrangements with other post-secondary education and training institutions;
- Improve access to graduate level courses for those from under-represented groups to facilitate better outcomes in research, the academic workforce, and professional pathways;
- Contribute to the body of knowledge on improving educational attainment, retention and success, and social inclusion of people from disadvantaged backgrounds; and
- Undertake research that reflects the broader needs of the society and looks to find solutions to current and future issues facing all Australians, in particular indigenous Australians.

Contributing to Innovation

Societal expectations are that leading research universities will have significant constructive impact on national and regional economies. The major contributions of research universities, in this regard, are through the production of highly capable graduates and the generation and translation of knowledge that is useful for private firms and public sector agencies. Research universities need to be open to and accessible by business and initiators of cluster relations with enterprises and other mechanisms to enable entrepreneurial firms to obtain the know-how necessary for them to respond competitively to market opportunities.

Intra-national Collaboration

Elite universities are likely only to gain the ongoing support they need when they contribute to the wider social benefit and are seen to do so, by such actions as enhancing the capacity of other educational and research institutions. In this regard, in the contemporary world of plural higher education systems, some very good performance is to be found in multiple places. Thus, concentrations of expertise and infrastructure should be accessible by researchers in other universities of a country, and elite universities should be inviting others to share in and contribute to their work.

International Partnerships

Few countries alone can afford the scale of infrastructure that is needed for big science. Australia, for instance, as a southern hemisphere continent, is very aware of the expanding research capacity across the northern hemisphere and its inability to replicate it. Hence, it becomes necessary to network with the world's major centres for high-end research, and collaborate in the management of the huge datasets generated in an instrumented world, whether down on the seabed or up in a spacecraft. However, entry tickets are distributed primarily through the recognition of academic performance and thus it is essential to ensure that the nation's leading researchers are internationally reputable, as the hi-tech centres are themselves expertise-seeking.

The last decade or so has seen an expansion of research university networks, e.g. the Association of Pacific Rim Universities (APRU); Canada 13; the Coimbra Group; the Committee on Institutional Cooperation (CIC); the Consortium of Nine Research Universities of China (C9); the Group of Eight (Go8), the International Alliance of Research Universities (IARU); the League of European Research Universities (LERU); the Russell Group; Universitas 21 and the Worldwide Universities Network (WUN). These networks provide complementary bases of capability. More recently there is the development of networks of networks (e.g. Go8/C9) opening up collaborative opportunities for students and academic staff, internationally, within prestige frameworks. Some strong universities (e.g. Harvard) stand outside such groupings and collaborate bilaterally.

Independent Verification of Performance Quality

Finally, research universities need to have robust evaluative processes, so they know how good they are and for maximum credibility, their own evaluations need to be subject to independent, external validation against international benchmarks.

These seven pillars may be regarded as the foundation needed by a nation's elite research universities in contemporary circumstances, but the institutions have to adapt continuously, as many have long done.

NOTES

[1] The views expressed in this paper are those of the author personally and do not necessarily represent the views of Go8 University Vice-Chancellors.

[2] The following countries have specific policies and measures for building 'world-class universities' or centres of research excellence that meet international cutting-edge performance criteria: Botswana, Brazil, Canada, Chile, China, Denmark, England, Finland, France, Germany, India, Indonesia, Japan, Korea, Malaysia, Portugal, Russia, Singapore, South Africa, Sweden, Thailand, Vietnam.

[3] Exponential growth in knowledge, increasing cross-disciplinary research, internationally co-authored articles, and expanding use of digitization and computational capacity are not recent developments, but the pace and scale of their expansion raises the participation cost threshold in many fields. The expansion of high performance computing has facilitated the processing of larger and more complex data in various fields of inquiry, such as: particle physics, astrophysics, biochemistry, nanotechnology, climate modelling, aerospace, genomics, proteomics and financial markets. Universities around the world are experiencing an increasing emphasis on the need for effective data management and stewardship to underpin the changing research environment, as research becomes more dependent on data in digital form, as computers and networks proliferate. Electronic networks provide the infrastructure by which researchers are increasingly able to communicate, access data, information and software in cyberspace, allow them to share and control remote instruments, and link distant learners to virtual classrooms and campuses. [Revolutionizing Science and Engineering Through Cyberinfrastructure: Report of the National Science Foundation Blue Ribbon Advisory Panel on Cyberinfrastructure. (January 2003) ES 2. Available at http://www.communitytechnology. org/nsf_ci_report/]. Enabling greater access to information of all kinds: published and unpublished, text and non-text, the Internet and the Web, have also greatly enhanced collaborative, inter- and multi-disciplinary research, and access to large shared datasets. These developments simultaneously enable more distributed research and require larger nodes of capacity and talent. [OECD (1998),The Global Research Village: How Information and Communication Technologies Affect the Science

System. OECD, Science, Technology and Industry Outlook 1998]. Houghton, J. W. et al. (2003), Changing Research Practices in the Digital Information and Communication Environment. Department of Education, Science and Training, Commonwealth of Australia].

[4] Elite universities tend to be located in "economically vibrant, culturally interesting, and socially progressive parts of the relevant country, and often the capital (cities)". Palfreyman, D. and Tapper, T. (2009) What is an "Elite" or "Leading Global" University?, in Palfreyman, D. and Tapper, T. (Eds.). Structuring Mass Higher Education: The Role of Elite Institutions. Routledge. N.Y.

[5] "In western Europe (following the collapse of the Roman Empire) the only people left with any of the skills to run society in an age of huge political instability were the priests of the Christian Church... university, in the middle ages, referred to a universal course of studies recognised throughout the Christian world. You would learn what a pagan Roman would have learned about logic and music and mathematics, about good and bad arguments and about the nature and proportion of harmony in different contexts, but then you would move on not only to philosophy but to theology, in which you were shown how to trace the connections and harmonies in the text of the Bible, so as to defend the consistency and rationality of doctrines taught by the Church...Anyone emerging from the courses of a "university" institution was regarded as competent to teach in any other institution." Archbishop of Canterbury (Dr Rowan Williams) (2006). "China - what is a University?" Speech given in Wuhan. http:www.archbishopofcanterbury.org/698.

[6] John Wiley, chancellor, University Madison-Wisconsin (2007). The future of research universities. Science and Society Interviews. EMBO Report Vol. 8. No. 9.

"Responsibility for long-range research has been defaulted to America's research universities. Back in the 1960s, when I graduated in physics, essentially all the consumer electronics companies, all the telecommunications companies, all the auto manufacturers, most of the basic materials companies - probably most of the Fortune 500 companies in general - had basic research laboratories and hired scientists, engineers and mathematicians to conduct long-range research. Today almost none of those private sector research laboratories exist anymore. The few that have survived are pale shadows of their former selves, and are tightly focused on near-term goals. Most of today's economy was born in those earlier research laboratories. Most of tomorrow's economy is being born today in university research laboratories."

[7] Productivity Commission (2007). Public Support for Science and Innovation, Research Report. Canberra. Page xxiii.

"Universities' core role remains the provision of teaching and the generation of high quality, openly disseminated basic research. Even where universities undertake research that has practical applications, it is the transfer, diffusion and utilisation of such knowledge and techno-logy that matters in terms of community wellbeing... Apparent cultural barriers between universities and businesses may reflect, in part, the preferences of researchers, who can be more motivated by curiosity and excellence than commercial opportunities. Addressing any cultural 'barrier' requires prudence because it poses risks for the research functions of universities and some of the motivations for science career choices".

[8] Association of Universities and Colleges of Canada (2008), Momentum: the 2008 report on university research and knowledge mobilization. Ottawa.

"Insofar as investments in university research can be considered a university 'R&D portfolio for Canada', investments in 'blue chip' basic research across the full spectrum of disciplines essentially provide, collectively, assurances of dependable and stable returns of research outputs that are less susceptible to market and other fluctuations and more likely to provide longer-term gains. Conversely, strategic investments in highly targeted research entail greater risks, given the potential for failure due to scale or global competition, but the returns, when successful, can potentially be secured more quickly. Using this analogy, one can pursue a dialogue to assess what level and mix of investments in university research will yield the desired level of risk and returns, given governments', universities', research funders' and the public's shared goals for and expectations of university research."

[9] HEFCE (1999), "The role of selectivity and the characteristics of excellence", HEFCE review of research policy and funding.

"In the past ten years the degree of selectivity has increased: the proportion of HEFCE funding going to higher rated departments has increased relative to that going to lower highly rated departments. At the same time, because of the aggregation of highly rated departments in a relatively small number of higher education institutions (HEIs), research funding overall has also become increasingly concentrated. However, this has occurred as a consequential effect of the policy of selective funding, rather than as the result of a deliberate policy of concentration. International comparisons suggest that the UK research base is not less selective or less concentrated than in the USA. In fact the USA has become less selective in the last decade."

[10] HEFCE (1999), "The role of selectivity and the characteristics of excellence", HEFCE review of research policy and funding.

"We recognise the danger that a major increase in selectivity could reduce the number of research-led institutions to a level that would be inconsistent with the general health of the UK research base, in terms of both its economic and its social contribution. In supporting excellence, we believe that a significant increase in selectivity would undermine the dynamism of the system as a whole, leading to complacency and ossification. It could also undermine research of national, regional and local relevance that is highly valued by users, and the removal from many institutions of the beneficial effects of research on teaching and other activities that have been identified by the sub-group investigating teaching, research and other activities. We conclude that for the benefits of HE research to have the greatest impact on the life of the nation, it is not only peak performance that should be supported, but also the 'average' quality of the system. This should be as high as is reasonably possible and well distributed geographically. Excessive attention, either to peaks or to average performance, could undermine effectiveness. This does not necessarily imply different funding and assessment mechanisms, but means that the roles and requirements of good research and the best research should be considered separately."

REFERENCES

Altbach, P., & Balan, J. (2007). *World class worldwide: Transforming research universities in Asia and Latin America*. Baltimore: Johns Hopkins University Press.

Arai. K. (2007). An interview in "The Future Of Research Universities". *EMBO Reports*, 8(9).

Archbishop of Canterbury. (2006). China - What is a university? Speech given in Wuhan. Retrieved http://www.archbishopofcanterbury.org/698

Association of Universities and Colleges of Canada. (2008). *Momentum: The 2008 report on university research and knowledge mobilization*. Ottawa.

Australian Qualifications Framework Council. (2009). *Strengthening the AQF: An architecture for Australia's qualifications*. Consultation Paper.

Bleiklie, I., & Byrkjeflot H. (2002). Changing knowledge regimes - Universities in a new research environment. *Higher Education*, 44(2–3), 1–14.

Bleiklie, I. (2007). Systematic integration and macro steering. In *Main transformations, challenges and emerging patterns in higher education systems*, UNESCO Forum Occasional Paper No. 16. Paris: UNESCO.

Bok, D. (1990). *Universities and the future of America*. Durham and London: Duke University Press.

Boulton, G., & Lucas, C. (2008). *What are universities for?* Leuven: LERU.

Brandenburger, A., & Nalebuff, B. (1996). *Co-Opetition: A revolution mindset that combines competition and cooperation. The game theory strategy: That's changing the game of business.* New York: Currency Doubleday.

Brink, C. (2009, July 1–3). On quality and standards. Keynote Address at *The Australian Universities Quality Forum.* Alice Springs.

Bush, V. (1945). *Science the endless frontier: A report to the President.* Washington, DC: United States Printing Office.

Clark, B. R. (1983). *The higher education system: Academic organization in cross-national perspective.* Berkeley, CA: University of California Press.

Cutler, T. (2008). *Venturous Australia: Building strength in innovation.* Report of the Review of Australia's National Innovation System. Melbourne.

De Weert, E. (2009). *Graduates in the knowledge society: Employer and higher education perspectives.* Presentation at ANECA Conference, Madrid.

Douglass, J. A., King, C. J., & Feller, I. (2009). *A room with a view: Globalization, universities, and the imperative of a broader U.S. perspective.* Berkeley, CA: Center for Studies in Higher Education.

Ehrenberg, R. G. (2004). Econometric studies of higher education. *Journal of Econometrics, 121,* 19–37.

Fairweather, J. (2009) U.S. higher education: Contemporary challenges, policy options, In Palfreyman, D. & Tapper, T. (Eds.). *Structuring mass higher education: The role of elite institutions.* New York: Routledge.

Feldman, D. (2009). Diversify, differentiate, innovate: Airport strategies for success in a new world. Exambela Consulting. Retrieved from http://www.exambela.com.

Geiger, R. L. (2009). The Ivy League. In D. Palfreyman, & T. Tapper (Eds.), *Structuring mass higher education: The role of elite institutions.* New York: Routledge.

Gibbons. M. (2004). Globalisation, innovation and socially robust knowledge. In King, R. (Ed.), *The university in the global age.* Houndmills: Palgrave Macmillan.

Guri-Rosenblit, S., Sebkova, H., & Teichler, U. (2007). Massification and diversity of higher education systems: Interplay of complex dimensions. In *Main transformations, challenges and emerging patterns in higher education systems.* Paris: UNESCO Forum Occasional Paper No. 16.

Hazelkorn, E. (2008). Learning to live with league tables and ranking: The experience of institutional leaders. *Higher Education Policy, 21,* 193–215.

HEFCE. (1999). The role of selectivity and the characteristics of excellence. *HEFCE Review of Research Policy and Funding.*

Henkel, M. (2002). Current science policies and their implications for the concept of Academic identity. In *Proceedings of the international workshop science, training and career: Changing modes of knowledge production and labour markets.* Enschede: CHEPS, University of Twente.

Humboldt, W. Von. (1810). Über die innere und aeussere organisation der hoeheren wissenschaftlichen Anstalten in Berlin. In Leitzmann, et al. (Eds.), *Wilhelm von Humboldts Gesammelte Schriften. Band X.* Berlin.

Kehm. B. & Pasternack, P. (2009), The German "Excellence Initiative". In Palfreyman, D. & Tapper, T. (Eds.), *Structuring mass higher education: The role of elite institutions.* New York: Routledge.

Kerr, A., Cunningham-Burley, S., & Tutton, R. (2007). Shifting subject positions: Experts and lay people in public dialogue. *Social Studies of Science, 37*(3), 385–411.

Laredo, P. (2007). Revisiting the third missions on universities: Toward a renewed categorization of university activities. In *Diversification of higher education and the changing role of knowledge and research.* UNESCO Forum Occasional Paper Series No. 6. Paris: UNESCO.

Lindblom, C. (1959). The science of "Muddling Through". *Public Administration Review, 19,* 79–88.

Litan, R., & Mitchell, L. (2008). Should universities be agents of economic development? In C. J. Schramm, et al. (Eds.), *The future of the research university: Meeting the global challenges of the 21st century.* Missouri: Kauffman Foundation.

Marginson, S. (2007). *Global university rankings: Where to from here?* Paper presented at the Asia-Pacific Association for International Education, Singapore.

Marginson, S. (2007). Global university rankings: Implications in general and for Australia. *Journal of Higher Education Policy and Management*, *29*(2), 131–142.

Martin, B. R., & Tang, P. (2007). *The benefits from publicly funded research*. SPRU Electronic Working Paper Series, Paper No. 161. University of Sussex.

Meek, V. L. (2000). Understanding diversity and differentiation in higher education: An overview. *Higher Education Policy*, *13*, 1–6.

Meek, V. L., & Davies, D. (2009). Policy dynamics in higher education and research: concepts and observations. In V. L. Meek, U. Teichler, & M. Kearney (Eds.), *Higher education, research and innovation*. Kassel: International Center for Higher Education Research.

Mian, S., & W. Hulsink (2009). Building knowledge ecosystems through science and technology parks: A comparative review of the emerging US and European regional models. Paper prepared for the XXVI IASP World Conference on Science and Technology Parks, June 1–4, RTP, North Carolina, USA.

Mohrman, K., Ma, W., & Baker, D. (2009). The research university in transition: The emerging global model. *Higher Education Policy*, *21*, 5–27.

Moodie, G. (2009). Four tiers. *Higher Education*, *58*, 302–320.

Mowery, D. C., & Sampat, B. N. (2005). Universities in National innovation systems. In J. Fagerberg, D. Mowery, & Nelson. (Eds.), *Oxford handbook of innovation*. Oxford: Oxford University Press.

Natelson, D. (2007). *Long-Term research, companies and universities*. Retrieved from http://nanoscale. blogspot.com/2007/03/long-term-research-companies-and.html

National Board of Employment, Education and Training. (1993). *The effects of resource concentration on research performance*. Commissioned Report, No. 25. Canberra.

National Intelligence Council. (2008). *Global trends 2025: A transformed world*. Washington: US Government Printing Office. Retrieved from http://www.dni.gov/nic/NIC_2025_project.html.

Newman, J. H. (1852). *The idea of a university*. Longmans, Green.

Nowotny, H., Scott, P., & Gibbons, M. (2001). *Re-Thinking science: Knowledge and the public age of uncertainty*. London: Polity press.

OECD. (1997). *National innovation systems*. Paris: OECD.

Palfreyman, D., & Tapper, T. (2009). What is an "Elite" or "Leading Global" university? In D. Palfreyman, & Tapper, T. (Eds.) *Structuring mass higher education: The role of elite institutions*. New York: Routledge.

Parliament of the Commonwealth of Australia. (1957). *Report of the committee on Australian universities*. Canberra. September.

Pavitt, K. (2001). Public policies to support basic research: What can the rest of the world learn from us theory and practice? *Industrial and Corporate Change*, *10*(3).

Pharmaceuticals Asia Product News. (2009). *Key trends in offshoring pharmaceutical R&D: Company strategies, emerging markets and impact on ROI*. Aarkstore. Retrieved from http://aarkstore.com/ reports/KeyTrendsinOffshoring

Porter. M. (1985). *Competitive advantage*. New York: Free Press.

Productivity Commission. (2007). *Public support for science and innovation*. Research Report. Canberra.

Ramsden, P. (2008). *The future of higher education teaching and the student experience*. Report prepared for The Review of Higher Education in the United Kingdom. HEFCE.

Rothblatt, S. (2009). Foreword to structuring mass higher education: The role of elite institutions. In D. Palfreyman, & Tapper, T. (Eds.) *Structuring mass higher education: The role of elite institutions*. New York: Routledge.

Salmi, J. (2009). *The challenge of establishing world-class universities*. Washington, DC: The World Bank.

Scott. P. (2005). *Mass higher education - ten years on*. Paper presented at the AUA Annual Conference, Coventry.

Scott, P. (2009). Structural changes in higher education: The case of the united kingdom. In D. Palfreyman, & Tapper, T. (Eds.) *Structuring mass higher education: The role of elite institutions*. New York: Routledge.

Shapiro, H. T. (2001). Professional education and the soul of the American research university. MichiganL: Ann Arbor.

Teichler, U. (2006). Changing structures of higher education systems: The increasing complexity of underlying forces. *Higher Education Policy, 19*(4), 447–461.

Trajtenberg, M. (2008). Entrepreneurial universities: The view from Israel. In C. J. Schramm, et al. (Eds.), *The future of the research university: Meeting the global challenges of the 21st century.* Missouri: Kauffman Foundation. Retrieved from http://ssm.com/abstracts=1352645

Trow, M. (1973) *Problems in the transition from elite to mass higher education.* Berkeley, California: Carnegie Commission on Higher Education.

Trow. M. (2003), On Mass Higher Education and Institutional Diversity. In *University education and human resources.* Tel Aviv: Technion-Israel Institute of Technology.

Usher, A. (2009, May 21–24). *Ten years back and ten years forward: Developments and trends in higher education in the Europe region.* Paper prepared for the UNESCO Forum on Higher Education in the Europe Region: Access, Values, Quality and Competitiveness. Bucharest.

Wiley, J. (2007). The future of research universities. Science and society interviews. *EMBO Report, 8*(9).

Michael Gallagher
The Group of Eight, Australia

AKIYOSHI YONEZAWA

3. THE "GLOBAL 30" AND THE CONSEQUENCES OF SELECTING "WORLD-CLASS UNIVERSITIES" IN JAPAN

INTRODUCTION

Fostering "world-class" universities is now a clearly set national goal for many countries around the globe (Sadlak and Liu, 2009). In response to requests from a wide variety of countries, Salmi (2009) identified three prerequisites for the establishment of world-class universities: (1) concentration of talent, (2) abundant funding and (3) appropriate governance. East Asian countries are recognized to be efficient in their strategic approach to fostering world-class universities (Altbach and Balan eds., 2007). In terms of funding, traditional tendencies of governments in this region to allocate significant portions of national budgets to a limited number of universities, is consistent with the global policy trends. With regard to governance, Deem, Lucas and Mok (2009) argue that East Asian state universities are enhancing their autonomy through corporatization and marketization. The concentration of talent should be considered from both national and global dimensions. On the one hand, many East Asian higher education systems (e.g., Japan, South Korea, Taiwan) are highly successful in concentrating domestic human talent into a limited number of leading research universities, based on well-established hierarchical structures of their higher education systems. On the other hand, the concentration of talent in the international dimension is still a new challenge for most top Asian universities.

As Kuroda and Passarelli (2009) point out, transnational education and international student mobility within Asian countries is rapidly developing. The Chinese government and top universities are beginning to attract overseas researchers (mainly from the Chinese diaspora) through the provision of strong support for their research activities (Ma, 2007). South Korea, following the 1995 government announcement of the "Initial Plan to Open the Higher Education Market to Foreign Countries", has transformed itself from being primarily a "sending" country into both a "sending and hosting" country (Byun, 2009). Brain circulation, partly through diaspora networks (Kuznetsov, 2006), is starting to improve the international attractiveness of East Asian higher education. Also indicative of this trend was the title of an article attached to the Times Higher Education Supplement's 2009 World University Rankings, which read "Asia Advances".

N.C. Liu et al., (eds.), Paths to a World-Class University: Lessons from Practices and Experiences, 67–81.

There is both diversity as well as similarity among the contexts of prospective higher education systems in East Asia. Japan, the first country in the region to experience an economic take off in the 1960s, is now struggling with the transformation of its conventional higher education system into a more globally open one. A rigidly hierarchical higher education system already works to assure the position of a small number of Japanese universities in the global rankings, based mainly on their high research performance. However, indicators related to the internationalization of leading Japanese universities, such as those provided in the QS/ Times Higher Education Rankings, which report the share of international students and faculty, do not indicate that there has been a positive performance. Therefore, recent national policy debates have focused on the weakest aspect of prominent Japanese universities: "internationalization". It is not an easy task to achieve both qualitative and quantitative goals for the internationalization of higher education. This is because quantitative increases in the number of international students may have undesirable consequences on the quality of education and research settings. If we focus on those leading Japanese national universities that have received favourable recognition in the world rankings, the majority of their international students are accepted at the postgraduate level in the science and engineering fields. Looking at the larger, national picture, however, a majority of the international students enrol in the humanities and social sciences at the undergraduate level, mainly at private universities.

In 2001, with the aim of utilizing the university system to stimulate the national economy, the Japanese government established a plan to foster around 30 universities to become "world-class" institutions and it has since accumulated various policy tools to work in that direction (Oba, 2008). At the same time, the government perceived the necessity to increase the number of international students in the Japanese higher education system as a whole and set out a plan in 2008 to invite 300,000 international students by 2020. Within this plan, the government revealed its intentions to enhance the international status of the proposed 30 selected universities, but owing to financial limitations it could only provisionally name 13 universities in the 2009 first round selection. The selection process for this first round was based on the setting of specific institutional goals and their accomplishment by a predetermined date. It has proven informative with regards to how the Japanese government identifies "world-class" universities, and also how universities themselves act to satisfy requirements by achieving internal consensus within a highly complex organizational context.

In this article, upon providing a brief policy background, the author examines the structure of university selection criteria so as to present an image of what the national government interprets as "world-class" performance. He then details how major universities establish institutional strategies to meet these requirements. Finally, he highlights the practical challenge of internationalizing leading research universities without damaging the quality of research and education, whilst at the same time drawing attention to the different contexts of world-class university policies among East Asian countries.

POLICY BACKGROUND

Fostering "world-class" universities has consistently been at the top of Japanese higher education policy agendas since the establishment of the modern university system in the latter half of the 19th Century. With a limited public budget and high social demand for higher education, the Japanese government has concentrated public investment into a select number of national public universities (Yonezawa, 2007a). This has resulted in the development of a large, demand-absorbing private higher education sector based on tuition fees. By the mid 1970s Japan had realized mass higher education, in which over 70% of students were enrolled in private institutions, typically characterized by large, mainly undergraduate student bodies.

In 2001, under growing pressure stemming from the globalization of the knowledge economy, the Koizumi government revealed a plan to foster the development of around 30 national, local public and private universities, from among more than 700 in operation at the time, into "world-class" institutions. The rationale and process for selecting these 30 universities sparked heated debate, leading to the government's subsequent decision not to select institutions, but rather to select research units as "Centers of Excellence in the 21st Century" (and from 2006, "Global Centers of Excellence") (Yonezawa, 2003). At the same time, the Japan Society for the Promotion of Science (JSPS), a governmental agency acting as a national research council, selected 20 universities in a programme supporting the strategic planning of internationalization from 2005 to 2009 (JSPS, 2007, 2010).

Arguments involving Japan's quest for enhanced international status in higher education continued after Koizumi resigned. Subsequently, the Abe Cabinet (2006–2007) set educational reform as its central policy agenda, with the government stressing the importance of securing a leading position for Japanese higher education in Asia through promoting internationalization of higher education and maintaining Japan's share in the international student market (The Council for the Asian Gateway Initiative, 2007). The Fukuda Cabinet (2007–2008) proved itself to be particularly enthusiastic towards the internationalization of Japanese higher education, based partly on strong diplomatic initiatives between Japan and neighbouring countries. Under this cabinet, the government set up a plan to invite 300,000 international students by 2020, which meant that the country would aim to triple the existing number of international students within only 12 years. This plan also targeted the selection of 30 national, local public and private universities for internationalization (the "Global 30"). At the same time, a series of high-level meetings were held to develop strategies for upgrading the position of Japanese universities in the world rankings.

The Aso Cabinet (2008–2009) essentially continued these policies and formed a working group to examine "international evaluation" (or rankings) under the Central Council for Education (CCE), an official advisory committee of the Ministry of Education, Culture, Sports, Science and Technology (MEXT). The Aso government also set up a project-based budget to support the "Global 30" universities for five years, from 2009, whilst the number of universities to be selected was limited to less than half of the original plan, at least in the first round selections in 2009.

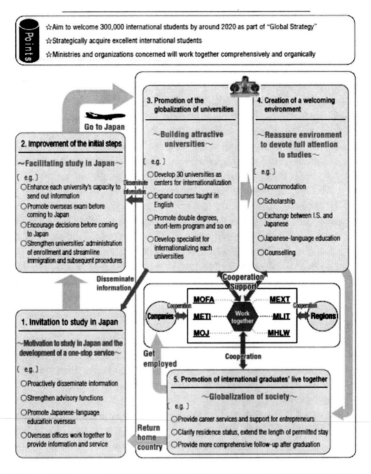

☆Aim to welcome 300,000 international students by around 2020 as part of "Global Strategy"

☆Strategically acquire excellent international students

☆Ministries and organizations concerned will work together comprehensively and organically

Figure 1. Framework of "300,000 INTERNATIONAL STUDENTS PLAN".

Source: Student Office of MEXT (2008).

SELECTION CRITERIA

The selection process of a project, such as the "Global 30", understandably involved great controversy, debate and division. In Japan, "internationalized" universities do not always find themselves highly placed in world rankings. For example, Ritsumeikan Asia Pacific University, a small sized university, implements a unique university education by accepting around 50% non-Japanese faculty and student body, and offering around 50% of its classes in English. Similarly, Akita International University, a small sized local, public university, offers all its classes in English and assures all undergraduate students that they will have the opportunity to study abroad as exchange students. Neither of these two institutions, however, find themselves highly placed in world rankings. In quite stark contrast, leading national universities with proven records in world-class research have provided degree programmes in English only at the postgraduate level and they have catered only for those who are not able to study in the Japanese language.

The limited number of institutions put forward for the "Global 30" in the first round was partly due to the structural complexities of the selection process, which stipulated that candidate institutions must first establish a leading position in accepting a significant number of international students, and that they already enjoyed strong international recognition (typically in world rankings). The selection committee published scores based on criteria, which included the following detailed quantitative requirements:

– Granting of 340 or more postgraduate degrees (master's or doctors) annually in the last three years (scored 1 to 5 based on performance);
– Acquisition of 130 or more Grants in Aid from JSPS annually in the last three years (scored 1 to 5 based on performance);
– Acceptance of 300 or more international students from more than four countries in 2008 (scored 1 to 5 based on performance);
– Sending of 50 or more students abroad in 2008, under official student exchange agreements (scored 1 to 5 based on performance);
– Employment of more than 45 international faculty members (scored 1 to 5 based on performance);
– Participation in international university consortiums;
– Having plans to establish at least one undergraduate and one postgraduate degree programme in English, in addition to the existing programmes (assessed by number);
– Establishment of offices abroad for recruiting students, and willingness to allow their usage by other Japanese universities (additional points are awarded for multiple offices);
– Having plans to realize a share of international students of 20 (with a minimum of 10%), and a total number of international students of more than 2,599 by 2020; and
– Plan to make the share of international faculty into 10% (with a minimum of 5%) by 2020.

These criteria, combined with a concrete plan for facilitating internationalization (i.e., including matters related to housing, training of staff members, etc.), clearly indicates that applying institutions were to be large scale, comprehensive universities with a high research capacity. Smaller and mid-sized institutions, despite satisfying many of the strong international criteria mentioned above, were actually eliminated from the selection process in 2009. It is noteworthy that neither the Tokyo Institute of Technology, a top national research university in engineering, nor Hitotsubashi University, a leading national university in the social sciences, applied to join the programme. Moreover, the withdrawal of the Tokyo Institute of Technology, which is always ranked among the top 100 to 200 universities in the world, reveals the extent to which many Japanese universities considered the indicators difficult to satisfy.

SELECTION RESULTS

In July 2009, MEXT released a list of 13 universities selected from among 22 applying institutions. Each successful university is to receive between 200 and 400 million Japanese yen for five years, from 2009, to pursue further international-ization through the measures outlined above and thus contribute to the national target of accepting 300,000 international students by 2020. Relative to the annual revenues of these selected universities (for example, Tohoku University's total annual revenue was 120 billion Japanese yen in 2008), the grant for this project is very small and in fact, MEXT requires selected universities to match award amounts with internal funds.

The list of applicant universities in the first round selection of the "Global 30" included the following (those who were successful in their bids are in bold):

- National (public):
  Hokkaido (former imperial)
  Tohoku (former imperial)
  Tsukuba
  Chiba
  Tokyo (former imperial)
  Tokyo University of Agriculture and Technology
  Kanazawa
  Gifu
  Nagoya (former imperial)
  Kyoto (former imperial)
  Osaka (former imperial)
  Kobe
  Hiroshima
  Yamaguchi
  Kyushu (former imperial)
- Local (public):
  None
- Private:
  Keio
  Sophia
  Tokai
  Meiji
  Waseda
  Doshisha
  Ritsumeikan

The results are interesting at a variety of levels. First, private universities, almost none of which (except for Keio and Waseda) regularly appear in world rankings, performed well in the selection and this is probably because their management capacity is more flexible and adaptive than that of national universities, with a long history of governmental bureaucracy. For example, Meiji University, a private university located in the centre of Tokyo is planning to provide services for international students through partnerships with private enterprises (e.g., travel agencies and education related information service providers). However, perhaps a more persuasive interpretation is that private universities have larger student bodies at the undergraduate level, relative to their size, and they are more focused on the admission of international students at this level. For example, Waseda University, one that is highly selective and the second largest private university in Japan, already hosted 3,125 international students out of a total student body of 56,974 in 2009, and is planning to increase this number to 8,000 by 2020.

On the other hand, national universities are seen to have received surprisingly negative results. One former imperial university (Hokkaido University), possessing a stable position in the world rankings, was not selected. Moreover, only one non-imperial national university (Tsukuba University, recognized as the eighth ranked national research comprehensive university upon its establishment in 1973) was selected. In the national sector, the dominance of large comprehensive research universities, almost all of which have origins as "imperial universities" before World War II, was evident. However, although all of the selected national universities had already operated programmes in English at the postgraduate level, none of them had degree programmes in English at the undergraduate level. In this regard, the provision of undergraduate degree programmes in English in the field of humanities and social sciences is especially challenging, as most Japanese academics in these fields use Japanese for instruction and research. Consequently, Tohoku University decided to limit the number of students admitted to its newly-established under-graduate programmes in English to around 30 every year, and only to the fields of engineering, natural sciences, and marine sciences. Kyushu University has also limited the provision of undergraduate programmes in English to engineering and agriculture in 2010, whilst it plans to open an "International Liberal Arts College" in around 2015, to embrace all main subjects.

In the case of private universities, most international students on current under-graduate programmes are studying in the Japanese language as fee paying students. On the other hand, fee levels at national and local public universities are relatively low and are not sufficient to cover actual education costs per student. Therefore, it is considerably difficult to discern a clear incentive, at least from a financial perspective, for such universities to accept international students who require additional care, compared with domestic students. Nevertheless, national univer-sities face more direct pressure from the national government to implement planned increases in the number of international students and faculty, in that they rely heavily on the national budget for financing. Linked to this, the government is planning to exercise a mid-term evaluation of the "Global 30" project in 2012, with the published results being linked to financial decisions.

THE "WORLD-CLASS UNIVERSITY" POLICY IN QUESTION

The plan to invite 300,000 international students to Japan by 2020 and the "Global 30" project officially initiated in July 2008, under the Fukuda Cabinet, had already been losing political support when Taro Aso became prime minister, in September 2008.

Although the original intention of the "Global 30" project was to select 30 universities as target universities for internationalization, the government decided to limit the number to 13 in the 2009 first round selection, partly in the light of financial constraints and realities. In the September 2009 general election, the long-standing rule of the Liberal Democratic Party (LDP) was replaced by that of the Democratic Party of Japan (DPJ). At present, it is too early to judge the impact, if any, of this government change on "world-class" university policies. However, the early evidence indicates that fiscal policies related to the project, (i.e., the high concentration of financial resources into a limited number of top research universities to be globally recognized), were not reflected in the prioritization areas advanced by the DPJ. That is, they did not promote the concentration of investment into "world-class" universities as a key policy item in their election manifesto, preferring instead to focus on the issues of access and financial support for child-raising and schooling. In this regard, in March 2010 the Diet passed budgetary legislation to deliver increased levels of financial support for child-raising. The new initiatives include the elimination of tuition fees at the senior-secondary level and the introduction of an allowance of 13,000 Japanese yen per month for every child, regardless of parent income, from June 2010. Although these policies entail a significant overall budget increase for education, science and health, it is inevitable that other projects' funding including that for "world-class" universities will come under unprecedented scrutiny.

Whilst the total budget for higher education in fact grew in 2010, this reflects increased support for national university hospitals, which appeals to the general public as users of healthcare services. By contrast, the budget for world-class university science education and projects for elite-oriented internationalization of education may easily be at risk of cuts under the new policy direction, which emphasizes direct contribution to the day-to-day life of the largest number of ordinary citizens. With respect to this, the new government has established the "Government Revitalization Unit" (GRU) under the cabinet office, and has revisited governmental budget allocations for projects including the "Global 30", research projects and reviewed the operational costs of national universities, among other public expenditure. The discussion process can be monitored via the Internet[1] with ministries soliciting public commentary on budgetary matters. Discussion on the "Global 30" project began in November, 2009, with the project receiving critical commentary on its rationale and effectiveness, leading the GRU to rethink its approach to provide financing for the internationalization of education. Other competitive funds for supporting top research units such as Global Centers of Excellence (GCOEs) and projects to attract global top researchers (World Premier Research Center Initiatives: WPIs) (Yonezawa, 2007b) were also criticized for exhibiting a lack of a concrete and demonstrable impact. Regarding the budgetary provisions for establishing a supercomputer, "SPring-8 synchrotron", which aimed to be the fastest in the world, Upper House member Renho questioned the rationality by asking, "Why should we aim to be number one in the world? What's wrong with number two?"[2]

Fearing deep budgetary cuts for "world-class" universities and research, academic leaders, including Nobel Prize winners and university presidents, have launched a counter campaign stressing the importance of world-class research for the development of nations with scarce natural resources, such as Japan. In this regard, the presidents of nine leading universities (seven national: Hokkaido, Tohoku, Tokyo, Nagoya, Kyoto, Osaka and Kyushu; two private: Waseda and Keio) published joint statements arguing for the necessity to invest in university education and research, in November 2009 and March 2010. The vice presidents of the selected 13 universities in the "Global 30" project also published joint statements in November 2009, criticizing budgetary cuts to this project.

Faced with academic leaders decrying there to be a lack of vision for national development, cabinet members including the then Deputy Prime Minister Naoto Kan, who became Prime Minister from June 2010, supported the reconsideration of budgetary cuts for academic and technology related projects. Subsequently, in December 2009 the Hatoyama Cabinet published their New Growth Strategy for national development, which referred to investment in science, technology and highly skilled human resources for fostering environmentally friendly, "green" innovation as a key strategy (Prime Minister of Japan and his cabinet, 2009). However, with regards to the actual financial terms, funds for such projects as the "Global 30", GCOEs and WPIs faced significant budgetary cuts of approximately 20%.

MEXT originally had a plan to hold the second round to select the remaining 17 universities for the "Global 30" in 2010. In this second round, there was to be the possibility that different types of key international universities, such as small-sized universities with highly internationalized student and faculty bodies, would be selected. However, after severe scrutiny of budgetary priorities the government decided not to implement the additional selection of universities, at least in 2010. Moreover, the 13 previously selected universities are now struggling to implement their submitted plans for internationalization on reduced budgets. Further, most of these universities have started to employ academic staff who are able to lead classes in English. However, to date, in contrast to other East Asian countries, such as China, Korea and Taiwan, Japanese universities have tended to foster the next generation of academics within their own post graduate education provision, thus resulting in a shortage of fluent English speakers who have honed strong linguistic skills overseas. For as can be seen in Figure 2, the number of non-Japanese Asian nationals who have obtained science and engineering doctoral degrees in the United States, far exceeds those of Japan. Moreover, although many leading Japanese researchers in engineering and natural sciences have experienced postdoctoral fellowships in North America and Europe, large sections of the Japanese academic community clearly still lack the resources that would equip them to learn and teach in English speaking countries, such as the United States.

Further, the condition of the humanities and social sciences in Japan in terms of internationalization is graver than in the sciences (Yonezawa, 2008), for apart from the exception of fields, such as economics and international relations, most Japanese academics working in these subject areas have been trained in Japanese universities and publish academic articles and doctoral theses in the Japanese language. Considering the higher and more sophisticated linguistic skills necessary

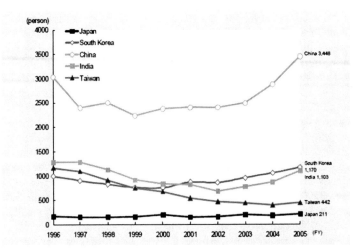

Figure 2. Trends in the numbers of Asian researchers receiving doctorate degrees in science and engineering in the United States.

Source: MEXT. White Paper on Science and Technology, 2009; National Science Foundation Doctorates Awarded 1996–2005.

to realize quality dialogues in these fields, it is not realistic to expect most existing academic staff members to be able to switch their teaching language from Japanese to English (Eades, 2000).

The very ambitious target number for international students and faculty could be a serious issue for the higher education management of the selected universities. Table 1 shows the number of international students enrolled in these universities in 2008 and the number they promised to enrol by 2020. In this regard, the academic and non-academic staff of the 13 universities involved so far are engaging in student recruiting tours worldwide, setting up international offices for recruitment in countries such as Russia, Tunisia and India and adding to existing offices in China. These universities are also trying to increase the number of short-term student exchanges, mainly at the undergraduate level, even though this does not have a direct, positive impact on their research performance.

It is more problematic to send domestic students abroad for international exchange, for the "Global 30" funds are not permitted to be utilized for scholarship to incoming and outgoing students and at the moment, the Japanese government does not have an effective support system for sending students abroad, only having a very limited provision of public student loans. As shown in table 2, the number of Japanese students studying abroad on an official study visa has not increased in the last five years and in particular, the number of Japanese students who study in the United States has dropped significantly, whilst the numbers of students studying in China and Korea have dramatically increased. In this context, it should be kept in mind that these Japanese students, in general, tend to study languages and cultures, rather than cutting edge research in the science and engineering fields.

Table 1. Current (2008) and targeted (2020) number of international students

	2008	2020
National		
Tohoku University	1,218	3,211
Tsukuba University	1,377	4,500
University of Tokyo	2,444	3,500
Nagoya University	1,214	3,000
Kyoto University	1,336	3,200
Osaka University	1,439	3,000
Kyushu University	1,292	3,900
Private		
Keio University	934	4,000
Sophia University	1,000	2,600
Meiji University	712	4,000
Waseda University	3,000	8,000
Doshisha University	563	3,500
Ritsumeikan University	1,119	4,005

Source: Toyo Keizai (2009).

Table 2. Number of Japanese students studying abroad

Country of Destination	2001	2002	2003	2004	2005	2006
USA	46,810	45,960	40,835	42,215	38,712	35,282
China	14,692	16,084	12,765	19,059	18,874	18,363
UK	6,206	5,741	5,729	6,395	6,179	6,200
Australia	2,407	3,271	3,462	3,172	3,380	3,305
Germany	2,182	2,317	2,438	2,547	2,470	2,377
Taiwan			1,825	1,879	2,152	2,188
Canada	1,478	1,460	1,460	1,750	2,126	1,812
France	1,439	1,483	2,490	2,337	1,750	2,112
South Korea	697	721	938	914	1,106	1,212
New Zealand	499	502	566	913	912	1,036
Total	78,151	79,455	74,551	82,945	80,023	76,492

Source: Student Exchange Office, MEXT.

There is another possible financial opportunity for leading Japanese universities. In 2004, all national universities were incorporated and they set up six year goals and plans on how these were to be achieved (Oba, 2007). Moreover, at the time of incorporation the government clarified its policy of establishing a linkage between the achievement of these mid-term goals with financial allocations to national universities. In March 2010, the first round results of performance-based funding were released, with the top ranked university being the Nara Institute of Science and Technology, a small sized, postgraduate university in science and technology, which was awarded 4 million Japanese yen in the financial reallocation, comprising 0.07% of its operational budget awarded by the government (5.7 billion Japanese yen in 2008), and 0.04% of its total revenue (9.5 billion Japanese yen in 2008). Although almost all the prestigious comprehensive universities, such as the former imperial universities, received additional funds as shown in Table 3, the amount of financial reallocation (1.6 billion Japanese yen) was surprisingly small compared

Table 3. Performance scores and financial reallocation according to the results of the mid-term assessments of selected national universities in 2010

Rank by performance score (out of 86 national universities)		Amount of financial reallocation (million Japanese yen)	Total score of assessment results
1	Nara Institute of Science and Technology	4.0	70.00
2	Shiga University of Medical Science	3.0	63.75
3	Hamamatsu University School of Medicine	2.5	60.64
4	Tokyo Institute of Technology	16.0	60.18
5	Ohanomizu University	3.0	59.93
6	**University of Tokyo**	25.0	56.87
10	**Kyoto University**	13.0	51.3
12	**Osaka University**	8.0	49.4
13	**Tohoku University**	7.5	49.3
14	Kobe University	3.5	48.66
15	Hitotsubashi University	1.0	48.3
18	**Kyushu University**	5.5	48.09
19	**Hokkaido University**	5.0	48.06
21	Tsukuba University	2.5	47.44
24	**Nagoya University**	2.5	46.69
39	Hiroshima University	-1.0	44.25

Source: Asahi Shimbun 2010 (Bold: former imperial universities).

with the total operational budgets for national universities as a whole (1.2 trillion Japanese yen), or even in relation to the expenditure made in preparing for these performance assessments. The University of Tokyo, for example, received 25 million Japanese yen in additional funds, the largest amount among all national universities, however this represented only 0.03% of its operational budget awarded by the government (86 billion Japanese yen in 2008), 0.01% of the university's total revenue (206 billion Japanese yen in 2008), or equivalent to the annual salary of two or three professors. Nevertheless, as pointed out in the Asahi Shimbun (2010)[3], the amounts awarded were not negligible for local or small-sized universities. In terms of penalties, Hirosaki University, which is a local comprehensive university located in northern Japan and was given the worst performance score among all the national universities, faced a reduction of 7 million Japanese yen, which is still just 0.06% of its planned operational budget awarded from the government in 2009, and 0.02% of the planned total revenue for the same year.

Briefly summarized, both policy shifts and mass student behaviour do not appear to be highly supportive for world-class universities and consequently the selected universities are now struggling to transform their education and research systems into more internationally friendly ones, with the costs for this reform having to be covered, substantially, by their own financing arrangements.

CONCLUSION

Japan's "Global 30" project is an interesting example of a national policy trial for fostering "world-class" universities through the support of institutional internationalization. Most leading East Asian universities have established relatively strong research credentials, whilst their international aspect and international recognition are, in many cases, still weak. However, whilst support for internationalization is both rational and forward-looking, it is highly difficult to develop effective performance criteria which are deemed acceptable by the various types of universities. Moreover, varying opinions and perspectives remain as to the exact meanings of terms such as "world-class", "international", or "internationally recognized", and perhaps more importantly as to what expectations accompany such designations. Inevitably, interpretations will sometimes overlap and therefore present dilemmas for university management. At the same time, the analysis presented in this chapter has also revealed the considerable difference in the context of world-class university policies between developed, or matured higher education systems, such as that of Japan and new, rising higher education systems, such as those in China and Korea.

One of the rationales for world-class university policies, namely, to invest in a limited number of national flagship universities, thus sacrificing financial support for a large number of mass higher education learners, is increased participation and access to the global knowledge economy. In the case of Japan, however, around five to ten universities are already ranked in the top 200 universities in the world and although there is still a great financial gap between the top American universities and those of Japan, it is unlikely that the latter will completely lose access to knowledge creation in the near future. Continuous investigation will be necessary to assess the extent to which a country should invest in the pursuit of "world-class" university status, so as to assure at least minimal levels of participation in cutting-edge knowledge creation.

NOTES

[1]   http://www.cao.go.jp/sasshin/index.html
[2]   Nature News "Japanese sciences face deep cuts". Published online November 17, 2009 | Nature 462, 258–259 (2009) | doi:10.1038/462258a http://www.nature.com/news/2009/091117/full/462258a.html
[3]   Asahi Shimbun "Kokuritsudai Jun'i Zuke Genba ga Fuman" (Dissatisfaction with the ranking results of national universities by academics), March 29 2010.

REFERENCES

Altbach, P. G., & Balan, J. (Eds.), (2007). *World class worldwide: Transforming research universities in Asia and Latin America*. Johns Hopkins University Press.

Byun, K. (2009). *Changing patterns in the Government's policies for the internationalization of Korean Higher Education*. A paper presented at 2009 HEPRI-KEDI International Symposium, October 8, Korea University, Seoul.

Council for the Asian Gateway Initiative. (2007). *Asian gateway initiative*. Prime Minister of Japan and his Cabinet. Retrieved from http://www.kantei.go.jp/foreign/gateway/index_e.html

Deem, R., Lucas, L., & Mok, K. H. (2009). The "World-Class" University in Europe and East Asia: Dynamics and consequences of global higher education reform. In B. M. Kehm, & B. Stensaker (Eds.), *University rankings, diversity, and the new landscape of higher education*. The Netherland: Sense Publishers.

Eades, J. S. (2000). Why don't they write in English? Academic modes of production and academic discourses in Japan and the West. *Ritsumeikan Journal of Asia Pacific Studies, 6*(6), 58–77.

JSPS. (2007). *Strategic fund for establishing international headquarters in universities: Innovative models for promoting the internationalization of Japanese Universities (Interim Report)*. JSPS.

JSPS. (2010). *Strategic fund for establishing international headquarters in Universities (Final Report)*. JSPS.

Kuroda, K., & Passarelli, D. (2009). Modelling TNE directions in Asia. *A report of observatory on borderless higher education*. International Strategic Information Service.

Kuznetsov, Y. (Ed.), (2006). *Diaspora networks and the international migration of skills: How countries can draw on their talent abroad*. Washington, DC: The World Bank.

Ma, W. (2007). The flagship university and China's economic reform. In P. G. Altbach, & J. Balan (Eds.), World-Class worldwide: Transforming research universities in Asia and Latin America. Johns Hopkins University Press.

Oba, J. (2007). Governance reform of national universities in Japan: Transition to corporate status and challenges. *Journal of Comparative Asian Development, 6*(1), 45–86.

Oba, J. (2008). Creating world-class universities in Japan: Policy and initiatives. *Policy Futures in Education, 6*(5), 629–664.

Prime Minister of Japan and His Cabinet. (2009). *The new growth strategy (Basic policies): Toward a radiant Japan*. Prime Minister of Japan and His Cabinet.

Sadlak, J., & Liu, N.C. (Eds.), (2009). *The world-class universities as part of a new higher education paradigm: From institutional qualities to systemic excellence*. UNESCO-CEPES.

Salmi, J. (2009). *The challenge of establishing world-class universities*. Washington, DC: The World Bank.

Student Office of MEXT. (2008). Outline of the student exchange system. MEXT.

Toyo K. (2009, October). *Special issue: Honto ni Tsuyoi Daigaku* [Really Powerful Universities] (Vol. 24). Toyo Keizai.

Yonezawa, A. (2003). Making "World-class Universities": Japan's experiment. *Higher Education Management and Policy, 15*(2), 9–23.

Yonezawa, A. (2007a). Japanese flagship universities at a crossroads. *Higher Education, 54*(4), 483–499.

Yonezawa, A. (2007b). Stability amidst a storm of evaluation: Policy trends and practice in higher education evaluation in Japan. In A. Cavalli (Ed.), *Quality assessment for higher education in Europe.* London: Portland Press.

Yonezawa, A. (2008). Quality assessment and assurance in Japanese Universities: The plight of the social sciences. *Social Science Japan Journal, 11*(1), 69–82.

Akiyoshi Yonezawa
Center for the Advancement of Higher Education
Tohoku University, Japan

PAUL ŞERBAN AGACHI, CAMELIA MORARU,
ROMANA CUCURUZAN AND ADRIAN CURAJ

4. IS DEVELOPING ELITE UNIVERSITIES A TOP PRIORITY AGENDA FOR HIGHER EDUCATION IN ROMANIA?

Analyses of the Evolution of the Higher Education Sector's Priorities and Romanian Top University Strategies in Developing Excellence

INTRODUCTION

This chapter aims to present and analyse the evolution of the higher education sector in Romania, regarding the adoption and implementation of the elite university concept or that of excellence. In particular, the aspects that we investigate relate to the policy agenda in recent years that has aimed at promoting excellence in research and elite universities in the national higher education system, as well as those strategic institutional developments that have occurred as a consequence of intense national and international competition. The questions that we aim to address are - is developing elite higher education or excellence in universities a top priority for Romania? What concrete measures have been taken in order to sustain this development at the government, regional and institutional levels? What would a world-class university look like in the Romanian context and is one feasible? How important is the research dimension in the day to day life of a Romanian university? This paper presents and evaluates the strategic measures adopted at the higher education systems level in relation to research, development and innovation (RDI) and assess their effectiveness for developing excellence in research. The last part of the article presents the vision in the context of higher education system development and that of RDI in Romania.

EVOLUTION OF THE ROMANIAN HIGHER EDUCATION SYSTEM

In the years leading up to the current global crisis, the Romanian higher education sector experienced a number of important developments. First, in relation to the funding system, there was an increasing demand for improved productivity through per capita reductions in financial allocations to students, whilst at the same time continuing to expand investment in the higher education sector. With regards to overall investment, between 2001 and 2007 there was a seven fold increase and in terms of research funding this was multiplied four times from 2004 to 2008. Second, there was a rapid rise in the number of new public and private higher

N.C. Liu et al., (eds.), Paths to a World-Class University: Lessons from Practices and Experiences, 83–105.

education institutions, in order to comply with labour market needs and with the rise in the spatial mobility of potential students. Third, and related to the last point on expansion of provision, there was massification[1], which refers to the widening of accessibility for other than traditional target groups, such as Roma students, students with special needs, lifelong learners, professionals involved in different types of activities choosing online or distance learning to complete or complement their first degree.

Before 1989, the higher education system in Romania was centralized, with the number of universities, programme content and access criteria being solely established by the state, in accordance with its centralized five year plans for economic and social development. Moreover, between 1948 and 1960, admissions to the higher education institutions were predominantly determined by political criteria over performance criteria, regardless of whether admission for particular courses required professional evaluation of competences. Further, each student's origins as well as the political views of their family members could qualify or disqualify them from entering the higher education system and consequently students coming from rural areas or urban poor families, or students belonging to the working class were often given privileged access, when compared with those coming from the traditional intellectual classes or those from families with a different political persuasion to that of communism. During 1971 and 1972 the new political orientation of the Communist Party led to them bringing about a major increase in the number of places allocated for technical programmes to the detriment of the social sciences. It is important to note that up until 1989, whilst the Communist Party remained in power, private universities were not permitted. Consequently, the resulting legacy of the communist development of the higher education system, by the time of its demise in 1989, was 46 public universities with a total number of 164,507 students out of a total population of 23 million. However, by 2008, the student population had risen to 907,353, attending 56 public and 28 privately accredited universities.

After 1989, Romania moved from a highly centralized and controlled economy to one with a free market, but not without facing serious disequilibria[2] during this transformation, such as:

– A steep decline in industrial production, where, for example, between 1990 and 1992 this stood at approximately 63% of that for 1989;
– A high inflation rate, which reached over 250% in 1992 and this contributed to the fact that it was not until 2001 that for the first time export activity exceeded that of 1989, the year when the Ceausescu regime was toppled; and
– A high rate of unemployment owing to the need to restructure the economy, which registered a peak of 11.5% in 1999. In particular, in this regard, the overstaffed industrial giants had to be closed down and because they were often the major employer in regional economies this led to serious social and economic deprivation where they had been located.

However, since 1990, foreign direct investment (FDI) inflows have continually increased, exceeding nine billion Euros in 2008. Moreover, despite the ups and downs of the economy the funding of the educational system, as a percentage of GDP, has experienced an overall up trend, as shown in Table 1.

Table 1. Public expenditure on education (percentage of GDP)

2000	2001	2002	2003	2004	2005	2006	2007	2008
3.4%	3.6%	3.6%	3.5%	3.3%	3.5%	4.3%	5.5%	6%

Source: Ministry of Education and Research, 2008.

For the reference period covered by the above table, it can be seen that public expenditure allocated to education reached 6% of the GDP in 2008 and this proportion was maintained in 2009. With regards to higher education expenditure on research and development, as a percentage of GDP, there was an increasing trend after 2000, which compensated to some extent for the marked decline experienced from 1995 until 1999, as shown in Table 2.

Table 2. R&D expenditure in higher education institutions (percentage of GDP)

1995	1996	1997	1998	1999	2000	2001	2002	2003	2004	2005	2006	2007
0.80	0.71	0.58	0.49	0.40	0.37	0.39	0.38	0.39	0.39	0.41	0.46	0.531

Source: National Institute of Statistics, http://www.insse.ro.

After 1989, there was a growing need for radical reform of the higher education system and the most profound shifts were started in the 1993 to 1994 period, in response to the changes brought about by the democratization process in Romania, prompted by significant exposure to European and global ideas and trends, as well as improved access to their financing schemes.

In particular, one of the major developments for many Romanian institutions was to put the research agenda at the top of their strategic priorities, so they could become major actors in the production of relevant scientific knowledge and systems of enquiry. To achieve this end, Romanian institutions developed ambitious programmes which included a) the acquisition of high performing staff involved in research activities (researchers, teachers), through the attraction, development and retention of highly skilled human resources (HR) departments, whose members had the capacity to recruit talent; b) high performing students, who enrolled on master's, doctoral and postdoctoral programmes after passing comprehensive and competitive selection procedures; c) the establishment of an intellectual climate that promoted openly declared and implicit values that encouraged research, fostered intellectual freedom, provided sustainable mechanisms for stimulating innovation and creativity, and supported young researchers in initiating complex research projects of a probing nature.

More specifically, among the most important changes operating at the European and international levels that led to a transformation within Romanian higher education institutions, were the following.

– At the national higher education systems level: a) an increase in level of university autonomy through both institutional and legislative measures; b) growing interest in ways of defining and developing university excellence[3], especially in relation to its most indicative outcomes, such as scientific results and the employability of graduates. Regarding the former, recently this has been helped by the rolling out of the Romanian RDI strategy, 2007–2013, which has trained up the different higher education institutions so as to provide consistency through-out the sector, with the incentive for compliance being improved funding of 0.8% of GDP in 2008; c) substantial exposure of the universities to the business environment and international cooperation, with respect to education and research; d) developments making a research career attractive, by instigating marketing measures and incentives designed to appeal to the most talented students or graduates.

- At the European level: a) engagement with the Bologna Process and the const-ruction of the EHEA[4] and ERA; b) Romanian integration into the European Union, with all the challenges and opportunities resulting for higher education institutions, such as increased competition for students and resources and addressing the educational needs of larger target groups; c) financial resources provided through different mechanisms at the European level, especially funds for research, such as FP 5, 6, 7, have increased the opportunities for former communist higher education systems to participate in existing European networks, from which they had been previously excluded[5]; d) European market pressure on institutions to ensure that by their efforts they are able to compete globally in terms of new products, new technologies, and having more flexible and adaptive human capital capable of devoting a lifetime's commitment to learning and professional development and e) an increased role for relevant stakeholders in the dynamic development of universities.

- At the global/international level: the need for a global perspective on performance and competitiveness, in the face of increased globalization, has put a lot of pressure on the Romanian higher education institutions, in terms having to modify their mission statements so that their educational outcomes and research strategies have an international relevance. In other words, higher education institutions are operating in a changing and challenging international environment (Hazelkorn, 2005).

By committing themselves to both of the perspectives of social cohesion and international competition, European and Romanian universities, are faced with a difficult dilemma, that is, how to achieve high standards of performance whilst still promoting equal opportunities and increased accessibility at all levels of study? Attempts to reconcile this dichotomy have led to much debate, in terms of universities' mission, role in society, evaluation of results, as well as their moral/ethical and cultural contribution to the development of the community in which they are located.

In the context of accessibility to higher education and the improvement of social cohesion, Romania engaged in developing concrete measures to reform its higher education system soon after the overthrow of the communist regime. In this regard, measures were adopted that fostered increased student participation through the introduction of favourable procedural reforms at the institutional level. This process was speeded up in 1993, after the government conveyed increased autonomy on higher education institutions, which resulted in further changes in curricula, admission procedures and financial support mechanisms for both students and institutions, all of which made higher education a more attractive option for prospective students. Through the implementation of several legislative measures, nowadays, there is a non-discriminative admission procedure for BA and MA levels, whilst for doctoral studies a set of admission criteria based on domain competency has been designed. After accession to the EU, Romanian legislation was adapted to comply with the *acquis communitaire*, which granted equal opportunities for all EU students in terms of admission procedures and access to funding.

The major themes of the debate regarding accessibility are rooted in the massification vs. performance issue and these include ensuring an adequate level of performance in the context of massification, assessing the ideal level of flexibility in terms of admission and the degree to which educational content should be adapted so as meet to target groups' needs. In order to evaluate the different available strategies in relation to these matters, a suitable analytical methodology that can support in depth comparative studies is required.

Nowadays, with the support of institutional evaluations and accreditation procedures, as well with the external institutional accreditation carried out by the Ministry of Education, Research and Innovation, the study programmes are classified as follows (according to the ARACIS proposal):

– Universities offering solely undergraduate programmes;
– Universities offering both undergraduate and graduate programmes; and
– Universities offering undergraduate, graduate programmes and doctoral programmes.

That is, the aim is for both a massification process, horizontally developed at the base of higher education studies (e.g. undergraduate programmes) and also compliance with performance criteria that can be attained vertically, in the sense that students can progress to next level after attaining their qualification. The massification of programmes aimed at fostering accessibility do not include doctoral programmes, because these need specific selective admission criteria, based on each research domain, if high performance standards are to be achieved and hence the outcomes having competitive value.

The Romanian higher education institutions are being asked today to provide accountability and socio-economic relevance whilst maintaining academic freedom, with the overall goal of top quality research and excellent teaching standards. Moreover, they are being encouraged to establish effective linkages between research, teaching and learning, so that they can foment accessibility and social cohesion right up to the national level and beyond. In other words, higher education institutions are being advised to reorient their understanding of the concept of university community to include a wider interpretation, one that addresses academia and the student body at all levels - local, regional, national and European/international. With this shift in perspective, amongst the key questions that the universities have to address are - What type of community should we primarily serve? What areas of work do we wish to cover? More specifically, with the current globalization of higher education each institution is faced with the dilemma of "Shall we count as higher education actors in the international field or not, should we aim to have world class universities or not?" (Agachi et al., 2007).

In recent years, the Romanian higher education agenda has been mainly concerned with defining the vision of what a university of excellence should be, i.e. the main traits that distinguish one from all other types of universities, rather than identifying the criteria that would need to be components of its provision, if it were to qualify as a potential candidate for a world-class university status. The higher education institutions in Romania follow the European trend in terms of "a keen and growing interest in the overall research profile and research capacity of their institutions[...] seeking ways to best manage research as an essential, or even the key function, of the institution"[6].

SHIFTS AND DEVELOPMENTS IN THE UNIVERSITIES' MISSIONS AND STRATEGIES

Higher education institutions, nowadays, are facing a constant challenge to find a balance between their mission demands and changes induced by external factors. Ideally, the mission of a university should constantly describe the way in which it, as a whole, with its own defined and distinct identity, is seeking and formulating answers to the challenges that are constantly rocking humanity (Scott, 2006). Moreover, it has to be flexible and responsive, so as to ensure a positive future for its academic staff as well as its beneficiaries, stakeholders and the community it serves. However, no matter what the challenges are over time, the main role of the university remains the same, in that it should encompass the triad of teaching, research and public service (Scott, 2006; Altbach et al., 2009). In today's climate, the challenges assigned to those responsible for the strategies and policies of a university are legion, with their being members of large communities that have the responsibility to uphold humanity and promote sustainable development. In particular, maintaining a continual process of internal self-evaluation of competences and potential, strategic decision making and implementation of the agreed measures, whilst anticipating and not just responding to changes in the external environment, are crucial dynamic elements in the development of universities of excellence.

The research mission of a university is not new and it first appeared in the Humboldtian model during the mid nineteenth century, when teaching and research were closely linked, in that the latter was seen as essential to enrich the inquiry mission. Nowadays, in the postmodern era the mission of many universities has markedly changed, being not only a matter of achieving their inquiry goals, but also acting as an important driving force in international competition. That is, for these institutions developing cutting edge research of international relevance has resulted in them being in a special class of university, which is helping to shape human destiny in terms of scientific, technological, social and cultural developments, on a global scale. The ultimate outcome is that this could result in the creation of a super league of research universities that have far wider influence than their counterparts in all levels of society (Scott, 1998). Moreover, research has not only the discovery function, but is increasingly becoming the "meeting point" for other important elements in societal development, because knowledge at the international level is shaping the orientation of research in science and technology, the advancement in humanity understanding and thus shifting societal values and perspectives. This change is triggering for a significant number of universities another very relevant change in their mission - an increased focus on internationalization (Sadlak, 1998), that brings with it implicitly an opening of the universities to a wider context. For the Romanian universities to pursue this endeavour has meant from the very beginning being confronted with the inherent difficulties associated with performing in a somewhat unknown international academic environment and dealing with the effects of long decades of isolation and lack of academic freedom under the communist regime. However, it is believed that adopting such a shift is important, as those institutions that do so will be exposed to a very rich learning environment.

The way in which Romanian universities have oriented themselves in relation to international and national evolution has varied significantly over time. In order to understand these changes it is useful here to provide a brief outline of the recent history of Romanian higher education. Up until 1990, access to higher education was very restricted and the student population was numerically very low. The doctoral studies provision was not fit for purpose, with admissions being opened once every five to seven years. After the collapse of the communist regime, a relaxation in the admissions policy and the demands of a free market economy, led a huge increase in demand for higher education study. For example, in 1999 the total enrolment rate in tertiary education (ISCED 5 and 6) (GER) in Romania[7] was 22%, with 23% of females and 21% of males. Only eight years later, in 2007 the overall figure had risen to 58%, with a 67% of females and 50% males represented in the cohort, representing an increase of 260% over the period in question. The increase in the number of private higher education institutions alongside this increasing trend in enrolment in both public and private institutions produced mainly academic staff oriented towards teaching, whilst research activities provided less of a focal point. As a consequence, in public institutions there was a drive to encourage staff to remain teaching within a particular institution while becoming involved in research activity. In this regard, some institutions generated specific retention measures and stimulating programmes to assure that their HR potential was not wasted. As a result, the major higher education institutions in Romania succeeded in becoming both research and teaching institutions, which helped them to overcome the challenges that massification and diversification of missions had brought.

In some cases, the mission has remained the same over the last two decades, whereas others have faced a constant change and improvements in relation to its content, in the search for better performance. Moreover, the commitment to be a research intensive university has remained a central aim for some of the major players in the higher education system in Romania. On the other hand, others' missions were markedly reoriented towards internationalization from the very beginning of the Bologna Process, taking the view that this approach would prove over the years to be an important step in their evolution into becoming classed as universities of excellence. After 1989 this perspective was taken up by universities, such as the Universitatea Babeş-Bolyai Cluj-Napoca and it was closely followed by the Universitatea Bucureşti and the Universitatea Al. I Cuza Iaşi. The impact of this early adoption of internationalization strategies can be seen in their advantageous position in terms of networks and partnerships and their readiness to fulfil implementation of the Bologna Process. In this regard, the participation of the Babeş-Bolyai University in international evaluations, such as the Salzburg Seminar and EUA alongside the setting up of an International Advisory Board at the university, were major turning points in the strategic development of the institution, as well as providing external confirmation of the relevance of its developments. One key outcome of these developments was the involvement of the higher education institution management in networks and associations that are at the heart of the latest developments in higher education. Moreover, as a consequence there was a change in perspective in the role and status of the university at the national as well as at the European level. Furthermore, the managerial decisions that had to be taken that resulted from these changes of mission were more easily taken, because the management team were able to ensure that they were consistent with international evolution of the sector. These tendencies may well yet in future decades extend to include a greater focus on social cultural missions of such universities (Gould, 2003; Scott, 2006).

In order to illustrate the status of some of the major higher education institutions in Romania regarding their mission, we focus here on the main values that have shaped their mission statements. The selection of the universities that have been taken into consideration was based on two criteria: one is institutional relevance at the national level and the other is geographical distribution of the institutions, so as to provide a comprehensive spatial view of the Romanian higher education system. The selected universities are North West Region[8] - Universitatea Babeş-Bolyai Cluj-Napoca, Universitatea Tehnică Cluj-Napoca, North East Region - Universitatea Alexandru Ioan Cuza Iaşi, Universitatea Gheorghe Asachi Iaşi, Center Region - Universitatea Transilvania din Braşov, South Region - Universitatea Craiova, Bucureşti and Ilfov Region - Universitatea Bucureşti, Universitatea Politehnica Bucureşti, West Region - Universitatea de Vest Timişoara, Universitatea de Ştiinţe Agricole şi Medicină Veterinară Timişoara.

Most of the selected universities focus on the higher education triad - teaching, research and serving society at large. This adoption of multipurpose missions is a very demanding endeavour and asks for constant managerial and financial effort so as provide an effective and efficient balance with regard to all three areas.

Table 3. Selected Romanian higher education institutions' mission statements

University	Core values of the mission statement	Main focus of the mission statement
Universitatea Babeş-Bolyai Cluj Napoca	– systematic and innovative knowledge – multiculturalism – permanent and innovative learning culture – personal and moral development – active attitude and participation	Higher education triad: innovative research,

Table 3. (Continued)

	– integration in diversity and for globalization, in terms of respecting identity and reciprocity	teaching and support services
Universitatea Tehnică Cluj Napoca	– educational mission – training provided for larger target groups – high quality standards in research	Creativity and innovation in teaching, research and training
Universitatea "Al. I. Cuza" Iaşi	– students' development – excellence in research – innovation in teaching and learning	Commitment to excellence in teaching, learning and research
Universitatea Gheorghe Asachi Iaşi	– teaching and research and dissemination of results – lifelong learning for larger target groups	Teaching, including lifelong learning programmes
Universitatea Transilvania Braşov	– teaching, research and serving society – alignment to the Romanian as well as European developments in higher education	Multipurpose mission, focus on the higher education triad: teaching, research and support services
Universitatea din Craiova	– continuous improvement of teaching, research and training programmes – development and diffusion of culture and civilization's values – contribution to the development of civil society – involvement in national and international networking	The higher education triad: teaching, research and support services
Universitatea Politehnica Bucureşti	– training in science and technology – preservation of the Polytechnic School's prestige in research – support services for local community and for the society, as a whole	High standards in research in S&T
Universitatea Bucureşti	– contribution to national and international science and knowledge – preservation and diffusion of culture and civilization's values – support for academic freedom, critical thinking, renewal and development of knowledge – training and development of skilled and highly skilled staff	Society' s development through knowledge

Table 3. (Continued)

Universitatea de Vest Timişoara	– training for academic and non-academic staff – development and diffusion of culture and civilization' s values, with respect to multiculturalism and pluralism	Higher education triad: teaching, research and support services
Universitatea de Ştiinţe Agricole şi Medicină Veterinară Timişoara	– contribution to rural and agricultural development in Romania – high standards in training and development of students and academic staff	Commitment to teaching, research and consultancy

Source: Mission statements were synthesized from the official website of the selected universities. http://www.ubbcluj.ro; http://www.utcluj.ro; http://www.uaic.ro;http://www.tuiasi.ro; http:// www.unitbv.ro; http://www.ucv.ro; http://www.pub.ro; http://www.unibuc.ro; http://uvt.ro; http://usab-tm.ro.

ELITE UNIVERSITIES? FROM EGALITARIAN PERSPECTIVES TOWARDS A PERFORMANCE BASED APPROACH FOR HIGHER EDUCATION INSTITUTIONS

Given the above somewhat general mission statements the question that remains unanswered is - without having a specific dedicated mission on research or education and research, are higher education institutions acting appropriately and effectively so as to support research competitiveness and performance? What actions should be implemented at the institutional level so as obtain optimal results when adopting this perspective? What weight should be placed on scientific research activity in the overall strategic institutional development? A possible solution may lie in a consideration of the evidence-based reports with regards to the research strategies of the main universities in recent years as well as their research results[9].

The international evolution in the higher education field related with diversification of the assessment exercises, the rise of rankings and classifications as well as the already existing tradition in major Romanian universities have a great impact on the excellence concept: excellence is mainly related to research relevance at national and international level.

After 1989, Romanian universities opened themselves up to differentiation and started to overcome the isomorphism that had characterized the entire educational system for more than four decades. Among the major challenges faced was dealing with profound transformation of the values and routines from an old system based on egalitarianism to a new approach, in which competition and cooperation, differentiation and preservation of a distinct identity, were the leading concepts. The first major step in relation to the Romanian higher education system moving towards the differentiation according to performance and excellence that was made after the signing of the Bologna Declaration in 1999, was the successful introduction of quality indicators in the university core financing mechanism[10], a mechanism that previously took into consideration only quantitative aspects such as student numbers. Since then the quality criteria have been constantly developed and by 2008 it represented 30% of the total budgetary allocation. The first set of quality indicators (IC1 - IC4) proposed (Nica, 1998, 2000) reflected the quality of academic staff (IC1), the quality and impact of the scientific research (IC2), the infrastructure quality (IC3) and the quality of the academic management (IC4). This first set of indicators was subsequently successfully extended (Nica, 2002), firstly by adding ten new indicators (IC5 - IC14) and by 2008 the number had risen to sixteen (IC1-IC16)[11].

One of the key indicators IC6 measures the level of performance in scientific research, which has progressively gained importance from 2001 to 2008, now being that with the largest weighting in the quality aspect of university financing, standing at 7% out of the 30% total. The increasing trend in this allocation came with the realization that intensive research activities are a must for any university wishing to achieve excellence status. That is, the inclusion of this indicator addresses the need for there to be a corrective qualitative indicator based on research linked to the core funding methodology. Even though this methodology is not perceived as a classification system for higher education institutions, it serves as a useful scientific assessment exercise for the evaluation of the Romanian academic research performance"[12], which focuses on the impact of quality of research on the overall educational process. In 2008 when the CNFIS (the National Council for Higher Education Financing) published an official report in which the results of the IC6 were presented to a large audience, it was rather recognized as a "transparency tool", not as a ranking or classification. Nevertheless, one of the effects that this generated at the time was an intensive debate with regard to the results between higher education institutions.

Another important step in the Romanian higher education system's orientation towards performance assessment and evaluation that followed the elaboration of the quality based indicators and financing procedures, was the proposal for a Romanian ranking system to represent the formal results of the cooperation between UNESCO-CEPES and Romanian experts already involved in the evaluation of the universities' results and performance[13]. The ranking put forward in 2005[14] took into consideration 5 indicators and 21 sub-indicators. Out of the 5 indicators, 4 were taken from the ranking by Shanghai Jiao Tong University (SJTU), with the supplementary indicator added in Romanian classification being institutional prestige and reputation[15]. The proposals were discussed at the national level, both in terms of procedures and evaluation mechanisms and in terms of administrative mechanisms, but so far no decision on the launching of a ranking initiative has been taken.

A further attempt to achieve such an ongoing system was made by the CNCSIS (National Council for Research in Higher Education), which published a ranking of the universities according to their scientific research activity[16], but the public debates around it were so contentious that continuation of the initiative was not perceived as a desirable outcome and so this initiative was dropped.

Nevertheless, reflections, initiatives and projects concerning the concepts of university of excellence, elite university, world-class university and the position that the Romanian authorities, institutions, experts and stakeholders should adopt on these perspectives, have flourished.

Similar initiatives and reflexive exercises at the higher education level with regards to excellence, research performance and evaluation were also supported and encouraged by important civil society entities such as those run by AdAstra[17], who carried out a ranking of Romanian universities based on the SJTU ranking criteria. These activities, as well as other measures at the system or institutional levels, were aimed at encouraging reflection upon what should be considered relevant in the international arena, generated a clear tendency at institutional level to reflect on the importance and relevance of national and international rankings and especially of those rankings that are evaluating the research component of the university.

As a result, the attention given to excellence and the required strategic measures to achieve this has increased in the last years in Romania at the governmental as well as at the higher education institutional level. Following these intense debates, three major initiatives were launched.

The Romanian National Research Strategy for 2007–2013 was set out in 2005–2006, which was followed by the National Plan 2 (PN2) of Research and Development, having as their main objectives production of knowledge and international visibility, and economic development through innovation and social quality. More specifically, the programmes of the PN2 were focused on Ideas (i.e. ground breaking advanced research), Human Resources (human resource development), Capacities (development of research infrastructure), Partnerships (the development of projects in partnership with research institutions and enterprises) and Innovation (development of innovation capacity). All projects were required to have result and impact indicators. The universities responded very rapidly to this by employing dedicated young research staff, and submitting a large number of research proposals. As a result scientific production has increased significantly, with much of the development being oriented universities in terms of scientific research.

Secondly, the Romanian Ministry of Education, Research and Innovation in partnership with the UEFISCSU (Executive Unit for Higher Education and Research Funding), CNCSIS and CNFIS launched five strategic projects financed by the European Social Fund's Human Resources Development Operational Programme, aimed at increasing the competitiveness and performance of the Romanian higher education system, in terms of better quality and leadership, doctoral studies in schools of excellence - the Organization of Doctoral Schools, improved higher education management and electronic student enrolment systems, with the goal of rolling out multilevel strategic mechanisms to support institutional excellence.

The project "Quality and Leadership" has as its general objective the construction of a long-term vision for Romanian higher education, to be undertaken by key actors from the higher education and business sectors and by society as a whole, which will establish universal policies at the university level as benchmarks for the strategic positioning of the different institutions throughout Romania. In other words, the outcome of the consultation will be the setting up of a system that will allow for assessment of the differential achievements of these universities when pursuing their particular programme of excellence.

Evaluation of the quality of research in universities and increase of visibility by scientific publications has a general objective of elaborating, testing and implementing of a methodology which ensures international evaluation of the research quality in Romanian universities, the development of a program for universities of excellence as well as the increases of the capacity of scientific publishing at the institutional and individual level. Doctoral Studies - the Organization of Doctoral Schools promotes a unique strategic approach of the reform of doctoral studies, to ensure a real contribution of doctoral and postdoctoral programs to the education of young researchers with scientific performances at international level. The improvement of higher education management and the installing of an electronic student enrolment system are complementary to the above-mentioned projects on the managerial and administrative side.

Thirdly, in 2009, two legislative initiatives were launched[18] containing somewhat contrasting proposals, with regards to excellence in the higher education system. First, the new proposal for the Education Code[19] contends that the mission for the higher education system should be "the professional development of human resources, to produce scientific knowledge through scientific research, to create and innovate"[20]. In accordance with these legislative measures, each university has to declare whether its mission involves teaching or teaching and research. Subsequently, excellence at the organizational and individual levels is to be recognized and promoted[21]. Moreover, the financial mechanisms to sustain institutional excellence are to retain the 30% component of funding being based on quality, as discussed above, with this being potentially doubled through the possible access to the institutional development fund, which is open to a certain selected group of institutions. Individual excellence is to be supported through grant allocation and overall excellence will be evaluated both at the institutional level and the system level.

The Presidential Commission for Education and Research, which launched the Higher Education Law project, adopted a rather radical position regarding excellence in universities, proposing classification of each institution into the following groups, that is, research intensive universities, education and research universities, educational universities and vocational universities[22]. Universities can elect which category to belong to, following which evaluation of their research, teaching and learning quality is carried out accordingly. Secondly, criteria to evaluate the excellence of performance in the different domains, such as research and teaching, are to be established and the subsequent aim is to double current performance through additional financial allocation aimed at sustaining excellence in institutional programme delivery. Under both, special measures are proposed to encourage and support top research through dedicated programmes, with elite support coming in the guise of a supplementary scheme from outside the institutional framework. The present minister for education, Daniel Funeriu, fully supports the educational proposals of the Presidential Commission for Education and Research and considers that the major changes for higher education, after the adoption of the new educational law, will be transformation at the level of academic management, evaluation of universities based on their main chosen mission - teaching, research and teaching or advanced research, followed by significant financial support and other measures at the national level aimed at concentrating resources and stimulating overall performance.

As already shown, all policies, initiatives and measures are complementary and serve the same goal to increase the competitiveness of the higher education system in general and of research in the sector in particular.

In order to take a closer look at the performance of the higher education institutions in Romania, we chose to take for further analysis the IC6 indicator relating to the level of performance in scientific research from the complex methodology designed by CNFIS. In this regard, the aggregated indicator is based on 10 sub-indicators, that is, number of grants and contracts; value of grants and contracts; number of scientific papers (ISI, IDB, national); number of Ph.D. theses finalized; number of books edited in national and international publishing houses; number of patents obtained; number of centres of scientific research; representation in academies number of national prizes in science, technology and arts. All sub-indicators are given the same weighting factor, and no parameter is considered more important than the others.

Based on this indicator as a part of the total quality based financing (7% out of 30% as explained above), we ran an analysis to assess research performance by university and the figures for the two academic years 2007–2008 and 2008–2009 (see Table 4). The top two institutions in both years were the Politehnica Bucureşti and the Universitatea de Ştiinţe Agricole şi Medicină Veterinară Timişoara, both maintaining their respective positions. The major changes were registered by the Universitatea Gheorghe Asachi Iaşi, which improved its position by 3 places and the Universitatea Bucureşti, which lost 3 places. Moreover, it should also be noted that in the cases of the Universitatea Al.I. Cuza Iaşi, Universitatea din Craiova, and the Universitatea de Vest they all retained the same positions in the rankings for the two years in question.

Table 4. IC 6 Score 2007–2008 and 2008–2009

University	Position 2007–2008	Position 2008–2009	IC6 Score 2007–2008	IC6 Score 2008–2009
Universitatea Babeş-Bolyai Cluj Napoca	3	5	6.41	4.97
Universitatea Tehnică Cluj Napoca	4	3	5.33	6.30
Universitatea "Al. I. Cuza" Iaşi	6	6	5.27	4.51
Universitatea Gheorghe Asachi Iaşi	7	4	4.76	5.09
Universitatea Transilvania Braşov	8	7	4.21	4.49
Universitatea din Craiova	9	9	3.76	3.59
Universitatea Politehnica Bucureşti	1	1	7.09 *	6.74
Universitatea Bucureşti	5	8	5.29	3.90
Universitatea de Vest Timişoara	10	10	3.60	2.91
Universitatea de Ştiinţe Agricole şi Medicină Veterinară Timişoara	2	2	6.71	6.48

It is not surprising that several technical and agriculture universities were situated in top positions, given the fact that a substantial number of papers and books published at the local level was counted in the assessment, as well as the fact that the indicator was compiled on the basis of the number of papers per number of academic staff and these institutions are relatively small. In spite of these results, it is important to point out that most of the variables taken into consideration were either input or status variables, with only four being in relation to outputs.

However, a comparison of the IC6 score with that obtained from the sub-indicator that links the Romanian quality indicators methodology with international evaluation, i.e. that contained within the ISI Articles (3.1), reveals a different hierarchy between the selected institutions. That is, when the selected indicator 3.1, which refers to the number of articles published in ISI journals, is used, the rankings for the two years under consideration become as in Table 5 below.

Whilst, as was revealed above, under the IC6 score classification the Universitatea Politehnica Bucureşti and the Universitatea de Ştiinţe Agricole şi Medicină Veterinară Timişoara came top, with the ISI articles compilation the latter was much lower in rank, being in 8th place in the first year and 10th in the second and the former occupied 3rd and 5th positions in the two considered years, respectively. By contrast, according to the SJTU ranking criteria the top universities in Romania are the Universitatea Bucureşti, Universitatea Babeş-Bolyai, Universitatea Politehnică Bucureşti and the Universitatea Al.I.Cuza Iaşi, which were found scattered in the domestic indicator hierarchy. Moreover, under the HEAACT Taiwan ranking system, we found that only the Universitatea Bucureşti and the Universitatea Babeş-Bolyai Cluj-Napoca figured anywhere in the tables.

Table 5. Score 2007–2008 and 2008–2009

University	Position 2007–2008	Position 2008–2009	3.1. Score 2007–2008	3.1. Score 2008–2009
Universitatea Babeş-Bolyai Cluj Napoca	1	1	0.32	0.40
Universitatea Tehnică Cluj Napoca	3	4	0.25	0.31
Universitatea "Al. I. Cuza" Iaşi	5	5	0.24	0.26
Universitatea Gheorghe Asachi Iaşi	2	2	0.31	0.32
Universitatea Transilvania Brasov	10	*	0.06	*
Universitatea din Craiova	6	8	0.17	0.19
Universitatea Politehnica Bucureşti	4	3	0.25	0.31
Universitatea Bucureşti	7	9	0.14	0.16
Universitatea de Vest Timişoara	9	7	0.12	0.21
Universitatea de Ştiinţe Agricole şi Medicină Veterinară Timişoara	8	10	0.12	0.12

Nevertheless, the above results are a good starting point for distinguishing the different factors involved in the assessment under the national and international systems. In this regard, the authorities in Romania can identify weaknesses in the domestic approach, when institutions are oriented towards having an international profile, whilst at the same time protecting different aspects at the national level for other institutions who wish to improve their performance, but at present are not too concerned about their visibility on the international stage.

In 2008, because the previous classification based on non-weighted parameters was considered insufficiently relevant to the workings of many Romanian higher education institutions, an aggregated quality indicator was proposed, which included the following five sub-indicators, in order to assess scientific research performance:

- Capacity to attract funds for scientific activity (25%);
- Capacity to train the highly skilled human resources for scientific activity (10%) - number of Ph.D. theses finalized;
- Relevance and visibility of the scientific results (50%) - scientific articles and patents;
- Capacity to design and develop innovative products and technologies that are transferable to the business environment (10%) - new products and technologies; and
- Institutional capacity to organize and support performance in scientific research (5%).

Table 6. Selected Romanian higher education institutions' capacity to attract funds from national grants

University	Amount of funds attracted national grants 2007 (In RON)	Amount of funds attracted national grants 2007 (In EUR[23])	Position in the hierarchy[24]
Universitatea Babeş-Bolyai Cluj Napoca	4.374.229	1.214.726	1
Universitatea Tehnică Cluj Napoca	1.594.306	442.740	8
Universitatea "Al. I. Cuza" Iaşi	2.412.017	669.819	5
Universitatea Gheorghe Asachi Iaşi	2.565.709	712.499	4
Universitatea Transilvania Braşov	1.982.834	550.634	6
Universitatea din Craiova	1.662.546	461.690	7
Universitatea Politehnica Bucureşti	3.515.354	976.216	3
Universitatea Bucureşti	3.535.712	981.869	2
Universitatea de Vest Timişoara	757.939	210.480	10
Universitatea de Ştiinţe Agricole şi Medicină Veterinară Timişoara	1.163.700	323.160	9

It can be observed that the emphasis is now being put on output, the indicators (indicators 2 to 4), account for 70% of the total weighting. However, as yet no classification has been carried out according to this new method, but it is hoped that a ranking more consistent with those of the SJTU or the HEAACT approaches will emerge; in other words, one that allows for more accurate international comparisons.

Regarding the indicator IC1 - Capacity to attract funds for scientific activity, with respect to sub-indicator IC1.2. - projects financed through national grants, we use for our analyses the figures provided by CNCSIS for the year 2007. The hierarchy for the selected universities is displayed in Table 6.

The figures show the same tendency of the universities from the selected regions to sustain research and to promote excellence. It is also obvious that universities that attract more research funds tend to score higher in the number of articles and other scientific outputs.

CONCLUSIONS

The development of universities of excellence is a major ongoing debate through-out academia and in the Romanian context, if a consensus can be reached at the governmental level, in terms of the appropriate legislative framework, this will represent a major reform at the national leve. However, at present although significant concerns have been raised regarding this issue by some major higher education institutions, as well as by some governmental bodies, as yet there has been no compre-hensive government commitment to long-term support for this approach. Moreover, the current discussions range around competitiveness, especially at the university level, in terms of whether other missions undertaken at the institutional level, such as promoting social cohesion and increasing the accessibility of higher education studies to wider sections of the population, will have a negative impact on overall per-formance. It is for these reasons, amongst others, that public opinion leaders in relation to higher education and other experts in the field have still to reach a common under-standing of what should be the future development of the higher education system in Romania and, in connection to this, the role that the creation of universities of excellence should play in modern society. Notwithstanding this impasse, progress is already underway in the classification or ranking of Romanian universities, so as to place them both within the national and international settings.

Furthermore, important formal and informal steps are being taken at both the sector and institutional levels towards the establishment of support mechanisms for producing excellence. In this regard, some of the most effective measures taken have been the adoption of very ambitious research strategies, including the doubling of financial support mechanisms at the institutional level (Universitatea Babeş-Bolyai Cluj-Napoca), international cooperation and partnerships in research (Universitatea Politehnica Bucureşti, Universitatea Bucureşti, Universitatea Babeş-Bolyai Cluj Napoca) and long term strategies to support the development of highly capable human resources for research (Universitatea Alexandru Ioan Cuza, Iaşi, Universitatea de Vest Timişoara, Universitatea Babeş-Bolyai Cluj-Napoca, Universitatea Bucureşti).

The results of the IC6 indicators for the country's top universities show a positive causal relation between the amount of national and international funds attracted and the research results produced. Moreover, if we also analysze the regional distribution of the universities from the innovation network perspective, this causal relation is also doubled by concentration of RDI actors at the regional level. In sum, universities that manage to attract research funds (grants, contracts) tend to be more productive and internationally visible than universities with low or almost non-existent interests in this field. Nevertheless, those that have a strong network at the regional level tend to be more active in the dissemination of their results and more oriented towards pragmatic solutions that can be more easily transferred into practice. If such institutions expand their activities to the international arena, thereby undertaking missions that facilitate the increase of their capacity through organizational learning brought about through the access to relevant resources at European or international level, they can expect to improve their overall performance, particularly in the field of research.

The relative weighting that should be placed on the local and international factors is hard to assess, but we would contend that excellence in research cannot be reached without proper financial mechanisms and a strong commitment towards internationalization. That is, the aim of developing and promoting research-intensive universities or universities of excellence in the international arena is an essential commitment, if a nation like Romania is to participate fully in the dynamic and challenging competitive world of today and thereby be able to contribute effectively in the major fields of science, technology and societal development in the future. This commitment should be all embracing and holistic, working at multiple levels, including the institution itself, governmental bodies and representatives of civil society. However, this by itself is not sufficient, because it also necessary to establish shared core values, regarding evaluation, identity, mission and institutional capacity, and in particular the development of institutional competence through participating in competition, should be viewed as an opportunity for promoting the institution through effective marketing, rather than something to shy away from. In other words, those that grasp the openings becoming available in the modern higher education environment will surely prosper.

However, discussion of the implications at the different organizational levels under different mission, in terms of their required adaptation, is lacking. Moreover, the specific measures to encourage departments and chairs to improve their performance in certain areas (research, teaching, vocational training, etc.) are only included in vague general terms in most strategic documents and there are rarely real measures and concrete results made available in the public domain regarding such matters as research capacity, financial performance, quality and success rates. As a result, the impact of macro and micro level decisions regarding excellence at the institutional level, type of mission and commitment to research or teaching performance is difficult to analyse. Even if the quantitative data were more reliable, there is a strong case for the use of qualitative techniques, such as interviews, focus groups or document analyses (where available), in spite of their almost always being heavily reliant on time and other resources.

Following the developments in recent years, the increase of the level scientific output in Romania is impressive, rising from 6552 ISI papers in the period 2002–2004[25] to 14352 in the period 2006–2008 (a 2.2 fold increase), from an average of 58 patent requests per year registered at the OSIM in the period 1996–2003, to one of 610 per year registered for the period 2006–2008[26] (more than a tenfold increase!) and there being a jump in the European Innovation Index, from 0.18 to 0.27 in the period 2005–2008[27]. This is a consequence of both the increase in public expenditure on research, owing to the more realistic understanding of the importance of the field on the political side. Furthermore, it comes as a result of the realization by the universities as to the importance of their scientific mission, at both the national and international levels, which has led to their increasingly being responsible for key scientific results coming out of the Romanian RDI system.

In spite of all this, and also the fact that there are several higher education institutions committed to developing excellence in teaching and research, as yet no major university in Romania can claim to have become a member of the world-class university elite, and this is for several reasons:

- The required budget of such a university has been estimated as having to be based on 2006 in real terms at greater than 500 million USD/year and growing, owing to the rapid evolution of international markets and economies, but the largest budget of any Romanian university is only around 150–200 million USD/year[28];
- The conditions required for developing high level research are difficult to reach, in spite of the tremendous efforts to improve the research infrastructure, because up until 2000 money allocated to this endeavour was very low and hence the nation has a long way to go to catch up;
- There is still a pressing need in many cases to address gaps in provision, by the development of excellence programmes within universities and placing high priority in terms of research focus, with appropriate levels of funding accompanying such activities;
- The mentality of the academic staff for whom research is an important part of their activity has only recently started to change and thus, their efficiency is still relatively low, producing 0.4 ISI papers per member of staff/year, as compared at the best universities in the world with an output of 4 papers per member of staff per year; and
- Although, it is estimated that in future years there are four Romanian institutions that will probably express their will to become world-class universities, up until now, only one has publicly declared its intention to do so and has taken specific strategic measures to this end, which suggests there may well be a lack of ambition amongst the institutions concerned.

Notwithstanding the above potential obstacles, the importance of having a category of universities of international standing is obvious, because it will allow Romania to position itself well in the international higher education market, to attract more students and hence more funds and allow that nation to make a more significant contribution to the creation of knowledge.

We would argue very strongly that there are two major key reasons why there must be a marked improvement of the higher education system in Romania as a whole and average university performance, these being the scientific and economic perspectives. For were there to be a movement towards the nation having institutions ranked in the world-class category, the obvious outcomes would be better scientific knowledge creation and, perhaps more importantly, increased economic and financial returns in relation to this. However, the substantial reforms needed to stimulate such tremendous changes at the level of the higher education Romanian system do not come cheap and unfortunately will be perceived by some as unpopular measures, owing to the need to redirect scarce financial resources in an economy that is not particularly strong. Therefore, we will need to convince society at large of the importance of such investment for the future of our nation, by ensuring that any money received is used with the utmost efficiency and the outcomes are of the highest quality. This can only be achieved by bringing together a whole raft of interested stakeholders, ranging from politicians to higher education managers and those with business interests and other interested parties in civil society, uniting in supporting the future of the higher education sector.

Notwithstanding this, if building world-class universities is considered to be too ambitious given Romania's current economic circumstances, building research intensive universities may provide an alternative more incremental way forward, with our suggestion that three or four universities should be provided with special support, so that eventually in the not too distant future they will be able to enter into the elite of world-class universities.

NOTES

[1]   See more in Altbach et al. (2009), ch. 1.
[2]   The analysis is based on official data provided by INSSE, UN - Economic Survey of Europe 2005.
[3]   University of Excellence or Excellence University - has been conceptualized at the Romanian HE system level as an emerging concept after a long history of theories and instruments developed in order to measure the quality of a system, to assure quality and to encompass performance in various areas - education, research and support services. Among the most frequent terms associated with university of excellence are: research intensive university, universities highly engaged in scientific knowledge and relevance at international level.
[4]   European Higher Education Area - EHEA, European Research Area – ERA.
[5]   See OECD report, 2004.
[6]   OECD, 2004, pag.9
[7]   UNESCO Institute of Statistics - GER - gross enrolment rate in tertiary education a measure of total enrolment in a specific level of education, regardless of age, expressed as a percentage of the eligible official school-age population, corresponding to the same level of education in a given school year. For the tertiary level, the population used is that of the five-year age group following on from the secondary school leaving age. GER aims to express the level of participation and indicates the capacity of the education system to enrol students of a particular age group http://stats.uis.unesco.org/unesco/TableViewer/tableView.aspx?ReportId=167
[8]   The regions selected are administrative regions of Romania with specific roles in the socio-economic development of the country, sustained through specific strategic development plans and financed accordingly.
[9]   Until now, the only university which undertook a proactive strategy of research with explicit goals (e.g. access to the first 500 universities in the Shanghai Jiao Tong Ranking) and measures for implementation was the Universitatea Babeş-Bolyai Cluj Napoca.
[10] The proposal of the first set of qualitative indicators was launched by professor Panaite NICA, at that time - 2001, vice-president of the National Council for Higher Education Financing (Consiliul National de Finantare a Învăţământului Superior – http://www.cnfis.ro.)

[11] CNFIS (2008). Propunere privind Metodologia de repartizare pe instituţii de învăţământ superior a alocaţiilor bugetare pentru finanţarea de bază în anul 2008.

[12] Dumitrache, I., Căta-Danil, G., Ciuparu - Raport: Analiză comparativă a practicii internaţionale în evaluarea cercetării, UEFISCSU (2009), p. 18.

[13] UNESCO-CEPES member of the International Ranking Expert Group Professor Jan Sadlak has been cooperating in a long term project with Romanian experts, such as Professor Panaite Nica who designed the first quality based financing mechanism for the Romanian higher education system and co-authored with Paul Şerban Agachi the first Romanian ranking proposal and Paul Şerban Agachi, also a member of the International Ranking Expert Group and one of the supporters of the importance of having world class universities for national higher education systems that are co-designed at the institutional level (Babeş-Bolyai University).

[14] Agachi, Nica (2005) - Ierarhizarea universităţilor din România. Metodologie de aplicare.

[15] The institutional reputation is a criterion that reveals the quality of a certain higher education institution perceived by other similar institution at national and international level, as well as by stakeholders (Agachi and Nica, 2005: 8).

[16] Agachi, P.Ş., Nica,P., Moraru,C.,Mihăilă, A. (2007).

[17] AdAstra is an NGO dedicated to Romanian researchers aimed at: demonstrating showcase modern science, performed either in Romania or by Romanian scientists abroad, presenting the latest scientific paradigms and methodological concepts to be used as benchmarks for objective estimation of the state of science and education in Romania, initiating and maintaining an information flow that will facilitate scientific cooperation within the Romanian scientific communities and encouraging and advising young researchers in Romania, to provide an open discussion forum on science and education policies, with the declared aim to present coherent reform proposals to the Romanian political establishment – http://www.ad-astra.ro.

[18] The two legislative proposals were launched by the presidential commission on education, led by former minister of education Mircea MICLEA, including: experts from the educational sector, coordinators of governmental bodies with major roles in the evolution of higher education system, and by the actual minister of education (Ecaterina Andronescu) consultancy team.

[19] Codul Educaţiei, Proiect, Cabinetul Ministrului, Ministerul Educaţiei, Cercetării şi Inovării, 14 August 2009.

[20] Codul Educaţiei, Titlul III - Învăţământul superior, Capitolul I - Dispoziţii comune, pag. 66.

[21] Codul Educaţiei, Titlul III - Învăţământul superior, Capitolul VI - Excelenţa în învăţământul superior, p.104.

[22] Legea Învăţământului Superior, comisia prezidenţială, 2009.

[23] The currency rate took into consideration was 1 RON = 3,601 EUR, BNR rate at 28 December 2007.

[24] Position in the hierarchy refers to the present selection of the universities on the basis of perceived relevance at the level of higher education in Romania and on the basis of geographical distribution. The position of the selected universities in the present ranking corresponds or does not to the positions in the national hierarchy. For example, it is the same for the Universitatea Babeş-Bolyai but is highly different for the Universitatea de Vest Timisoara.

[25] Agachi et al., Sistemul naţional de Cercetare, Dezvoltare şi Inovare în contextual integrării în Aria Europeană a Cercetării, Editura Academiei, Bucuresti, 2006.

[26] ANCS - Analiza cheltuielilor publice destinate cercetarii si dezvoltarii in Romania, Raport catre CE, 2009.

[27] European Innovation Index Scoreboard 2008.

[28] For more comments on the budget of a world-class university see Altbach (2006) Part 4 - Research Universities chapter 13 - The Costs and Benefits of World-Class Universities, p. 71. For the budget of Romanian top universities in the public sector, see the CNFIS report on the financing of the public universities http://www.cnfis.ro.

REFERENCES

Agachi, P. Ş., et al. (2006). *Sistemul naţional de Cercetare, Dezvoltare şi Inovare în contextul integrării în Aria Europeană a Cercetării*. Bucuresti, Romania: Editura Academiei.

Agachi, P. Ş., & Nica, P. (2005). Ierarhizarea universităţilor din România. Metodologie de aplicare. *Revista de Politica Ştiintei şi Scientometrie, 2*, 178–189.

Agachi, P. Ş., Nica, P., Moraru, C., & Mihăila, A. (2007). Ierarhizarea universităţilor din România, din punctul de vedere al activităţii de cercetare ştiinţifică. *Revista de politica ştiinţei şi scientometrie*, *4*, 154–170.

Altbach, P. (2006). *International higher education - reflections on policy and practice*. Chestnut Hill, MA: Center for International Higher Education, Lynch School of Education, Boston College.

Altbach, P., Reisberg, L., & Rumbley, L. (2009). *Trends in global higher education. Tracking an academic revolution*. Center for International Higher Education, Boston College.

European Committee for Social Cohesion. (2004). *A new strategy for social cohesion*. Strasbourg.

ANCS. (2009). *Analiza cheltuielilor publice destinate cercetarii si dezvoltarii in Romania. Raport catre CE*. Bucureşti.

CNCSIS. (2007). *Raportul Conferinţei Naţionale*. Cluj-Napoca.

Cabinetul Ministrului, Ministerul Educaţiei, Cercetării şi Inovării. (2009). *Codul Educaţiei. Proiect*. Bucureşti.

Conell, H. (2004). *University research management. Meeting the institutional challenges*. OECD Publishing.

Maastricht Economic and Social Research and Training Centre on Innovation and Technology. (2008). *European innovation scoreboard* http://www.proinno-europe.eu/EIS2008/website/docs/IS_2008_final_report.pdf

Gould, E. (2003). *The university in a corporate culture*. New Haven, CT: Yale University Press.

Hazelkorn, E. (2005). *University research management. Developing research in new higher education institutions*. OECD Publishing.

Comisia prezidenţială. (2009), *Ministerul educaţiei, cercetării şi inovării*. Legea Învăţământului Superior - Proiect, Bucureşti.

Nica, P. (1998). *Implicaţii manageriale ale trecerii la finanţarea globală a universităţilor*. Bucureşti: Paidea.

Nica, P. (2000). *Managementul calităţii şi ierarhizarea universităţilor româneşti*. Bucureşti: Paidea.

Nica, P. (2002). *Calitate şi adaptabilitate în managementul facultăţilor cu profil economic*. Iaşi: Sedcom Libris.

Sadlak, J. (1998). Globalization and concurrent challenges for higher education. In P. Scott (Ed.), (2000). *The globalization of higher education*. Buckingham, UK: SRHE and Open University Press.

Scott, P. (1998). Massification, internationalization, and globalization. In P. Scott (Ed.), (2000). *The globalization of higher education*. Buckingham, UK: SRHE and Open University Press.

Scott, J. C. (2006). The mission of the university: Medieval to postmodern transformation. *Journal of Higher Education, 77*.

INTERNET WEBSITES

Codul Educaţiei, Proiect, Cabinetul Ministrului. (2009). Ministerul Educaţiei, Cercetării şi Inovării Ministerul official website. Retrieved from http://www.edu.ro

Indicator IC6 – Research Evaluation, National Council for Higher Education Financing. (2009). Official website. Retrieved from http://www.cnfis.ro/Public/cat/22/Indicatorul-IC6.html

Legea Învăţământului Superior – proiect. (2009). Comisia prezidenţială pentru analiza şi elaborarea politicilor din domeniul educaţiei şi cercetării official website. Retrieved from http://edu.presidency.ro

România Educaţiei, România Cercetării. (2007). Comisia prezidenţială pentru analiza şi elaborarea politicilor din domeniul educaţiei şi cercetării official website. Retrieved from http://edu.presidency.ro

UNESCO CEPES Publications. (2009). UNESCO CEPES official website. Retrieved from http://www.unesco.org

Universitatea "Alexandru Ioan Cuza" Iaşi – Mission Statement. (2009). Universitatea "Alexandru Ioan Cuza" official website. Retrieved from http://www.uaic.ro

Universitatea Babeş-Bolyai – Mission Statement, Universitatea Babeş-Bolyai. (2009). Official website. Retrieved from http://www.ubbcluj.ro

Universitatea Bucureşti – Mission Statement, Universitatea Bucureşti. (2009). Official website. Retrieved from http://www.unibuc.ro

Universitatea de Ştiinţe Agricole şi Medicină Veterinară a Banatului, Timişoara – Mission Statement. (2009). Universitatea de Ştiinţe Agricole şi Medicină Veterinară a Banatului, Timişoara official website. Retrieved from http://www.usab-tm.ro

Universitatea de Vest, Timişoara – Mission Statement. (2009). Universitatea de Vest, Timişoara official website. Retrieved from http://www.uvt.ro

Universitatea din Craiova – Mission Statement. (2009). Universitatea din Craiova official website. Retrieved from www.ucv.ro

Universitatea Politehnica Bucureşti – Mission Statement. (2009). Universitatea Politehnica Bucureşti official website. Retrieved from http://www.pub.ro

Universitatea Tehnică din Cluj Napoca – Mission Statement. (2009). Universitatea Tehnică din Cluj Napoca official website. Retrieved September 12, 2009, from www.utcluj.ro

Universitatea Tehnică "Gheorghe Asachi" Iaşi – Mission Statement. (2009). Universitatea Tehnică "Gheorghe Asachi" Iaşi official website. Retrieved from http://www.tuiasi.ro

Universitatea Transilvania Braşov – Mission Statement. (2009). Universitatea Transilvania Braşov official website. Retrieved from http://www.unitbv.ro

Paul Şerban AGACHI
Academic Council
University Babeş-Bolyai, Cluj Napoca, Romania

Camelia MORARU
Faculty of European Studies and Center for University Development
University Babeş-Bolyai, Cluj Napoca, Romania

Romana Emilia CUCURUZAN
Faculty of European Studies
University Babeş-Bolyai, Cluj Napoca, Romania

Adrian CURAJ
National Authority for Scientific Research
Centre for Strategic Management and Quality Assurance in Higher Education
Politehnica Universit, Bucureşti, Romania

NATALIA RUIZ-RODGERS

5. THE ROLE OF RESEARCH UNIVERSITY IN THE THIRD WORLD:

A Case Study of the National University of Colombia

The image of Colombia that is portrayed by the daily news is dire violence, kidnappings, and of course, drugs, are words that are conjured up at the mere mention of the country's name. Some of it is indeed true. For the last sixty years Colombia has been immersed in a civil war between rebels, drug traffickers and the government that has shed much blood and created great misery. What is less known is that Colombia is a nation of a great intellectual and scientific heritage. From the country's first days as a Spanish colony, when some of the earliest universities in the continent were established, to our present time as an independent republic, for centuries Colombia has had an extremely rich academic tradition. What are the perspectives for continuing that tradition into the 21st century? This essay presents a case study of the National University of Colombia, an institution that to maintain its leading role in the domestic arena, must become relevant in the international context. Even though the task of building of a world-class research university in Colombia offers unique -even daunting - challenges, the experience from the National University shows that, with long-term vision and support from the government, a way can be made.

The first part of this chapter offers some general background on Colombia and on the problems associated with developing science and technology in the country. The second part deals specifically with the question of building a world-class research university in a Third World country, and some of the institutional arrangements that could make it possible. The third section provides an overview of the National University, identifying its strengths and weaknesses in the context of Colombia. Finally, the fourth section describes the strategies used by the National University to achieve the goal of becoming a world-class research university.

COLOMBIA: THE BACKGROUND FOR UNDERSTANDING HIGHER EDUCATION

Situated in the northwestern corner of South America, Colombia is a land of great cultural and biological diversity. Traversed by the equator, dissected by the Andes, and with access to the Pacific Ocean, the Caribbean Sea and the Amazon River basin, the country has a unique wealth of environmental conditions and natural resources. Due to its tropical climate, most of the population centres are scattered

N.C. Liu et al., (eds.), *Paths to a World-Class University: Lessons from Practices and Experiences, 107–124.*

throughout mountainous terrain (which is cooler) rather than in the flat, hot and humid lowlands. This geographic fragmentation of its population (and its land) has often been considered as a challenge to the development of infrastructure, as well as to the establishment of a strong, centralized state capable of enforcing the rule of law across the territory (DNP, 2005).

At nearly 45 million, Colombia has Latin America's third largest population after Brazil and Mexico, and its GDP of around USD 240 billion is the fourth in the region (World Bank, 2009). The per capita income is USD 4,724, but this average masks some stark regional and social disparities. The mean yearly income in and around the main cities of Bogotá (the capital), Medellín and Cali is close to USD 6,000 per person, but in some of the poorest regions in the Pacific lowlands it drops to USD 1,600. The population is not only separated by physical features, but also by deep social fractures. Colombia inherited an extremely unequal social structure from its colonial past, and modern society has not been able to shake off the profound disparities in wealth distribution. Today, nearly a fifth of the population lives below the poverty line and, despite recent gains in security and socio-political stability, the GINI index is 0.56, making it the one of the most unequal countries in Latin America.

A country with the level of poverty and security problems that Colombia has faces stark choices when it comes to tertiary education and research. This is not only due to matters of resource allocation, but because basic and applied research may not be within the radar of what society deems to be important tasks. This relation between science and technology and the context within which they exist may be examined from multiple perspectives. On the one hand, science and technology can be understood as part of the set of restrictions that countries face in order to advance to their desired future and in this sense, future scenarios are conditioned by current scientific and technological developments. On the other hand, societies may recognize their potential and build a vision of a nation based on their own desires and under this premise, science and technology are the vehicles that make the move in the desired direction possible.

In every historical time period, those societies that have been able to master strategically decisive technologies have forged their own destiny (Castells, 2002). These societies have been able to act, because their development has been based on knowledge. In today's society, this translates into having people with the ability to produce and reproduce knowledge, to have access to technologies that enable production, to have the norms and agreements that make these relations of production possible, and to make networks. The priority of universities thus becomes the development of capacities that allow the production and reproduction of knowledge.

In this context, scientific development adopts a key role because it produces institutionalized and legitimate knowledge for society. The relationship between society and science is established as the means to produce knowledge that is responsive to the market and the needs imposed by society. Moreover, in the global context, universities are precisely the main points of articulation between societies and the development of scientific knowledge. In accordance with this fact, scientific development and the strengthening of universities are consistently on the political agendas of national governments and international organizations, such as UNESCO, the World Bank, the Inter-American Development Bank, and the OECD.

The relationship between economic and scientific development highlights the importance of scientific and technological knowledge for the building of strong societies. Latin America has been no stranger to scientific knowledge, but for most of its history it has performed a relatively passive role in the global arena. From the colonial era to the first half of the twentieth century, technological and scientific activities were largely subservient to - and lagging behind - the advances in the former European colonial powers. Even after these nations achieved formal independence, during the first half of the nineteenth century, Europe (and, later, the United States) continued to exert a very prominent economic and cultural influence. After the Second World War, there was a deliberate effort to spur national science and technology as necessary elements towards modernization and development. An example of this was the establishment of science and technology agencies throughout South America and in Colombia, the government established COLCIENCIAS, the National Administrative Department for Science and Technology, in 1963. In addition, this decade saw the arrival of funding agencies like the Johnson, Rockefeller, Ford and Kellogg Foundations, whose "missions" provided key support for research in agriculture and economics (Villaveces and Forero-Pineda, 2007).

These investments were accompanied by a series of reorganizations and restructuring of universities, so that by the end of the 1960s, all mayor public universities had undergone critical transformations. In this regard, the Universidad del Valle near Cali (1962–1978), the National University in Bogotá (1964–1966) and also the Universidad de Antioquia in Medellín all embarked on significant reforms of their academic programmes and organizational structures, a step seen as indispensable to promoting research (Villaveces and Forero-Pineda, 2007, p. 115).

The Colombian state considers universities to be strategic allies in the development of science, technology and innovation. Apart from generating knowledge, universities promote the formation of the human capital which enhances the country's competitiveness and productivity. That is, universities educate students at many different levels (from undergraduate to doctoral), generate knowledge through the rigorous work of research groups and doctoral programmes, disseminate knowledge through articles, books and academic conferences, and use this knowledge through the development of patents, specialized consulting and continuing education programmes. Recent evaluations made by the SNCyT found that universities have been the sector most strongly committed to the acquisition, creation and use of knowledge (COLCIENCIAS, 2009, p. 31), thus reinforcing the view that institutions of higher learning have the greatest ability to contribute to the consolidation of Colombia as a knowledge-driven society. In 2007, nearly 90% of the researchers and over 97% of the research groups that were active in the country belonged to universities; 84% of indexed journals were produced in universities; and over half of the resources used by COLCIENCIAS between 2000 and 2007 to fund research was given to universities (OCyT, 2008, p. 62, 70, 83, 118).

In sum, in Colombia there has been a significant change in the pursuit of building capacities to do research. The change is particularly noticeable in the increasing numbers of Ph.D. qualified faculty members in universities: in the National University, 27% of the faculty holds a doctorate; in the Universidad de los Andes, 53% (Bucheli et al., 2009); and in the Universidad de Antioquia, 20% (a 17 point increase from 1994).

WORLD-CLASS UNIVERSITIES: WHAT ARE THEY, AND WHY BUILD ONE IN COLOMBIA?

The term "world-class universities" has become, over the last decade, attractive and useful in relation to competing in a globalized market of higher education (Samil, 2009, p. 15), for they are recognized both by their academic peers and by their results. The two main sources of such recognition are two worldwide university rankings: the one produced by the Shanghai Jiao Tong University (SJTU), and the other that compiled for the Times Higher Education Supplement (THES)[1]. Thus, acceptance into this exclusive club of world-rank universities is not a result of self-proclamation, but rather, in the words of Samil, "the elite condition is bestowed by the external world based on international recognition" (2009, p. 15). This author suggests a more precise and manageable definition of world-class universities, claiming that the superior results of these institutions, such as highly sought-after graduates, cutting-edge research and technology transfer, are attributable to three main factors. First, a high concentration of human talent, both of professors and of students, second, a wealth of resources in order to offer advanced research and teaching opportunities and third, "appropriate governing characteristics that promote strategic vision, innovation and flexibility, and that enable institutions to make decisions and manage their resources without being hindered by bureaucracy" (2009, p. 19–20).

The international rankings are heavily based on academic output in refereed journals. With regards to SJTU, 60% of the score is related to publications indexed in the Science and Social Science Citation Index, whereas for the THES 20% is based on indexed publications and 40% is based on a peer review of research in different areas. In the short term, these scores can be affected by factors like 1) publications in the journals *Nature* or *Science*; 2) articles indexed by ISI or SCOPUS; and 3) the number of international students or faculty.

A different sort of classification, which is used primarily in the United States, is based on the guidelines set forth by the Carnegie Foundation. This classification "has been widely used in the study of higher education, both as a way to represent and control for institutional differences, and also in the design of research studies to ensure adequate representation of sampled institutions, students, or faculty"[2]. The emphasis of this classification is on the attributes that typify a research university. This category is defined by 1) the number of doctoral programmes in different disciplines; 2) the number of students who graduate within a given period; and 3) the research activities. According to the Carnegie Foundation, research universities can be either extensive (if they graduate 50 or more doctoral students per year in at least

15 disciplines) or intensive (if they graduate 10 or more doctoral students per year in at least three disciplines, or 20 doctoral students irrespective of the discipline).

In sum, the category "world-class" corresponds to the pursuit of a niche within the global market for tertiary education. It compels universities to develop capabilities to be competitive and internationally recognized as the best within that niche. The "research university" category is focused on the production and dissemination of knowledge, that is, on doctoral education and research.

Why and how would we build a world-class university in the Third World? Each country must be able to give meaning to what it understands as a world-class or research university, not just in the what, but also in the how it can be achieved. Some roads are well-trodden, but to follow others' footsteps without reflection might take us along unknown paths, away from the potential knowledge that might turn comparative advantages into competitive advantages for a nation. This requires a country to define the strategic lines, not the disciplines, which will take it along the desired path.

In Colombia, the trend or at least the intention has been towards the development of research universities. This has been, first of all, a state policy, for in the words of the Colombian Minister of Education:

> in research universities we seek the generation of knowledge that contributes to society at large through technical and social innovation through, for example, scientific publications and patents. At the same time, we should place the emphasis on doctoral education, mobilize external resources for scientific production and establish a great network of researchers. (Vélez, 2009)

Colombian universities have also shown signs of mobilizing and prioritizing resources towards the development of their institutions based on research. In this regard, the strategic development plans of all major universities, public and private, revolve around citing the promotion of research as the core of their mission. The National University's 2007–2009 plan states that "a fundamental step towards becoming a research university is to complete the full cycle of education, up to the highest degree" (Vicerrectoría de Investigaciones UNAL, 2007). Similarly, the Universidad de Antioquia (public) and the Universidad de los Andes (private), have incorporated research and the creation of knowledge as a key part of their institutional missions (Vicerrectoría de Investigaciones UNIANDES, 2008).

However, it is apparent that to achieve the status of research or world-class universities, Colombian universities need to increase the pace and scope of the structural changes that will allow them to produce and reproduce knowledge at the highest level.

THE NATIONAL UNIVERSITY OF COLOMBIA: ITS CONTEXT AND ITS CHALLENGES

The National University of Colombia has been at the undisputed centre of the academic tradition in Colombia. With a history spanning 140 years, a staff of nearly 3,000 professors, and over 43,000 students (38,000 undergraduate and

5,000 graduate), it is the largest and most important university in the country. It is truly national, being present in four of the country's main urban centres, as well as on three satellite campuses in some of the most remote areas of the country, ranging from the Caribbean to the Amazon. Created shortly after Colombia became an independent nation, it continues to offer high-quality education irrespective of social and economic backgrounds. Moreover, the university represents the largest and longest running effort of the Colombian people to build a nation through education and research, even under very difficult conditions.

Today, the National University stands as proof that the nation's dedication to the pursuit of knowledge, art and social service far outweighs the destructive power of a few. Even during periods of acute social strife, economic downturns and civil violence, it has remained open for the study of the widest range of academic disciplines, from classical studies to agronomy, from medicine to architecture. A melting pot of classes, diverse ideologies and regional origins, the university itself mirrors the country's deep struggles and is no stranger to political conflict. However, our campuses have been, and remain, bastions of free speech and dissent in a country in which political freedom cannot be taken for granted.

The university is also very closely monitored, being considered by many as the standard against which all higher learning in the country is measured. In other words, it sets the broader trends in higher education in the country, and at the same it carries the weight of great expectations. It is precisely because of this that it has to extend its mission as an engine of development and innovation, by setting higher targets so as to become an internationally recognized centre of research and teaching.

The following overview of the National University is focused on three issues a) the achievement and maintenance of quality of its academic programmes; b) research excellence; and c) financial support.

Quality Assurance

Colombia has 282 institutions of higher education (Figure 1), 81 public and 201 private, which offer 2,932 undergraduate and 1,934 graduate programmes (Figure 2). Among this very broad offering of tertiary education, the National University stands

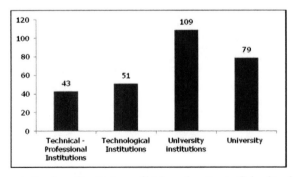

Figure 1. Number of institutions of higher education in Colombia, 2008.

Source: National System of Information of Higher Education in Colombia.

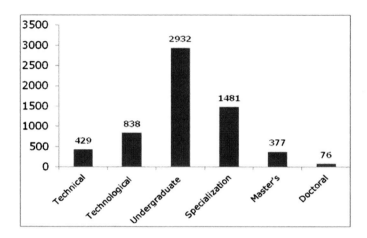

*Figure 2. Number of educational programmes in institutions of
higher education in Colombia, 2008.*

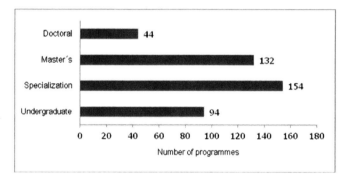

*Figure 3. Number of academic programmes at the
National University of Colombia, 2009.*

out for its sustained effort to monitor and ensure the quality of its programmes and
it is one of only 17 schools to have been certified by the Ministry of Education as
high quality institutions (eleven are private and six are public). The parameters
used by the National Accreditation Council (CNA) to assess the quality of undergraduate programmes are mission, students, professors, academic process, quality
of life, administration, alumni, infrastructure and financial resources and this
certification is given for a period of between four and eight years.

The university offers 352 academic programmes (Figure 3) and 75 of its 94 undergraduate programmes, across different fields, have been given the official quality
recognition (Figure 4), which represents 80% of the total offer at this level over
the last four years (Figure 5). According to this measure, our programmes
represent 13% of the total number of programmes certified in the country (574).

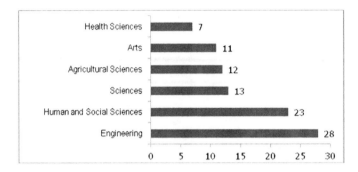

*Figure 4. Number of undergraduate programmes by field at the
National University of Colombia, 2009.*

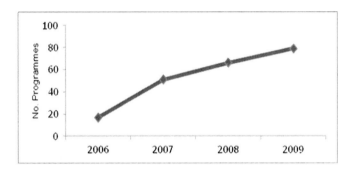

*Figure 5. Number of undergraduate programmes at the National University
of Colombia certified as high quality, 2006–2009.*

In 2010, the university will embark on a process of evaluation and certification of 12 programmes based on the implementation of an ambitious improvement plan. An essential component of this plan, which was developed over the course of the last four years, is a curricular reform that establishes an academic credit system and increases the interdisciplinary and flexibility of the programmes concerned.

The university is also conducting an internal review of its graduate programmes, in tandem with the government establishing a national certification system. The evaluation model is based on the research activities and the graduation rate for each programme. In this regard, although the trend shows that there has been an improvement in the graduation rates in recent years (Figure 6), the number of doctorates granted is still very low for the National University (181) and for Colombia as a whole (489). The oldest Ph.D. programmes in the university are in philosophy, physics and chemistry (begun in 1989) and the fields with the highest number of Ph.D. awards are science and agricultural science (Figure 7). Finally, in an effort to increase the number of Ph.D. students in all fields, five years ago the university initiated a programme to support these students through scholarships and provided financial support for research projects (Figure 8).

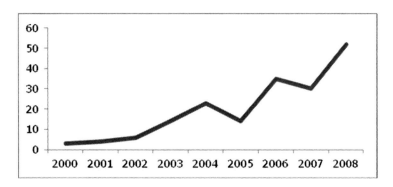

Figure 6. Doctoral degrees granted by the
National University of Colombia, 2000–2008.

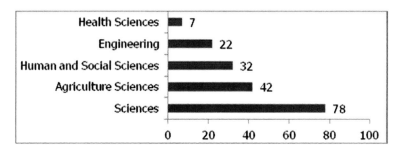

Figure 7. Doctoral degrees granted by the
National University of Colombia, by field.

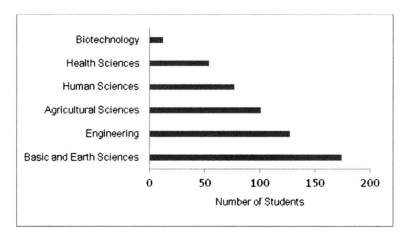

Figure 8. Doctoral students at the
National University of Colombia, by field, 2008.

Research Excellence

The National University of Colombia is the major producer of original research in the country. According to the National System of Science, Technology and Innovation there are nearly 3500 recognized research groups, classified in four categories by research products (Figure 9) and of these, 479 belong to the National University, 91 of which have been classified in the highest quality levels (A_1, A), more than any other institution of higher learning in the country (Figure 10).

The quality of the faculty is another indicator of the university's research vocation. With respect to this, out of approximately 5,000 researchers with a Ph.D. working in Colombia, 855 are employed as full-time professors at the National University, mainly in the areas of natural sciences, engineering, and social sciences (Figure 11). In addition, of the university's 2325 full-time faculty 1,400 hold a master's degree as their highest qualification.

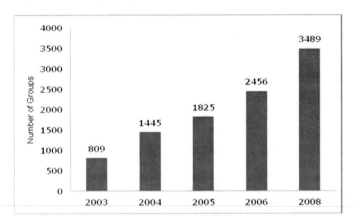

Figure 9. Number of research groups recognized by the national system of science, technology and innovation, 2003–2008.

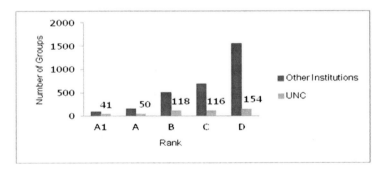

Figure 10. Number of research groups recognized by the national system of science, technology and innovation by category (A1 is the highest).

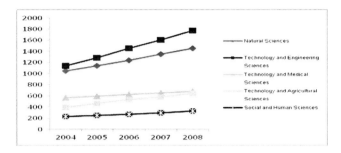

Figure 11. Number of researchers with a doctoral degree in Colombia by field of knowledge, between 2000 and 2008.

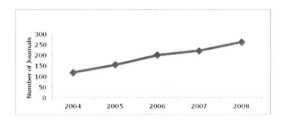

Figure 12. Number of Colombian scientific and technological journals in international indexes, between 2001 and 2008.

The National University has also played a key role within the recently created Research Centres of Excellence. In this regard, in 2005 the government opened a national competition to establish a network of research groups articulated around a common programme of work in scientific and technological fields considered strategic for the country. The basic criteria for establishing these centres are the national economic impact, the dynamism of the selected activities and scientific capacity, the ability to attract resources from international cooperation, the ability to train doctors and provide postdoctoral training and the relationship with international research peers. The university is actively involved in six of these ten centres, that is, CENM (Centre of Excellence in New Materials), CEIBA (Centre of Excellence in Modeling and Simulation of Phenomena and Complex Processes), GEBIX (Centre for Genomics and Bioinformatics of Extreme Environments), ARTICA (Research and Innovation Centre of Excellence "Regional Alliance of Applied Ticks"), CIIENN (Research and Innovation Centre of Excellence in Biotechnology and Biodiversity), and CIIEN (Centre for Research and Innovation in Energy).

Finally, the National University is one of the leading producers of publications in internationally indexed academic journals. Since 2003, the country started using a classification or indexing system for national journals that has stimulated the quality and the visibility of the products through international exposure (Figure 12). Although the majority of these journals are in the human and social sciences (Figure 13), the researchers with the greater number of cited documents comes from medicine, agriculture and the biological sciences (Figure 14).

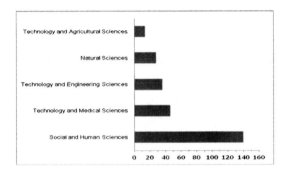

Figure 13. Number of Colombian Journals in international indexes (2008).

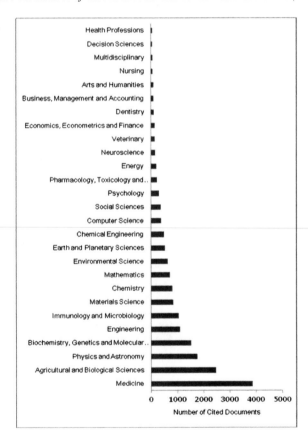

Figure 14. Number of cited documents of researchers in Colombia in international indexed journals, between 1996 and 2008.

Source: SCImago Research Group.

Financial Support

One of the greatest constraints to developing excellence in knowledge creation is limited budgets. In relation to this, the Colombian higher education system is not unique among developing (and developed) countries in that it faces financial difficulties and chief among the challenges confronting the National University is how to attain the goal of becoming a world-class university, in the context of dwindling state support and ever-increasing costs. The national budget allocated to education in Colombia corresponds to about 4.8 % of the GDP, with the net coverage rate for primary and secondary education being about 90% and that for higher education it is about 25%, although these trends are, as stated in the introduction, markedly different across regions. Additionally, the investment in research, as a percentage of the GDP, is 0.4% and the total budget of COLCIENCIAS now stands at about US$ 120 million, after substantial incremental increases in the last two years (Figure 15).

Although the National University of Colombia has the highest budget of any public university in the county, a mixed funding model has been applied to improve the development of the institution, which has enabled it to increase the total budget in the last three years (Figure 16A). In this regard, of the total current annual budget of the university (USD 500 million), 55% corresponds to government transfers, whilst 45% is mainly the result of external resources (Figure 16B), with tuition fees accounting for less than 4%.

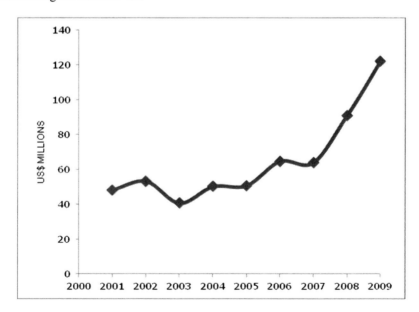

Figure 15. Budget of Colombian Administrative Department of Science, Technology and Innovation (COLCIENCIAS), between 2001 and 2009.

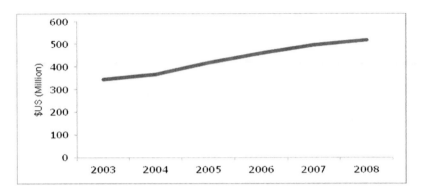

Figure 16A. Total budget of the National University of Colombia, between 2003 and 2008.

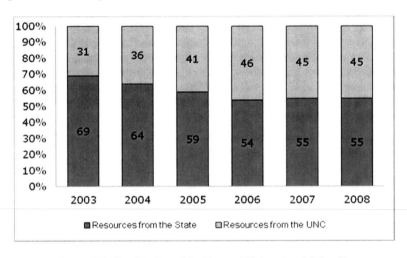

Figure 16B. Total budget of the National University of Colombia between 2003 and 2008: Percentage of resources provided by the state and resources produced by the university.

TOWARDS BECOMING A WORLD-CLASS UNIVERSITY: THE STRATEGY OF THE NATIONAL UNIVERSITY OF COLOMBIA

The institutional perspectives of building a university with international recognition, in the initial stage and in a complex environment, are based on international parameters. To this end, the National University is focusing on five broad strategies: a) internationalization, b) improving the qualifications of the faculty, c) funding for graduate study, d) increasing the number of international publications, and e) accreditation.

Internationalization has been built primarily through increasing the number of cooperation agreements with international universities, which has led to improvements in the academic exchange of professors and graduate students (Figure 17). Traditionally, the university has made such arrangements with counterparts in Spain (59), France (41), the USA (33), Mexico (31) and Germany (29) and in 2008, it was able to increase financial support for academic interchange (122 visiting professors and 196 NUC professors at international events). As an institution, it participates in eighteen international networks, one being the Network of Macro-Universities in Latin America and the Caribbean (*Red de Macro-Universidades de América Latina y el Caribe*), which supports training grants for 23 UNC graduate students and joint research projects between several universities within the network.

Additionally, the university has a financial assistance programme with the DAAD (German Academic Exchange Service) to send professors to study for Ph.D.s in Germany. Moreover, this year the National University won an international competition of the DAAD for a Research Centre of Excellence in Marine Science in conjunction with the University Justus-Liebig of Giessen in Germany, being awarded € 1,479,488 that will be used to support a new Ph.D. programme to begin next year, in collaboration with another five universities in Colombia.

The second strategy has been to improve the qualification of the faculty through increasing the number of professors with a Ph.D. (Figure 18). With respect to this, in 2005 the university changed the academic regulations for professors, opening a national contest to recruit new professors with a doctoral degree and they also took action that led to an increase the number of foreign professors from to 135. In addition, this year 250 professors are studying for a Ph.D., mainly in universities abroad and by 2017, the university is expected to have 1500 Ph.D. professors, which will represent 65% of its academic staff.

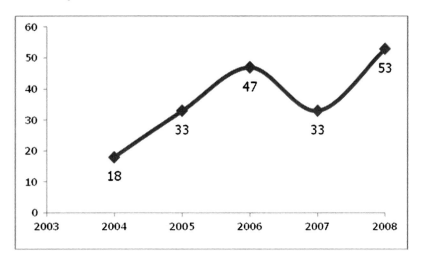

Figure 17. Number of new international agreements signed by the National University of Colombia, between 2004 and 2008.

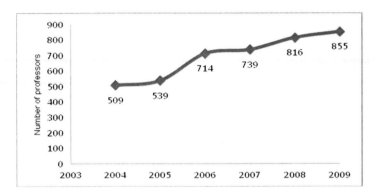

Figure 18. Number of professors with a doctoral degree at the National University of Colombia, between 2004 and 2009.

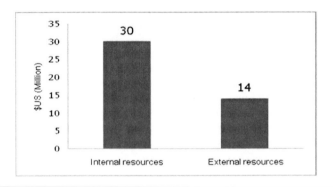

Figure 19. Financial support for research projects at the national university of Colombia (2007–2008).

A third strategy has been to increase the funding for research projects and scholarships for graduate students. In 2005, the university established a vice-rectory for research and a fund to ensure that 25% of the resources that are given by the government go to support research endeavours. In addition, this fund receives 6% of the external resources coming from extension activities. Moreover, the university encourages its researchers to send proposals to compete for national and international funding opportunities, so as further to increase the research activities (Figure 19).

In 2004, the National University established a scholarship programme for out-standing students on its Ph.D. and master's programmes, of which 70% are for the former and 30 for the latter (Figure 20). Furthermore, it is currently working to establish a scholarship system that will enable it to increase the number of scholarships with internal and external resources, with the goal of having, by 2010, at least 500 per year. In addition, COLCIENCIAS has a new financial programme to give 500 Ph.D. scholarships per year, for a period four years (2009–2012).

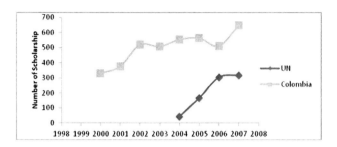

Figure 20. Number of scholarships provided to graduate students from a national agency (mainly COLCIENCIAS) and from the National University, between 2000 and 2007.

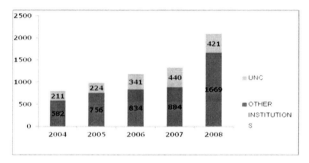

Figure 21. Number of papers in international indexed journals by researchers from Colombian institutions and from the National University.

The fourth strategy towards becoming a world-class university has been to increase the number of scientific papers in international and indexed journals. The salary of professors in a Colombian public university is established by law, and it increases in relation to academic production (books, papers, patents, etc.). Whilst this has had the positive effect of increasing the number of publications (Figure 21), the university recognizes that it still needs to improve the quality and the impact of its academic products. To this end, it is promoting a stronger evaluation process by academic peers for research proposals and unpublished books. Moreover, it is planning a special programme to improve the English language competencies of the faculty. Furthermore, in the last five years researchers from the university have received 90 international and 200 national awards and among their achievements are one publication in *Science* and four in *Nature* in the past six years.

The fifth strategy has been to achieve high quality international certification for all of the graduate programmes. With respect to this, architecture was the first programme certified by an international agency, The Royal Institute of British Architects (RIBA), a few years ago. This year, the university will submit its agronomy programme to the Iberoamerican Network for Quality Accreditation of Higher Education (RIACES), and it is planning a financial project to increase the number of international certifications for graduate and undergraduate programmes starting in 2010.

Finally, the university is carrying out strategic planning to develop the institution over the next ten years, in compliance with the government policy aimed at improving the quality of the universities throughout Colombia. In this regard, according to an institutional SWOT analysis, the National University still needs to improve its teaching and research labs, put in place a better administrative system, make longer strategic plans, develop the indicator system and connect more alumni to the university. Furthermore, although it is the largest university in Colombia, it needs to work hard to engage in more research, to attract a significant proportion of graduate students from different countries, and to generate more publications that have an impact upon the international academic community.

In conclusion, with suitable governance, better financial support and efficient management, the National University of Colombia expects to attract more resources and more academic talent to develop further and thus achieve international recognition in the near future.

NOTES

[1] Developed by QS Quacquarelli Symonds Ltd.
[2] http://www.carnegiefoundation.org/, retrieved 05/09/2009.

REFERENCES

Bucheli, V., Zarama, R., & Villaveces J. L. (2009). *La relación entre recursos y retornos en los procesos de investigación de UNIANDES.* Unpublished manuscript.

Castells, M. (2002). *La Era de la Información* (Vol. I). La Sociedad Red. México, D.F: Siglo XXI Editores.

COLCIENCIAS. (2009). *Plan estratégico 2007 – 2010.* Retrieved August 28, 2009 from http://quihicha. colciencias.gov.co/web/guest/sobrecolciencias

DNP. (2005). *Visión Colombia II Centenario: 2019.* Bogotá: Planeta.

OCyT. (2008). *Indicadores de ciencia y tecnología.* Observatorio colombiano de Ciencia y Tecnología. Retrieved August 28, 2009 from http//www.ocyt.org.co

Samil, J. (2009). *The challenge of establishing world-class universities.* Washington, DC: The World Bank.

Vélez, M. (2009). *Speech given during the Foro Internacional de Investigación.* Retrieved 12/03/2010 from http://www.mineducacion.gov.co

Vicerrectoría de Investigación UNAL. (2007). *Plan de desarrollo 2007–2009.* Universidad Nacional de Colombia.

Vicerrectoría de Investigaciones Uniandes. (2008). *La Investigación en Uniandes 2007: Elementos para una política.* Bogotá: Universidad de los Andes.

Villaveces, J. L., & Forero-Pineda, C. (2007). Cincuenta años de ciencia en Colombia 1955–2005. In C. Forero-Pineda (Ed.), *Fundación Alejandro Ángel Escobar- 50 Años.* Bogotá: Arfo Editores.

World Bank. (2009). *Data - WDI, GDF and ADI online databases.* Retrieved on March 12, 2000, from http://web.worldbank.org

Natalia Ruiz Rodgers
National University of Colombia, Colombia

MARIJK VAN DER WENDE

6. TOWARDS A EUROPEAN APPROACH
TO RANKING

INTRODUCTION

Recently the European Commission launched a project to develop a multi-dimensional university ranking. More precisely, the project concerns a feasibility study on the design and testing of a new multi-dimensional global university ranking. This paper will inquire the background of this decision and the particular approach chosen. It will also explore the expected consequences for institutional development and for patterns of cooperation and competition (and beyond) in the European Higher Education Area (EHEA) and the European Research Area (ERA).

RATIONALE AND KEY PRINCIPLES

A European ranking initiative was announced by the European Commission in December 2008, shortly after a European conference on the international comparison of educational systems organized by the French EU Presidency in late November 2008. The final conclusions of the French Presidency (2008) confirmed that the phenomenon of ranking has become increasingly an accepted method of evaluation and an expression of the performance of higher education institutions, but also that league tables produced for whole institutions might be of high interest for media but are of little use to most stakeholders in higher education (p. 1). And that next to the need to assess research performance, there is also a need to establish reliable European measures to assess teaching and learning, as well as other aspects of the mission of higher education institutions (p. 3). Consequently the French Presidency called on the European Commission to launch a call for tender to explore and test the feasibility of a multi-dimensional "mapping" of European higher education and research.

The call for tender was presented a few weeks later by Ján Figel, the then European Commissioner for Education, Training, Culture and Youth, by explaining that:

There are not many ranking systems of universities of the type we are interested in. At present most rankings are typically mono-dimensional. But while they may have some merit, we are more interested in developing a ranking system that goes beyond the research performance of universities, to include elements such as teaching quality and community outreach. What we

N.C. Liu et al., (eds.), Paths to a World-Class University: Lessons from Practices and Experiences, 125–135.

are looking at is multi-dimensional, because we want to take account of the rich diversity of our universities, so that potential students, researchers and staff can get better picture about the respective university. (EC Press Release, 11 December 2008)

The winning bid was announced in June 2009 and comes from the CHERPA-Network consortium, which is led by the Center for Higher Education Policy Studies (CHEPS) of the Twente University in the Netherlands and the Centrum für Hochschulentwicklung (CHE) in Germany. At that occasion the Commissioner stressed again that:

It's important that we look into the feasibility of making a multi-dimensional ranking of universities in Europe, and possibly the rest of the world too. Accessible, transparent and comparable information will make it easier for students and teaching staff, but also parents and other stakeholders, to make informed choices between different higher education institutions and their programmes. It will also help institutions to better position themselves and improve their quality and performance. (EC News, 2 June 2009)

After years of unresolved discussions on the emergence, popularity, and the effects of university rankings, the European Commission publicly embraced the notion that comparable information on higher education institutions and their teaching and research programmes should make it easier for students, researchers, academics, and parents to make informed choices on where and what to study and where to work. Better information would also help policy makers at institutional, national and European levels develop future strategies in higher education.

The idea that good information will support informed choices, would not easily be contested by stakeholders. However, many concerns arise around the basis on which comparisons will be made. Widespread critique concerns in particular the fact that existing rankings tend to focus on research in the "hard sciences" and ignore the performance of universities in areas like humanities and social sciences, teaching quality and community outreach.

Consequently, the project should take an incremental approach (feasibility study) and draw on the experience of existing university rankings and of EU-funded projects on transparency in higher education, e.g. the Classification Project[1] and trans-national projects on the use and effectiveness of student information systems and (performance) indicators.

The envisaged new European ranking system should therefore be:
– Multi-dimensional: covering the various missions of institutions, such as education, research, innovation, internationalization, community outreach and employability;
– Independent: it should not be run by public authorities or universities;
– Transparent: it should provide users with a clear understanding of all the factors used to measure performance and offer them the possibility to consult the ranking according to their needs; and
– Global: covering institutions inside and outside Europe (in particular those in the US, Asia and Australia).

Clearly, the key idea is that the new ranking should avoid a one-dimensional view on excellence in higher education. Rather, it should emphasize variation in areas in which universities can excel, thus stimulating diversity in institutional profiles and missions[2].

This view was also endorsed by European ministers responsible for higher education who gathered in April 2009 in Leuven for a meeting on the next phase of the Bologna Process (2010–2020). The conference communiqué acknowledges the need for "Multidimensional transparency tools", while emphasizing indeed the importance of diversity.

> We note that there are several current initiatives designed to develop mechanisms for providing more detailed information about higher education institutions across the EHEA to make their diversity more transparent. We believe that any such mechanisms, including those helping higher education systems and institutions to identify and compare their respective strengths, should be developed in close consultation with the key stakeholders. These transparency tools need to relate closely to the principles of the Bologna Process, in particular quality assurance and recognition, which will remain our priority, and should be based on comparable data and adequate indicators to describe the diverse profiles of higher education institutions and their programmes (Communiqué of the Conference of European Ministers Responsible for Higher Education, Leuven, 2009).

BACKGROUND: TO RANK OR TO BE RANKED

The question about the factors leading to this decision and the particular approach chosen can be discussed from a range of perspectives. First of all, there is of course a pragmatic argument for developing a European ranking. As university rankings have established themselves at global level (dominated by the ones published by the Shanghai Jiao Tong University (SJTU) and the Times Higher Education (THE), European universities are subject to ranking, whether they like it or not. And even though rankings are far from problem-free, they seem to be here to stay. In other words, they cannot be (and in fact are not) ignored; research has already shown a great impact on policy makers at all levels (Hazelkorn 2007; HEFCE, 2008; IHEP, 2007). "To rank or to be ranked" is thus the question (Marginson and Wende, 2007). Obviously, this argument has at the same time a political dimension: it cannot be left to others (only) to define the criteria against which performance is measured and the methods on which comparisons are based, and (thus) reputation is established. Especially not when the region's own institutions are rarely ranked at the top[3].

A CRITICAL STANCE TOWARDS EXISTING GLOBAL RANKINGS

Second, the wealth of critiques on existing rankings urges for a new and more sophisticated approach. These critiques focus in particular on the fact that rankings are biased towards research and more particularly towards the natural and medical sciences and use of the English language. Essentially all of the measures used to assess quality and construct rankings enhance the stature of the large comprehensive research universities in the major English-speaking centres of science and scholarship and especially the US and the UK. In this way global rankings suggest that the model global university is English-speaking and science-oriented and that there is in fact only one model that can have global standing: the large comprehensive research university. Common limitations on the methodological side are that most ranking systems evaluate universities as a whole, denying the fact that they are internally differentiated, that the weightings used to construct composite indices covering different aspects of quality or performance may be of arbitrary character, and that they provide little to no guidance on the quality of teaching (Marginson and Wende, 2007; 2009). See for a more detailed discussion of methodological and conceptual issues: Wende, 2008.

It should be noted that the higher regard for research institutions cannot be blamed on the rankings as such, but arises from the academy's own stance towards the importance of research. Although it can be argued that a league of world-class universities needs to exist as role models, the evidence that strong institutions inspire better performance is so far mainly found in the area of research rather than that of education (Sadlak and Liu, 2007). Critics even claim that world-class research universities need not be doing a good job at (undergraduate) education at all (Bok, 2005).

Especially the concerns related to biases *vis a vis* particular functions (research) and types of institutions (global research universities) ensure that rankings are seen as problematic in relation to information to stakeholders (especially students), institutional development, and diversification at system level. Holistic institutional rankings do not only ignore the fact that higher education institutions are internally differentiated, but also that they have different goals and missions. Rankings tend to norm one kind of higher education institution with one set of institutional qualities and purposes and in doing so strengthen its authority at the expense of all other kinds of institutions and all other qualities and purposes. This type of one-sided competition jeopardizes the status of activities that universities undertake in other areas, such as undergraduate teaching, innovation, their contribution to regional development, to lifelong learning, etc. and of institutions with different missions and profiles. Consequently, variation in institutional development and the need for diversification at the system level are under pressure, since academic and mission drift (isomorphism) can be expected to intensify. Vertical stratification rather than horizontal diversification may be the result. Hierarchy rather than diversity; specialization and diversification are not generated unless the incentive structure favours this.

THE NEED FOR DIVERSIFICATION

Diversity is of particular importance in the European context. It is generally understood that in order for higher education systems to respond effectively to external demands from students with an increasingly wide range of educational backgrounds, from the labour market, from the economy (e.g. contributions to regional development, innovation and economic growth), diversity is a favourable condition (Van Vught, 2009). However, insufficient diversity at the system level has been identified as a problem for European higher education. The European Commission considers uniformity in provision due to a tendency to egalitarianism and a lack of different-iation as one of the key problems of higher education. Insufficient differentiation is especially observed in the fact that most universities tend to offer the same mono-disciplinary programmes and traditional methods geared towards the same group of academically best-qualified learners, but that Europe has too few centres of world-class excellence (EC, 2005). Also, from within the sector itself it is acknowledged that it is evident that the European university system must allow for more diversification within the system in order to broaden access on a more equitable basis and to reach out to increased excellence at the same time (EUA, 2006).

It is important to distinguish the various dimensions and definitions of diversity, such as external diversity (differences between higher education institutions) and internal diversity (differences within higher education institutions) (Birnbaum, 1983). Huisman (1995) distinguishes between systemic diversity (differences in institutional type, size and control found within a higher education system) and programmatic diversity (differences in degree level, degree area, comprehensiveness, mission and emphasis of programmes and services provided by institutions). And Teichler (2007) between vertical diversity (differences between higher education institutions in terms of (academic) prestige and reputation) and horizontal diversity (differences in institutional missions and profiles) (see also Van Vught, 2009).

It is felt that the global rankings enhance in particular vertical diversity (or stratification), whereas more horizontal diversity would be more desired from the point of view of the functioning of the system as a whole. This follows more the Australian idea of a "world-class system" rather than focusing too much on the "world-class institution". Consequently, new policies and instruments (for instance multi-dimensional ranking) should strive to correct the perverse effects arising from league tables and to advance horizontal institutional diversity and informed student choice. And they should stimulate and enable higher education institutions to excel in different missions and to develop distinct profiles. Therefore more sophisticated indicators for measuring performance in areas other than basic research, such as undergraduate teaching, lifelong learning, knowledge transfer, innovation and regional development, need to be developed and integrated into such instru-ments. Besides a wider range of indicators, also the development of a good classifi-cation of institutions is needed. Because rankings only make sense within defined groups of comparable institutions, in other words, classification is a prerequisite for sensible rankings. Such a classification of higher education institutions in Europe has been developed over the last years (see Van Vught et al., 2005; CHEPS, 2008).

DIVERSITY: A FACT OF LIFE IN EUROPEAN HIGHER EDUCATION

Third, while more rather than less diversity may be desired with respect to the variety of institutional missions and profiles, European higher education most certainly possesses an abundant diversity in a range of other dimensions. Diversity is a fact of life in European higher education. Different national and regional languages, cultures, educational systems, academic traditions, admission systems, and even academic calendars, characterize the way in which higher education is performed in the different countries. In addition, legislation, governance models and funding systems (and consequent tuition fee policies) may differ depending on constitutional realities (at federal, national and regional levels) and on political and ideological positions. Countries' demographic development and economic strengths and growth patterns usually explain further particular directions in steering higher education system.

Whereas this diversity certainly holds challenges to be overcome (see next section), it is also, certainly at the political level, seen as a potential strength of European higher education:

> In a world where people and ideas are circulating at an ever increasing pace, it is a major challenge for Europe to make its high degree of linguistic, educational and cultural diversity, a unique source of open-mindedness and cross-fertilization (French Presidency, 2008, p. 1).

Obviously, the Bologna Process aimed at enhancing convergence, and has indeed been successful in bringing systems closer together in a range of areas, particularly those related to degree cycles, qualification levels, and frameworks for quality assurance (accreditation) (EURYDICE, 2009; Rauhvargers, et al., 2009). Despite such achievements, certain tensions between convergence and diversity have continued. In-depth studies and comparisons between countries showed that the actual implementation of the new structures can still vary significantly (see for instance: Witte, 2006; Huisman and Van Vught, 2009).

The relationship between the strive for more convergence on the one hand and for diversity on the other, is quite ambiguous. From their analysis of this relationship Huisman and Van Vught (2009) conclude that

> In sum, two supranational policy contexts (EU policies and the Bologna process) both support the idea of institutional diversity. But this support appears to be conditional. First, the policy documents are in favour of "organized diversity", thus setting some boundaries to institutional variety. Second, the policy documents are rather vague when it comes to specifying which elements of diversity are appreciated. It would not be too far-fetched to conclude that institutional diversity is appreciated as long as it does not go against the need for convergence of the fragmental European higher education system (p. 22).

The fact that diversity is and will to a certain extend be sustained (see also the next section for some of the reasons why) implies that any policy measure or concrete instrument should have a type of in-built flexibility, thus reflecting this diversity while at the same time enabling transfer and cooperation between the various systems. The European Credit Transfer System (ECTS) and the International Diploma Supplement (IDS) are good examples in case. Information and transparency are seen as the basis for these mechanisms. The new European ranking system should be based on the same principles (see first section of this article). In this sense, it should also follow the principles for good ranking as outlined in the Berlin Declaration (IREG, 2006):

Specify the linguistic, cultural, economical, an historical contexts of the educational systems being ranked. International rankings in particular should be aware of possible biases and be precise about their objectives. Not all national or systems share the same values and beliefs about what constitutes "quality" in systems should not be devised to force such comparisons.

EUROPEAN HIGHER EDUCATION: A YOUNG AND STILL FRAGMENTED REALITY

Fourth, European higher education encompasses between 3000 and 4000 institutions in between 27 (counting the countries that are members of the European Union) and 45 countries (the number of countries that have joined the Bologna Process, together constituting the European Higher Education Area, EHEA). The EHEA is a very young initiative and can hardly be called a reality in the operational sense yet. The Bologna process of convergence between the different national systems started only ten years ago, although it should be acknowledged that previous periods of increasing cooperation (the ERASMUS programme started in 1987) were certainly meaningful as well. Moreover, Bologna is a voluntary process without any legally or politically binding elements. The ownership of the process rests with the ministers of higher education and the European Commission's political authority and legal competences in the area of higher education are still quite limited. As the main steering mechanisms - legislation, planning, funding, quality assurance - are concentrated at national (or in some cases even sub-national) level, the coordinating powers are thus extremely decentralized and dispersed. At European level, in fact only cooperation mechanisms (the Erasmus Programme and the Bologna Process being prime examples) and some peer-pressure type of coordination (i.e. the Open Method of Coordination) exist, apart from some legal provisions arranging for recognition and free mobility. But despite the converging degree cycles and qualification frameworks, one cannot really speak of a "European higher education system" as such, i.e. with an integrated steering core, including funding mechanisms, legislation, etc. In this sense European higher education cannot be compared with systems like the USA (although specific per State), let alone China. Consequently, policy measures and concrete instruments can never be launched in a top-down fashion or through straightforward legislation. Instead, this happens through incremental, non-rigid, bottom-up policy-making processes backed up with substantive consultation rounds. A wide diversity of interests and contexts need to be taken into account. Consequently, multi-faceted, multi-dimensional solutions are in fact a *sine qua non*. In the same fashion, some dimensions of (criteria incorporated in) the new European ranking will be found more important in some countries than in others.

At the same time, the new European ranking system could only be developed and defined at European level. None of the participating countries alone is large and influential enough to compare itself to the other major higher education systems (USA, China). Only Europe as a whole has this capacity and considers itself now ready and able - despite the early phase of its integration process as described above - to engage more actively and play a more influential role at global level in the setting of systems and criteria against which performance is measured and the methods on which comparisons are based, and (thus) reputation is established.

IMPLICATIONS FOR INSTITUTIONAL DEVELOPMENT: PATTERNS OF COOPERATION AND COMPETITION

As has been stated above, European higher education is strongly focused on co-operation between countries and institutions. Inter-institutional cooperation has been the most important basis for achieving the mobility of students and scholars. Over the last two decades, various transfer mechanisms and later on common frameworks have been developed in order to overcome obstacles related to differences between national systems and institutional models (see above). More recently, European higher education institutions have become more aware of the challenges of global competition, not in the least place fuelled by the impact of global rankings. Both cooperation and competition are now important determinants for institutional strategy development, and at policy levels intra-European cooperation is considered to be a condition for strengthening positions in global competition (Huisman and Wende, 2004; 2005).

The question is what the consequences of the new European ranking system will be for institutional development and for patterns of cooperation and competition in and beyond the European Higher Education Area (EHEA) and the European Research Area (ERA). As both cooperation and competition constitute major strategic options for HEIs and governments in Europe, the question is in fact to what extend the new ranking would be useful for expressing distinct institutional profiles with a clear mission and could thus and on that basis help institutions to cooperate better with their partners, to identify new ones, and to compete better against their competitors, as far as these categories can always be clearly distinguished. At this point, these questions can only be explored in a very preliminary (even speculative) fashion.

It is expected that the new European ranking system will stimulate a range of different institutional missions and profiles, rather than imposing only one reference model. Hitherto, in many cases governmental policies were necessary to avoid mission (usually academic) drift within the system. Apart from comparative multi-country studies, no systematic studies have yet been made into this phenomenon at the European level as a whole. The formation of European leagues and consortia may be expected to play a role in this respect; they reflect dynamics in the system more than established associations of certain categories of institutions (e.g. the European Association of Universities (EUA) or the European Association of Institutions in Higher Education (EURASHE), who's mission it is to preserve those categories. The formation of new leagues and consortia so far demonstrates quite different characteristics. The League of European Research Universities (LERU) focuses on a top-level echelon of prestigious research universities, whereas the European Consortium of Innovative Universities (ECIU) emphasizes rather the innovative and entrepreneurial character of its member institutions. Other consortia may focus on locations (e.g. UNICA, including capital-city universities), disciplines (e.g. the IDEA League of Engineering Institutions, or ELIA, the League of Institutes of the Arts), or on cooperation and exchange as such (e.g. the Santander and Coimbra networks). There is no systematic knowledge on what role the position of institutions on rankings has played in the formation of these consortia and networks, as compared to other factors, such as for instance perceived reputation and personal relationships.

It is in any case remarkable that the sector which is most involved in rankings, i.e. the business schools (MBAs in particular), which is constantly being compared within Europe as well as against their global counterparts (e.g. in the Financial Times ranking of business schools) and which even has a European quality label (through the EQUIS accreditation) and usually use "Europe" into their institutions' names, hardly have a defined European league or even network (apart from a small - three institutions - and recent initiative connected to the EuroMBA). Apparently, competition prevails here and less focus is placed on cooperation as such.

It may be expected that the new European ranking with its multi-dimensional features would provide more detailed insight into potential cooperation partners as well as into the strategic assets of competitors. However, the added value of it as compared to the current situation will have to be examined. Many university consortia were established in the 1990s (some of which mentioned above) with the idea that the formation of strong international consortia (cooperation) of universities would make individual institutions less vulnerable and would enhance their strategic options (competition). Research into these consortia has shown that a successful composition of such relationships has to be based on both complementarity and compatibility between institutions, which is certainly not always the case (Beerkens, 2004). Consequently, a new ranking system providing more detailed information could in principle be useful for both cooperation and competition purposes. And learning from the research cited, it would be as important to know in which aspects a potential partner institution is different (complementarity) as well as similar (compatability).

At the same time, it should be realized that the policy context for higher education institutions in Europe is extremely complex. While institutions are encouraged and challenged to cooperate and compete internationally, their actual performance is still by and large defined by national systems. Governments all wish to make the higher education system more nationally effective, Europeanized and globally competitive at the same time. They usually present a, not necessarily coherent, mix of policy options, including models for cooperation and competition at national, European and international levels. The various policy choices at national level are at this point only to a limited extend guided by an overarching European vision, as embodied in the Bologna Process and Lisbon Strategy. It is certainly not realistic to speak about an effective division of labour or a considered balance between global competitiveness, European agendas, and national priorities and interests. Institutions have to pave their own avenues in this reality. Consequently they as well as their stakeholders will always benefit from more information and indeed only multi-dimensional transparency instruments could in principle prevail.

NOTES

[1] See: http://www.u-map.eu.
[2] More details on the project are presented in the paper: Multidimensional Excellence of Higher Education Institutions. Recognising and Acknowledging Word-Class Performances, by Federkeil et al.
[3] 32 European Universities appeared in the top 100 of the Shanghai Jiao Tong Ranking 2009, of which only two were in the top 20.

REFERENCES

Beerkens, H. J. J. G. (2004). *Global opportunities and institutional embeddedness: Higher education consortia in Europe and Southeast Asia*. University of Twente: CHEPS. Dissertation.

Birnbaum, R. (1983). *Maintaining diversity in higher education*. Washington, DC: Jossey-Bass Publishers.

Bok, D. (2005). *Our underachieving colleges: A candid look at how much students learn and why they should be learning more*. Princeton University Press.

CHEPS. (2008). *Mapping diversity. Developing a European classification of higher education institutions*. Enschede: University of Twente: CHEPS.

Communiqué of the Conference of European Ministers Responsible for Higher Education, Leuven and Louvain-la-Neuve. (2009, April 28–29). *The Bologna process 2020 - The European higher education area in the new decade*. Retrieved March 5, 2010, from http://www.ond.vlaanderen. be/hogeronderwijs/bologna/conference/documents/Leuven_Louvain-la-Neuve_Communiqu%C3% A9_April_2009.pdf

EUA. (2006). *The contribution of universities to Europe's competitiveness*. Speech of EUA President Prof. Georg Winckler to the Conference of the European Ministers of Education, Vienna, 16–17 March 2006. Retrieved August 30, 2009, from http://www.eua.be/eua/jsp/en/upload/EUA_Winckler_ Speech_160306.1142503291615.pdf

European Commission News. (2009, June 2). *Commission launches feasibility study to develop a multi-dimensional university ranking*. Retrieved August 30, 2009 from http://ec.europa.eu/education/news/ news1416_en.htm

European Commission Press Release. (2009, December 11). *Ranking Europe's universities*. Retrieved August 30, 2009, from http://europa.eu/rapid/pressReleasesAction.do?reference=IP/08/1942&format= HTML&aged=0&language=EN

European Commission. (2005). *Mobilising the brainpower of Europe: Enabling universities to make their full contribution to the Lisbon strategy* (p. 518). SEC.

EURYDICE. (2009). *Higher education in Europe 2009: Developments in the Bologna process*.

French Presidency of the European Union. (2008). *Presidency conclusions on typology and ranking of the higher education institutions: The European approach*.

Hazelkorn, E. (2007). The impact of league tables and ranking systems on higher education decision-making. *Higher Education Management and Policy, 19*(2), 87–110.

HEFCE. (2008). *Counting what is measured, or measuring what counts? League tables and their impact on higher education institutions in England*. Report to HEFCE by the Centre for Higher Education Research and Information (CHERI), Open University, and Hobsons Research. HEFCE Issues Paper, 2008/14.

Huisman, J., & Van Vught, F. A. (2009). Diversity in European higher education: Historical trends and current policies. In F. A. van Vught. *Mapping the higher education landscape. Towards a European classification of higher education*. Springer.

Huisman, J. (1995). *Differentiation, diversity and dependency in higher education*. Utrecht: Lemma.

Huisman, J., & Wende, M. C. van der (Eds.), (2004). *On cooperation and competition. National and European policies for internationalisation of higher education*. Lemmens, Bonn: ACA Papers on International Cooperation.

Huisman, J., & Wende, M. C. van der (Eds.), (2005). *On cooperation and competition II. Institutional responses to internationalisation, europeanisation and globalisation*. Lemmens, Bonn: ACA Papers on International Cooperation.

Institute for Higher Education Policy (IHEP). (2007). *College and university ranking systems. Global perspectives and American challenges*. Washington, DC: Institute for Higher Education Policy.

International Ranking Expert Group. (2006). *Berlin principles on ranking of higher education institutions*. Retrieved June 24, 2006, from http://www.che.de/downloads/Berlin_Principles_IREG_534.pdf

Marginson, S., & Wende, M. C. van der (2007). To rank or to be ranked: The impact of global rankings in higher education. *Journal on Studies in International Education, 11*(3–4), 306–330.

Marginson, S., & Wende, M. C. van der (2009). Europeanisation, international rankings, and faculty mobility: Three cases in higher education globalisation. In *Higher Education to 2030, Volume 2: Globalisation*. Paris: OECD.

Rauhvargers, A., Deane, C., & Pauwels, W. (2009). *Bologna process stocktaking report 2009*. Report from working groups appointed by the Bologna Follow-up Group to the Ministerial Conference in Leuven/Louvain-la-Neuve 28–29 April 2009.

Sadlak, J., & Liu, N. C. (Eds.), (2007). *The world-class university and ranking: Aiming beyond status*. Bucharest; Shanghai; Cluj-Napoca.

Teichler, U. (2007b). *Higher education systems, conceptual frameworks, comparative perspectives, empirical findings*. Rotterdam: Sense.

Wende, M. C. van der (2008). Rankings and classifications in higher education. A European perspective. In J. C. Smart (Ed.), *Higher education: Handbook of theory and research, 23*, 49–71.

Wende, M. C. van der, & Westerheijden, D. F. (2009). Rankings and classifications: the need for a multidimensional approach. In F. A. van Vught (Ed.), *Mapping the higher education landscape. Towards a European Classification of Higher Education*. Springer.

Van Vught, F. A. (Ed.), (2009). *Mapping the higher education landscape. Towards a European classification of higher education*. Springer.

Vught, F. A. van (2006). Higher education system dynamics and useful knowledge creation. J. Duderstadt, & L. Weber (Eds.), *Universities and business: Towards a better society*. New York: Economica.

Vught, F. A. van, Bartelse, J., Bohmert, D., Burquel, N., Divis, J., Huisman J., et al. (2005). *Institutional profiles. Towards a typology of higher education institutions in Europe*. Report to the European Commission. http://www.utwente.nl/cheps/documenten/engreport05institutionalprofiles.pdf.

Witte, J. (2006). *Change of degrees and degrees of change: Comparing adaptations of European higher education systems in the context of the Bologna process*. University of Twente, CHEPS: Dissertation.

Marijk van der Wende
Amsterdam University College
VU University Amsterdam, The Netherlands

SECTION II:
INSTITUTIONAL PRACTICES OF BUILDING WORLD CLASS-UNIVERSITIES

JOHN T. CASTEEN III

7. EFFECTIVE UNIVERSITY MANAGEMENT IN DIFFICULT TIMES

INTRODUCTION

Any thoughtful discussion of university management in difficult times must occur in at least two contexts. The first is framed by the past half-century, a period in which we have seen the progressive collapse of state financial support for public colleges and universities in the United States, with simultaneous demands for increased student enrolment. The second is the more recent timeframe of the past year, a period whose global financial crisis and concomitant recession have exacerbated the problems that took shape in the last half-century, as historic decreases in US states' tax revenues have led to additional reductions in state support for public colleges and universities. Private universities have shared in the more recent suffering, because of considerable endowment losses that have coincided with losses in the equities markets. While US universities struggle through the recession, institutions in other parts of the world are somewhat protected by more robust government support. The damage that has occurred in the past half-century and especially in the past year has left public colleges and universities and also many private institutions, particularly in the US, in a precarious condition. We are struggling to preserve our commitments to teaching, research, and service, because of financial constraints, increased operating costs, and other pressures. Effective management is the best, perhaps the only solution to the predicament in which we find ourselves in these difficult times.

For the purposes of this paper, discussion of world-class universities in the US will include the members of the Association of American Universities (AAU), top-tier Land-Grant institutions, and a few anomalies with distinguishing characteristics. In particular, this paper describes institutional practices at the University of Virginia and at other US colleges and universities as they seek to sustain their commitments to teaching, research, and service in spite of the financial constraints arising from the economic downturn of recent years.

THE ISSUE OF GOVERNANCE

Management in colleges and universities is a function of governance. Governance systems for higher education differ greatly from nation to nation, and even among US colleges and universities, governance takes many different forms. Private universities are typically governed by one of two types of boards: self-perpetuating boards made up of laypersons, with heavy alumni involvement; or self-perpetuating boards made up of university employees (senior administrators). These boards are flexible and characteristically small, sometimes as small as five persons. In private universities with self-perpetuating boards, there is usually an inner circle responsible for governance and a larger outer circle of people responsible for fund-raising. Governance systems for public universities in the US range from relatively simple structures that place a single campus under the governance of an appointed board of trustees, to the complex configurations seen in state university systems (California and Texas, for example), with their overlapping boards of regents and trustees.

Some US colleges and universities are Land-Grant institutions, and some are not. The distinction is important, because it is directly related to the institutions' founding missions and their modern-day purposes. Land-Grant colleges are the result of the federal government's Morrill Acts of 1862 and 1890, which gave eligible states 30,000 acres of federal land to sell off to finance the establishment of public colleges (The Library of Congress Web Guides, 2009). The 1862 Act dictated that Land-Grant colleges and universities should provide farmers and their children with an education in science, engineering, military tactics, to meet the need for trained military officers to fight in the American Civil War (1861–1865), mechanical arts, agriculture, and other practical matters to prepare them to participate in the work of the Industrial Revolution. The concept had already begun to take shape prior to passage of the Morrill Acts, for in 1855 Michigan State University became the first Land-Grant university (known then as the Agricultural College of the State of Michigan), and similar institutions were soon after established in Pennsylvania (the Farmers' High School of Pennsylvania, later Pennsylvania State University) and Iowa (Iowa State Agricultural College, later Iowa State University).

The first Land-Grant institution created under the Morrill Act was Kansas State University. Some states today have both kinds of public universities: Michigan with Michigan State University as the Land-Grant and the University of Michigan; and Virginia with Virginia Tech as the Land-Grant and the University of Virginia. Among the private universities, several have Land-Grant origins, and some still retain limited Land-Grant functions. In 1852, Yale instituted its engineering school and the degree of Bachelor of Philosophy (science) and instruction in these programmes was consolidated in 1854 into the Yale Scientific School that, on being renamed the Sheffield Scientific School, became Connecticut's Land-Grant college. MIT began as a Land-Grant college, and still retains a strong emphasis on scientific and technological research. Today, Land-Grant colleges and universities continue to fulfil their mandate by providing accessibility to higher education for great numbers of American young people, and several of these institutions are among the nation's most distinguished public research universities. Some still carry out assignments that stem naturally from their origins. For example, Land-Grant universities manage databases of genetic strains of plants and animals throughout the US — the University of Connecticut for chickens, the University of Illinois for corn, and University of California-Davis for viticulture and enology, amongst others.

In spite of the discrepancies among colleges and universities in the US — private and public, Land-Grant and non-Land-Grant — many institutions have faced common challenges in recent decades. Many public universities, in particular, have been beset by massive reductions in state support with simultaneous demand for increases in student enrolments. These pressures have forced these institutions to seek greater operating autonomy from their respective state governments; reform tuition policy whilst ensuring access and affordability; and to increase dependency on private support.

THE CONTEST FOR CONTROL

In the past half-century, the management of public colleges and universities in the US has often been a story of give and take between institutions that desire greater freedom from state control and state legislatures that seek greater control over those institutions. Whilst this statement is truer of non-Land-Grant public universities than of the Land-Grant colleges and universities, it does not greatly misrepresent the normal course of relations between the states, which own and support all US public institutions other than the service academies, and the now-more, now-less independent public universities. Others, most notably California, support multiple complex systems of universities, some subject to direct legislative directives and others protected by provisions in state constitutions or in their charters. The differences between these two kinds of public universities are ultimately less significant to this topic than the various ways in which the states have defined the legislature's or the governor's role in directing university affairs. In some instances, most notably Texas, legislative involvement in the affairs of two large public university systems is often said, however fairly, to be considerable. In other instances, with perhaps Michigan the best case, trustees elected by all the registered voters in the state govern the universities, thus at least in theory protecting against inappropriate intrusion on the part of the state government.

Two decades of more or less steadily declining state tax support, often coming with demands for the public universities to expand their enrolments and more recently the extreme US version of the global economic crisis, have exacerbated the levels of financial and political demands made on the public universities. That said, it is important to acknowledge that more than a few states, Iowa for example, but also others in the American Middle West, have scrupulously protected tax funds for the public universities, until very recently. In the same vein, not all reductions in tax funds have resulted from considerations of education. For example, so-called tax-payer revolts in California and Virginia, and legislative responses to them, have had more to do over time with reductions in tax support for the universities than general economic conditions, although more recently these states' cuts have been driven primarily by the national recession.

In the states whose situations I know best, Connecticut and Virginia, political responses to recessions have differed radically, in spite of the fact that the economic conditions in the two states have been remarkably similar. In its recession of 1989–1992, Connecticut's governor repeatedly promised to restore funds cut from the university as rapidly as possible, and indeed by 1996 he had done so. By contrast, responding to Virginia's somewhat less severe recession of 1990–1992, three consecutive governors put politically popular reductions in tax rates ahead of supporting the public universities, and in fact made three state functions (education, healthcare facilities and support for indigent persons, and highway construction maintenance) absorb most of the reductions initially driven by the recession, then subsequently by tax cuts. This history has had ironic consequences: what were once the most reliable supporters of public higher education have become the least reliable, with the consequence that the best public universities now compete with the private national universities (Stanford, Harvard, etc.) for philanthropic gifts, with remarkable success; and what were once the least costly American universities for students to attend have had to charge higher tuitions and fees than they once did, with the consequence that many students who could once earn the cost of attendance by working whilst attending, now must borrow to pay their fees, thus limiting their options for postgraduate studies.

Disparate though conditions are among the states and among their public universities, these events of the last two decades have forced some of the states to reconsider and restructure their relations with their public universities and at the same time compelled many of the universities to find new ways to deal with state governments. These changes actually began more than half a century ago and in one specific case, the political leaders in Vermont, then as now a sparsely populated, largely rural state, convinced themselves and the voters that it could profit by the uncommon excellence of its state university, which at the time competed successfully with many of its regional private competitors (Dartmouth, Middlebury, Colgate, Hamilton—then as now, prominent liberal arts colleges). By the early 1990s, Vermont was a noteworthy, but peripheral exception, to the general rule among the states of supporting education ahead of all other obligations that particularly existed in the heady 1980s when virtually all of the states were wealthy. Consequently, Vermont moved to make its public university more expensive for non-Vermont students than most if not all of its private competitors. Over time, in-state students also paid uncommonly high fees, because having cut tax appropriations to the university and committed the money elsewhere the state could not repair the damage done to the university, other than by raising taxes, a strategy not acceptable to the voters. The result is that a university that, while small, supports major research programmes, and still has some of uncommonly high quality, has become increasingly a local option for Vermont students, rather than a regional or national option for all students.

External intrusions into university affairs, often politically motivated, have exacerbated tensions during the last half-century. In 1949, Clark Kerr, a University of California professor who later served as UC president from 1958 to 1967, fought on behalf of the faculty against a loyalty oath required by the Board of Regents. In this regard, the Board had imposed a requirement that all university employees sign an oath affirming loyalty to the US Constitution and denial of membership or belief in organizations (including Communist organizations) advocating overthrow of the US government. However, many employees resisted the oath for violating principles of shared governance, academic freedom, and tenure. Clark Kerr experienced another form of intrusion nearly two decades later, when Ronald Reagan, three weeks after he was elected governor in 1967, directed the board of regents to fire him from the UC presidency. Moreover, Reagan did not believe that a great university needed to be supported by public funding, so he cut the UC budget by 10% and proposed that it should sell the collections of rare books in Berkeley's Bancroft Library. Furthermore, he insisted on the setting of a political standard for appointing faculty members in the departments of sociology and philosophy, which he considered as being hotbeds of liberalism.

SECURING GREATER AUTONOMY

Public colleges and universities have been forced by economic realities, political intrusions, and other pressures to re-evaluate their relationships with their state governing bodies. Some schools have responded with new management models that fundamentally redefine these relationships. One watershed case occurred in Virginia, where administrators and trustees from colleges and universities in the state worked to secure passage of the Restructured Higher Education Financial and Administrative Operations Act of 2005 (The State Council of Higher Education for Virginia, 2005). The legislation has given Virginia's higher education institutions the capacity to plan effectively for their future and manage their operations more efficiently. It marks a major adjustment of the colleges and universities' relationships to state regulatory agencies, especially with regard to spending, tuition, construction, and personnel and asset management. With new freedoms come new responsibilities. Colleges and universities that benefit from restructuring must meet a set of state goals that include creating six year financial plans; setting and meeting financial and administrative performance standards; working with specified K-12 schools or districts to improve student achievement; stimulating economic development in distressed areas of the state; meeting enrolment demands; and making attending college affordable for all Virginia students while also enrolling more transfer students from Virginia's community colleges. The State Council of Higher Education for Virginia (SCHEV) assesses performance in meeting these goals annually and if it deems an institution successful at meeting the state goals, the institution becomes eligible for a series of financial incentives.

One distinct advantage of the Restructuring Act is that it avoids the one-size-fits-all approach that has characterized other arrangements between public universities and their states. Restructuring has offered Virginia's public colleges and universities the opportunity to apply for three distinct levels of autonomy. That is, all of these colleges and universities, after their respective boards have committed to meet the aforementioned statewide goals included in restructuring, achieve Level I status. After securing this status, the institutions that continue to advance their financial and administrative strength may then enter into memoranda of understanding to achieve Level II status. Institutions that achieve what is termed Level II autonomy may then seek additional, more comprehensive autonomy, through a management agreement, which outlines board approved policies in the following areas: 1) capital outlay; 2) leases; 3) information technology; 4) procurement; 5) human resources; and 6) finance and accounting. In 2006, the general assembly approved the management agreement negotiated by the University of Virginia with the governor, which re-affirmed its authority to set its own tuition and gave authorization for it to independently manage operations in these six core areas. William and Mary and Virginia Tech also achieved Level III autonomy, whereas other institutions in Virginia fall somewhere in between Level III autonomy and Level I autonomy.

REFORMING TUITION POLICY

In its English origins the word tuition means the teaching or instruction of students. (When conceiving the University of Virginia, Thomas Jefferson described students "... rising under a luminous tuition, to destinies of high promise.") (The University of Virginia Library, n.d.). However, in modern times in the US, tuition refers to the fees that colleges and universities charge students for their instruction. In Asia, universities use the word fees to describe the same charges, whilst in the UK, "top-up fees" are a new way of charging students who study at universities in England and Wales. Prior to 2006, most British students paid some portion of their tuition — a capped fee based on their families' incomes. Top-up fees allow universities to charge students additional fees to finance more closely the actual costs of providing courses. Top-up fees are controversial, with critics arguing that the fees will discourage students from going to college, because of the large debts they will incur.

Tuition policy is a serious matter for both public and private colleges and universities in the US. Although these institutions are different in many ways, the current economic crisis has put both the public and private in the same leaking boat. That is, the demand for higher education has never been greater, but securing the funding to pay for it has seldom, if ever, been more difficult. The operating budgets of private universities depend heavily on income from their endowments, where for some these supply as much as 30% to 40% of their annual operating budgets. By contrast, state universities depend on allocations of tax monies set by their states' legislatures and the economic downturn has dramatically reduced tax revenues to the states. With endowment losses and the concomitant drop in payout, and with availability of state funding so thoroughly diminished, all institutions are hard pressed to fund the costs to meet their business practice.

The simple solution would be to increase tuition to meet institutions' budget needs, but students, tax paying parents, legislators, and the media are highly aware and often critical of the steady increase in tuition over the past two decades, an increase that has exceeded the annual rise in the cost of living. In this regard, faculty and students in the University of California system recently protested against the state legislature's approval of a 20% cut in funding and the university administration's response, which proposed a 32% increase in tuition and mandatory furloughs for faculty members.

When reforming the policy for setting tuition, institutions need to think beyond the usual considerations: the market, what peer institutions charge, what potential students expect to pay based on previous years' charges, and the availability of financial aid to offset tuition for needy students, without overburdening them with loans. Various ideas have emerged regarding how to reform tuition policies, including charging differential tuition rates programme by programme to reflect the variations in the actual costs of a student's education (both undergraduate and graduate), holding tuition at the same cost as the student's year of entry, and removing the caps on out-of-state enrolment at public institutions, thereby increasing the number of such students who pay higher tuition. However, in many cases the current model for setting tuition is a one-size-fits-all approach: charge rates that are consistent with benchmark institutions and meeting enrolment targets is vital to this approach. Steady enrolment or enrolment growth is the common assumption, but very seldom does academic and long-term resource planning precede and then determine realistic enrolment targets to fit the plan, i.e., scale the size of the programme to available resources. An alternate approach would be to set enrolment and tuition limits first and then plan to raise the funds from other sources necessary to meet the budget.

Yet another model starts with the institution's mission and subsequently sets tuition with the goal of linking the mission to the budget. This might mean eliminating programmes that are not essential to the mission, or it might mean lowering enrolment levels. In this regard, if the quality of instruction is primary to the institutional mission, then this becomes the key factor in building the budget and planning enrolment and such an approach might require hiring more faculty members to lower the faculty-to-student ratio. One of the more radical proposals has been to differentiate among the community colleges, four-year universities (dedicated primarily to teaching), and research universities and even to reduce the number of research universities altogether. In this regard, tuition is lowest at the two-year colleges, and highest at the research universities, where support for research activities is very costly. However, regardless of what measures we may take to rethink the cost of tuition, universities need to work to establish education as a priority in the minds of the public and of their legislatures, by promoting the truism that education is an investment in future generations. In particular, this should involve disseminating the fact that higher education prepares citizens to be contributing members, both intellectually and financially, to the nation and to the localities where they work. Moreover, as part of any public-relations campaign, higher education institutions should define clear terms of public accountability and make readily available the proof that they are living up to the standards they have set.

With regard to tuition policy, there is often a discrepancy between concept and practice, for whilst the trustees of US public colleges and universities technically have authority to set tuition, legislators and governors have frequently interfered with this authority. Such erratic fiscal policy coincided with a period when the universities were growing more complex and the various demands for state resources were increasing. However, since the necessary recent restructuring Virginia's institutions have gained more control over tuition which has helped them to deal with the volatility of appropriations, ensure greater stability and predictability, and to enable long-term planning. With this greater control, Virginia's colleges and universities have gained more freedom to price tuition according to market demands and at a benchmark closer to its peer universities. Several political realities in Virginia have tempered our ability to set tuition at true market rates, however. For example, members of the General Assembly's House of Delegates must run for election every two years, so they are continually held accountable by their home-town constituents for unpopular decision, including those related to tuition increases at Virginia's public colleges and universities. These elected officials tend to make tuition control a campaign theme every two years. In this regard, from time to time, members of the general assembly have tried to insert language in appropriation bills that would limit tuition increases and supersede the tuition policies outlined in Virginia law. Another political reality is that in Virginia the governor is elected to a single four-year term without the opportunity to run for a second term and he/she also has the authority to appoint the members of the governing boards of the state's universities. These appointments often reflect political affiliations, which can often change, rather than commitment to the institution and this has limited our ability to create long-term plans or to build durable collaborative partnerships with the incumbent governor. Despite these constraints, the additional freedoms that have resulted from restructuring have enabled us to enhance the quality of education we offer, strengthen economic development, and improve access to higher education.

INCREASING ACCESS AND DIVERSITY

Nowadays, the leaders of US colleges and universities often speak of commitments to diversity, but the concept of diversifying the student body by attracting students from every racial, ethnic, geographic, and socio-economic background, is relatively new. Until about a half-century ago, few institutions bothered to seek out talented students from the full spectrum of the population. It was easier to let the students who excelled and who were from families with adequate financial means find their way to the universities of their choice. Seeking out the talented students in under-served and under-represented populations has required more work. Now, providing access to higher education for students from all populations has become a sort of national mission in the US, with colleges and universities making commitments to robust financial aid programmes to offset tuition increases and to ensure that college education remains affordable during difficult economic times.

At the University of Virginia, we created the AccessUVa financial aid programme in 2004, before passage of the restructuring legislation, to provide support for students from low- and middle-income families (The University of Virginia, 2004). Through this programme the university promises to meet 100% of demonstrated need for all admitted undergraduate students. Moreover, it replaces needs based loans with grants for students from families with incomes up to 200% of the poverty level, and limits the amount such loans that any student is required to take on. This latter piece of the programme is targeted at middle-income students whose families earn between $75,000 and $149,999, many of whom are supporting more than one college student at a time. The university assesses the programme's success in increasing enrolment and enhancing the experience of AccessUVa students, by tracking the number of applications received from low- and middle-income students, the percentage of low-income students in the student body, and the financial aid recipient participation in such activities as internships and study abroad. AccessUVa students graduate with manageable amounts of debt so they can go on to medical school, law school, or do public-service work if they so choose, rather than rushing into jobs to begin paying off loans.

UNC-Chapel Hill created the Carolina Covenant in 2003 to meet 100% of demonstrated need for those students whose families' incomes are 200% or less of federal poverty guidelines (The University of North Carolina, 2003). Both AccessUVa and the Carolina Covenant guarantee students whose families have such income levels that they can attend the institutions without incurring debt. Moreover, both include comprehensive efforts by the universities to recruit more students from low-income families. The University of Michigan launched M-PACT in 2005, so that now eligible students' financial aid packages include higher percentages of grant support and decreased percentages of loans (The University of Michigan, 2005). For this, Michigan provided an initial $9 million in seed money to jump-start the prog-ramme so that 2,900 in-state undergraduates at the Ann Arbor campus could benefit and the state authorities hope to raise a permanent endowment of at least $60 million for the programme.

These initiatives have spurred other programmes, like the University of Florida's Florida Opportunity Scholars programme (FOS) (The University of Florida, n.d.), which provides full grant/scholarship financial aid packages to freshmen Florida resident students, from families which make less than $40,000 per year. The prog-ramme was made available to first generation in college Florida resident, first-time in college (FTIC) freshmen students, enrolling beginning in summer 2006 or later Recipients receive a full grant and scholarship package each year for enrolment on a baccalaureate degree programme and two million dollars in grant assistance was committed for the 2006–07 inaugural years. The University of Maryland created a financial assistance programme called Maryland Pathways in 2005 (The University of Maryland, 2005), which is a three-tiered programme that reduces the debt component and increases the grant component of the student's financial aid package, including the elements: Work Grant, Pell Grant Supplement and Senior Debt Cap. When fully implemented, Maryland estimates that it will cost $1.6 million annually. The University of Texas has a similar programme called the Longhorn Opportunity Scholarship, which provides scholarships to students from high schools in census tracts with average family incomes of less than $35,000 and whose students have been historically underrepresented at the university (2009). The programme also combines coordinated focused mentorship opportunities, designed to provide sub-stantial assistance to students in their first year of enrolment.

Further, some states have become involved in increasing access through needs based financial aid programs for in-state high school graduates attending in-state institutions and New York State's Tuition Assistance Programmes and California's Cal Grant programmes are two notable examples. Another needs based programme worth mentioning is the D.C. Tuition Assistance Grant Programme that allows residents of the District of Columbia to attend public institutions in other states, but they pay only the tuition charged to in-state students in those other states.

Some of the most selective private institutions in higher education with vast resources have taken aggressive steps to increase access. In this regard, Princeton University was the first to do so in 1998 when it eliminated all loans from financial aid packages, followed closely by Harvard who matched this and also went further when it announced in the spring of 2004 that parents of students of families earning less than $40,000 a year would not be required to pay anything towards their students' education. However, students coming under this scheme are still required to contribute through academic and summer job earnings.

The US federal government runs Federal Student Aid, an office of the U.S. Department of Education that provides federal aid for students, including Pell grants, Stafford loans, PLUS loans, and work-study programmes, which can supplement aid provided by state or local government and scholarships and other support provided by colleges and universities. Students fill out the Free Application for Federal Student Aid (known as the FAFSA) form to determine their eligibility for federal student financial aid, which consists of numerous questions regarding the student's finances, as well as those of his or her family.

Whilst federal support and aid programmes like the Carolina Covenant, AccessUVa, and others mentioned above would be important in any economy, the need for this kind of aid has become dramatically apparent during the past year, as the global economic meltdown has taken its toll on family finances in US households. The combination of the recession's effects and the failure of US federal and state financial aid programmes has made this a particularly difficult time for families to plan and pay for college education for their children. Moreover, the demand for financial aid will continue to rise as unemployment rises into 2010 and as more parents face salary cuts and freezes and other forms of diminished income. Comprehensive financial aid programmes, like AccessUVa, are expensive to finance. With respect to this particular form, in 2009–10 the university's unrestricted contribution to this programme will be $29.7 million and this cost will continue to rise as the recession continues. For instance, in the years since AccessUVa was introduced, the number of students demonstrating some level of financial need has increased by 15.3%, to almost 27% of the student body in the most recent academic year. The University funds this programme with revenue from various endowments designated for needs based financial aid, from internal reallocations, from profits or by using excess reserves in a variety of units that receive external revenue, from tuition, and from private gifts. We have launched a fundraising programme this fall to build an endowment for AccessUVa, so that we can meet this predictably increasing need in the years ahead. Many other colleges and universities have launched similar campaigns specifically to attract support for financial aid.

INCREASING PHILANTHROPIC SUPPORT

Philanthropy, in general, can be categorized as giving by persons, foundations, and other donor groups to non-profit entities, with those giving benefiting from associated tax advantages. Fundraising is the active solicitation of those gifts, which often subsequently are converted into endowments that allow their value to grow in the markets. In this regard, in colleges and universities virtually all endowed funds are invested, and a portion of the earnings is released each year to support their needs as well as to meet the purposes specified by donors. Based on historical averages, a $1 million endowment gift made today can be expected to pay out about $500,000 over the next 10 years, and during the same period its principal will have grown to more than $1.8 million, because of reinvested earnings. Funds generated through endowments provide important sources of funds that universities would not be able to generate through less aggressive investments. For example, one dollar invested in Harvard's long-term endowment pool on July 1st 1989, would have grown to over nine dollars by June 30th 2009 and this includes accounting for losses reported this past year. The same dollar invested in a passively managed portfolio of stocks and bonds would only have grown to $3.60. Moreover, an endowment of $1 billion invested in Harvard's endowment pool from July 1989 through June 2009 would be valued at $2 billion today, even after providing a 5% per year spending distribution increased by a 3% per annum inflation rate. That same $1 billion of endowments invested in a passively managed portfolio of shares and bonds would have declined to $750 million after accounting for spending and inflation. Further, today, a 5% spending distribution from the $2 billion of endowments would be $100 million a year versus $38 million per year from the $750 million of endowments.

Because of historic reductions in state support for public universities in recent decades and simultaneous increases in operational costs, US public universities now pursue philanthropic gifts at least as aggressively as private universities do and often with equal success. As of August of this year, 33 American universities were pursuing capital campaigns with goals of at least $1 billion and amongst those universities, roughly half are public. In September 2006, we launched the public phase of a $3-billion campaign at the University of Virginia, which at the time of its announcement was the largest goal ever announced by any American university, public or private. Since that time, five private universities have launched campaigns with goals of $3 billion or more: Columbia ($4 billion); Cornell ($4 billion); Stanford ($4.3 billion); the University of Pennsylvania ($3.5 billion); and Yale ($3.5 billion). During the same period, four public universities have announced $3-billion goals, these being the State University of New York; City University of New York; University of California-Berkeley; and the University of Texas. All of these campaigns are ambitious, especially for public universities, and particularly with the current state of the economy.

The extreme US version of the global economic crisis has taken a toll on fund-raising in the past year. An April 2009 *Chronicle of Higher Education* analysis found that gifts to a dozen colleges that have been pursuing campaigns of at least $1 billion since 2007, had fallen by 32% from the previous 12 month period. A spring survey by the Council for the Advancement and Support of Education of fund raisers across higher education in the US and Canada, found that in the year ending June 30, they expected their gifts to be down by 4%. Nevertheless, colleges and universities have seen an average of 7% annual growth in giving over the last 20 years and whilst the recession has led to the postponement and cancellations of capital campaigns in some American colleges and universities, others are still thriving in spite of the economy. With respect to this, the crisis has affected philanthropic giving at the University of Virginia, to some extent, but perhaps less than one might expect considering the scale of the financial meltdown and its effects on personal wealth in the US. At the end of the 2008 calendar year, we were about three-quarters of a percentage point behind our campaign target (61.8% of the goal achieved with 62.5% of the time having elapsed). On 1 April 2009, we were exactly 2% behind (63.6% achieved in 65.6% time having elapsed), thus the gap has widened, but only marginally so. As of 31 July 2009, the university had raised $1.985 toward its goal, or 66.2% of the total, with 69.8% of the time having elapsed and in early September, we reached the $2 billion mark, about eight weeks behind schedule. Other universities are making similar progress, with Columbia having raised $3.2 billion and Cornell $2.5 billion towards their $4 billion goals. Moreover, Stanford has raised $3.8 billion toward its $4.3 billion goal and UC-Berkeley and City University of New York have raised roughly half of the funds toward their $3 billion goals.

Although fundraising at American colleges and universities has become more sophisticated and complex in recent decades, the concept of soliciting friends and benefactors for support is nothing new. In fact, fundraising for higher education in the US dates back at least to the time of Thomas Jefferson, who asked his friends and colleagues for financial support to create the University of Virginia in the early 1800s and in the 200 years since then capital campaigns have been important pieces of our evolving financial self-sufficiency model at the university. In the early 1990s, sudden, singularly vicious, state funding cuts were even more common than they are now. In this regard, the state governor, in 1990–91, called for a radical scaling-back of research and scholarly activities in Virginia's universities and for a general renunciation of the state's commitment to excellence in higher education. The university responded to the losses in state support with a fundraising campaign that totalled $1.43 billion in 1995–2000. This successful campaign and subsequent prudent investments allowed the university to mitigate damage from the collapse in state support. The Board of Visitors used these new resources to support essential new construction, to pay for maintenance of buildings no longer supported by adequate public funds, and most critical of all, to make institutional funds the core support for both faculty and students, thereby working to reverse the process of deterioration that had occurred whilst the state did not have the means to pay salaries consistent with the market or to meet its share of the cost of financial aid to students. In sum, under the current economic circumstances the importance of philanthropic support has become increasingly important at our university and at every college and university in the US.

MANAGING THE ONGOING ECONOMIC CRISIS

In the past two years, some of the best institutions in the US, including private institutions, have been forced to take dramatic steps to reduce expenditures and otherwise mitigate damage from the historic meltdown in the global economy and the particularly severe US recession. Many selective private universities rely heavily on their endowments to sustain their operating budgets, and as a result those institutions have been severely affected by the economic downturn. Harvard has taken several steps to combat the economic crisis and a loss of 27.3% in its endowments, the biggest percentage decline in over 40 years. In fact, it had relied on its endowments for roughly a third of its annual operating budget. To absorb these losses, it has frozen staff hiring, laid off 275 employees, offered 1,600 staff members a voluntary early retirement plan, scaled back its expansion plan for a separate campus in Allston, reviewed compensation costs, and cut spending.

As of early December 2008, the market value of Duke University's endowments was approximately 19% lower than on July 1st 2008. Its overall approach to weathering the financial downturn has included identifying cost reductions, savings and efficiencies in all school and administrative budgets; recognizing that the current downturn may be of sustained duration and that they must look for both one-time and more durable interventions; reviewing and potentially delaying proposed capital projects, until funding sources are clearly defined; and seeking resources for their strategic priorities, whilst continuing to protect core commitments, including faculty excellence and student financial aid. Moreover, to offset a $125 million budget shortfall the university has worked to cut $100 million from its $2 billion operating budget and used $500 million in new bond debt, normally reserved for capital needs, to cover operations. Similarly, the Johns Hopkins University's endowments lost 20% of their value in the first six months of the fiscal year beginning last July, and revenue for the 2010 and 2011 fiscal years will be $100 million short of previous estimates. In response to the economic crisis, it has frozen all hiring and most salary increases and reduced top administrators' pay by 5%.

The value of Stanford's endowments is expected to plummet by 30% in 2009, the largest single-year decline in the university's history. In monetary terms, valued at $17.2 billion in 2008, this is expected to fall to $12 billion this year, which is the same level as 2005. Moreover, having spent $933 million from its endowments in 2009, it will reduce that spending to $829 million in 2010 and make further reductions in 2011. In response to a directive to adjust to a new baseline budget, Stanford schools and units have laid off 412 staff members and eliminated their positions over the last eight months, a decision spurred by the steep decline in the value of the university's endowments. Approximately 60 more people will lose their jobs by the end of the year; many of them have already been notified that their positions will be eliminated as part of the university's response to budget reductions. Between December 18th 2008, and August 14th 2009, Stanford also laid off 72 staff members whose positions were funded by sponsored research. In addition to laying off staff, the university froze 50 open faculty positions, implemented a campus-wide salary freeze, eliminated unfilled staff positions and suspended construction projects valued at $1.1 billion. In addition, the university's schools and units cut spending on travel, food, marketing activities, computers and other equipment, professional services, conference fees and printing.

The University of Virginia relies less on its endowments to sustain its operating budget and has fared differently. In addition, officials at the university took aggressive measures to identify problems early, plan for them, and anticipate necessary corrective actions. These actions have included the following.

– Spending: Imposing strict limits on spending regardless of funding sources;
– Hiring: Holding open any existing and future vacant positions. Recruitment and hiring that are essential to preserve safety and revenue capacity must be approved

in advance by the provost or chief operating officer. Approval standards are rigorous;

- Managing Employee Levels: Establishing a transfer programme that will take stock of current talent available within the university and match it for use in departments that may need certain skills or resources. This programme will help preserve the university's workforce by retaining employees (transferring them) within the university instead of hiring from outside;
- Salaries: Planning no across the board general fund faculty and staff salary increases in two years (2008–2010). Certain special salary adjustments for reasons other than routine cost of living are granted on a case-by-case basis. Examples include: salary changes associated with staff and faculty promotions, counter offers, and unique competitive situations;
- New Hires: Setting salaries at levels equivalent to or below the salary of the person being replaced when the university must hire replacement personnel;
- Construction: Deferring new construction or renovation projects that depend on departmental operating funds or reserves and that have not been started, unless specifically approved in advance by the COO. This is a strategy to preserve departmental reserves for essential uses during the downturn;
- Travel: Limiting travel as much as possible. Priority will be given to tele-conferencing when it is feasible; and
- Private Support: Reviewing estimates of private funds used to support unit operations and (as appropriate) making adjustments for diminished revenue streams in the short term. In addition, the university is increasing efforts to raise expendable funds from donors, to address shortfalls in funding for essential initiatives, most notably AccessUVa.

Thus far, we have been able to manage state budget cuts without layoffs, but it has not been easy. For the university to absorb these repeated cuts, total employment (the total payroll) has had to shrink to sustainable levels. Using retirements, routine turnover, and transfers, administrative units (not counting those in the Medical Center) have let go more than 100 positions during the last year. Moreover, in activities that are not absolutely essential to our core business of offering and supporting academic programmes, the coming year will bring reductions the will, at the very least, match this scale, but layoffs will continue to be a last resort. In this regard, layoffs are bad business logic in universities, because our chief investments are in people whose whole career accomplishments add up to the universities' net value. In addition, they are not compatible with an institutional culture in which the continuity of core business and perpetual innovation and reinvention matter, because we aim to grow stronger, especially so in bad times. Further, layoffs cost money, possibly more than they might save, because most staff and faculty members work in teams that have to be rebuilt from scratch, if allowed to collapse during a recession.

As the financial meltdown began to subside but the recession continued in the early months of 2009, secondary shocks became apparent in the US, particularly at the state level. In Virginia, tax collections fell by 21.3% in April compared to the previous year and in June, they fell another 8.8%, which represented the largest drop in state tax collections in recorded history. Virginia law requires our governors to manage shortfalls by reducing allotments from the state's general (tax) funds to its agencies, which include public colleges and universities. Because little elasticity for growth currently exists in other revenue sources for the University of Virginia, the recession promises now to be the most serious financial setback of modern times, and because the university's mission and functions are far larger than they were in 1929, perhaps of all times. Since this recession began, it has already dealt with several prior state cuts spanning three fiscal years. This past summer, Virginia's governor required that all agencies provide plans for dealing with additional reductions equal to 5%, 10%, and 15% of their remaining state general fund appropriations for this year. In early September, he announced that the cut would be 15% or $19 million, but with federal stimulus funds offsetting a portion of the cut, thereby bringing the actual reduction down to $10.3 million. Further, the prior reductions were all ordered as permanent cuts in spending. The governor has stipulated that these additional reductions *may* continue through the next biennium (2010–2012), one of several signs that state leaders recognize the damage done by the seriatim cuts, and want to leave public agencies options for an eventual recovery.

Virginia's revenue crisis is by no means unique in the US and California, New York, Florida, North Carolina, and another 20 or so states have reported similar or worse numbers. As a result, public colleges and universities in these states are contending with reductions that are as severe as that of our university, and in some cases, worse. At the University of Virginia, we are better able than many of our peer universities to deal with cuts for two key reasons. First, despite market losses the university's fiscal managers are continuing to generate funds for academic programmes and to predict and effectively manage downturns. For example, wise endowment management has given the university strength and stability in the last decade, regarding which some history will provide a perspective. In 1998, the university established an investment management company as a subcommittee of the University's Board of Visitors' Finance committee. The investment company, called the University of Virginia Investment Management Company (UVIMCO), was created for a number of reasons, including to pool and manage numerous foundation monies into one endowment, improve hiring practices, increase salaries, and to establish the investment entity's own auditors, legal counsel, and payroll system. Also of importance was the opportunity to improve the university's ability to honour its confidentiality assurance to its investment managers. The intent behind the formation of UVIMCO was also to provide continuity to the management of the endowment and to provide outside investment expertise to the finance committee. Many US universities have disaggregated the investment function from the other duties carried out by boards of trustees (the Harvard Management Company being one of the more prominent examples). Evidence from the last half-century shows that this disaggregation is good practice, as it puts investment planning in the hands of professionals and allows board members to carry out responsibilities better suited to their areas of expertise.

Despite a ca. 25% drop in the value of the endowment, as a result of the recent global economic crisis, that of the University of Virginia has performed very well over the long term. As of 30 June 2009, UVIMCO oversaw investments totalling $4 billion, which included the university's endowment and foundation assets as well as current funds invested in the long-term pool. During the 12 months ending on 30 June, the long-term pool had declined by 21%. Over longer-term periods, however, UVIMCO's returns compare favourably to benchmarks, for as of June 30th the endowment's multi-year returns were 3 year =1.6% compared to -8.2% S&P; 5 year =6.5% compared to -2.2% S&P; 10 year =9.5% compared to -2.2% S&P.; 20 year =11.6% with no S&P comparison. So far, the university has incurred somewhat less damage from losses in the markets than we would have predicted from prior experience and indeed, less damage than other large endowments are reporting.

Second and perhaps most essential for managing budget cuts, the university does not rely on a single major source of funds, such as the state or the endowment, with some wealthy private universities in the US reportedly drawing more than 40% of their expenditures from their endowments, but instead we rely on a diverse variety of sources: tuition set at a realistic level; patient fees at the Medical Center calculated to cover the real cost of providing care; endowment payouts set at levels that dampen the effects of downturns as well as upturns (and this year will fund 5.2% of the university's total operating budget); predictably strong annual and capital giving from alumni, parents, and friends; auxiliary revenues that cover the full cost of non-core functions; ticket sales; and state funding (which provides a smaller and smaller portion of the budget). Because these revenue streams are well diversified and predictable, we can manage them in unison to maximum advantage. Moreover, the diversity of revenue sources has allowed the university to keep its credit rating high, for despite a struggling economy and state budget cuts, it has repeatedly received AAA bond ratings from the top three rating agencies.

Actions taken by the US federal government to mitigate damage from the economic crisis have created opportunities for the University of Virginia and other colleges and universities to gain strength. In February 2009, US President Obama signed into law the $787 stimulus package known officially as the American Recovery and Reinvestment Act (ARRA) of 2009 (US Government, 2009). The university received $10.7 million in ARRA funds from the state to partially offset increases in tuition for in-state students and is now also pursuing such funds from federal agencies like the National Institutes of Health and the National Science Foundation. Researchers have applied for competitive grants, to date totalling over $277 million, and have received awards of $25.2 million over two years. Overall, the university's sponsored source of revenue, sponsored research funding, grants and agreements received from a variety of public and private sources, reached $295.93 million in 2008–09. Moreover, it was the first institution of higher education in the nation to offer benchmark level taxable Build America Bonds, which are partially subsidised by the U.S. Treasury, through the AARA. Savings from this programme are approximately $2.1 million annually and more than $60 million over the life of the bonds.

In sum, dire economic conditions often give us the opportunity to re-examine common practices in every area of our universities, rethink priorities, cut back on nonessential spending, and find less expensive ways of achieving our goals. Officials at the University of Virginia and at other colleges and universities in the US are working to ensure that they sustain excellence in teaching, research, and service, despite the economic downturn. Further, through knowledge creation, research, and workforce development, colleges and universities will serve as agents of the recovery that is now beginning to take shape.

ADDENDUM: WHERE WE HAVE FAILED

Effective management has helped sustain colleges and universities in difficult times. In some instances, however, we have failed to anticipate problems or to adequately address them as they have appeared. One of higher education's failures has been our inability to effectively prepare students from diverse backgrounds for success in college level work. In this regard, students from a wide range of socio-economic, racial, and geographic backgrounds enter college with varying levels of aptitude, but in spite of orientation, counselling, and advice programmes, we have not succeeded in levelling the playing field for all incoming students. One alternative that has been embraced in the UK is to outsource college preparation to a third-party vendor. In this regard, Kaplan International Colleges is part of Kaplan, Inc., a leading provider in lifelong education owned by the Washington Post Company. These colleges teach academic preparation programmes especially designed for international students, in partnership with a select group of top UK universities: City University London, the University of Southampton, the University of Glasgow, the University of Liverpool, the University of Sheffield, and Nottingham Trent University. Each international college is based on the campus of these partner universities and the participating students have access to all the university's facilities, including guaranteed accommodation. Furthermore, they are guaranteed admission at the partner university upon successful completion of their study programme and they also provide teaching space and quality assurance. The international colleges are designed for international students and offer foundation certificates, diploma and graduate diploma programmes, and academic courses for pre-master's preparation. Moreover, the foundation certificate, diploma, and graduate diploma programs differ between the colleges, as does the progression upon completion. For example, at Nottingham Trent International College students who successfully complete diplomas in business or computing progress to the second year of a three year undergraduate degree course. At Glasgow International College, business and engineering students progress to the diploma programme and then into the third year of a four year undergraduate degree. The international colleges also offer pre-sessional English programmes, intended to increase English language ability of international students and to build their confidence in using English before joining an academic course. These programmes are not perfect, but they offer a viable solution to a problem that higher education leaders have been confronted with for decades.

Deferred maintenance is another failure that afflicts even the most prestigious colleges and universities. The Association for Higher Education Facilities Officers, along with the National Association of College and University Business Officers, defines deferred maintenance as "maintenance work that has been deferred on a planned or unplanned basis to a future budget cycle, or postponed until funds are available." Postponing maintenance and repairs is easy to do when other, seemingly more urgent, fiscal needs arise. The assumption is usually that any repair postponed until 2010 will indeed be completed in that year. However, when, as so often, repairs are postponed again and again, and when multiple repairs are postponed for multiple buildings or for entire systems of infrastructure, the aggregated cost necessary to pay for repairs to a university's physical plant can be staggering. In other words, if ignored for too long, deferred maintenance will necessitate very expensive, wholesale repairs to (or replacement of) buildings or other segments of the physical plant, where failing to attend to basic maintenance needs in the short term will lead to mounting costs in the long term and in some cases additional early replacement costs of buildings that fail to reach their projected life expectancy, because the most basic repairs were postponed year after year. At the University of Virginia, in 2005, we determined that the aggregate cost of completing all deferred-maintenance projects [E&G only] was $114 million. In 1981, Harvard University rather famously discovered that it had accrued $70 million in deferred maintenance for the Harvard Business School alone. In 2001, Harvey Mudd College (a small but highly respected liberal arts college in California renowned for its engineering programmes) found that the total cost for its deferred-maintenance projects had reached $12 million, a sum that was, at the time, almost half of the college's entire yearly operating budget.

In the United States, a common measure for calculating a college or university's backlog of deferred maintenance is the Facilities Condition Index: the total deferred maintenance cost divided by the total net replacement value. This index may be calculated for an individual building, a group of buildings and associated infra-structure, or for an entire physical plant. In 2005, the University of Virginia's Facilities Condition Index was 10.4 and because a score in excess of 10 is considered to denote "poor condition", the university's administrators and its governing body elected to take decisive action to improve it, by normalizing maintenance schedules and bolstering funds that could be used to pay for deferred maintenance. Methods for building reserve funds to pay for deferred maintenance vary greatly. At Duke University, a portion of every federal research grant or private foundation gift is set aside, in order to offset costs associated with deferred maintenance, whereas at Penn State University, a portion of every tuition fee paid by entering students is set aside for deferred maintenance. At the University of Virginia, we have instituted a series of policies that require, for instance, annual re-investment of at least 1.5% of the replacement value of buildings and equipment. Furthermore, we now endeavour to build an endowment for maintenance into calculations when seeking private or governmental funding for any construction project. Through these and other efforts, the university has set a goal of reducing its Facilities Condition Index to 5 by 2014 and only time will tell whether we can reach this goal.

Yet another failure in higher education relates to the introduction and steady evolution of computer-based management systems to support virtually all university business. This has revolutionized our operations, from the way we handle student admissions, course registration, and academic transcripts, to the way we keep financial records, manage our library holdings, and support the work of faculty in the class-rooms. Software providers have thrived on the opportunity to convince universities that each one requires specialized, custom-made, integrated management systems, designed to meet each institution's individual requirements. However, most universities could have adopted a variety of standard, off-the-shelf software and saved a great deal of time and money in doing so, the potential drawback to this was considered to be that standard software might have required adapting some university procedures to fit the strengths of those various software packages, rather than the other way around. Nevertheless, customized integrated systems may be beneficial in some ways, but experience tells us that they do not work well at the intra-university level, and certainly can be problematic at inter-university level, when there are multiple systems involved. As a consequence, if we consider the cost and time required to design, install, test, and de-bug the management systems, the investment can be staggering and perhaps unjustifiable. Moreover, constant improvements, increased speed, and new applications, mean that universities will continue to struggle in the future to remain technologically up date and also having to always weigh up the purposefulness of any new expenditure.

REFERENCES

The Library of Congress Web Guides. (2009). *Morrill Act*. Retrieved from http://www.loc.gov/rr/program/bib/ourdocs/Morrill.html

The State Council of Higher Education for Virginia. (2005). *The restructured higher education financial and administrative operations act*. Retrieved from http://www.schev.edu/ Restructuring/restructuring.asp

The University of Virginia Library. (n.d.). *Jefferson digital archive*. Retrieved from http://etext.lib.virginia.edu/etcbin/ot2www-foley?specfile=/texts/english/jefferson/foley/public/JefCycl.o2w&act=surround&offset=9844651&tag=8747.+UNIVERSITY+OF+VIRGINIA,+Necessity+for.+--+[continued].+&query=luminous+tuition&id=JCE8747

The University of Virginia. (2004). *AccessUVa*. Retrieved from http://www.virginia.edu/financialaid/access.php

The University of North Carolina. (2003). *Carolina covenant*. Retrieved from http://www.unc.edu/carolinacovenant/

The University of Michigan News Service. (2005). *U-M expands M-Pact, replacing loans with grants*. August 8, 2006. Retrieved from http://www.ns.umich.edu/htdocs/releases/story.php?id=460

The University of Florida. (n.d.). *Florida opportunity scholars 2008–9 annual report*. Retrieved from http://fos.ufsa.ufl.edu/doc/FOS%2008-09%20Annual%20Rpt%20FINAL.pdf

The University of Maryland. (2005). *Maryland pathways*. Retrieved from http://www.financialaid.umd.edu/MarylandPathways.html

The University of Texas. (2009). *Longhorn opportunity scholarship*. Retrieved from http://www.texasscholarships.org/types/osfs/los.html

US Government. (2009). *American recovery and reinvestment act of 2009*. Retrieved from http://www.recovery.gov/Pages/home.aspx

John T. Casteen III
University of Virginia, USA

ETIENNE ZÉ AMVELA

8. THE ROLE OF ELITE UNIVERSITIES IN AFRICA

A Case Study of the University of Yaounde I in Cameroon

INTRODUCTION

The University of Yaounde I (UYI) was created by presidential decree on 29 March 1993, following the split of The University of Yaounde, which itself was an emanation of The Federal University of Cameroon, created in 1963 (Presidency of the Republic, 1993a and 1993b). The UYI is often referred to as "The Mother" of all State Universities in Cameroon, which, by virtue of her relatively old age and high number of competent alumni, gives her the rightful place of an "elite university" in the country[1]. This chapter addresses the following question: given her role as an elite university in Cameroon, is the University of Yaounde I a potential world-class university?

To attempt an objective answer to this question, the author will first present the main missions of the UYI, then will revisit the ranking criteria and weights used by the 2007 Academic Ranking of World Universities by Shanghai Jiao Tong University (SJTU), before discussing what the university has done in the past and what it is doing today so as to be counted tomorrow among world-class universities.

THE MISSIONS OF THE UNIVERSITY OF YAOUNDE I

The missions of the UYI may be summarized as follows: to elaborate and transmit knowledge, to develop research, cooperation and the training of the student body, to uplift the higher forms of culture and research to the highest level, following the best rhythm of progress, to ensure access to higher education to all those who have the calling and ability, to contribute to the economic, social and cultural development, and to enhance the practice of French-English bilingualism enshrined in Article 2 of the Constitution of the Republic of Cameroon, and spread the use of technologies of information and communication throughout the country.

To accomplish the above missions, the UYI puts at the disposal of its teaching staff the means necessary for their teaching and research activities and guarantees the best possible conditions of serenity and intellectual freedom needed to attain genuine reflective thinking and intellectual creativity. With regards to the students, it provides facilities for their orientation and strives to offer them the best choice of the most appropriate intellectual and professional training.

The institution promotes sports and socio-cultural activities on campus and remains open to former students and all those who did not attend university, but who wish

N.C. Liu et al., (eds.). Paths to a World-Class University: Lessons from Practices and Experiences, 159–175.

to further their knowledge and improve their respective socio-professional standings. Within the limits of the means available, the UYI endeavours to provide the best possible living and working conditions for the three main components of its community: the students, the teaching staff, and the administrative and technical staff. To fulfil all these missions, it has been granted a distinct legal and moral role that goes along with financial autonomy. Moreover, the university may also establish cooperation links with other national and international institutions of a similar nature and it has the authority to award academic and professional grades and qualifications. Finally, it should be added that just like the other six state universities in Cameroon, its vision and strategic objectives must be consonant with those of the government, being placed as it were, under the supervisory authority of the Ministry of Higher Education. Having specified the missions of the UYI, the next section will revisit the 2007 Academic Ranking of World Universities.

THE 2007 ACADEMIC RANKING OF WORLD UNIVERSITIES

It will be recalled that the ARWU ranking (SJTUGSE, 2007) uses objective ranking criteria and weights based on four indicators of academic or research performance: quality of education or the number of alumni winning Nobel Prizes and Fields Medals; quality of faculty which refers not only to staff winning Nobel Prizes and Fields Medals but also to highly cited researchers in 21 broad subject categories; research output evaluated through two indicators: first, the number of articles published in *Nature* and *Science* (N & S) but which may be relocated in humanities and social sciences for institutions specializing in humanities and social sciences, and second, articles in *Science Citation Index-expanded, Social Sciences Citation Index*; and size of institution calculated by dividing the weighted score of all the above indicators by the number of full-time equivalent academic staff. Should the number of academic staff not be available, then only the weighted score of the remaining indicators is taken into consideration.

A comparison between the missions of the UYI and the four indicators of academic or research performance reveals that while ARWU talks of quality of education and quality of faculty, the UYI lays emphasis on elaboration and transmission of knowledge and uplifting of higher forms of culture and research to the highest level following the best rhythm of progress. In our opinion, the university has thus adopted one of the surest ways leading to the winning of Nobel Prizes and Fields Medals and the simultaneous training of potential highly cited researchers in the most important broad subject categories. Furthermore, given that the ARWU rankings rely heavily on research output, the UYI aims at developing research, co-operation and the training of men and women to this end. The common objective at this level is the aim to increase the number of high quality publications in well established scientific journals around the world. However, it should be pointed out that while putting emphasis on N & S the UYI does give humanities and social sciences the place they deserve. Finally, the last indicator used by the ARWU, viz., the size of the institution is also taken care of by the UYI, with it paying attention to the quality teaching staff in terms of numbers and qualifications not only at the entry point, but also after recruitment through in-service training for staff development[2].

This brief comparative and contrastive analysis has shown, among other things, that the only two missions of the UYI that have no counterpart in the ARWU are the practice of French-English bilingualism and the use of the technologies of information and communication. The first is dictated by the historically bilingual nature of Cameroon which is enshrined in the constitution, and the second by the necessity to adapt to the modern way of life characteristic of the 21st century where ignorance of the technologies of information and communication can be equated with modern day "illiteracy".

In this comparison, another idiosyncratic feature of the UYI is its efforts to dissipate the outdated concept of the university as an "Ivory Tower" understood as a place of retreat from the world and one's fellows with a life style remote from that of most ordinary people, leading in the long term to the ignorance of practical concerns, problems, etc. In fact, while this concept receives no further attention from the ARWU, the UYI makes the necessary effort to ensure access to higher education to all those who have the calling and ability, irrespective of any other considerations, and who wish to contribute actively to the economic, social and cultural development of the country. It is believed that this will make the *raison d'être* of the university more relevant to the community at large, thus making the university less of an "Ivory Tower". Now that we have revisited the ARWU and compared it with the missions of the UYI, we are in a better position to attempt an objective answer to the most important question of this paper, viz., "Is the UYI a potential world-class university?"[3]

IS THE UYI A POTENTIAL WORLD-CLASS UNIVERSITY?

The administrative and academic authorities of the UYI are fully conscious of the fact that according to the July 2008 SJTU ranking (SJTUGSE, 2008), out of the first one thousand (1,000) best universities in the world, the African continent can boast of only five, all of which hail from the Republic of South Africa (Mianzenza, 2007). The authorities in Cameroon believe that the only way out of this unenviable situation is to make the world-class university ranking criteria and weights the goals of the UYI and to work hard to achieve these. The task may be arduous, but not impossible and this optimistic attitude may be justified by the fact that, as we have just highlighted in the previous section the world-class university ranking criteria and the UYI missions do have a lot of converging points. It is against this background that we shall attempt to answer one of the most important questions of this paper which may be rephrased as follows: "In her nationally recognized role as an elite university, what has the UYI done, and what is she doing today to become a world-class university tomorrow?"

To give a global answer to this fundamental question, the author will find partial answers in each of the ten avenues to be explored. Instead of making a scanty and therefore superficial survey of all the points, it is wise to select only those that can be more readily equated with the four main indicators of the SJTU ranking and discuss them in some detail, which it is believed should cover enough objective elements for an unambiguous answer to the question "Is the UYI a potential world-class

university?" Therefore, to this effect the author will discuss in turn, with appropriate examples, the following points:
- The strategic development plan of the UYI which is an articulation of the vision of the institution for the next ten years;
- Quality teaching and quality research;
- Promotion of interdisciplinary and international research projects;
- Development of cooperation links with other universities around the world; and
- Innovations as an elite university in Cameroon and the sub-region.

The UYI Strategic Development Plan

The top decision-makers of the UYI are fully aware that strategic planning has indeed become a modern tool in the management of complex organizations. In fact, such a plan defines the main strategic orientations which will determine the actions taken by the organization, the global objectives which should be reached, the sectorial objectives for each of the structures and actors involved in its implementation. Moreover, it determines the means to secure funds for the realization of objectives, the role to be played by the different actors, specifies the structural changes to bring in to the running of organizations, the different stages to go through and the deadlines to respect. Thus, it puts the organization into perspective, by giving to the whole endeavour a global coherence between the objectives to be reached on the one hand, and the means available or to be sought throughout the period of the plan, on the other.

It is precisely so as to improve its management and give more visibility and coherence to the whole range of its actions that the UYI has embarked on the setting up of a Strategic Development Plan (SDP). The SDP is underpinned by four main reasons. First, the institution has to accommodate an ever increasing number of students year on year. Second, the adoption of the new BMD (bachelor, master's doctoral) system in higher education in Cameroon calls for the revision of many teaching and research programmes and the definition of new objectives to be reached. Third, it is necessary to fine tune the UYI's output so as to be in accordance with other important developments in the country, such as the strategy of the education sector adopted in June 2006 and revised in April 2009, and the operational strategy for the New University Governance spearheaded by the minister of higher education. Last, the UYI needs to make a better programming of expenses by designing a meaningful framework for medium term expenditure. After this brief introduction of the SDP, we shall successively discuss the following aspects, that is, the points tackled by the SDP, the UYI policy drive, and the guiding principles and strategic axes of the SDP.

The points tackled by the SDP. Keeping in mind the four main reasons given above, which justify the existence of the SDP, and in order to express the vision that the UYI authorities have carved for the development of their institution over the next ten years, their SDP is aimed at tackling the following five points:
- The management of admissions and the respect of equity in the context of a strong and ever-increasing demographic pressure from new students;
- The improvement of internal efficiency and the preservation of quality performance in all the sectors of its activity;

- The challenge of securing and reinforcing partnerships with the private sector and the socio-professional milieux;
- The improvement of academic management and governance; and
- The preservation of durable and efficient financing.

The ambitious strategies proposed in the SDP see the UYI transforming itself in due course into a true "technopole", which will establish a strong bond between the institution and the world of science and technology. By developing research and teaching in highly specialized technical domains, this technopole should then enable the UYI to find her rightful place in the heart of the nation and hopefully of Central Africa. The realization of this objective is seen as one of the conditions to be fulfilled for the setting in motion of a vast programme of reforms. The UYI top management believes that it is only through such a programme that any financial assistance, whether national or foreign, could be used efficiently as an incentive for investment which will result in mid-term and long-term development.

The UYI policy drive.   The UYI policy drive stems from the observation that everywhere in the world and at all times, the most impressive added values depend, among other things, on the production techniques used by their proponents. This makes knowledge itself an essential strategic economic resource, a comparative and decisive advantage in the face of fierce competition in which the big technological blocks of our times are engaged. Thus, the challenge faced by the UYI is to put in place, with help from financial and technical partners, a proactive institution which takes local realities into account and anticipates the needs of the national economy. The current SDP may therefore be considered simultaneously as a comprehensive framework of actions for the development of training in perfect conformity with national development objectives, as a framework for consultation and harmonization of viewpoints with civil society and partners in development, as a framework for designing tools for financial coherence and medium term budgeting; and finally, as a framework for the definition and organization of analytical frameworks intended to guide and foster long-term sustainable development.

The guiding principles and strategic axes of the SDP.   The UYI's SDP is a 93-page document comprising seven main parts, that is, the global context of the development of the UYI, diagnosis of the UYI, guiding principles and strategic axes, priority programmes, financial evaluation and programming of the SDP, financing policy of the SDP, and operational framework for the SDP[4]. In line with the National Strategy for Development which contains a vision of Cameroon for the year 2035, it can be summarized that the two main options of the SDP may be to adapt the training offered by the UYI in quality and quantity to meet the real needs of the Cameroonian economy, and to develop the university expertise and provide it as a service for the national economy - enterprises, industries and the like.

In this context, the following five principles underlie the actions undertaken within the framework of the proposed SDP: the reduction of disparities of all sorts through the promotion of equality and equity, with special attention to gender;

efficient and well-coordinated partnerships so as to tap into all kinds of resources from a wide range of sources in relation to the development of the university; the promotion of a responsible attitude for efficient and transparent management, with special emphasis on the necessity to produce good and tangible results that will benefit the university and the community at large; the necessity for all the stake-holders to achieve the highest possible norms of quality performance in their respective fields of activity, and a good mastery of expenditure through a rational and rigorous use of available resources by fighting against wastage, idleness, laxity, corruption and other such evils.

As for the three priority axes of the SDP, they may be summarized as follows: the improvement of access and equity for all types of teaching according to the available resources and the needs of the society; the improvement of the quality and relevance of the teaching offered, taking as a yardstick the UNESCO standards; and the improvement of management methods and university governance.

In sum, the vision of the SDP is to make the UYI dynamic and efficient to the satisfaction of all and this can only become a reality if the: material, financial and human resources available are managed with maximum efficiency and transparency. Moreover, this necessitates the existence of a reliable information system, effective decentralization at all levels of the hierarchy and the obligation of effective results for the officers in charge of piloting the university.

Quality Teaching and Quality Research at the UYI

As far as the special attention devoted to quality teaching and quality research is concerned, at the UYI, the academic or university department is the fundamental unit in which teaching and research are conceived, structured and carried out. The policy of decentralization advocated by the Ministry of Higher Education is applied at the UYI in all the professional schools and faculties down to the level of their respective departments and thus, each department has been enjoying greater admini-strative and financial autonomy since 2006.

A study of the previous budgets executed by the UYI reveals that in 2005 both pedagogic and research activities were still coordinated by the respective deans or directors of the faculties and schools. Since 2006, however, the budgetary allocations to departments have been steadily on the increase (The UYI, 2005, 2006, 2007 and 2008). To illustrate this fact, we have selected at random two faculties and one school: the Faculty of Arts, Letters and Social Sciences (FALSH), the Faculty of Science (FS) and the National Advanced School of Engineering (ENSP)[5]. Their respective departmental budgetary allocations and relative increases are shown in the tables below in CFA Francs (US $1 = 550). Please note that the most commonly known French acronyms are maintained to refer to the Schools and Faculties of the UYI. Thus, FALSH stands for "Faculté des Arts, Lettres et Sciences Humaines", FS for "Faculté des Sciences" while ENSP stands for "Ecole Nationale Supérieure Polytechnique". (For more acronyms, see later section).

If we consider the total allocations for the three departments in each faculty/school, we notice that the FALSH has the lowest absolute value every year,

Table 1. Budgetary allocations of three selected faculties and school

FALSS	2005	2006	2007	2008
History	2,550,000	7,000,000	8,368,000	31,263,000
Psychology	2,125,000	6,000,000	7,368,000	21,638,000
Arts and Archaeology	2,125,000	7,000,000	8,368,000	26,556,000
TOTAL 1	6,800,000	20,000,000	24,104,000	79,457,000
Increase		194%	21%	230%

FS	2005	2006	2007	2008
Biochemistry	2,975,000	12,000,000	12,000,000	61,440,000
Maths	2,975,000	11,000,000	11,000,000	56,520,000
Computer Science	2,975,000	12,000,000	12,000,000	43,350,000
TOTAL 2	8,925,000	35,000,000	35,000,000	161,310,000
Increase		292%	0%	361%
TOTAL 1 and TOTAL 2	15,725,000	55,000,000	59,104,000	240,767,000

ENSP	2005	2006	2007	2008
Industrial & Mechanical Engineering	44,000,000	52,000,000	80,000,000	82,000,000
Civil Engineering	42,750,000	52,000,000	80,000,000	82,000,000
Maths & Physics	42,000,000	52,000,000	80,000,000	82,000,000
Computer Science	41,500,000	52,000,000	80,000,000	82,000,000
TOTAL 3	170,250,000	208,000,000	320,000,000	328,000,000
Increase		22%	45%	3%

followed by the FS while the ENSP receives the highest amount every single year. If on the other hand we consider the relative yearly increase as one moves from year to year, we notice that for the years 2006, 2007 and 2008 the FALSH recorded the following increases in terms of percentage expressed from the previous year: 194%, 21%, and 230%; the FS 292%, 0%, and 361% while the ENSP recorded 22%, 45% and 3%.

These statistics call for at least the following three observations: the highest increases were in the FALSH and the FS; in 2005, 2006, 2007 and 2008, the respective cumulative totals for both the FALSH and the FS were 15,725,000; 55,000,000; 59,104,000 and 240,767,000; and the corresponding yearly allocations for the ENSP alone are higher than these cumulative totals, viz., 170,250,000; 208,000,000; 320,000,000 and 328,000,000 francs. This shows that just like the ARWU, the UYI lays special emphasis on science and technology. Moreover, the UYI goes even further by clearly favouring the development of the School of Engineering (applied sciences) followed by pure sciences (FS) and then by social sciences and humanities (FALSH). However, all of these important components of knowledge do receive some kind of attention, with none of them being completely neglected in favour of another. We may therefore conclude that in the domains of quality teaching and research the ARWU and the UYI do share the same vision.

Promotion of Interdisciplinary and International Research Projects

At the UYI, teaching and research activities are mostly carried out in three faculties, two schools and one specialized research centre (still with their respective best known French acronyms): The Faculty of Arts, Letters and Social Sciences (FALSH), the Faculty of Science (FS), the Faculty of Medicine and Biomedical Sciences (FMSB), the National Advanced School of Engineering (ENSP), the Advanced Teachers' Training College (ENS), and the Biotechnology Centre (CBT). Within the framework of this paper, it would be rather unrealistic to attempt a comprehensive presentation of the research activities in all these entities. However, it is acknowledged that it is appropriate to give some concrete examples here that illustrate some of the measures that have been taken by the UYI and which illustrate the genuine effort being made towards achieving world-class university status for the institution. In this regard we focus on research carried out in 2008 in two of the seven structures housed in the scientifically advanced Bio-technology Centre: the Immunology Laboratory and the Molecular Biology and Metabolic Disease Research Laboratory[6], which are considered among the most representative of the vision of the UYI as a whole.

The immunology laboratory headed by Prof. Rose Leke. Research activities within the Immunology Laboratory for 2008 were multifaceted and involved close collaboration with other laboratories within the university and around the world. For illustration purposes, we shall focus on two projects: the malaria project and collaborative research on medicinal plants; before providing a list of the main meetings, conferences, and workshops in which laboratory members participated (Leke, 2008).

Malaria project activities. Research activities in the laboratory were conducted within the framework of the malaria project entitled "Malaria Immunity in Pregnant Cameroonian Women", a collaborative project between the UYI and the University of Hawaii in the USA. The project is aimed at studying how the absence of malaria during pregnancy (due to the use of intermittent preventive therapy [IPT]) may bring about the following: alteration in the development of pregnancy-associated immunity in the mother; reduction in placental pathology; and increase in the susceptibility of babies to malaria. The activities carried out included:
- Preparation of the various study sites where the project had to take place. In this regard, sensitization rallies were organized with the villagers and health authorities of the concerned villages and hospitals, to explain the purpose of the project; and
- Launching of the project in September 2008. This opportunity was used to recruit study participants (pregnant women) and to collect study samples.

The project was visited by two clinical independent monitors from the National Institute of Health in the USA, and one from South Africa. It is currently on-going with the participation of a multi-disciplinary team of researchers, scientists, obstetricians, gynaecologists, paediatricians, clinicians, entomologists, laboratory technicians, students, a laboratory manager, statisticians, data managers, a secretary, an administrator, a financial coordinator and drivers.

Collaborative research on medicinal plants. In collaboration with the Laboratory of Nutrition and Nutritional Biochemistry of the UYI, a study was conducted to evaluate the antihyperglycemic and antihypolipidemic properties of two medicinal plants of the Cameroonian pharmacopeia, namely, Chromonela odorata and Harungana madagascarensis. One student successfully defended her postgraduate diploma dissertation on this work.

Participation in national and international conferences/workshops. Each of the five conferences listed below received at least one participant from the Immunology Laboratory, which shows, among other things, the international character and the level of the standards involved.
- Introduction to biostatistics and epidemiology, Yaounde, April 2008;
- Health research ethics for ethics committees, Accra, Ghana, February 2008;
- 57th Annual meeting of the American Society of Tropical Medicine and Hygiene, Louisiana, New Orleans, USA, December 2008;
- Fundamentals of international clinical research, Cape Town, South Africa, January 2009; and
- Insecticide resistance project inception meeting, Geneva, Switzerland, February 2009.

The molecular biology and metabolic disease research laboratory headed by Prof. J.C. Mbanya. After a brief summary of the project, we shall discuss the major activities carried out in 2008.

Summary of the project. The project is code-named CAMDER - Cameroon Diabetes Epidemiology and Registry and it is the fruit of a collaboration between the Free University of Brussels (VUB) in Belgium and the UYI. The goal of the project is to contribute to the epidemiology of diabetes in Cameroon by studying diabetes patients under the age of 40 and their relatives within one generation. The expertise and the experience of the Belgian Diabetes Registry and the Diabetes Research Centre of the VUB were used to set up the Cameroon Diabetes Registry, its objectives being to: determine the number of newly diagnosed diabetic patients under the age of 40 residing in Cameroon; study the relationship between genetic, lifestyle and/or environmental factors and development of the disease; develop and apply new early markers to improve prediction of diabetes and its evolution; prepare, develop and support new experimental therapies and participation in international studies; and provide information and advice to authorities, physicians, patients and their families and the general public. In addition, the project is geared towards capacity building, with four Cameroonian students currently undertaking their master's and doctoral degrees at VUB in Belgium.

Major activities in 2008.   The major activities in 2008 include the following:
- The laboratory comprising four rooms was officially handed over to the team in June 2008 by the rector of the UYI, in presence of Professor Chris Van Schravendijk of the VUB. At the same ceremony, an important consignment of laboratory goods and a Toyota 4WD purchased in Belgium were presented by Professor Chris Van Schravendijk, on behalf of the VUB, to launch the activities of CAMDER;
- Recruitment of research subjects started since July 2007 and continued throughout 2008 at the National Obesity Centre of Yaounde Central Hospital. In December 2008, recruitment was also initiated at the National Diabetes and Hypertension Centre of the same hospital. By the end of 2008, fifty subjects were successfully recruited and their blood samples donated for: genetic, immunological and hormonal analyses. These samples were carefully stored at the Biotechnology Centre; and
- The students on research assignment in Cameroon have been provided with: laptops, a flat bed scanner, one tower case computer and a printer. Thanks to this equipment all project related documents are being developed and printed together with scientific articles at the Biotechnology Centre.

This concludes our discussion on the sustained promotion of interdisciplinary and international research projects. We shall now move on to the overall development of cooperation being conducted by the UYI.

Development of Links with Other Universities around the World

The development of collaborative links with other universities around the world is a permanent activity which has been gathering momentum at the UYI as the years go by. To illustrate this point with concrete examples, we shall focus on the activities in the last seven months and will discuss in turn the reception of foreign delegations, cooperation missions abroad, and the formalization of partnerships.

The reception of foreign delegations.   On 5 May and 4 August 2009, two delegations from the University of Venice in Italy carried out working visits at the UYI to explore cooperation avenues and offer their know-how in tele-education, in relation to the setting up of national and regional virtual universities on the campus. On 22 July 2009, the rector received experts from the Centre for Disease Control and Prevention of Atlanta in the USA, who came to explore the potential of the UYI in epidemiology and to discuss how the Bill and Melinda Gates Foundation could finance research activities in competent laboratories at the UYI. Moreover, the rector of the UYI granted an audience on 28 April 2009 to Mr. Bonaventure Mve Ondo, vice-rector in charge of relations with the "Agence Universitaire de la Francophonie (AUF)", Mr. Jean Gratien Zanouvi, regional director for Central Africa and Mr. Abdoulaye Salifou, director delegate of programme. Their discussions laid the foundation for the creation of a Pan-African Institute for University Governance. The visit paid on 12 March 2009 by H.E. Arturo Spiegelberg of Ortueta, the Spanish Ambassador to Cameroon, accompanied by Luis Padilla, Secretary General of the Casa Africa Network, was to establish cooperation links between the UYI and their organization, founded in 2007, under the distinguished patronage of His Majesty the King of

Spain, the Spanish Minister of Foreign Affairs and the President of the Canary Islands government. The main objective was not only to make Spanish better known in Africa, but also to facilitate contacts at various levels. Finally, the workshop on Linking Institutions for Veterinary Education (LIVE) was organized in February 2009 at the UYI, with this project being aimed at establishing a network in the zootechnical and veterinary sciences and it has received funding from the Edulink Programme within the context of the 8th European Development Fund.

Cooperation missions abroad.   During this period, officials of the Rector's Office have visited the following countries: Italy, Spain, South Africa, Nigeria and South Korea. In our opinion, this is enough evidence to show that the UYI is indeed making strenuous efforts to open up to the outside world[7].

Formalization of partnerships.   It should be pointed out that the different offers made and studied have led to the signing of several outline agreements for inter-university cooperation, agreements for co-supervision of theses, and conventions for the funding of research projects. A comprehensive list of these agreements and conventions has been compiled by the Department of Academic Affairs and Co-operation (2009) in a document entitled "Repertoire of Agreements and Conventions". Here, those relating to five faculties and schools of the UYI are listed.

The National Advanced School of Engineering (ENSP). Endorsement for distance learning in a master's degree in telecommunications signed with the "Agence Universitaire de la Francophonie", conventions with the structures ACEP Management and Microlog Sarl for the setting up of international training programmes and certifications, agreement with the Grenoble Institute for inter-university exchange programmes, financing conventions with the University of Paris Sud Orsay within the framework of the Edulink programme of the project for the network of master's degrees and doctorates in applied statistics in Francophone Sub-Saharan Africa, convention with the CIRAD ("Centre de Coopération Internationale en Recherche Agronomique pour le Développement") for activities within the domain of Technologies of Information and Communication within the context of the TICER ("Technologie de l'Information et de la Communication pour l'Enseignement et la Recherche") project and a financing convention with the IRD ("Institut de Recherche pour le Développement") for the implementation of the project entitled "Aires Sud", coordinated by Mr. Ntede Ngah Hyppolite.

The Faculty of Science (FS).   Conventions for inter-university exchanges with the Paul Sabatier University in Toulouse, Paris Diderot University in Paris 7 and the INRA (Institute for Natural Research in Africa) in disciplines such as: organic chemistry, biology, animal physiology, and biochemistry, the convention for the opening of an e-Miage with the University of Rennes 1, the convention for the creation of a Mixed International Unit code-named UMMISCO, i.e., "Unité de Modelisation Mathématique et Informatique des Systèmes Complexes" and conventions for the financing by the IRD of "Aires Sud" projects, coordinated by Mr. Flobert Njiokou and Mr. Emmanuel Ngameni.

The Faculty of Arts, Letters and Social Sciences (FALSH). Conventions for inter-university exchanges in the following disciplines: social science, German, and tourism have been signed with the Universities of Hamburg, Bielefeld and Hanover in Germany, Oslo in Norway, Buffalo in USA, and Bordeaux 3 in France, a convention was signed for tele-education and professionalization in tourism with CFA Stephenson of Paris and Stephenson International, an agreement with the Association of Catalan Public Universities concerns institutional development and training in university management and a convention of academic tutelage with the Higher Institute of Language and Communication of the Ndi-Samba Group concerned with studies leading to the Bachelor of Arts in English Modern Letters.

The Higher Teachers' Training college (ENS). Two financing conventions signed with the IRD for the "Aires Sud" projects coordinated by Mr. Omokolo Ndoumou Denis and Mr. Assako Assako René Joly and two other conventions for exchange programmes with the Universities of Salamanca in Spain and Tuscia in Italy, more specifically, regarding the latter, in the disciplines of language, humanities and dialogue of cultures.

The Faculty of Medicine and Biomedical Sciences (FMBS). A convention signed with the National Insurance Funds (CNPS: "Caisse Nationale de Prévoyance Sociale") that will help develop a partnership in the domain of training and research in health sciences.

From this brief analysis of the collaborative links at the UYI, one may safely conclude that each of the Schools/Faculties of the UYI is actively involved in the development of such links aimed at the promotion of their respective fields of specialization, with other schools/faculties around the world. Such an intense activity is bound to make the UYI better known and to also make it fully aware of what is happening elsewhere in higher education. Moreover, it is believed that such a strategy will increase the university's chances of producing first class articles and of making her researchers known and appreciated within their respective disciplines, among their counterparts around the world. Consequently, this will be a positive input in the UYI's genuine and structured efforts to be counted among the best universities in Africa and the world;.

Innovations as an Elite University in Cameroon and the Sub-region

To play her role as elite University in Cameroon and the sub-region, the UYI should, on the one hand, endeavour to consolidate her past and present achieve-ments; and on the other hand should spare no efforts to innovate constantly, so as to set the pace for other universities to follow. Furthermore, she should equally open up to the outside world in order to benefit from the positive contributions which other universities may bring. In our opinion, this is the attitude to adopt and the price to pay for a genuine advancement of knowledge in our perpetual quest for academic and technological excellence.

To give concrete examples of some of the actions taken and which contribute to conferring to the UYI the role of an elite university in Cameroon and the sub-region, we shall consider in turn two of its pace-setting innovations: the creation of a University Free Zone and the setting up of two virtual universities on campus.

The future creation of a University Free Zone. Article 1 of Order n° 011/PM of 20 February 2006 signed by the prime minister, created an inter-ministerial committee to study the setting up of a University Free Zone (ZFU) in Cameroon (Prime Minister's Office, 2006a and 2006b). Subsequently, after decision n° 06/0229/ MINESUP/CAB of 17 April 2006 the Minister of Higher Education appointed the members of this committee (Ministry of Higher Education, 2006). With assistance from international experts who worked relentlessly with their Cameroonian counterparts, this committee put in place the University Free Zone, which is expected to be at least partially operational by the beginning of the 2010/2011 academic year. When completed, it will cover a vast territory of several hundred hectares hosting an international technological university complex, which should enjoy a special status of administrative, financial and legal autonomy (Ministry of Higher education, 2007 and 2009). Its main activities will include the following:

- Training engineers and higher technicians in sufficient numbers to satisfy the needs of enterprises and industries in the Central African region. Priority will be given to the most modern and most relevant scientific domains. Specific conventions and agreements can be signed with foreign institutions to secure long term partnerships;
- Carrying out applied and developmental research together with partners from the relevant economic and administrative sectors (industries, technical ministries, big international organizations, etc.). The setting up of laboratories in the domains given priority will be carried out progressively, following the signing of local partnerships and the recruitment of the required competences. After the signing of relevant conventions, foreign laboratories could set up research branches within the ZFU campus;
- Setting up welcome training centres for enterprises and big industrial groups: the training of engineers and qualified technicians on the use of highly specialized equipment, corresponding to specific industrial activities, such as telecommunications, computer science, oil exploration, cement works and electricity that can be carried out professionally only with the material used in real commercial production. It should be possible to bring together certain centres within the ZFU campus, since their activities concern training as opposed to actual production;
- Building a centre for the creation of enterprises to facilitate the insertion of qualified technicians into economic life through innovative approaches. These enterprises which may be based either within or outside the zone, will all benefit from follow up support and assistance in management control, which are very important in the launching of successful enterprises;
- Creating a big university campus capable of receiving not only students from the whole of the Central African and the whole Sub-Saharan regions, but also national and foreign lecturer-researchers and other personalities on mission. The campus should also provide all the necessary utilities with regards to: health, leisure and culture;

- Ensuring that the development brought about by the economic, social and cultural role played by the ZFU is durable; and
- Establishing a multimedia centre whose main objective is to put in digital form the courses taught by lecturers of the ZFU and those of other universities who may need their services. This will help partially satisfy the need for qualified teaching staff, because students would be more autonomous in their studies, thanks to the CDROMs being put at their disposal.

It is envisaged that in the near future preparatory classes will be set up for entrance examinations into the universities of the sub-region. These will also be provided to prepare students for entrance into the different levels of the ZFU (bachelor - master's - doctoral). Such preparatory classes will be run by selected and qualified secondary schools in the region. Moreover, it is expected that the mere presence of the ZFU will lead to the creation of jobs with a high level of technical-know which it will bring to enterprise into the region. Partnerships will be signed with the socio-economic sector in the form of consultancy in enterprises and services, technical expertise on technical problems submitted to the ZFU, in-service training for those who need it, open days, guided tours of the zone and carefully selected conferences open to the general public.

In sum, the ZFU will constitute a competitiveness pole likely to improve higher education teaching systems in the whole sub-region. Moreover, all the higher technological schools in the sub-region could sign partnership conventions with the ZFU so that their lecturers and/or students could have access in one way or another to the installations or equipment available in the zone. More partnerships could be signed with enterprises, industries and other technological structures in the region, which could then be used as additional stimuli for the universities around the zone and beyond to find additional means of adding more practical applications to their functions. Furthermore, these partnerships will also help external partners improve their productivity and the quality of their services. In other words, the ZFU is seen not only as a regional pole of excellence for teaching, research and innovation, but also as a dynamic meeting point between universities, enterprises, industries and other technological structures in the region.

The virtual universities. This project was justified owing to the necessity to develop innovative tele-educational forms of teaching to satisfy the ever-increasing needs of higher education not only in Cameroon, but also in the sub-region[8]. After a brief statement on the context of the project, the author will discuss, in turn the anticipated activities; the ten main objectives of the project; the national, sectorial and ministerial strategy and the specific strategic objectives.

Within the framework of a partnership between the African Union and India, Cameroon has been selected to host the Pan-African e-Network project. This is aimed at creating in Cameroon a joint initiative for tele-education comprising two virtual universities, one national and the other subregional. The sub-regional virtual university is in fact a telecommunications relay centre intended for the following countries: Gabon, Equatorial Guinea, the Congo, Sao-Tome and Principe, Chad, the Central African Republic, the Democratic Republic of Congo, Burundi and Rwanda. The target population consists of all persons willing and endowed with the intellecttual capacity and possessing the minimal financial requirements to have access to higher education and this represents about one million potential beneficiaries. A partnership with thirteen Indian universities will supply course content and guarantee the quality of the diplomas awarded. At the time of writing this paper, the Indian government had already fulfilled her obligations by supplying and installing the much needed equipment in brand new ultra modern buildings on the UYI campus.

The physical structures and the already installed equipment were inaugurated by the Minister of Higher Education in a solemn and very colourful ceremony on 30 July 2009. The first phase of the project will involve the mastery of the system put in place by the Pan-African e-Network, whereas the second phase will focus on the extension of the network to cover the whole of the Cameroonian national territory. To achieve this effectively, a complete feasibility study will be needed in order to refine the vision and determine the means necessary for its realization. In both cases, the projects should aim at developing teaching staff and diversifying partnerships so as to be able to offer improved training.

In a nutshell, the project aims at:
- Making it possible for Cameroon to intensify her network and achieve equitable access to higher education through tele-education throughout the national territory;
- Developing tele-education leading to the award of diplomas and other higher educational qualifications;
- Bringing together all initiatives relating to educational technologies and developing their applications and other innovative processes;
- Producing high quality pedagogic content and ensuring their broadcasting and availability on-line in the region concerned;
- Making the training process available to the target population any time in the life of individuals and organising access to continuous apprenticeship and in-service training;
- Organising, managing and developing tele-education at the national and sub-regional levels;
- Serving as an essential relay for the development of tele-education to satisfy the needs of Cameroon and the sub-region;
- Securing training on-the-job for teachers and administrators through tutorials and tele-education;
- Ensuring the development of inter-university partnerships in the design of course content and in the awarding of diplomas; and
- Developing and increasing the level of service for learners in terms of free access to resources, an on-line library, and other relevant services.

Since the UYI is a state university, this project also has to fall in line with the: national, sectorial and ministerial strategy. Viewed from this standpoint, the global strategic objective of the project is to take an active part in Cameroon's technological transformation aimed at ensuring her status as a middle income country by the year 2030. This will be achieved by providing a relative advantage in certain technological fields with a strong added value, in an international environment marked by competition. The impact of this will be significant in relation to not only training and research, but also at the level of new industrial applications.

In this regard, there are two main preoccupations. First, this project reinforces the capacities of Cameroonian citizens through higher education, thus consolidating the country's geostrategic position on the continent and providing it with a stronger role at the global level. Moreover, there is the goal of make the country a magnet for big investment in scientific and technological learning. Second, the project brings into higher education the digital culture, thus preparing the country for strong participation in the digital age.

As a final observation, it may be said that this brief presentation of the two virtual universities constitutes an additional factor that helps to justify the contention that the UYI has the role of an elite university at the national and sub-regional levels. Moreover, the impact of these virtual universities on the UYI is bound to be multifarious, for it will help to improve, among other things: the quality of education, the quality of faculty and research output. It is therefore evident that just like the ZFU, the virtual universities will help pave the way for the UYI to enter the exclusive club of world-class universities.

CONCLUSION

On the basis of the above discussion, which could not be exhaustive owing to space constraints, it can still be safely concluded that The UYI is indeed a potential world-class university. In this regard, it has taken concrete measures, and is planning to do more to match the requirements of such status which, fortunately, as shown, fall in line with the current mission of the university. To achieve these goals may be an uphill task indeed, but not an impossible one, especially since the UYI authorities remain optimistic and are determined to meet the challenge.

If the author may express a wish, it is that the difficult task should be better structured and injected with more momentum so that the UYI can become integrated into the exclusive club of world-class universities in the shortest possible time and subsequently steadily be able to continue its upward movement towards the top of the classification. The whole process may not be completed in our lifetime. However, there is no justifiable reason why it should not be set in motion now and godspeed to the UYI and to all those universities around the world who are rightly vying for a place in the select club of world-class universities!

NOTES

[1] The seventh and youngest of all the state universities is The University of Maroua created in August 2008 and located in the Far-North region of Cameroon.

[2] It should, however, be pointed out that the mass admission of students into the university does have a negative impact on the quality of teaching and the rate of success.

[3] Owing to space constraints, we cannot indulge in a discussion on all the African countries that are building world-class universities and thus we shall limit ourselves to the UYI in Cameroon.

[4] The SDP of the UYI was examined and adopted by the UYI Senate on 17 February 2010. It will be presented to the UYI Board of Governors Meeting of 18 March 2010 for final adoption, before its submission to the Minister of Higher Education.

[5]   The UYI counts three faculties: 1) Arts, Letters and Social Sciences (FALSH); 2) Sciences (FS) and 3) Medicine and Biomedical Sciences (FMSB) and two schools of higher learning: 1) the National Advanced School of Engineering (ENSP), and 2) the Advanced Teachers' Training College1 (ENS).

[6]   We limit our discussion to the year 2008, because work done in 2009 could not[1] be included. In fact, the first draft of this chapter was completed before the end of 2009.

[7]   Mention is not made here of cooperative missions carried out abroad by officials and lecturers from schools and faculties of the UYI.

[8]   There will be no competition between the virtual universities and other institutions of higher learning, either in Cameroon or in the other countries involved. Both types of institution are needed, as they are fundamentally complementary.

REFERENCES

Department of Academic Affairs and Cooperation. (2009). *Repertoire of agreements and conventions.* Yaounde: The University of Yaounde I, Cameroon.

Leke, R. (2008). *Différentes activités des laboratoires du Centre de Biotechnologie de Nkolbisson.* Unpublished pamphlet, Yaounde: The University of Yaounde I, Cameroon.

Shanghai Jiao Tong University Graduate School of Education. (2007). *Academic ranking of world universities.* Retrieved http://www.arwu.org

Shanghai Jiao Tong University Graduate School of Education. (2008). *Academic ranking of world universities.* Retrieved http://www.arwu.org

Mianzenza, A. D. (2007). *Les universités d'Afrique à l'épreuve du classement des meilleures universités du monde.* Brazzaville: Centre d'études stratégiques du bassin du Congo, Congo.

Ministry of Higher Education. (2006a). *Décision n°06/0229/MINESUP/CAB du 17 avril 2006 constatant la composition du comité interministériel de réflexion sur le projet de création des zones franches universitaires au Cameroun.* Yaounde: Ministry of Higher Education, Cameroon.

Ministry of Higher Education. (2006b). *Rapport de Mission - Cameroun 30 janvier -16 février 2006 - Etude de préfaisabilité d'une zone franche universitaire.* Yaounde: Ministry of Higher Education, Cameroon.

Ministry of Higher Education. (2007). *Zone franche universitaire: Un modèle porteur pour un continent!* Yaounde: Ministry of Higher Education, Cameroon.

Ministry of Higher Education. (2009). *Note de conjoncture 2008 de l'Enseignement Supérieur au Cameroun n°7, 2009.* Yaounde: Ministry of Higher Education, Cameroon.

Presidency of the Republic. (1993a). *Décret n°93/027 du 19 janvier 1993 portant dispositions communes aux universités, modifié et complété par le décret n 2005/342 du 10 septembre 2005.* Yaounde: Presidency of the Republic, Cameroon.

Presidency of the Republic. (1993b). *Décret n°93/036 du 29 janvier 1993 portant organisation administrative et académique de l'Université de Yaoundé I.* Yaounde: Presidency of the Republic.

Prime Minister's Office (2006) *Arrêté n°011/PM du 20 février 2006 portant création du comité interministériel de réflexion sur le projet de création des zones franches universitaires au Cameroun.* Yaounde: Prime Minister's Office, Cameroon.

The University of Yaounde I. (2005). *Estimates for 2005 financial years.* Yaounde: The University of Yaounde I, Cameroon.

The University of Yaounde I. (2006). *Estimates for 2006 financial years.* Yaounde: The University of Yaounde I, Cameroon.

The University of Yaounde I. (2007). *Estimates for 2007 financial years.* Yaounde: The University of Yaounde I, Cameroon.

The University of Yaounde I. (2008). *Estimates for 2008 financial years.* Yaounde: The University of Yaounde I, Cameroon.

Etienne Zé Amvela
The University of Yaounde I, Cameroon

DIMITRIOS NOUKAKIS, JEAN-FRANÇOIS RICCI
AND MARTIN DETTERLI

9. RIDING THE GLOBALIZATION WAVE: EPFL'S STRATEGY AND ACHIEVEMENTS

INTRODUCTION

The academic world is more than ever a global war for talent, international mobility of students and faculty, diversification of funding, are a few of the main features of this changing environment faced by universities. International rankings are blooming and contribute - despite their obvious limitations - to globalization as well as competition.

Nowadays three main markets are predominant: North America, with most of the world's leading universities, Asia, the fastest growing and changing academic environment with a huge potential in the near future, and Europe, with a long academic tradition. One has to cope with three different backgrounds, three challenging environments, and a global competition framework.

Europe is made up of nations with very heterogeneous cultures, traditions, languages and political systems and this multiculturalism has to be fully taken into account in the way academic organizations are defined and managed. But however strong their academic roots may be, these academic structures and organizations need to evolve in order to accommodate this new context and the challenges brought in education and research. The Bologna Declaration[1] and its ongoing implementation in 46 countries, over the last decade, initiated the emergence of the European Higher Education Area (EHEA). Much progress has been made from the early Erasmus student schemes to the creation of the European Qualifications Framework, designed to ensure academic openness and recognition of degrees across national borders, thus promoting academic and professional mobility.

This paper summarizes several of those main academic challenges, as seen by *Ecole Polytechnique Federale de Lausanne* (EPFL), a medium-sized specialized institute of technology located in the heart of Europe (albeit in a non-EU state) and aiming to become a global academic player.

CHALLENGES IN A GLOBAL WORLD

Academic institutions have defined various ways of responding to new challenges and positioning themselves in the changing global academic environment. By many standards, Switzerland is quite a special case within the EHEA. For instance, less than 20% of its 7.5 million inhabitants have a university degree,

N.C. Liu et al., (eds.), Paths to a World-Class University: Lessons from Practices
and Experiences, 177–193.

but the scientific output of its twelve universities (measured as the ratio of citations per paper) is consistently at the top of the world, in terms of quality (Nature, 2004; Science Watch, 2009). If we look at the effects of the Bologna process on the student population of Swiss universities, 20% of total enrolments are currently international students (of whom 75% are from the EHEA), whilst the "Bologna" median is just at 3% (Eurostat, 2009). Switzerland is definitely a global player in higher education and as such it has to take global trends into account.

This section gives a broad - albeit inexhaustive - view of several of the main challenges facing universities and institutes of technology, as well as a few specific measures and initiatives implemented by EPFL and other academic institutions worldwide.

Recruit the Best Students

Recruiting first rate students is and will remain one of the main competitive advantages of universities in the global education world. In this regard, some universities like Imperial College base admission on interviews and performance evaluations. However, partly because of the current legal framework in Switzerland, which grants access to higher education to all students with a Swiss baccalaureate (end of high school degree), EPFL sets the selection process on a first "propédeutique" (preparatory) year, to give all students a chance of meeting the selection criteria. Students with a foreign high school degree are admitted, but they have to pass their first preparatory year to move on. Yet for both approaches, the dilemma is to find the right process to attract and select the best students who will become the leaders, scientists, engineers or entrepreneurs of tomorrow.

Owing to this global competition, financial aid is on the agenda of most of the universities. For example, Cornell, Duke or Yale aim at education programmes that are accessible, whatever the financial circumstances of the students and their families. Princeton has developed a broad system of financial aid grants calculated on an individual basis. Despite low tuition fees (approximately $1,000 per year), recent surveys in Switzerland show that there remain social inequalities in accessing universities. Thus, there is an urgent need for a constructive debate and concrete solutions in order to give better and fairer access to higher education, both in Switzerland and in Europe. In this regard, fellowships for students from low-income families need to be further developed, in order to improve the situation.

Europe is pursuing the reform of education according to the Bologna Declaration. This new educational framework will greatly contribute to promoting and reinforcing the international mobility of students in Europe. As a consequence of this internationalization of education, more and more programmes are about to be taught in English, especially at the master's and doctoral levels. Universities will also have to enhance their creativity and find niches to emphasize their specificities. Again, the development of scholarships at the European level is a crucial step to promote the mobility of European and extra-European students within the EHEA.

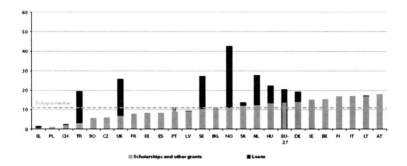

Figure 1. Public financial aid to tertiary students, by type (loans and grants), as a percentage of public expenditure on tertiary education, ISCED 5-6 - 2005 (Eurostat, 2009).

Flexibility of the curricula is another key issue in the implementation of the Bologna Declaration. With respect to this, one of the most distinctive characteristics of educational programmes at the University of Cambridge is their breadth in the first years. Here, it is acknowledged that many students do not have a clear idea of the options and topics they want to follow and the "Tripos System" gives them "the opportunity to explore some topics in a very wide way, to delay specialization or to select some other fields according to new areas of interests". Yale University provides some vertical flexibility within it programmes, whereby "[i]n addition to being able to enrol on advanced level courses, students with exceptional preparation in certain areas may be eligible to accelerate - that is, to complete their degrees and graduate early by acquiring sufficient acceleration credits". However, recent results from EUA surveys suggest that certain structural changes in the curricula (such as the widespread use of the European Credit Transfer and Accumulation System - ECTS), within the "Bologna area", are more often than not an obstacle to the development of flexible learning paths for students, whilst also making both mobility and recognition more difficult - a trend that goes against the original aims of the Bologna Declaration!

A lot of work still needs to be done, in order to effectively transform the wide range of higher education programmes into a consistent framework for Bachelor, master's and doctoral studies. As part of this reform, European universities should consider the development of true graduate schools covering both master's and doctoral programmes. It is striking to see that in most of the leading US universities graduate students account for more than 50% of the total student body.

Providing the students with an opportunity to expand their knowledge is also on the agenda of many institutions. In this regard, beyond scientific and technological competences, courses in the humanities offer the opportunity to study subjects which can make an important contribution to science and engineering students' general education and social awareness. As an example, the Imperial College humanities courses include topics, such as philosophy, ethics in science and technology, history, modern literature and drama, art and music. A very similar offer has been developed at EPFL within the SHS (social sciences and humanities) programme. University College London aims at "promoting social responsibility, global citizenship (including sustainability) and leadership in the student body, through both the formal curriculum and extra-curricular opportunities". The strategy of Duke University strives to "infuse the campus with expanded opportunities to participate in and enjoy the arts". The University of Toronto aims at "developing some understanding of the histories, cultures, values and epistemologies that shape the world we have inherited, in which we live, and which we shape". It should also be noted that this open-mindedness and flexibility also include the opportunity for the students to complete part of their curriculum abroad.

Attract and Retain the Best Faculty

Beyond statements like "our staff is our most valuable resource", universities have to innovate in order to attract and retain their best staff, especially faculty and researchers. As a consequence of globalization and international recruitment, institutions have to benchmark their start-up and hard money packages in order to be competitive worldwide. This also includes considering spouse programmes together with competitive salaries.

European universities should also develop a clear framework for academic promotion. With respect to this, EPFL has adopted the US three-level faculty system, including the development of a true tenure-track approach aimed at giving young scientists the autonomy and academic freedom to develop their own research and teaching.

Promote Innovation and Reinforce Technology Transfer

Innovation is a key driver for the economy and society, and universities play a crucial role at the very origin of the economic and industrial pipeline. Many institutions have therefore developed specific initiatives to support knowledge and technology transfer projects in their very early stages. Interdisciplinarity is a buzzword in all institutional visions and strategies, for beyond cutting-edge research within scientific domains, more and more discoveries occur at the interface between disciplines. Many institutions, including Imperial College, Yale University, KTH Stockholm, Duke University and MIT promote such interdisciplinarity beyond structural organizations, through dedicated centres and programmes. EPFL launched several initiatives in the field of design, information security, global health, cognitive neuroscience, neuroprosthetics, space research and energy: they aim at bringing together scientists and researchers from various fields and domains in order to develop innovative solutions and ideas.

Develop Strategic Partnerships

Strategic partnerships are increasingly becoming part of the academic environment. Academic alliances are expanding beyond countries and continents, but national collaborations both with other academic institutions as well as with industries are also relevant. Partly because of the results of most rankings, Europe has been used to looking west, but the current global trends and developments mean that its universities also have to learn to look east, in order to explore their partnership options with Asian universities: developing joint degrees, creating joint research programmes and joint laboratories, offering courses and programmes in Asian studies as well as providing incentives for these developments.

Become Less Dependent on State Funding

The current constraints of public financing for higher education and research is putting major pressure on universities and beyond rationalization programmes and efficiency increases - typical economic approaches - European universities are having to find new sources of funding. The Bologna reforms and increased student mobility have raised the question of tuition fees, which are today quite heterogeneous even within the EHEA. Another issue is the development of fundraising and sponsorship for chairs, fellowships or even buildings. Such external funding should greatly contribute to creating real endowments, which would significantly increase the flexibility and reactivity of European universities. Despite significant success for a few rare European institutions, major cultural change is still needed to give the universities substantial financial leverage.

Improve the Management of Universities

Because of the complexity of both the internal academic world as well as the external political environment, managing a university requires strong commitment and leadership. But such leadership is also needed at all levels of any institution, partly owing to the need to manage rapid change, thus promoting, developing and even training professional university administrators should, more than ever, receive great attention.

As part of the necessary management of change, internal communication is a key component of any corporate culture, but this notion is often quite difficult and complex to manage in an open academic environment. Cornell University and UC Berkeley, for instance, have created an Employee Assembly - a mechanism for the informal exchange of information and views between employees and university administrators. However, whatever the channels of this internal communication, this should never be taken for granted and thus universities should consider duplicating and multiplying communication channels, in order to reach out to a majority of the institutional community.

European universities often have deep historical roots and over the centuries they have usually developed well-respected traditions, which are definitely part of their corporate culture and identity. Nevertheless, these traditions can also strongly restrain the university's top/senior management from undertaking the reforms needed due to external change. Beyond retaining their corporate identity, universities should therefore develop a more flexible organization. Together with this evolution, the university's top/senior management will have to integrate more and more characteristics and tools derived from the economy and the business world.

Through the "Workforce Planning Initiative", Cornell University has been developing "a global strategy in order to achieve sustainable improvement in both the effectiveness and the efficiency of campus wide support functions". At Yale University, senior management and the unions agreed "to launch and support a strategic initiative aiming at improving the overall quality, efficiency and workplace culture". Within the UK national context VfM - Value for Money is the term used to assess "whether or not an organization has obtained the maximum benefit from the goods and services it acquires and/or provides, within the resources available to it". Here once again, staff commitment, awareness and participation are crucial for real success and implementation.

Data management and information systems have become unavoidable components of any university's senior management good practice: finance, human resources, student management and academic information, but also research grants, contracts as well as governance indicators, belong to this data management portfolio. The integration and combination of these large amounts of data and their use to competitive advantage is another challenge for the university senior management team. However, this information is also required for the purpose of public reporting. For instance, in Switzerland, within the framework of the four-year performance contract, the ETH Domain - ETHZ, EPFL and the four Research Institutes[2] - reports its performance to parliament on a yearly basis.

Local Responsibility and Commitment

Last but not least, universities have important social responsibilities towards local and regional communities. Many North American universities have developed significant commitments for a number of years: Duke University through the "Duke-Durham Neighbourhood Partnership", Caltech through its Office of Public Relations, and Princeton through the Office of Community and Regional Affairs (CRA), are a few examples of this culture of openness. Despite very different backgrounds and history, European universities are increasingly playing a significant citizen role towards their local and regional communities.

ON ORGANIZATIONS, STRUCTURES AND MANAGEMENT

Many of these challenges require special efforts in shaping and re-organizing academic institutions and the way they are managed. Because of the fast changing environment, European universities are increasingly having to reflect on their mission and role in and for society, develop strategies and define goals, as well as adapt their structures and management.

University organizations are people structures, where students, faculty and researchers as well as technical and administrative staff, belong to the same complex and changing academic environment. Together with at times very deep historical backgrounds, they all contribute to creating a unique organization in size, networks, competences, leadership and culture. Despite a very broad range of organizations, one may ask what are the common organizational features of institutions like Oxford University, MIT or Nanyang Technological University? In other words, are there any common organizational criteria that could contribute to success and international recognition?

In order to move towards these objectives, structure and organization need to be carefully defined. According to Laurie J. Mullins (2004), "structure is the pattern of relationship among positions in the organization and among members of the organization. Structure makes possible the application of the process of management and creates a framework of order and command through which the activities of the organization can be planned, organized, directed and controlled. The structure defines tasks and responsibilities, work roles and relationships, and channels of communication". A variety of structures can obviously fit into this very general and global framework. A study by Burns and Stalker (1966) described two extreme and divergent systems of management practice and structure: the mechanistic system (a rigid structure with features often assimilated to bureaucracy) and the organic system (a more fluid structure appropriate to changing conditions). Whereas the former pattern is more appropriate for stable conditions, the latter is more suitable for tackling new problems and situations. In reality, most organizations combine characteristics of the two extreme patterns of mechanistic and organic systems.

Universities are a very typical example of such a hybrid organization, where the unique combination of academic and administrative staff creates a very interesting - but complex - pattern. On the one hand, the academic staff often feel that organic structures are the only framework they can effectively work within. That is, loose coordination and as little bureaucracy as possible are considered to be the most suitable organizational, along with the granting of academic freedom. On the other hand, the technical and administrative staffs have a central function in keeping the organization operational, but they often have difficulties in integrating a real customer-oriented culture to specific academic needs. This dilemma is a potential source of tension and misunderstanding, and a perpetual challenge for universities of today.

Defining a structure and an organization is a first step, but it is not enough and synergies, collaborations and interactions need to take place so as to form an effective integrated system. Lawrence and Lorsch (1969) described the parameter of integration as "the quality of the state of collaboration that exists among departments that are required to achieve unity of effort by the demands of the environment. It is the degree of co-ordination between different departments with interdependent tasks. The mechanisms used to achieve integration depend on the amount of integration required and the difficulty in achieving it.
- In mechanistic structures, integration may be attempted through the use of policies, rules and procedures;
- In organic structures, integration may be attempted through teamwork and mutual co-operation; and
- As the requirements for the amount of integration increase, additional means may be adopted, such as formal lateral relations, committees and project teams."

In every system and organization, achieving the right balance and level of integration is crucial. Redundancy and unnecessary complexity as a result of too much integration may easily lead to frustration and additional costs. However too low a level of integration can result in loose and inefficient coordination, which leads to wasting of resources by the organization as a whole. In sum, every institution has to define and find the right balance, which mostly depends on historical background and academic tradition, political governance and legal framework, as well as its corporate culture and internal structure.

EPFL'S INGREDIENTS FOR BECOMING A WORLD-CLASS UNIVERSITY

Structural Reorganization - Break Departmental Barriers

In its mission statement, EPFL aims to:
– Educate and train future scientists, engineers and architects;
– Conduct cutting-edge research; and
– Transfer knowledge to create jobs and companies.

The management of EPFL has reinterpreted these three missions to position them in the global, internationalization trend of the academic landscape. Since 2000, its management is composed of the president and four vice-presidents (the direction), who are assisted by a general secretary and a general council. From the academic point of view, the old departments were reorganized in 5 schools, each of them managed by a dean with extended power and autonomy (see Figure 2).

Note: For the sake of simplicity, several functions have been omitted. There are several transdisciplinary centres but only two are shown to illustrate the principle.

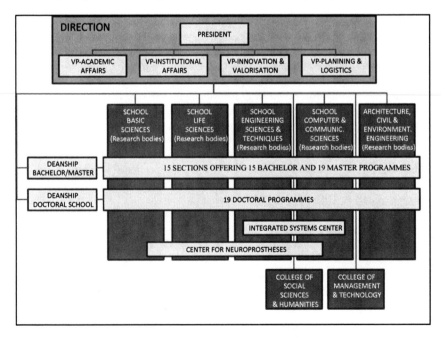

Figure 2. Organizational structure of EPFL in 2009.

These schools are vertical structures that carry, essentially, the research efforts at EPFL, whilst the educational aspects are dealt with by transversal structures, such as the sections and programmes - the latter draw the necessary resources from the schools to elaborate and offer the educational content necessary for a first-class education. Similarly, transversal structures have been created to promote trans-disciplinary research initiatives, which are centres (such as those for biotechnology and bioengineering, or neuroprosthetics) operating across two or several faculties, bringing together complementary competencies and sharing infrastructure and expertise.

The net outcome of such a matrix structure is an increased number of inter-faculty connections, which in turn leads to a high number of creative educational and research initiatives of an interdisciplinary nature. Of course, there is a cost to pay for managing through such a complex structure, and this often translates into additional internal communication efforts and sometimes decisional delays.

Bring in Complementary Competencies

Not all the ingredients and competencies necessary for the realization of EPFL's project were present at the beginning of this millennium. For instance, there was little activity in life sciences, the non-engineering parts of exact sciences were hosted by the University of Lausanne, and there were no internal competencies in social sciences. Taking advantage of a vast reorganization plan for the academic landscape at the regional level geared towards setting up an academic network between Geneva and Lausanne, EPFL managed to bring in several of its missing competencies, either by acquisition or by creating new structures:

- Creation of the School of Life Sciences in 2002, in coordination with the university hospitals of Lausanne and Geneva. This School is now composed of four transdisciplinary institutes, hosts 40 research groups, offers 1 bachelor degree, 2 master's curricula, 3 doctoral schools, and is a dynamic growth driver;
- Creation of the Colleges of Social Sciences and Humanities as well as the College of Management of Technology (CDM). Whilst the mission of the former is to provide the courses necessary to develop the students' soft skills, the latter is now playing a key role in the development plans of EPFL's research and educational activities in the areas of entrepreneurship and finance;
- Transfer of the Departments of Chemistry, Physics and Mathematics of the University of Lausanne to the School of Basic Sciences;
- Transfer of the ISREC (the Swiss institute for experimental cancer research) to the School of Life Sciences; and
- Integration of the IMT (Institute of Microtechnology of the University of Neuchâtel) into the School of Engineering.

By bringing in complementary competencies, adding new entities, and shedding off some of its own, EPFL has contributed to the consolidation of the regional academic landscape and the creation of strong academic clusters. At the same time, it reached a critical mass in many research domains and was also able to work out innovative and attractive educational programmes. As a consequence, EPFL is becoming increasingly successful in attracting research funds, renowned scientists and a good number of outstanding students.

Recruitment Strategy of Junior and Senior International Faculty

As Professor Donald Kennedy put it, "a university is its faculty"! The trans-formation of EPFL could not have happened without putting in place the appropriate schemes that allowed an aggressive hiring policy of world-class senior faculty members, as well as attracting promising young scientists. EPFL's senior manage-ment and the school deans were able to attract several of the world's finest scientists onto the campus by offering competitive packages in terms of salary, start-up and hard money, top-rated facilities and technical infrastructure, in a very stimulating and open environment. As a result, the faculty has become increasingly international, as can be seen in Figure 3. Moreover, this evolution towards "anti-inbreeding" in the recruitment of professors facilitates contacts with other worldwide partners, as well as enhancing EPFL's knowledge and comprehension of the global academic landscape.

In parallel, EPFL introduced the position of "tenure-track assistant professor" (or PATT, its French acronym), in an effort to bring onto campus several of the world's best young researchers. In these cases, the offer included a competitive salary, start-up money and facilities, as well as mentoring by senior faculty members. Both programmes have proved extremely successful, with the école growing from 143 professors in 2000 to 266 faculty members by December 2008, of whom 60 are PATTs and through this process, 63% of EPFL's faculty has been renewed. The benefits of having a body of young and motivated scientists onboard can be

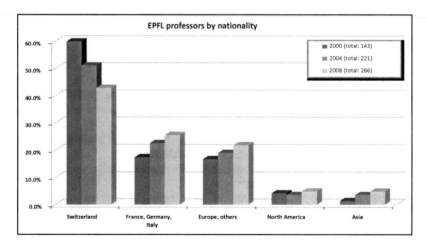

Figure 3. Evolution of the origin (nationality) of EPFL professors: Snapshots as of December 2000, 2004, 2008.

seen by their outstanding success rate in obtaining funding through the prestigious ERC advanced grants: in 2008 EPFL attracted more ERC advanced grants than any other institution in Europe!

Table 1. Number of European Research Council advanced grants awarded in 2008 by host institution

Rank	Institution	ERC advanced grants
1.	EPFL - Ecole Polytechnique Fédérale de Lausanne (Switzerland)	11
2.	Weizmann Institute of Science (Israel)	8
3.	ETHZ - Eidgenössische Technische Hochschule Zürich (Switzerland)	7
	University of Oxford (UK)	7
5.	Imperial College London (UK)	6
6.	University of Cambridge (UK)	5
7.	Université Catholique de Louvain (Belgium)	4
	Université de Genève (Switzerland)	4
	Helsinki University of Technology (Finland)	4
	University College London (UK)	4

Development of a Structured Doctoral School

Whilst in the past the education of doctoral students was the responsibility of the individual laboratories and research groups, the direction of EPFL recognized the need to reform doctoral education. This resulted in the establishment of EPFL's Doctoral School which was formalized in 2003 with the creation of 17 doctoral programmes under the leadership of a central dean and doctoral programme directors. It aims to provide high educational standards (curriculum, content, and teachers) and to ensure sustained growth so as to rapidly reach its optimum size.

The key objectives of the Doctoral School are:
– To provide structured education at doctorate level that contributes to the development of the students as future researchers and professionals;
– To guarantee the highest possible quality of standards for student recruitment and to coordinate the promotional activities and branding of graduate education at EPFL;
– To provide adequate support and supervision to doctoral students within a well-defined academic framework; and
– To create a network of doctoral students throughout EPFL.

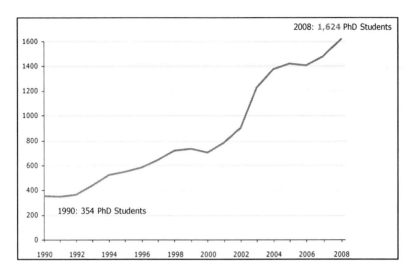

Figure 4. EPFL's population of doctoral students has multiplied four-fold since 1990.

Note: In 2008, doctoral students represent nearly 25% of the total student body (10% in 1990)

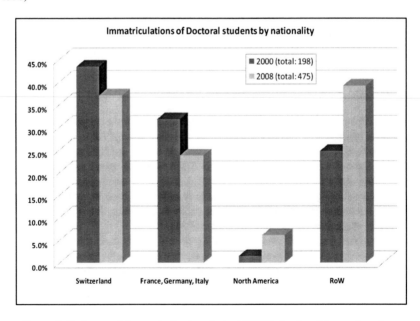

Figure 5. Evolution of the origin (nationality) of EPFL's intake of doctoral students: snapshots as of December 2000 and as of the 2008 creation of centres and programmes as strategic tools for academic cross-fertilization.

The results of the new organization are already clearly visible with the number and quality of applications to the doctoral programmes steadily increasing. EPFL is now also reaching populations of doctoral students far beyond its past regional attraction pool (see Figure 5). Even more importantly, the creation of the Doctoral School enabled senior management and faculty members to rethink the entire process and to reflect on the very nature of doctoral education (expected educational outcomes, standards of excellence) and to come up with concrete solutions to long-standing issues.

As illustrated in Figure 2, the creation of centres with well-defined structures spreading across several schools is a valuable tool for promoting research at the frontiers of established disciplines. Not only do these centres provide a framework for faculty members to work on interdisciplinary projects, but they also provide the critical mass to secure research funding in Switzerland and abroad. Moreover, because of their specialization and higher visibility, the centres are also becoming an excellent gateway to establishing links with other research institutions. Furthermore, they form good teaching and advising platforms for students engaged in research across different domains.

EPFL currently hosts a range of centres such as the:
- Space Centre;
- Bernoulli Centre;
- Microscopy and Surface Analysis;
- Energy Centre;
- Micronano Technology;
- Global Computing Centre;
- Integrated Systems Centre;
- Plasma Physics Research Centre;
- Neuroprosthetics;
- NCCR[3] Quantum Photonics;
- Centre of Translational Biomechanics;
- CIBM[4] (Centre for Biomedical Imaging);
- CMMX3 (Competence Centre for Materials Science and Technology);
- NCCR MICS (Mobile Information and Communication Systems); and
- NCCR Molecular Oncology.

Besides the centres, several other programmes have been launched with the objective of pulling together students and researchers around interdisciplinary research projects, including:
- Nano-Tera (Engineering and IT to improve the health and security of humans and the environment);
- Sport and Rehabilitation Engineering programme;
- Blue Brain Project (The first comprehensive attempt to reverse-engineer the mammalian brain);
- Alinghi (Scientific partnership for the America's Cup);
- Solar Impulse (Flying round the world in an airplane solely powered by solar energy); and
- Hydroptère (The fastest sailing boat on the planet).

The above all contribute to the development of a culture that puts innovative thinking to tackling the scientific challenges at the centre of the educational and research process. Beyond developing new scientific topics at the interface between domains, such initiatives are also very successful in providing concrete results for the economy and industry.

Expansion of Technology Transfer Activities

The third mission of EPFL consists in creating wealth, jobs and companies by transferring the ideas and technologies stemming from its laboratories to the industrial and economic networks. EPFL's Vice-Presidency for Innovation and Technology Transfer has recently developed several tools to close the innovation gap: science translator officers as a bridge between business technology needs and scientific research potential and, as an additional component to the more traditional technology transfer activities, new schemes for the management of IP, creation of Innogrants as a custom-tailored support for the best EPFL entrepreneurs, better access to the local SME network, etc.

For example, EPFL hosts Alliance, a Swiss initiative that groups universities of applied science in Western Switzerland, in order to facilitate contact between regional industries and research institutes. Under this arrangement, experts with many years of industrial experience visit companies to understand their needs and link them with the best-suited research laboratories. Through this industrial liaison programme, valuable exchanges of information between industries and scientists are created, enabling innovations to be brought to the market.

As another example of support for innovation, EPFL launched Innogrants, a programme of internal seed funds, which provides generous support to EPFL's best entrepreneurs through a network of expertise and grants tailored to the financial and technical needs of the inventions and to the management of innovation. Moreover, Innogrants encourage researchers to explore promising technologies at the interface of traditional academic fields.

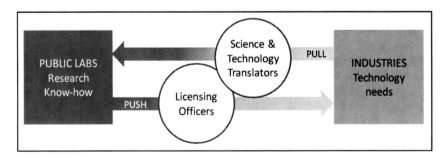

Figure 6. Collaboration with SMEs – Alliance.

Note: This is a scheme that ensures technology transfer and industrial liaison between the local research communities and the local industrial network.

Finally, different models of strategic partnerships have been developed with the aim of attracting leading industries to the EPFL campus. The goal is to establish relationships that go beyond one single laboratory in order to foster innovation, technology transfer and knowledge exchange. Such models can be in the form of a multidisciplinary research initiative, a technology incubator, or a sponsored centre of expertise. Good examples have materialized through projects with global companies such as Nestlé, Logitech, Merck Serono and Nokia.

The results of all these initiatives are clearly visible and have put EPFL in a good position within the European innovation environment.

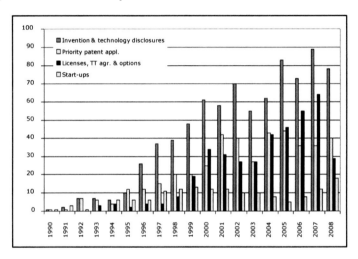

Figure 7. Technology transfer activity at EPFL.

Note: Over the last 10 years, an average of 12 companies were created every year. During this period the number of invention and technology disclosures, priority patents applications, and licences and TT agreements and options went up by a factor of between two and three

CONCLUSIONS

Whilst in a not-so-distant past, competition for funds and talent, as well as performance benchmarking, were limited within national borders, today the academic landscape looks more like a global competition battlefield. The reasons for such a situation are numerous and include among others: globalization of educational services, emergence of an international labour market for knowledge and talent, and demographic challenges in developed economies. The implications of the Bologna Declaration are also far-reaching, as they affect mobility within Europe and competition for European and non-European students.

As many countries are trying to become educational hubs, competition for students is becoming tough, even more so in attracting the very best. Interestingly, several of these potential educational hubs could end up being in Asia and in Eastern Europe.

International rankings also play an increasing role, as they provide the metrics (whether appropriate or not) for international comparisons. Governments react to these rankings and adjust their policies to tailor entities that can be positioned as global players, thus departing from the mission of providing education for their national market. However, according to Van Raan (2009), given the current global academic capacity, the world cannot sustain more than about 200 world-class universities. In other words, as the limiting factor for building world-class universities is the number of world-class scientists, competition for the best minds is expected to grow!

To become and remain part of the world's academic elite, institutions have to come up with a well thought out model, and count on visionary management and dedicated staff for flawless execution. One could agree that EPFL has proven that such a plan is feasible and can be successful, with reorganization into 5 schools with strong management; creation of centres and programmes as strategic tools for academic cross-fertilization; implementation of a highly competitive recruitment strategy for international junior and senior faculty; development of a structured doctoral school; and partnerships with first-class local and global institutions, being amongst its achievements.

Within the last decade, EFPL has reinvented itself by asserting its mission, changing its structure and developing a new corporate culture. Not only is it well positioned in the academic rankings, and is now considered a top quality educational and research hub in the heart of Europe, and most importantly, it makes significant contributions to the industrial development and economic growth of the entire Lake Geneva area.

NOTES

[1] The Bologna Declaration of June 1999 has put in motion a series of reforms needed to make European Higher Education more compatible and comparable, more competitive and more attractive for Europeans and for students and scholars from other continents. The three priorities of the Bologna process are: introduction of the three cycle system (bachelor/master/doctorate), quality assurance and recognition of qualifications and periods of study.
(http://www.ond.vlaanderen.be/hogeronderwijs/bologna/)

[2] The ETH Domain is composed of two institutes of technology: EPF Lausanne and ETH Zurich; and four research institutions: PSI - the Paul Scherrer Institute, Eawag - Aquatic Research, EMPA - the Swiss Federal Laboratories for Materials Testing and Research, and WSL - the Swiss Federal Institute for Forest, Snow and Landscape Research. The ETH Board is the strategic management and supervisory body of the ETH-Domain. It is responsible for fulfilling and implementing the science policy performance mandate set by the federal council and the federal parliament and for the four-year strategy and allocation of federal funding for the ETH-Domain.

[3] NCCR - National Centre of Competence in Research.

[4] An ETH Domain Competence Centre.

REFERENCES

Burns, T., & Stalker, G. M., (1966). *The management of innovation*. Tavistock Publications.

Eurostat. (2009). The Bologna process in higher education in Europe - Key indicators on the social dimension and mobility.

Lawrence, P. R., & Lorsch, J. W. (1969). *Organization and environment*. Irwin.

Mullins, L. J. (2004). Management and organisational behaviour. In *Financial Times*, 7th ed. Prentice Hall.

Nature. (2004). 430, 311–316., and Sciencewatch.com, Thomson Reuters. (2009)

Science Watch (2009) Country profiles: Top 20 countries in all fields, 1999-August 31, 2009. Retrieved from http://sciencewatch.com/dr/cou/2009/09decALL/.

Van Raan, A. F. J. (2009). Ranking and classification of universities based on advanced bibliometric mapping. *Proceedings of the Leiden University 3rd International Symposium on University Rankings.*

Dimitrios Noukakis
Office of International Affairs and Accrediation
EPFL - Ecole Polytechnique Fédérale de Lausanne, Lausanne, Switzerland

Jean-François Ricci
Secretary General
EPFL - Ecole Polytechnique Fédérale de Lausanne, Lausanne, Switzerland

Martin Vetterli
School of Computer and Communication Sciences
EPFL - Ecole Polytechnique Fédérale de Lausanne, Lausanne, Switzerland

CHRIS MARLIN

10. WORLD-CLASS RESEARCH PERFORMANCE THROUGH RESEARCH FOCUS AND THE STRATEGIC USE OF RESEARCH RESOURCES

INTRODUCTION

Many universities are adopting a more strategic approach to focussing their invest-ment in research, as part of improving the research performance of the university and hence being able to compete more successfully as a world-class university. However, focussing research activity in universities necessarily means concentrating research resources (including not only funding, but also staffing and other forms of support and investment) on some areas of research, at the expense of others. Given that this concentration of resources will be as much about what is not being supported as it is about the areas that do receive support, it is important that the academic schools of the university are engaged in the decisions about this resource concentration.

Flinders University is an Australian university which has improved its research performance through a process of focussing its research activity and investment on a relatively small number of areas and these, termed Areas of Strategic Research Investment (ASRIs), were chosen through a competitive process with clear criteria. This paper describes aspects of the Flinders approach to identifying and supporting these areas of research focus, concentrating particularly on how the various forms of research resources were invested differentially and how the broader academic community was engaged in the process of their selection.

The first part of the paper discusses the reasons why universities seeking to improve their research performance are opting to channel their available resources in support of research in a limited number of areas. The context of Flinders Univer-sity at the beginning of the process in 2002 is then described, as is the approach employed to identify the areas on which the resources were to be targeted. Finally, some comments are offered on the effect of this strategy on the research perfor-mance of this institution.

FOCUSSING RESEARCH - WHY DO IT?

Universities aspiring to be world-class are increasingly focussing their investment in research, which means directing more of their research support into a restricted set of activities, thereby reducing the amount of such resources available for other areas. There are many factors that are prompting universities to take such action, the principal ones being as follows:

N.C. Liu et al., (eds.), Paths to a World-Class University: Lessons from Practices and Experiences, 195–203.
© 2011 Sense Publishers. All rights reserved.

- Many fields of research are becoming very expensive, making it difficult for most universities to establish and maintain the necessary infrastructure across a large number of such areas, especially those where the number of researchers at the institution using the infrastructure is relatively small.
- The marketplace for research funding, particularly that for large-scale projects from governments and private sponsors for establishing centres of excellence of various kinds, is becoming progressively more competitive. Thus, universities are driven to promote their research capabilities in ways that distinguish them from other competing institutions. Consequently, the formation of differentiated collections of areas of research focus can be useful in that they project a distinctive research profile, contributing to what Connell (2004) calls "shaping a distinctive and well integrated institutional profile".
- Some governments have encouraged the universities within their respective higher education systems to differentiate themselves from other universities within the system, in terms of the areas of research on which the institution is focussed and into which it is investing government funding. For example, such a process began in Australia with the Green Paper on research (Kemp, 1999a) and the subsequent White Paper (Kemp, 1999b), which encouraged universities to set their own strategic directions in research, form judgements as to their particular strengths and capabilities in research, and to allocate resources accordingly.

Despite these compelling reasons to focus the research activities of a university, the internal process of doing so can still be quite controversial and potentially disruptive to its research performance in the short term. There is understandably a tension between the desire of the university management to improve research performance as a whole on the one hand, and the desire of individual researchers to pursue their own research agenda on the other hand. For, as noted by Taylor (2006), research is "an intensely personal activity, strongly dependent on the ideas and imagination of individuals or groups of individuals" and it "does not lend itself to control and management". In other words, universities often rely heavily on the drive and enthusiasm that researchers have for their research activities; as Hogan and Clark (1996) point out, research initiatives are usually generated by individual academics who grasp the best opportunities as and when they come along.

FOCUSSING RESOURCES - WHAT CAN BE FOCUSSED?

As already mentioned above, some of the reasons for focussing research relate to being able to concentrate limited resources on fewer areas and thus, there is a strong link between focussing research and focussing resources. In fact, it is the view of some that this is the sole purpose of focussing research; for example, Hogan and Clark (1996) state that the purpose of a research plan is "to set priorities for development and influence the deployment of resources". Nevertheless, within each university there are typically many different kinds of resources being used to support research:

- One of the more obvious sources is externally-derived funding, often referred to as *research income* and in this regard, Taylor (2006) says that "much research income is 'in and out', to be spent on a particular grant or contract". Moreover, because these funds have been obtained for a specific purpose, there is not much that can be done to redirect them strategically. However, in some cases, there may be "overheads" or other charges imposed by the institution and these may be used to invest strategically.

– Another obvious source of research support frequently available is a central university fund specifically set aside for this purpose, often known as the university's *research budget*. There are typically many demands on this budget, but it is also a resource which can, at least to some extent, be used strategically.

– As noted by Shattock (2003), there has been an increasing tendency to devolve detailed decision-making about resource allocation downward, as universities have grown larger. That is, there are resources which are distributed across the institution, particularly within the academic areas, and hence there is the potential for these resources to be used strategically. Although these resources will include some discretionary funding, the most important is usually that represented by the *staff time for research*, the monetary value of which will often dominate the resources available to academic areas.

Any process of focussing resources is, of course, as much about what is not being supported as it is about the areas that do receive support and hence may well cause some tensions within the institution, as already mentioned. Thus, it is important that the academic staff of the university is engaged in the decisions about resource concentration.

CASE STUDY: FLINDERS UNIVERSITY

Flinders University is located in Adelaide, South Australia, and was established in 1966 during a period of nationwide expansion of higher education. Over the period 2002–2009, the university embarked upon a process of identifying a collection of targeted areas in which to differentially invest its research resources. This collection of areas of research focus was termed the Areas of Strategic Research Investment (ASRIs), signifying that they were being identified for the purposes of selective investment.

This section describes the context for the institution, both in terms of its positioning within the Australian higher education system and its performance at the beginning of this process. It then outlines the path taken to identify the ASRIs and finally presents some information on the impact of adopting this targeted strategy in relation to the research performance of the university as a whole.

Policy and Funding Context in Australia

As already mentioned above, the Australian Government signalled, over the period 1999 to 2002, an expectation that universities would identify their areas of research focus and invest accordingly. This occurred, for example, through reporting mechanisms, such as Research and Research Training Management Reports, which were obligatory for institutions receiving government funding for research purposes and

required reporting on each of the following, so as to identify "areas of research strength" (DEST, 2005):
- Numbers of research students;
- Research income;
- Research-active staff; and
- Qualifications and activity of staff who supervised research students.

Furthermore, this period involved government policy shifts away from an emphasis on traditional grant sources towards a broader view of the kind of research success which would garner government support. Moreover, significantly, this also coincided with a period in which the pressure on traditional funding sources increased as a result of the greater volume of demands coming from a substantially expanded higher education sector. These factors meant that non-traditional sources of research funding took on increasing importance.

Flinders University within the Australian Higher Education System

Flinders University is a relatively small university within the Australian system of around 40 universities. In terms of staffing, for example, in 2002 it had a little over 2% of the staff within the Australian higher education system and was ranked 24th for size, on the basis of academic staff; that is, there are certainly much larger universities in the Australian higher education system. Furthermore, by 2002, it was clear that the university was progressively representing a smaller and smaller proportion of the Australian system, in the sense that its size relative to other Australian universities was decreasing. Despite its relatively small size, it had maintained a wide range of disciplines and consequently had attempted to support a similarly wide range of areas of research. One measure of discipline spread relative to size is illustrated in Figure 1, where the number of staff is plotted against the number of fields of education taught, for each Australian university in 2002[1]. Flinders University is circled in this figure, showing that it was teaching in about half of the possible fields of education, but it had less than 30% of the staff of the largest Australian university. Consequently, the number of staff contributing to research within most of the disciplines covered by Flinders was relatively small compared to competitor universities. Furthermore, most of these areas of research were under-resourced, when compared with what would have been required to establish them as research concentrations of national and international significance. For these and other reasons, the university was not performing as well as would have been expected, in relation to playing a leading role in the national centres of excellence which were being established at this time (e.g., within the Cooperative Research Centres programme).

Nevertheless, despite these issues the university maintained a good position in national and international ranking systems, being ranked ninth overall in the Melbourne Institute rankings of Australian universities in 2004 (Williams and Van Dyke, 2004) and 2005 (Williams and Van Dyke, 2005), for example. Moreover, in the Shanghai Jiao Tong University's 2004 Academic Rankings of World Universities, it was placed between 12th and 14th in Australia and between 404th and 502nd in the world.

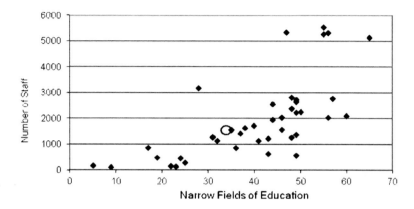

Figure 1. Narrow fields of education vs. numbers of academic staff for Australian universities, 2002.

Focussing Research at Flinders University

By about 2002, it was clear that Flinders University needed to focus its research and not only was there encouragement from the Australian government to do so, but, more importantly, it was finding it increasingly difficult to support the wide range of areas of research which had grown to expect this support. It was also becoming increasingly important to be able to project itself externally as having a particular set of research concentrations, as part of positioning the institution in the external environment.

The first attempt at identifying the areas for research focus, the ASRIs, took place over the first half of 2002 and total of 23 ASRIs were selected through a process which involved a special-purpose committee that examined research performance data for the university. This process also involved extensive discussion across the university, with Flinders University Council members, the major academic committees and other groups and there was an article written for the main internal publication explaining the process and inviting input. Nevertheless, when the 23 ASRIs were announced, there was a wide-spread negative reaction, mostly to the effect that the researchers had not understood that the process was going on and that they had not been consulted. Consequently, the results of this first attempt were put aside and another approach was adopted; this experience is consistent with Mintrom's (2008) comment that "university administrators must be realistic about how much management-driven change they can impose upon the research function at any given time".

The second, very successful, approach was carried out over the period 2004 to 2005 and involved groups of researchers getting together, typically as a result of some orchestration by the leadership within their faculty or at the university-wide level, subsequently submitting a proposal for funding to establish an ASRI. Thus, this was essentially a bottom-up process with direct financial incentives, as opposed

199

to the largely top-down process used at the first attempt. As a result, the ASRI selection process became much more like the kind of competitive grant process so familiar to successful researchers and hence they appeared to be much more comfortable in engaging in it.

A single set of clear criteria, summarized in Figure 2, was used across the five rounds of consideration of proposals for ASRIs over the two-year period and the consistency of these criteria and their application by the panel considering proposals was deemed essential. Feedback to unsuccessful bids in each of the first four rounds (the fifth round was only for ASRIs which had been proposed previously) led to a process of significant institutional learning over the two year period about what kinds of proposals were likely to be successful.

The selection of the ASRIs was carried out by a panel consisting of the Deputy Vice-Chancellor (Research), the head of the research office, the heads of the four faculties and three members external to the university. Because of the significant research resources represented by the staff time for research, it was considered important that the heads of the faculties be full participants in the decision-making process and hence be committed to supporting those ASRIs that were selected. Equally important was the involvement of the external members of this panel, because their presence discouraged deals of convenience between the heads of the faculties.

(a) the impact of the proposed ASRI on the research activity of the University, in terms of the number of researchers and the extent to which the research activity of each will be enhanced;

(b) how the proposed ASRI draws on the University's research capability to define an area which is distinctive for the University;

(c) how the proposed ASRI will benefit the University's postgraduate research students;

(d) the extent to which the University has national or international recognition for our leadership in the area covered by the proposed ASRI, or the extent to which such leadership can be developed;

(e) how investment in the proposed ASRI will return benefit to the University;

(f) the existing research strengths on which the proposed ASRI builds;

(g) the synergy between the proposed ASRI and areas of education - either undergraduate or postgraduate - which are distinctive for the University;

(h) whether the University is likely to be a major contributor in the area covered by the proposed ASRI for the next several years.

Figure 2. Criteria used in the ASRI selection process.

Funding the Areas of Strategic Research Investment

The initial funding available to the ASRIs was up to $100,000 per year for three years, with all of this funding coming from the central research budget and the average annual amount granted was approximately two-thirds of this maximum. Some of the faculties also contributed additional funding in this initial phase and this was taken by the panel to be a positive sign of that faculty's commitment to the proposed ASRI. Although there were no constraints on the nature of the funding requests submitted with the proposals, a pattern soon emerged: virtually all of the ASRIs principally wanted someone to assist both with internal networking of members and identifying external funding opportunities. These *research facilitators* were variously called either research development officers or business development managers, the role of whom is explored in more detail in Marlin (2009). Even though some faculties contributed to supporting the ASRIs in various ways, the core funding was entirely from the central research budget and ultimately, there were 17 ASRIs, as listed in Figure 3, thus illustrating that the amount of central funding required was substantial. However, the same central research budget also provided for allocations to faculties for research and therefore the latter's discretionary budget was substantially decreased as more and more of the former went to fund the ASRIs. This trend reached its peak in 2007 when about $1.2M was taken annually from the research budget for the ASRIs.

As a result of this process, some faculty-based schemes which had been responsible for distributing fairly small amounts of research funding to reasonably large numbers of researchers, were abandoned. This outcome contributed significantly to the overall effect of aggregating support to a smaller number of areas of research and hence allocating more and more of the university's research resources on a strategic basis. It also led to a much greater alignment of research strategy and strategic allocation of resources between the central university executive and the faculties.

As the initial three-year period of centrally-funded investment in the ASRIs was coming to an end for the first tranche, discussions were held with the faculties to determine the extent to which they would be prepared to support this group of

Aboriginal Health Research Unit	Bioknowledge
Applied Cognitive Psychology	Educational Futures
Cancer Control Alliance	Eye and Vision
Clinical Change & Health Care	Health and Society
Coastal & Catchment Environments	Immune Strategies
Cultural Heritage & Cultural Exchange	International Asia Pacific
Medical Devices & Technologies	Musculoskeletal Health
Nanostructures & Molecular Interactions	Neuroscience
Social Monitoring & Policy Futures	

Figure 3. The Areas of Strategic Research Investment (ASRIs) for Flinders University.

ASRIs more directly. The specific form of these discussions was to establish how much funding the faculties would be prepared to put into each ASRI, if this were to be matched equally from the central research budget. Thus, there was a transition from the ASRIs being centrally funded to their being supported through co-investment with the faculties. This approach ensured that those ASRIs that continued to be funded were those that the faculties really supported and resulted in even more strategic use of faculty research funding over time, thereby continuing the process that was begun during the initial phase of ASRI development.

Impact on Research Performance

In terms of whether the ASRI strategy and the consequent concentration of research support has been a success, it is clear that the ASRIs have had a significant positive impact on the research performance of Flinders University. For example, Flinders University's research income performance has improved very significantly since the ASRIs were introduced, with a 67% increase over the last three years; the approach has been particularly effective in developing new contract research with government and industry, where the increase has been 83% over the last three years for which data is available. For further discussion of this impact, see Marlin (2009).

CONCLUDING COMMENTS

Focussing research - and the resources which support it - is a key strategy for universities attempting to improve their research performance, and hence increase their international standing and relative position. This paper has explored some of the issues to be considered when conducting strategic research planning with the goal of focussing a university's research activities, such as identifying the sources of research support which may be concentrated and engaging the university research community in the process of selecting the areas of focus.

The experience in developing a particular approach to focussing research - involving the creation of a collection of Areas of Strategic Research Investment (ASRIs) - at Flinders University has been outlined. This approach was very successful at several levels:
− the level of engagement by the researchers in the process;
− the extent to which the University's research resources have been concentrated, right across the University; and
− its impact on the University's research performance.

The ASRIs are now entering a new phase of their development, with further concentration of research support through the reduction in the number of ASRIs being supported.

ACKNOWLEDGEMENTS

The work described in this paper was principally carried out while the author was Deputy Vice-Chancellor (Research) at Flinders University in Adelaide, South Australia.

The development and implementation of the ASRI strategy described here owes a great deal to many people. These include: Anne Edwards, the Vice-Chancellor of Flinders University during the time that the ASRI strategy was developed; Christine Steele and Katrina Hall, heads of the research office at Flinders University over the relevant period; Ann-Maree O'Connor from the research office, who played a major role in the implementation of the ASRIs; and Nicole Morcom, Executive Officer to the Deputy Vice-Chancellor (Research), who coordinated support for the strategy from my office.

NOTES

[1] The data used is taken from *Aggregated Student Enrolments* and *Selected Staff Higher Education Statistics*, Department of Education, Science and Training, Australian Government, Canberra.

REFERENCES

Connell, H. (Ed.), (2004). *University research management: Meeting the institutional challenge*. Paris: Organisation for Economic Co-operation and Development.

DEST. (2005). *Institution assessment framework information collection - 2005 instructions*. Canberra: Department of Education, Science and Training, Australian Government.

Hogan, J., & Clark, M. (1996). Postgraduate and research organization and management. In Warner, D., & Palfreyman, D. (Eds.), *Higher education management: The key elements*. Buckingham: The Society for Research into Higher Education and Open University Press.

Kemp, D. A. (1999a). *New knowledge, new opportunities: A discussion paper on higher education research and research training*. Canberra: Department of Education, Training and Youth Affairs, Australian Government.

Kemp, D. A. (1999b). *Knowledge and innovation: A policy statement on research and research training*. Canberra: Department of Education, Training and Youth Affairs, Australian Government.

Marlin, C. (2009). Focussing research in universities: Implications for research management. *Perspectives - Policy and practice in higher education, 13*, 42–47.

Mintrom, M. (2008). Managing the research function of the university: Pressures and dilemmas. *Journal of Higher Education Policy and Management, 30*, 231–244.

Shattock, M. (2003). *Managing successful universities*. Maidenhead: Society for Research into Higher Education and Open University Press.

Taylor, J. (2006). Managing the unmanageable: The management of research in research-intensive universities. *Higher Education Management and Policy, 18*, 1–25.

Williams, R., & Van Dyke, N. (2004). *The international standing of Australian universities*. Melbourne: Melbourne Institute of Applied Economic and Social Research, The University of Melbourne.

Williams, R., & Van Dyke, N. (2005). *Melbourne institute index of the international standing of Australian universities*. Melbourne: Melbourne Institute of Applied Economic and Social Research, The University of Melbourne.

Chris Marlin
University of Sussex, UK

SEERAM RAMAKRISHNA AND VENNI VENKATA KRISHNA

11. EMERGENCE OF ASIAN UNIVERSITIES AS CENTRES OF NEW KNOWLEDGE GENERATION AND A BASE FOR NATIONAL COMPETITIVENESS

A Case Study of the National University of Singapore[1]

INTRODUCTION

The rise of Asia in the global, knowledge-based economy in the last decade is closely associated with the rise of knowledge institutions of higher learning and scientific research[2]. Three features stand out and are indicative of the trend. The first is the tremendous growth of "human and knowledge capital" made possible by teaching and research excellence in the leading universities. Historically speaking, most leading universities in Asia have been performing these roles so as to make an impact on the society and economy. However what is of significance is the development of coupling teaching/research with innovation and at the same time forging university-private sector links with various actors and agencies, in the respective national systems of innovation (NSI)[3]. That is, universities are being re-positioned as frontiers of innovation in NSI, wherein most new technologies (biotechnology, nano, new materials, ICTs etc) have become science based. The third is the impact of globalization and the globalization of innovation and the emergence of "new" knowledge sites now being extended to the Asian region. Leading universities have the additional task of tapping into, or networking with, these globally dispersed knowledge networks and institutional sites.

With the dawn of the twenty-first Century, universities have come to occupy a very significant role in building and strengthening the national science, technology and innovation system and at the same time to catalyse knowledge based economies. In this paper, we take up the National University of Singapore (NUS) as a case study in the national context of Singapore, to explore some of the features outlined above. Over the years, the NUS has witnessed considerable growth in human resources and has championed the Humboltdian ideal of combining teaching and research excellence in knowledge production and advancement. The university has emerged as a leading university in Asia and is highly ranked at the global level, according to three important surveys[4].

This paper is structured into four sections. In the first, we briefly trace the trends in science and technology to show the growing importance of Asia in comparison with Europe and North America. In this regard, compared to the 1970s and 1980s, the period from the 1990s onwards was concerned with building knowledge based

N.C. Liu et al., (eds.), Paths to a World-Class University: Lessons from Practices and Experiences Classroom, 205–236.

economies in Asia and during this phase universities and knowledge institutions have come to occupy a prominent role in Singapore. The second section contains as a case study of the NUS to show how this important national institution has evolved over the years to become a catalyst for knowledge generation, professionalization and the economic progress of the country. The various subsections of part two provide a quantitative detail of the growth of the university and its research eco-system, thereby illustrating that it has become an important contributor to Singapore's science community. The university extended its twin missions of combining teaching and research excellence in the advancement of knowledge to the Third Mission of transferring it to industry and society and this is dealt in the third section. Concluding remarks and discussion are presented in the last section of the paper. In this regard, given the university has underlined the vision of becoming a "global university" centred in Asia we evaluate the most effective ways in relation to working towards "forging innovative new pathways". In other words, what are the new challenges and agenda for future? What are the important lessons the NUS case offers to other Asian countries in combining teaching, research and innovation?

EMERGING KNOWLEDGE BASE IN ASIA: THE CASE OF SINGAPORE

Asia has emerged as the most dynamic region of the world in the last decade and a half. In particular, the region registered unprecedented knowledge growth rates in recent years, surpassing its counterparts in Europe, South and North America. The leading Asian economies, such as Japan, the Republic of Korea, Singapore, China and India, have given top priority to science and technology policies, particularly in building institutions of higher learning and universities. Therefore, it is not surprising that knowledge institutions have played an important part in Asia's dynamic growth (Turpin and Krishna, 2007). Further, as Richard C. Levin, President of Yale University, recently remarked, "the United States and Europe face an emergent Asia, with China, India, Singapore, Japan, Korea and Australia rapidly positioning their knowledge enterprises to compete with those of the West in decades ahead"[5].

Asia's 10 leading countries increased their science output from 76,182 articles in 1995 to 144,767 in 2005, which representsed an increase of 90% (NSF, 2008). Moreover, the world shares of output in science publications increased by 76%, as a whole for the dynamic Asian region (including Japan) between 1999 and 2004. At the same time, Europe and North America witnessed a decline in share of (-5%) and (-7%), respectively, whereas Singapore registered an increase of (59%), preceded by China (89%) and South Korea (73%), for the same period[6].

Similar growth has occurred in Asian technological capabilities, as reflected in the trend in registered patents. In this regard, the number of patents filed in the U.S. from China and the Asia-8 increased by 800% during the period 1990 to 2003, which constituted about one fifth of all foreign-resident patents (NSF, 2006). Moreover, according to UNESCO, in 2000 Asia accounted for over 30% of world research and developmet (R&D) expenditure, which has now increased to 33.3% in 2009[7].

Generation and use of knowledge in high technology products is no more vertically integrated by a few big firms and is increasingly being dispersed, with Asia becoming important, both as a source of markets, of knowledge and human resources. Given the increasing importance of science-based innovation in new technologies, such as nanotechnology, biotechnology, material sciences and medical technologies, university-private sector relations are going to assume a very prominent economic role in national development[8]. Given this increasing role of universities in the social and economic sphere, it is pertinent to explore briefly the trajectory of Singapore's manufacturing and knowledge base through three identified main phases, as it has moved from a labour-intensive to a knowledge-intensive system (see Table 1).

Table 1. Phases in the transition of Singapore

Phases	Policy focus and shifts in technology and knowledge	Industrial focus	Type of knowledge and institutional imperatives
1960s–1980s	Focus on FDI, low cost manufacturing, developing production capabilities 1960s - Labour intensive 1970s - Skill intensive	Electronics cluster Chemicals cluster Shipbuilding and oil rigs cluster	Skills in manufacturing In-service training Polytechnic and industrial schools based skills
1980s–1990s *Transition phase*	Technologically sophisticated manufacturing with higher value addition Developing R&D capability 1980s - Capital intensive 1990s - Technology intensive	Continuation of above clusters + ICT, semiconductor and media technology enterprises	Engineering and information technology skills University based science and engineering Skills Nanyang Technological. University established
1990s and beyond, into the 21st Century	Knowledge based economic and S&T policies Developing innovation capability 2000 - Knowledge Intensive	Biopolis, science parks, Mediapolis and Fusionopolis CREATE Campus	Advancing science and engineering knowledge Universities playing a role in innovation and the economy; Singapore Management University established

The Case of Singapore

There is a general consensus among scholars, such as Yue (2005), Wong (2007) and Parayil (2005), that public policies played a significant role in transforming the economy of Singapore from being one that involved low-cost, labour-intensive manufacturing in the 1960s, to that of a high level technology manufacturing base by the 1980s. Subsequently, this was further modified to the current phase of knowledge based industry development that has been apparent since the 1990s[9]. Education in Singapore always implicitly followed Hobbes and Marx's orientations, whereby the social and economic value of specialized knowledge become paramount to industrialization and the capitalist structure of the economy (Kong, 2000), for "alongside the goal of enhancing national cohesion through educational policy, economic functionality remains a cornerstone of educational policy in Singapore" (ibid: 1)[10].

1960s to the 1980s.   In the first phase (See Table 1), FDI was crucial for the establishment of electronics and chemicals clusters, including those around petroleum refining in the 1960s and 1970s, which depended on manufacturing skills and technicians trained in polytechnics, mostly foreign workers. Subsequently, the country moved from a labour intensive pattern of manufacturing to one of skills in the later stages of this phase.

1980s to the 1990s.   In the 1990s the electronics cluster expanded, thus enabling higher value added in terms of technological capabilities being put into ICT hardware. Similarly, technological learning and capabilities acquired as part of the development of the chemicals and petroleum refining cluster led to the shipbuilding and oil rig cluster being developed. As Yue (2005) has pointed out, skills learnt in repairing super tankers allowed for the development of capabilities in the construction of oilrigs, which was catalysed by the boom in petroleum exploration in Southeaast Asia at the time. Subsequently, Singapore firms, such as Keppel and Sembawang, which mastered technical operations in this field, became world leaders in oil rig building.

High technology skills were obtained through mobility of foreign personnel, on-the-job training and in-house processes of "learning by doing" or "learning by interaction" within and outside firms. The two major universities, the NUS and Nanyang Technological University (NTU), supplied science and engineering professionals and aided applied and development research, to some extent, but they did not serve as being a major source of new innovations. Moreover, the Singapore Management University (SMU) and other management knowledge institutions supplied management professionals and fed business-oriented knowledge into various firms and enterprises.

Even though the industrial and economic structure led to considerable growth and prosperity for Singapore's citizens, from the beginning of the 1990s, the government realised the need to support the emerging knowledge-based economy. At this time, the nation's R&D base was quite weak, accounting for a mere 0.86% of GDP in 1990, much closer to various developing countries than those in the developed world. As a consequence, in the next phase the government initiated a number of research policy measures to meet the challenges of 21st century.

1990s: S&T policies towards enlarging the national R&D base. The first ever *National Technology Policy* (1995) was formulated in 1991, with the initial allocation of a S$2 billion R&D fund and a prescribed target of their being 2% of GDP given over to R&D by 1995. Under this policy, the focus was to foster public-private partnership in technology development. The *Second National Technology Plan* (1996) doubled the money set aside to S$4 billion and the focus was on science development in addition to technology. In an effort to implement systematically the second plan, government-constituted initiatives, such as the *Competitiveness Report* in 1998, which sought to promote IT innovation; *Technopreneurship 21* (T21) in 1999, aimed at boosting technopreneurs and start-ups; and the *Manpower 21 Report* in 1999, with the goal of promoting skilled human resources in universities, particularly through skilled migration. The *National Science and Technology Plan* (2005) allocated some S$7 billion with the main focus being on developing long-term strategic and basic research, by integrating the universities and by promoting R&D and innovation in the NUS and NTU, along with national and business sector based laboratories. The current *Strategic Directions for S&T Policy* (2006–2010) has earmarked a budget of S$13.5 billion, thus almost doubling that provided for the most recent previous plan. As a result, the gross expenditure on R&D, as a proportion of GDP, witnessed a considerable increase from a mere 1.1% in 1991 (First National Technology Policy) to 2.61% in 2007.

Shift towards a knowledge-based economy. With the increasing impact of globalization and market integration of economies in the new millennium, Singapore began to reorient its economic and industrial policies so as to back knowledge industries. In 2001, the government allocated over S$300 million to support undergraduate science scholars in pursuing doctorates. Another key higher education policy feature was to invite several world-class universities[11] to set up offshore centres/ campuses that would offer courses. A high-level committee recommendation, chaired by the then Deputy Prime Minister, Dr Tony Tan[12], led to the establishment of Singapore's biomedical cluster, better known as "Biopolis", in the beginning of 2000. Further, as a part of the innovation strategy to promote a knowledge based economy: science parks, Fusionopolis with a focus on engineering and physical sciences and media technologies, were promoted by the government. A major boost these policy orientations came about when the National Research Foundation was set-up in the Prime Minister's Office during 2005 and 2006. Moreover, as part of the new strategy to make a shift to a "new paradigm" of knowledge based economic growth, a ministerial committee on R&D, working in 2004, underlined the strategic directions for S&T policy, from 2006 to 2010[13]. This committee identified five thrusts to govern national science, technology and the innovation framework, which are as follows:

– To increase GERD/GDP from the current 2.25% to 3%, to ensure sufficient R&D support for the knowledge-based economy in the future;
– To focus the public research budget around a small number of strategic areas, so as to develop a critical mass of research capabilities and thus be globally competitive;
– Within the selected strategic areas, to fund a broad spectrum of research, ranging from basic investigator-led research to applied research;

- To prioritize increasing the scope of private R&D, by creating an enabling environment and fostering an open innovation platform, so that talented research scientists and engineers can flow across academia, the public research institutions and industry, in open collaborative networks; and
- To strengthen the nexus between Singaporean knowledge institutions and research performing agencies, such as the polytechnics, universities, research institutes and industry. The overall aim is to foster commercialization of research results through closer collaboration between the government, universities and industry.

Compared to the 1970s and 1980s, today, Singapore can boast of an emerging, but still nascent, national science community and an S&T system comprising various public-private research laboratory networks in select frontier areas. Moreover, over the last decade and a half the country has established a national innovation system aimed at building a future competitive economy based on knowledge. Further, as a leading national university, the NUS has played an important part in providing much of the training, skills and research base. We will now turn our attention to the main case study and explore the various institutional features of this important higher educational institution.

UNIVERSITIES AS CENTRES OF KNOWLEDGE AND S&T SYSTEMS: THE CASE OF THE NUS

Institutional Structure

The origins of the present day NUS go back to The Yong Loo Lin School of Medicine, established in 1905 (which is now part of the NUS), Raffles College for arts and social sciences, established in 1929 and the merger of the University of Singapore and Nanyang University in 1980. It is the oldest and largest public university in Singapore, with a total enrolment of about 31,000 students in 2008[14], comprising three leading graduate schools, six overseas colleges, three centres of excellence and 21 university based and 16 affiliated full time research institutes, as shown in Table 2 below.

Table 2. Schools, faculties and research institutes at the NUS 2008–09

Faculties and Schools	Graduate Schools	Research Institutes and Overseas Colleges
Faculty of Arts and Social Sciences Business School School of Computing School of Dentistry School of Design and Environment School of Engineering Law School School of Medicine Conservatory of Music School of Science	Lee Kuan Yew School of Public Policy The NUS Graduate School for Integrative Sciences and Engineering Duke-NUS Graduate Medical School Singapore	Six overseas colleges Three research Centres of Excellence 21 university level research institutes 16 national level affiliated research institutes

Student Enrolment and Faculty 1980–2008

Since the 1980s, the NUS has grown not only in terms of the number of students and faculties, but also in relation to its stature, now being one of the leading universities in Asia. It has progressed from an undergraduate teaching university to presently institutionalising a wide range of disciplines and fields of research across the spectrum of the arts, social sciences, natural and physical sciences, medicine, public policy and law. Whilst the 1980s may be characterized as a phase that was dominated by the function of teaching, in the 1990s the NUS emerged as a research-based university. Tables 3 to 5, draw our attention to some interesting growth trends for these three decades.

Table 3. Numbers of NUS faculty, research and other staff 1980–2008

Staff	1980	1985	1990	2000	2005	2008
Faculty	562	1203	1414	2569	1765	2103
Research	na	100*	224	373	1087	1710
Admin. Professionals	78	182	283	183	859	1344
General	1436	2001	2059	2518	2494	2491

Source: The NUS Annual Report.

Note * denotes the figure for 1987.

- The NUS witnessed more than a fourfold increase in total student enrolments from 7,137 in 1980 to over 30,350 in 2008. It crossed the ten thousand mark in the 1980s; twenty thousand by the mid-1990s and then reached thirty thousand in 2008.
- The number of faculty staff increased by little less than three times in a decade, being 562 in 1980 and 1414 in 1990 and this figure had reached 2103 by 2008.
- The university progressed from an under graduate based university in the early 1980s, to being a graduate one from the late 1980s, with 2069 graduate students being enrolled for the 1990 cohort. Subsequently, there was a threefold increase in graduate students between 1990 and 2008, rising to 7020.
- The 1990s can be viewed as a stage when the NUS had begun to emerge as a research university. Along with the increasing trend in the growth of the graduate student population in the 1990s, research staff witnessed an eight fold increase, from 224 in 1990 to 1710 in 2008. Also from the 1990s there was a substantial growth in the number of research graduate students, from 2763 in 1997 to 4751 in 2008.

Table 4. Graduate and under graduate enrolments at the NUS 1980–2008

Students	1980	1985	1990	1995	2000	2005	2008
Undergraduate	6751	12721	14645	16137	20681	21761	23330
Graduates	386	1062	2069	3453	8450	6461	7020
Total	7137	13783	16714	19590	29131	28222	30350

Source: The NUS Annual Report.

Table 5. The numbers of NUS research graduate students enrolled, 1997–2006

1997	1998	1999	2000	2001	2002	2003	2004	2005	2006	2007	2008
2763	3665	4321	4507	5005	5209	5407	5418	4485	4382	4459	4751
Number of Ph.D.s in all fields and Disciplines											
118	106	115	112	152	212	214	265	285	363	457	538

Source: hhtp://www.nus.edu.sg/registrar/statistics.html.

As shown in Table 5, the number of Ph.D.s increased more than four times, from 118 in 1997 to 538 in 2008, indicating the increased research intensity of the NUS in the last decade. However, it should be pointed out that in proportion to graduate students and research graduate students, the number of Ph.D.s coming out of the university has been low, but the recent trends during the last three or four years show that this is growing by between 20 to 25% every year. The number of Ph.D.s, as a proportion of total number of students, is certainly low compared to the leading universities in Asia, such as the University of Tokyo. The low proportion of graduate students along with that for Ph.D.s has also had a bearing on new knowledge production, measured in terms of numbers papers (See Table 8). However, the NUS's new knowledge production in social sciences compares very well with that of the University of Tokyo, with the former publishing 368 papers in 2007, just five less than the University of Tokyo and more than double the number of Seoul National University, which published 176 papers in the same year.

The NUS's Share of National R&D and S&T Human Resources

Over the last decade, the NUS has emerged as a key actor in the national S&T system, with the university's R&D budget, on average, accounting for around 35% of the total higher education R&D budget for the decade 1997–2007. Moreover, in terms of its trajectory, the actual figure doubled from S$101 million to around S$220 million in 2003 rose to S$366 million in 2007. Further, the NUS attracted nearly S$450 million for three major centres of excellence (see section 3.4.1), during the period 2006 to 2009.

Human resources, particularly research scientists and engineers, including medical professionals, are playing an important part in the national R&D effort towards the creation of an integrated national science community. As Table 6 shows, the NUS's contribution to skilled human resources in the tertiary sector has been quite substantial over the last two and a half decades, from 1980 to 2006, accounting for 25 to 27% of skilled human resources and nearly 50% of higher education research scientists and engineers, throughout the period. The significance of the NUS's human resource base to the country's S&T system as a whole is also reflected in the knowledge production, with the university contributing 50 to 60% of total R&D output, measured in terms of peer reviewed S&T publications for the decade 1997–2007 (see Table 7).

Table 6. The NUS share of RSEs in Singapore 1991–2006

Year	Total RSEs in Singapore	Higher Education RSEs	NUS Research Staff	NUS research staff share of total higher education b/a	NUS faculty in Science, Engineering and Medicine (SEM)	NUS research staff + SEM faculty share of total higher education RSEs (%)
		(a)	(b)		(c)	
1991	5218	1851	274	14.8%	670	51%
1996	10153	3106	1002	32.3%	735	55.9%
2001	15366	3518	842	23.9%	793	46.5%
2006	22675	4451	1218	27.4%	1000	49%

Source: Adapted from (Wong, Ho and Singh, 2009).

Note: SEM = science, engineering and medicine; RSE= research scientists and engineers.

The NUS and the Singapore Science Community

Compared to other countries, the evolution of a national science and technology system in Singapore is a recent development, just covering the last two decades. The country designed its trajectory of economic growth against a backdrop of export promotion, liberal policy towards the inflow of foreign firms and enterprises and drawing on a globally sourced skilled workforce. Regarding the lattermost point, this is similar in relation to the evolution of science and technology institutions, whereby the country has relied on global sources of scientific and engineering professionals[15]. The social, economic and cultural context structured a different pattern or model for the evolution of Singapore science community compared to other countries (See section 3.4.3).

The S&T system in Singapore basically comprises public scientific research institutes, universities and institutions of higher education, on the one hand and R&D centres and research institutes of transnational corporations (TNCs) and other business enterprises, on the other. These R&D based TNCs came in as a part of government liberal economic policies from 1980 onwards, aimed at promoting FDI in the financial, economic and science and technology sectors, an approach that became more prominent during the 1990s. As argued and implied in section two above, the main imperative for expanding science and technology institutions and infusing public funding into higher education in relation to R&D, was the economic motive of generating future wealth from knowledge. Biomedical sciences, information and media technologies, electronics and engineering sciences are just some of the important sectors that drew public policy attention, which enabled the creation of the research-ecosystem and a professional climate through the establishment of complexes, such as Biopolis, Fusionopolis, three science parks and the involvement of institutions of higher learning and research, including the NUS, NTU and SMU, among others.

As a leading national university, the NUS has played an important part in the evolution of Singapore's national science community[16], in particular, with regards to its professionalization and advancement of knowledge. The large or small size of scientific and engineering personnel in terms of numbers, infrastructure with buildings and allocation of R&D funding are important but do not indicate the existence or define science community. Steady production of knowledge in certain specialized fields, creation of university chairs and graduate and post graduate research students, attainment of recognition and rewards both nationally and internationally, research institutes, journals and specialized academies and professional groupings and, above all, a system of intellectual and academic culture signify science communities or specialized groupings. Professionalized national science communities evolve over sustained periods of intellectual and institutional efforts to cultivate and advance knowledge and they are a crucially important part of a national science and techno-logy (S&T) system (Krishina, 1997). Moreover, breakthroughs in new technologies, including in particular nano, biotechnology and information varieties, in large measure are the outcomes of science based innovation. Further, the evolution and promotion of a dynamic S&T system have been taken on board as the most important consideration in building an effective innovation system and a knowledge based economy.

In general, the NUS itself could be conceptualized as a form of Singapore national science community at the meso level. From such a perspective, next, we explore the ways in which it has progressed, in terms of professionalized teaching, education, research and knowledge production and at the same time consider how it has geared itself to catalyse innovation in the interests of the economic progress of the country.

Knowledge production. Universities such as the NUS that are engaged in teaching and research are now seen to occupy an important place in the knowledge production system, both directly and indirectly, through research publications, conference and symposia papers, reports, processes and products and other research output, thereby contributing to economic progress and national development. The NUS, particularly in science and engineering and technology education, is known for its academic excellence, as seen in the world rankings presented above. The mode of knowledge production at the NUS can be characterized as having followed an "Humboldtian Model" of combining teaching and research excellence (for instance in open science and research publications), but recently fostering the *Third Mission* of innovation or what has come to be termed as the Triple Helix of university - industry – government relations has come to the fore. We will consider this third mission in detail (including output indicators as patents and spin-offs) in a later section, but here we focus on the *Second Mission* of research output as measured by open publications.

As shown in Table 7, the last decade witnessed a doubling of NUS research publications in refereed international journals, from 1619 in 1997 to 3746 in 2007. Moreover, the total output of NUS publications which includes conference papers, chapters in books etc, has witnessed steady growth from 4313 papers in 1997 to over 7500 in 2007[17]. Furthermore, the NUS has accounted for more than 50% of the total number of research papers published nationally over the same period, indicating its significance in the national S&T system. As the pie chart (See Figure 1) shows, a similar trend is depicted for the decade between 2000 and 2010 of NUS dominating the science publication to the extent of 51% in Singapore.

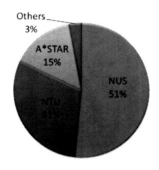

Figure 1. Science publication in Singapore (2000–2010).

Source: Accessed Thomson Reuters - Web of Science data on 1 Sep 2010; Journal Publications with Impact Factor

Note: Nanyant Technological University (NTU); and Agency for Science, Technology and Research (A*STAR), Singapore

Table 7. Publication profile of the NUS and Singapore 1997–2007 (SCI extended version, for science, engineering and medical sciences)

Year	NUS publications SCI extended	Sum of times cited	Average citation	H-Index[18]	Total Singapore Publication SCI ext. (Total Singapore/ NUS)	Sum of times cited	Average citation	H-Index
1997	1619	21167	13.07	58	2491(64.9%)	31239	12.54	64
1998	1701	27859	16.38	66	2772(61.4%)	41038	14.8	78
1999	2029	28747	14.17	67	3372(60.2%)	42839	12.7	75
2000	2191	34473	15.73	71	3958(55.4%)	54665	13.81	81
2001	2339	31675	13.54	65	4293(54.5%)	53804	12.53	79
2002	2519	34451	13.68	69	4717(53.4%)	58076	12.31	78
2003	2848	35674	12.53	65	5384(52.9%)	62303	11.57	74
2004	3179	37956	11.94	63	6200(51.3%)	65101	10.50	75
2005	3500	33332	9.52	63	6939(50.4%)	61320	8.84	73
2006	3764	24932	6.62	46	7392(50.9%)	44609	6.03	56
2007	3746	15660	4.18	34	6356(58.9%)	28913	4.55	42

Source: (Krishna, 2009).

As can be seen from the table above, NUS S&T publications have attained a high degree of international professional recognition, as indicated by the high citation scores and h-index for the decade[19]. The table also shows that the sum of the times cited and the total S&T citations obtained by NUS publications have been favourably comparable with other top universities in the world. For instance, according to the data available for the typical period of 2004–05 (about 22 months in total), the total numbers of times papers from Cambridge, MIT, Stanford and Harvard were cited was 15000, 16600, 19100 and 45000 respectively. Taking another recent period of 2007 for the NUS, Seoul National University and the University of Tokyo, the data shows that all the S&T papers of these universities were cited 15660, 17143 and 40973, respectively, for the period 2008–2009 (about 20 months)[20]. The data presented in Table 9 gives a comparative publication profile of all: S&T, arts and social science publications for the decade 1997–2007, with the foremost including medicine and the NUS emerges as one of the top Asian universities, together with the University of Tokyo and Seoul National University. Moreover, in arts and social sciences publications, the NUS emerges as top in Asia (See Table 8)[21]. From the national perspective, it is the most important actor in arts and social sciences, producing between 50 to 75% of the total the Singapore publications for the decade 1997–2007 (see Table 7).

Table 8. International publication trends for Asian universities
1997–2007 for S&T* and s**. (SCI extended
version, for science, engineering and medical sciences)

Year	University of Tokyo		NUS		Seoul National University	
	S&T	Social sciences	S&T	Social sciences	S&T	Social sciences
1997	7158	168	1619	170	1702	28
1998	7258	211	1701	182	1951	30
1999	7534	231	2029	197	2197	47
2000	7951	322	2191	214	2584	41
2001	7844	220	2339	233	2968	68
2002	8516	251	2519	184	3361	74
2003	9225	238	2848	262	3702	103
2004	9312	329	3179	268	4151	114
2005	8914	275	3500	251	4489	120
2006	8662	336	3764	339	4887	150
2007	8929	373	3746	368	5251	176

Source: (Krishna, 2009).

Note: S&T includes science, technology, engineering and medicine and ** social sciences includes arts and social science fields.

Table 9. Publication profile of NUS and Singapore 1997–2007 (Social Sciences)

Year	NUS publications	Sum of times cited	Average citation	H-Index	Total Singapore Publications (Total Singapore/ NUS)	Sum of times cited	Average citation	H-Index
1997	170	1529	8.99	20	231	2073	8.97	25
1998	182	1811	9.95	22	262	2537	9.68	24
1999	197	1703	8.64	21	293	2501	8.54	24
2000	214	2150	10.05	23	327	3043	9.31	27
2001	233	1815	7.79	20	385	3105	8.06	27
2002	184	1283	6.97	18	325	2422	7.45	24
2003	262	1987	7.58	21	436	3082	7.07	24
2004	268	1490	5.56	18	476	2598	5.46	22
2005	251	1251	4.98	18	478	2321	4.86	19
2006	339	771	2.27	11	593	1471	2.48	14
2007	368	632	1.72	9	691	1214	1.76	13

Source: (Krishna, 2009).

The NUS and Singapore's main research eco-system. "Research eco-system" implies a dynamic arrangement of various actors (public and private S&T and R&D institutions, universities, teaching and research hospitals, government agencies in industry, finance, economy and trade etc) of a research or S&T system who are interconnected with each other and collaborate and influence each other, often in unexpected ways. In a country such as Singapore, the geographical proximity of the NUS to the research eco-system is quite convenient in terms of communication and access. Interestingly, the university is located in the middle of Singapore's main research eco-system, with over 75% of the actors, agencies and institutions being physically located within a 6 to 7 kms radius. The main actors of this NUS research eco-system are as follows:

Research Institutes: The NUS established about 20 research institutes[22] and centres in natural, physical, engineering and social sciences, covering from solar energy, digital media, tropical medicine and marine studies to specialized research institutes on different regions of Asia. About 500 full-time research scientists and fellows, including visiting scholars, are engaged in research in these university level research institutes and centres.

Biopolis and Fusionopolis: Located at "one-north" and less than two kms from the NUS, the National University Hospital and the Singapore Science Parks, Biopolis is generally referred to as Singapore's biomedical cluster, which fosters a collabo-rative culture among the private and public research communities. It houses some 8 national laboratories[23] engaged in biomedical related R&D activities.

Fusionopolis brings together, under one roof: research scientists, engineers and technology experts from the public labs of the Agency for Science, Technology and Research (A*STAR) and those from the private sector. Even though they vary in their organizational goals, they share the common objective of advancing technology in a number of research programmes, working together in teams in the different disciplines housed in the complex. There are five leading national laboratories here in engineering, chemical information and media technology[24] and the co-location of scientific labs and other organizations are meant to promote public-private collaborations. Moreover, the proximity of Fusionopolis and Biopolis enables close collaboration between life sciences, physical sciences and engineering and with the faculties at the NUS.

CREATE Campus: National Research Foundation established a Campus for Research Excellence and Technological Enterprise (CREATE) with a budget of S$ 360 million to construct a new research complex around the NUS. The idea behind this is to create a unique research site for housing offshore research centres from world-class research universities and corporate labs[25] and the Massachusetts Institute of Technology has established the first centre within CREATE, known as the Singapore-MIT Alliance for Research and Technology (SMART) Centre. The SMART Centre is MIT's first such research centre of its kind outside its home campus in Cambridge, Massachusetts and MIT's largest international research offshore research complex outside USA.

Science Parks: Drawing on the successful role science parks or high technology clusters or innovation parks play in infusing dynamism to an innovation system, in the 1980s the government of Singapore began to make big investments in science parks[26]. The three science parks house some 350 to 375 firms and institutions, including some 200 registered as containing R&D facilities with global firms, such as Sony, Exxon, Silicon Graphics, Lucent Technologies and Quintiles having set up R&D units in the parks[27] and a predominant proportion of the tenants are involved in knowledge related operations. As the studies of Philip and Yueng (2003) and Yueng (2006) have drawn to our attention, Singapore's Science Parks provide a very high quality of R&D infrastructure in close geographical proximity to the NUS. In this regard, there are a number of collaborative projects between the NUS and laboratories located in three science parks, in which research students are involved. Moreover, there are cluster related dynamic interactions between institutions and researchers at the three science parks and the NUS, which include access and sharing of research facilities, access to seminars and workshops and access to library and other person-to-person based communications, which enhance the quality of research.

Internationalization of the NUS and socio-cultural context for research. Internationalization of higher education and of universities has attracted a good deal of attention in the last decade, the world over. The idea of reviving the "cosmopolitan university" of the medieval times, but in the context of the modern era of the information revolution and globalization, is increasingly being seen as a virtue for a global university. According to Knight and Wit (1997, p. 8), "internationalisation of higher education is the process of integrating an international/intercultural dimension into the teaching, research and service functions of the institution." At the NUS one key institutional initiative in the transformation of education was the internationalization strategy of attracting the best students from a whole host of countries to Singapore. Today, nearly a third of the total student population are from overseas, which has led to top young minds being together in a global learning community and with their diverse social and cultural perspectives this enriches the community, making campus life vibrant and promoting international understanding. Moreover, this strategic initiative is helping to prepare the next generation for working collaboratively, so as to be able to contribute more effectively in the era of globalization. Another way that students have been attracted to Singapore is through the provision of joint/double/concurrent degree programmes and in 2004 there were 21 of these programmes, which increased to 66 by 2008.

The NUS has placed a high level of importance on internationalization, both in its academic policies and practice over the years, as a means to increase intercultural cooperation and understanding among students and faculty members. To this end, the university institutionalized a rigorous peer evaluation-based system to ensure the recruitment and retention of faculty and research staff of international repute, paying special attention to quality, excellence and high professional standards. From around 10% in the 1980s, foreigners among the faculty increased to 39% in 1997 and then to over 50% of the total in 2007–08. The non-Singaporean Asian faculty (from Malaysia, India, China and other Asian countries) accounted for approximately 30% in 2007–08 and the European and North American cohorts comprised 20%. In terms of the researchers, the proportion of foreign nationals stood at around 75% in 2007. Among the student population, foreign students increased from 13% to 34% over the decade 1997 to 2007, which translates into 10,000 out of a total of 31000, coming from over 80 countries. This high level of concentration of foreign talent and substantial number of overseas students is comparable to U.S. Ivy League institutions and moreover, very few institutions in Asia can match NUS's proven record on internationalization. In fact, this underlines Singapore's development into a global city and a hub for business, information technology and high technology manufacturing through attracting and gathering global talents and professionals[28]. From a sociological perspective, going beyond R&D funding, infrastructure and material conditions, the nation's research eco-system and the NUS have evolved in such a way as to provide a congenial socio-cultural context for pursuing research. Moreover, over the last two decades the country has attracted talent by creating enabling conditions that foster multi-culturalism and a cosmopolitan perspective, whilst at the same time introducing a "laboratory life-world" which can be described as "home away from home" for many of the foreign scientists who work in S&T institutions. In other words, the research eco-system provides a "climate" which is quite comparable to North America and Europe, insofar as the day-to-day laboratory practices in terms of research autonomy, protocols, avenues for funding, the utilization of funds for approved projects, mobility of personnel for seminars and conferences and access to communication and literature, are concerned. In sum, all these features of socio-cultural context, knowledge production and the advancement of knowledge and the location nexus of the NUS with Singapore's main research eco-system together with the features of professionalization, provide a universe of meaningful context for Singapore's science community.

Professionalization of Education and Research

The process of professionalization is distinguished from institutionalization in the higher educational and research contexts, in the sense that once the disciplines and faculties of learning are institutionalized and function over a period time, they begin (including practitioners) to mature and transform. The manifestation of this change can be observed in terms of various institutional measures and initiatives in teaching and research excellence, source of skills for career advancement, creation of advance research centres, professional recognition and rewards[29], through national and international peers, the creation of journals, specialized societies and the process of national identity for the advancement and contribution of knowledge to society and the economy.

The current President of the Singapore National Academy of Sciences (SNAS), in 2009, is from the NUS and out of 19 council members of that body, seven are from the university, which shows that it plays an important part in the country's top science professional body. The NUS's science, technology and engineering faculty and professionals also play an important part in the top S&T journals, with a significant number being on their editorial boards[30]. As with other universities, the NUS has adopted the Quality Assurance Framework for University (QAFU) set out by the MOE.[31] In relation to this, autonomy plays an important part in the professionalization of teaching and research. In 2005, the three publicly-funded universities: the NUS, NTU and the SMU became autonomous universities, which enabled them to chart their own strategies towards achieving quality in teaching and research excellence. The NUS's key measures for teaching and research excellence are assessed through a bench marking process achieved by three main methods: visiting committees and international advisory panels; accreditation; and international rankings[32] and the review covers both teaching and research quality. A rigorous system of structured follow-up to the reports and recommendations are carried out under the direct purview of the Provost's Office. There is also a system whereby teaching is assessed by students periodically. To continue to promote professionalism in education and research, the NUS is focusing on four new initiatives:

- Strong commitment from the NUS leadership to make the development, retention and recruitment of excellent faculty, staff and students;
- Transforming its administrative culture and systems to be among the best-in-class;
- Enhancing faculty support in the pursuance of "high risk, high impact" research, as well as improving professional development support and mentorship for faculty members so as to encourage innovation and excellence in teaching; and
- Recruiting world leaders in strategic academic areas.

Another important feature of the NUS has been its transformative education approach, which includes a broad-based curriculum networked through multi-disciplinary courses[33]. Its education framework is based on being multi-disciplinary, entrepreneurial, self-directed, experimental and managerial. In order to enrich and develop students' entrepreneurial spirit, the NUS has established six overseas colleges (see section 4.1), in which the students, spend one year as interns in a technology-based start-up, whilst attending entrepreneurial and discipline based courses at partner universities, with the key areas being biotechnology, business, computing, engineering and pharmaceutical science.

Professional Rise of the NUS

Advance research initiatives and centres of excellence.   With Singapore's transition into a knowledge-driven economy, the NUS embraced the role of serving as a key engine of knowledge creation and innovation, in particular, by promoting cross disciplinary collaboration in research. It has adopted a global multi-disciplinary research strategy and has set up 130 research collaborations in the last three years. The university's core research mission is to undertake fundamental cutting-edge research that addresses important questions relevant to Singapore and globally, and to use this research capacity to train quality human resources and skills at graduate and undergraduate levels. Since 2000 it has launched some advance research initiatives in the frontier areas of science[34], engineering and social sciences. Table 10 shows some prominent advanced research institutes and centres of excellence established in the NUS over the last decade.

Table 10. Advanced research institutes[35] and centres of excellence

Advanced Research Institutes	Centres of Excellence
Nanoscience and Nanotechnology Initiative[36] (NUSNNI)	The Cancer Research Centre of Excellence[37] (CRCE)
Solar Energy Research Institute of Singapore[38] (SERIS)	Mechanobiology Research Centre of Excellence[39]
Interactive Digital Media Institute[40] (IDMI)	Centre for Quantum Technologies[41]
Tropical Marine Sciences Institute[42] (TMSI)	NUS-GE Water Technology Centre[43]
The Logistics Institute - Asia Pacific[44]	Duke-NUS Graduate Medical Programme[45]
The Risk Management Institute[46] (RMI)	The Singapore-MIT Alliance[47] (SMA)
The Asia Research Institute[48] (ARI)	
Global Asia Institute[49] (GAI)	

International research networks.   The university is an active member of various international academic networks and associations of universities, such as Asia Pacific Rim Universities[50]; ASEAN University Network[51]; Global Enterprise for Micro-Mechanics and Molecular Medicine network; the Universitas 21[52] which is a global network of 21 leading research-intensive universities in thirteen countries; and the IARU[53]. The most important function of these academic networks is to foster research and international cooperation in all disciplines, participate in summer and specialized workshops and to maximize the exchange of students, both at under graduate and graduate levels. In an effort to become globally connected with international innovation expertise and leading markets, the NUS has established overseas colleges in: Silicon Valley and Philadelphia, USA; Beijing and Shanghai, China; Stockholm, Sweden and Bangalore, India. These five colleges have established leading innovation and entrepreneurial hubs involving up to 150 students a year.

The NUS's international rankings. Recognition of quality teaching, research capabilities and other physical and intellectual infrastructure of universities at the global level is monitored and evaluated through international rankings by two agencies, namely, the Times Higher Education Supplement, London and Jiao Tong University's World Ranking of Universities. Over the last few years, the NUS has attracted world attention due to its high rankings in both indexes. As the table 12 shows that in the first ranking the university has been placed among the 30 top universities in the world in 2008, in its entirety, whilst being ranked between 9th and 11th in technology and information technology and between 17th and 25th in biomedicine and life sciences, over the last five years, thus signifying its excellence and world recognition in these fields. According to the other international ranking by Jiao Tang University, Shanghai, China, the university was ranked between 9th and 11th among the top 15 Asian universities, between 2005 and 2008. Moreover, in relation its position among the world's top 500 universities, it was ranked between 109 and 112 during the same period.

Table 11. The NUS's ranking in the world university rankings by
Times Higher Education 2004

Fields/Disciplines	2004 ranking	2005 ranking	2006 ranking	2007 ranking	2008 ranking
Overall	18	22	19	33	30
Biomedicine	25	15	9	12	17
Science	35	34	22	25	31
Technology	9	9	8	10	11
Social Sciences	10	13	11	20	-
Arts and Humanities	17	56	22	21	31

Source: Based on Times Higher Education Supplement Rankings during 2004 and 2008.

THE NUS's IMPACT ON THE ECONOMY AND SOCIETY

Leading world-class universities, such as MIT and Cambridge, have become proactive in fostering a variety of institutional initiatives, organizational forms and policies to promote university-industry relations or "Third Stream" activities[54]. Moreover, most leading universities have become sensitive to the societal and global challenges confronting the human race in the 21st Century. As a leading national university, in recent years the NUS has also been diligent in advancing these "new missions" or "agendas of research" aimed at having an impact on the economy and industry, on the one hand and society, on the other hand.

Nexus with the Private Sector

The university's relevance to industry and knowledge transfer activities began to assume importance from the mid 1990s onwards, with the establishment of the Technology Licensing Office. However, there was significant boost to entrepreneurship, commercialization of research and innovation after 2000, with the establishment of the NUS Enterprise which was invested with the mission to "move beyond traditional academic missions and adopt an entrepreneurial orientation in order to become a growth engine". This was established as a university level cluster for promoting the innovation and enterprise dimensions in teaching and research, by engaging students, staff and alumni. The main strategy to institutionalize this initiative was to foster the development of an entrepreneurial culture in teaching, training, internship and to encourage start-up enterprises or spin-offs, patenting and commercialization of intellectual property. The university's activities in innovation are close networks, which have been catalysed by the National Framework for Innovation and Entrepreneurship that has had approximately S$350 million allocated for its activities, which have included proof-of-concept grants, technology incubation schemes, early stage venture funding and disruptive innovation (DI) incubation. The main activities of NUS Enterprise are structured in terms of three main units:

The NUS Industry Liaison Office (ILO). It promotes industry collaboration, technology transfer and commercialization of the university's intellectual assets and expertise. It manages and protects the university's intellectual property and is charged with licensing technologies and know how developed by university researchers and faculty. At the same time, the ILO facilitates the university's collaboration with industry, through industry-sponsored research and joint research and development projects.

NUS Overseas Colleges. This is a university level unit of the NUS Enterprise cluster that manages the highly innovative NUS Overseas Colleges at Silicon Valley and Philadelphia, USA; Beijing and Shanghai, China; Stockholm, Sweden and Bangalore, India. About 150 bright students are sent for internship to these global knowledge hubs, to work in the start-up companies for one year. Here, students take courses on innovation and start-up related technology development problems with partner universities.

The NUS Entrepreneurship Centre. The centre was originally established in 1988 as a university level centre, called the Centre for Management of Innovation and Technopreneurship (CMIT). In 2001, it became a division of NUS Enterprise, and was renamed as the NUS Entrepreneurship Centre (NEC). The major objective of the NEC is to nurture entrepreneurial learning and venture creation among the NUS community. Its activities are organized along the four key areas of education, entrepreneurship, development and incubation and innovation research. The university has adopted a policy of owning intellectual property developed through its research staff and faculty, but offer liberal incentives to individuals and teams involved in the inventions. If we regard patents, spin-offs and research collaboration agreements with industry as important indicators for university-industry relations or the NUS's nexus with industry, it can be claimed that the university has been very proactive over the last few years, evidence for which can be seen from Tables 12 and 13 below.

Table 12. NUS's patents granted by the USPTO and technology category

Year/Period	NUS Patents applied	NUS Patents granted	NUS patents by technology category*	No. of patents
1990–2000	330	61	Electrical and Electronic	90
2001	83	17	Computers and Communications	60
2002	91	34	Chemical	38
2003	119	28	Drugs and Medical	44
2004	166	51	Mechanical	24
2005	150	40	Science	10
2006	150	46	Others	11
2007	126	49	-	-
Total	1215	326	Total	277

Source: NUS Research Reports.

Note: * For 277 patents for which information is available up to 2007.

Table 13. NUS spin-offs

Year/Period	NUS Spin-offs	By Nature of Business	NUS Spin-offs Number*
1980–99	11	Information Technology	22
2000–02	15	Biochemical	11
2003–06	18	Electrical and Electronics	3
		Mechanical	2
		Scientific equipment	2
		Others	4
Total	44	Total	44

Note: * Does not denote period.

Over the last seven years the NUS has emerged as a leading actor in the Singapore S&T system with strong innovation performance, as indicated by her patent portfolio. As Table 13 shows, the university filed 330 US patents (33 patents per year) and was granted 61 patents (6.1 per year) for the decade 1990–2000. This patenting activity witnessed a substantial activity after the turn of the millennium, reaching 1115 US patent applications (159.3 per year) and granted 244 patents (34.7 per year) for the seven year period 2001–2007, which represents a six fold increase compared to the previous one of the same duration. More specifically, as Table 13 shows with regards to the available data referring to 277 NUS patents, 42% concerned electrical, electronic and mechanical engineering science; 25% computing; about 30% were chemical, drug and medical related; and 3% covered other matters. A noticeable feature of patenting in the country is that by 2007 the NUS had become the 4th largest holder of Singapore-based US patents, surpassing MNCs, such as Motorola, Texas Instruments and Matsushita Electrical Industrial Co, among others, with 229 patents. With regards to other organizations, the A*STAR obtained 98 patents; Creative Technology 91; ST Assembly Services 86, the Institute of Microelectronics 86; and NTU obtained less than 50 patents in 2007.[55]

Building on the R&D base and innovative potential exemplified in the patent portfolio, the process of knowledge transfer to industry intensified during the same period (2000–2007) and thus a similar surge in the commercialization of research came about, as can be seen in the establishment of spin-off firms based on the NUS's R&D input (see Table 13). In this regard only 11 spin-off firms were established during the twin decade period of 1980 and 1999, but this picked up quite noticeably after 2000, with around 55 spin-offs being reported as being set up by the NUS for the seven year period ending 2008. Out of 44 spin-off firms, 50% were in information technology; 25% in biochemicals; 15% in engineering fields including the electrical, electronic and mechanical varieties; and 10% in other areas.

NUS and Societal Challenges

The NUS has given special attention to the societal challenges and problems of the 21st century. In which regard, research and teaching has been undertaken in various fields reflecting both an Asian focus and global concerns, ranging from the environment and sustainability of natural resources, through to the changing structure of the family and migration to ageing and healthcare delivery, amongst other issues. In detail, some of the important research and teaching programmes of the NUS in relation to societal challenges are depicted as follows:

Cleaning, renewing and optimizing water. The engineering faculty, in collaboration with General Electric, has established a Global R&D Centre with a 10 years budget of S$130 million. This centre will conduct research targeted at alleviating water concerns related to quality, treatment, systems integration and membrane applications. The second important programme in this regard is the Singapore-Delft Water Alliance, which is a multi-institutional, interdisciplinary centre of excellence for teaching about and research into water knowledge. NUS established Institute of Water Policy to undertake research in Asia and train the next generation of Asian policy-makers in water with the objective of raising the standards of governance.

Environment and sustainability. There are a number of research and teaching initiatives to this end involving the NUS, including zero-energy building and green building developments; biodiversity conservation in the Himalayas; research on alternative and governance of energy policies in Asia; and natural disaster and hazards research, which have all been specifically structured to counter the negative impacts of increased industrialization by finding sustainable solutions through the generation of new and systematic knowledge.

Sustainable cities research cluster. An interdisciplinary research cluster has been established at the Asia Research Institute with the main objective to explore and advance knowledge on emergent urban situations, in the areas of social-cultural and environmental sustainability that deserve continual attention in the 21st century. Some of the problems and issues that concern this cluster are eco-urbanism, cultural preservation, and quality of social life. Moreover, the interface between technology and society, for example, in relation to emerging environmental technologies, and water and energy resource use and industrial and landscape ecology as well as the quality of human health and social life in urban areas also come under its remit.

   Closely related to this cluster is research on creative cities and cultural trans-mission in Asia. In this regard, the dynamics of globalization has opened up the perspective of "culture as commodity and trade" in the new Asian economies, with the consequent spread of media technologies leading to many unintended outcomes and the fostering of a sense of pan-Asianness, with the commensurate harmonizing of relations and goals among these nations.

Ageing, changing family and migration. All these three issues in the Singaporean and Asian contexts have received considerable attention from members of the Arts and Social Science Faculty and the Asia Research Institute over the last few years. With regards to the foremost, Singapore as with other Asian societies, such as Japan, is confronting the big societal challenge of having an ageing society, which involves the need to address how does the society organize its resources and generate social capital to deal with the problems of leisure, health delivery and social dynamics and what are the policy implications of this situation? Being a small country with a population of about 4 million, Singapore's dynamic growth both as a global city and its economic success has been dependent on the migration of a skilled and non-skilled work force over the last four decades and thus issues relating to changing family structure and social and cultural assimilation of the migrant population have become a key pre-occupation of researchers. In particular in this field, we think it is important to mention the new societal development of cross border marriages which have investigated the inter-regional and inter-cultural differences between Singapore and Malaysia.

CONCLUSION

Different countries, depending on their natural, intellectual and human resource base endowments have chalked up different trajectories in the mosaic of development in Asia. In the specific case of Singapore, our exploration in this paper has shown how the country progressed during the 1970s and 1980s from an economy based on labour-, skill-, capital- and technology-intensive phases, to a knowledge-intensive phase in the 1990s, in particular this has intensified with the dawn of 21st century. It is in this sphere of operation that science and technology institutions, especially the universities, have come to play an important part. Our main objective in this paper has been to focus on the case of the NUS.

The NUS witnessed considerable growth over the last three decades, in terms of the number of students, faculty and infrastructure, as well as in its stature in Asia and the world at large. In terms of its mission, the university progressed from being a "respected teaching institution" during the 1970s and 1980s to a research intensive university and is now seen as an important national "icon" for the generation of new knowledge in the 21st Century. This function and status has been well recognized by the major international rankings institutions, such as the Times Higher Education Supplement, Shanghai's Jiao Tong and Taiwanese rankings. Growth in knowledge production more than doubled (by 231%) in the decade between 1997 and 2007 and this decade also witnessed the professionalization of teaching and knowledge, with the establishment of a number of advanced research centres for excellence in engineering and technology, the natural and physical sciences, public policy, arts and the social sciences. An important feature of these centres has been the building of an interdisciplinary focus that links researchers and students across disciplines and faculties.

Together with the rise of the NUS as a research university, our exploration has shown that the NUS occupies a very significant position in Singapore's science and technology system, contributing both in terms of knowledge production and as a major national source of scientists, engineers and medical professionals. Moreover, Singapore's main research eco-system is a stone's throw from the university campus, where in the former the government has invested heavily to the extent of over S$ 4–5 billion over the last decade, building three science parks, a biomedical cluster (Biopolis) and a media-technology cluster (Fusionopolis). Over the years, the NUS has had a radiating influence on the nation's research eco-system, as much as it has benefited by forging valuable research and training relationships with the university. Our major conclusion here is that the NUS has played and is continuing to play an important part in the evolution of Singapore's national science community, its professionalization and its advancement of knowledge, thus in essence the NUS is manifesting itself as a form of science community.

The NUS crossed the threshold of 10,000 students in 1980s, 20,000 in 1990s and 30,000 in 2008 and the faculty and research staff witnessed more than a fourfold increase during this period, thereby it "has been transforming and reinventing" itself in recent decades. One major development has been a high degree of inter-nationalization and no other major Asian university can match the cosmopolitan composition of international students and faculty as can be found at the NUS. With respect to this, from being around 10% in the 1980s, the foreigners among faculty had increased to 39% by 1997 and this had increased to 50% of the total staff for the academic year 2007–08, of which the non Singaporean Asian faculty accounted for around 30% and European and North American for 20%. Furthermore, the foreign researchers share increased to 75% in 2007 and regarding students the overseas cohort increased from 13% in 1997 to 34% in 2007.

The NUS compares very well with top universities, such as MIT and Yale, and even has a much better record compared to University of Tokyo in terms of its internationalization of students and infusing of a cosmopolitan culture on the campus. However, it still has yet to catch up with these top universities in terms of the proportion of graduate students among the total student population. For instance, the share of graduate students is 15.7% of the total, as compared to 60% at MIT; 50% at Yale University and likewise 50% at the University of Tokyo. At the NUS, the number of Ph.D. scholars as a proportion of the total number of students is certainly low compared to the leading universities in Asia, such as the University of Tokyo and the low proportion of graduate students coupled with Ph.D.s studied, also appears to be having a bearing on new knowledge production, measured in terms of papers. In this regard, although in the Asian context the NUS is one of the leading universities, it comes after the University of Tokyo and Seoul National University.

The NUS's policy of internationalization has not just been something confined to students and faculty, for it has developed international and global networks and has fostered research and collaborative links with top universities throughout the world. For instance, it has combined degree programmes in medicine with Duke University; public policy and cluster related collaboration with Harvard University; and is part of MIT the Singapore Alliance for joint research and teaching. At the same time the NUS is part of more than half dozen global networks of universities, such as Universitas-21. Moreover, the process of internationalization has been systematically structured and cultivated by the NUS authorities to combine it with the policy to attract global talent in faculty and research staff.

With increasing professionalism in its research output, since the 1990s the university extended its twin missions of combining teaching and research excellence to the "Third Mission" of knowledge connecting its innovation processes with those of the private sector. By doing so, to a large degree it is following other world-class universities, such as the University of Cambridge, who are responding to the challenges of the 21st Century knowledge driven economy and the demands of society. In this vein, there are two main institutional means by which the NUS has become proactive. *First* is the nexus with industry, which is mainly promoted through NUS Enterprise. Currently, the university owns about 305 U.S.-registered patents developed since 1990, has launched over 44 spin-off firms and has entered into 500 collaborations with industry over the last decade and a half. Further, our investigations have shown that these examples of knowledge transfer and innovation provide the potential for developing and extending this "new economic role" for the university in collaboration with the private sector. *The second* is the engagement of the NUS with societal challenges of the 21st century. In this regard, the current research and education programmes include; environment sustainability, sustainable cities, ageing, clean water and energy, all of which are pressing problems for both Singapore and Asia.

The comparative advantages experienced by Singapore during the 1980s and the 1990s are not going to sustain and serve the knowledge driven future economy of the nation, for today the economic and industrial landscape is heavily dependent on globally dispersed production, knowledge networks, higher education, science parks, innovation hubs, information networks linked to national innovation capacities and dynamic human resource skills. Key actors in these networks and innovation systems include firms, research institutions, government agencies and universities and regarding the lattermost the NUS along with other universities and knowledge institutions are going to be key drivers of the emerging knowledge economy of Singapore. For as the President of the NUS recently observed, "as globalization proceeds, the NUS must keep at the forefront of innovation in global education, research and institution networks".[56]

Having explored the NUS in its various facets and dimensions of teaching, research and innovation, it is pertinent here to reflect upon what this case study on the university has offer other universities.

Firstly, the NUS's experience clearly demonstrates the importance of taking institutional and organizational initiatives, so as to follow a path of first building a respected teaching university and subsequently raising the academic and intellectual threshold so as to become a leading research intensive university for the advancement of knowledge and its application to industry and society[57]. Equally important in this university's case, has been the role of the academic leadership[58], which has provided innovative insights for promoting and carrying out effective responses to contemporary challenges. That is, the way in which the leadership orchestrated combination of the three missions of teaching, research and innovation in serving society and economy, in our view, has much to offer universities in the developing world.

Secondly, universities that are not already doing so could play multiple roles in teaching, research and innovation so as to accomplish various societal goals and challenges[59]. However, in our view they need to attain a high degree of excellence and quality in teaching and research standards before taking on the role of innovation[60]. Otherwise, they will end up playing either a "hand maiden" or "service role" to private sector, rather than educational role towards achieving teaching and research excellence for national progress.

Thirdly, what comes out of the NUS experience is the insight that features, such as internationalization, multiculturalism and a cosmopolitan outlook are important ingredients that could be combined with quality and excellence and subsequently applied to the intellectual culture of institutions of higher learning. In this regard, it is our conviction that the future of world-class universities will foster not just an interdisciplinary approach in teaching and research, but promote cosmopolitan culture when seeking excellence[61].

Fourthly, there are several small countries in Africa and Asia which are still struggling to building research universities and their respective science and technology systems. The NUS case in Singapore offers many lessons for developing countries with limited resources on how an institution of higher learning could become an important actor and a necessary link in the building of a national S&T system and science community.

In sum, as a major national university of an Asian country, the NUS over recent decades has played an important part in nation building and economic competitiveness, from the perspective of knowledge. Our message for universities and decision makers aspiring to nurture and support leading research intensive universities is that they need:

- Internationalization and global benchmarking for recruitment, promotion and tenure of faculty;
- To build a strong and effective educational and research network with world leading institutions of higher learning;
- To mobilize investment for research infrastructure towards attaining peaks of excellence;
- To combine internationalization, multiculturalism and a cosmopolitan outlook with quality and excellence, so as to attract best world talent (students, researchers and faculty);
- To go beyond influencing public policies in the national context and address global challenges in an integrated and multi-disciplinary perspective; and
- Positive and harmonious partnering and evolving working relationships with the private sector and policy makers.

NOTES

[1] We wish to sincerely acknowledge the inputs given by Daniel Ng, Tay Poh Choo and Swapan Kumar Patra in writing of this paper. Without their help in collating information and data this paper would not have been possible. Views expressed in this paper are entirely ours and not those of the National University of Singapore.

[2] Even in the midst of economic downturn, public policies of the leading economies of Asia, continue to assign a very high priority to promote institutions of higher learning and research. In a way this is closely associated with the success of knowledge based industries, firstly in: Japan, Australia, New Zealand, South Korea, Singapore and Taiwan and in recent years in China and India (See also Ramakrishna & Ng, forthcoming).

[3] NSI is defined as 'the network of institutions in public and private sectors whose activities and interactions create, import, modify and diffuse new knowledge and relevant new technologies (Freeman, 1987, 1995). By stressing the role of the private sector, we do not however exclude university's relations with public sector industrial and business enterprises and other agencies.

[4] According to Times Higher Education world ranking of universities 2007, NUS stands at 33rd position among the top 100 universities; 25th among the top 50 universities in natural sciences; and 12th among the top 50 universities in life sciences and biomedicine. According to the Shanghai Jiao Tong University ranking for 2009, NUS stands at 6th position in Asia and 135th out of the top 500 universities.

[5] Plenary lecture given at the World Knowledge Forum, Seoul, South Korea on 15 October 2008. What is noticeable in the emerging new geography of knowledge production is the emergence of Asia as an important global player in the world S&T system, mainly propelled by China and India (NSF, 2006).

[6] See (Gaillard, 2010).

[7] This new figure is according to the recent report in 2009 by Battelle, USA, entitled '2009 Global R&D Funding Forecast'.

[8] As already noted, we do not exclude the university's relations with public sector agencies, industry and business enterprises.

[9] See also Lee (2000), whose influential book tells the story of Singapore transforming from a "third world" to "first world" nation.

[10] As cited by Kong (2000), see Yip, John Soon Kwong, 'Reflections and renewal in education'. In Tan, Jason; Gopinathan, S. and Ho, Wah Kam, (Eds). Education in Singapore: a book of readings. Singapore: Prentice Hall, 1997. pp. 385–400.

[11] These are: MIT, Wharton, Shanghai Jiao Tong University, INSEAD, France, Chicago Graduate School of Business.

[12] This Committee was formed with members from: various economic, trade and industry departments, the NUS, NTU and business enterprises. Biopolis is administered by the Biomedical Research Council and Singapore's major science agency A*STAR

[13] It was chaired by the Deputy Prime Minister at the time.

[14] Over the years the NUS witnessed growth that has encompassed a wide range of faculties, schools and areas of teaching and research in the: arts and social sciences, science and engineering, computing, design and environment, medicine, dentistry, business, public policy, law and a conservatory of music.

[15] For instance, Sydney Brenner, Nobel Laureate, has been associated with the NUS for quite some time. Edison Liu spent 20 years in the faculties of medicine at North Carolina University and Johns Hopkins and five years at the US National Cancer Research Institute before becoming the executive director of the Genomic Institute of Singapore and a professor at the NUS. There are hundreds of such talented people that the NUS and other institutions in Singapore have attracted over the last few years and owing to the lack of space we are just mentioning couple of names. See also section 3.6.1.

[16] A national scientific community can be defined as: "the scientists within a country form a national scientific community, a community within the world scientific community. They enter the national scientific community through the relatively similar scientific education which they have undergone and their acquisition of the shared culture of science - at an elementary level. They perform their research in the framework of national institutional arrangements for research such as universities with similar pattern, the same national associations and journals, supported by the same national foundations and the same bodies which set the national science policies; thus they perform their research within a common institutional and intellectual setting" (Thomas Schott 1991:442). The term is used to denote not just infrastructure, but intellectual climate and a national identity when scientific advances emanate from a specific country. See also (Knight & de Wit, 1997).

[17] See various NUS annual reports and research reports.

[18] H-index: Included in the Web of Science citation report, it reflects both the number of publications and the number of citations per publication. An h-index of h signifies that the author has published h papers each of which has been cited at least h times. So, for example, an h-index of 4 signifies that the author has published 4 papers each of which has been cited at least 4 times. The author may in fact have published 5 or even 100 papers, but papers 5 to 100 have fewer than 4 citations and are therefore discounted. For further information on the h-index see http://en.wikipedia.org/wiki/Hirsch_ number.

[19] The scores have been somewhat lower for the two years both for NUS and Singapore publications as a whole.

[20] These figures are based on the SCI extended data base accessed in August 2009.

[21] This is after comparing: the total number of times the papers are cited, the citation index and the h-index for each of these three universities.

[22] Asia Research Institute (ARI); Centre for International Law; Centre for Maritime Studies (CMS); Centre for Remote Imaging, Sensing and Processing (CRISP); East Asian Institute (EAI); Energy Studies Institute (ESI); Institute for Mathematical Sciences (IMS); Institute of Real Estate Studies (IRES); Institute of South Asian Studies (ISAS); Interactive & Digital Media Institute (IDMI); Life Sciences Institute (LSI); Middle East Institute (MEI); NUS Environmental Research Institute (NERI); NUS Nanoscience and Nanotechnology Initiative (NUSNNI); Risk Management Institute (RMI); Singapore Synchrotron Light Source (SSLS); Solar Energy Research Institute of Singapore (SERIS); Temasek Laboratories (TL@NUS) The Logistics Institute - Asia Pacific (TLI - Asia Pacific) and Tropical Marine Science Institute (TMSI).

[23] Bioinformatics Institute (BII); Bioprocessing Technology Institute (BTI); Data Storage Institute (DSI) Genome Institute of Singapore (GIS); Institute of Bioengineering and Nanotechnology (IBN);

Institute of Chemical & Engineering Sciences (ICES); Institute of Materials Research and Engineering (IMRE); Institute of Medical Biology (IMB); Institute of Molecular and Cell Biology (IMCB); and Singapore Institute for Clinical Sciences (SICS).

[24] Institute for Infocomm Research; Data Storage Institute; Institute of Materials Research and Engineering; Institute of High-Performance Computing; Institute of Microelectronics; Singapore Institute of Manufacturing Technologies; and Institute of Chemical and Engineering Sciences.

[25] CREATE aims to be a talent magnet and innovation hub. The research centres in CREATE will host: professors, research investigators, doctoral and postdoctoral researchers, who will form groups to pursue research programmes in areas that are aligned both with Singapore's strategic interest and those of the respective institutions. CREATE entities will have intensive collaboration with: Singapore-based universities, polytechnics, laboratories and research institutes, in cutting-edge research projects and in the attraction of global talent.

[26] The success of Silicon Valley in ICT, science-based innovation at Cambridge Science Park and high technology R&D and manufacturing characterised by Taiwan's Hsinchu Technology District, prompted the Singapore government to expand the three Science Parks (I, II and III) surrounding the NUS in the early 1990s.

[27] Quintiles is one of the world's largest clinical research organizations, having its Asian headquarters at Science Park I.

[28] See also Yeoh et al. (2000) who draw our attention to the fact that it was part of state policy and strategy for 21st century Singapore to be made into a cosmopolitan city.

[29] Singapore has three fellows of the Royal Academy of Engineering (Professor Cham Tao Soo, former president of NTU, Professor C C Hang, former deputy chairman of the NSTB; Professor Seeram Ramakrishna, vice president of the NUS) and one fellow of the National Academy of Engineering, Professor Miranda Yap, Chemical and Biomolecular Engineering, the NUS.

[30] We have chosen 15 leading S&T journals, such as: the Singapore Medical Journal; the International Journal of Nano Science; the International Journal of Applied Mechanics etc, published in Singapore. It was observed that the NUS faculty figure as members of editorial boards of 12 of these journals.

[31] The Ministry of Education (MOE) of Singapore worked out a quality assurance framework for all the universities in Singapore in 2003: the Quality Assurance Framework for University (QAFU). Under the QAFU, the MOE was to set up an external panel to validate the universities' self assessment against their institutional goals and performance targets. The panel conducts an on site validation of each university once every three years to check the validity of its self-assessment report, and to assess the university's strengths and weaknesses. The panel reports its findings and recommendations for quality improvements by the university to the Minister for Education.

[32] The visiting committees comprise international experts drawn from top institutions around the world. They provide quality assurance and high international standards. The NUS makes improvements in accordance with their recommendations. The university has a formalized schedule and systems for the visiting committees and international advisory committees and once every five years an independent external review is conducted for all of its departments.

[33] This transformative student-centric education approach aims to nurture thinking individuals who are alive to societal and global opportunities and help them to be ready to make a difference after they graduate from the university. The goal is to make them valued members and leaders of society and global citizens who can be effective in the changing any diverse setting in which they are placed.

[34] The NUS created the Centre of Life Sciences in 2007, which invested in research infrastructure and advanced research equipment to cater for a community of 450 researchers in life sciences programmes in: cancer, cardiovascular biology, immunology, neurobiology and ageing.

[35] All these advanced research centres and initiatives are led by professionals and faculty who have spent a long time in Europe and North America, in leading universities and research institutes, with very high international reputations in the science and technology fields. Dr. Joachim Luther, Head, SERIS, is an internationally recognized scientist in solar energy. Dr. Daniel Tenen, Head of the Cancer Research Centre of Excellence, moved from Harvard Medical School to the NUS. Similarly, Dr. Michael Sheetz who spent long years as a Professor in Columbia University's biological sciences

moved to the NUS to head the Mechanobiology Research Centre of Excellence. There are other notable figures, but we are mentioning only few names owing to the lack of space.

[36] This was set up to develop research into human capital and long term research capabilities in nanoscience and nanotechnology. NUSNNI helps accelerate research efforts across departments with research institutes and overseas collaborators at the Universities of Cambridge and Oxford and the University of California at Santa Barbara and at Irvine.

[37] This centre conducts cancer research extending from basic mechanistic studies to experimental therapeutics. It links unique resources in Singapore so as to develop new approaches to the under-standing and treating of this complex disease. The main objective of the centre is to build new capacity for interdisciplinary, collaborative approaches, in order to address the most challenging and significant research problems in cancer, with a particular focus being on cancers that afflict Asian populations. The vision is to make the CRCE one of the top cancer research centres in the world.

[38] The institute undertakes use-inspired basic research in the field of solar energy conversion. The institute's research includes the: development of materials, components, processes and systems for photovoltaic electricity generation and energy efficient buildings. SERIS is globally active, but is mainly focussing on technologies and services for tropical regions, in particular, for Singapore and Southeast Asia.

[39] The centre is headed by Professor Paul Matsudaira as the co-director. He moved from MIT to take up the position at the NUS. The objective of the centre is to develop a new paradigm of biomedical research, by focusing on the quantitative and systematic understanding of dynamic functional processes. Instead of purely being based on molecular networks of interactions, the processes of systematic decomposition of the biomechanical processes into smaller functional steps, at both the biophysical and biochemical level, are being investigated.

[40] The media of combining digital and interaction technologies is known as Interactive Digital Media (IDM). The institute was established to advance interdisciplinary research between natural science and social science, as it is generally believed that collaboration of these two areas is the key for the success of IDM, which will subsequently have a revolutionary impact on society in the twenty-first century. More specifically, the interdisciplinary research at the institute relates to the development of the next generation of IDM that takes: engineering, social and psychological aspects into consideration.

[41] This centre's focus is on developing quantum technologies for coherent control of individual photons and atoms and it explores both the theory and the practical possibilities of constructing quantum-mechanical devices for the purpose of cryptography and computation.

[42] TMSI undertakes research relevant to: physical oceanography, acoustics, marine biology, marine mammals, biofuels, water resources and climate change. The institute has been established as a centre of excellence for: teaching, research, development and advancement of knowledge in tropical marine sciences, as well as other environment related subjects. TMSI is a multi-disciplinary and inter-disciplinary research institute at the NUS with international links.

[43] This centre's focus is on developing novel applications from their fundamental research, so as to: contribute to enhancements in water quality and water resources, attain global leadership in water science and provide technological solutions in conservation and purification.

[44] This is an advanced research institute in collaboration with Georgia Institute of Technology (Georgia Tech) for research and education programmes on global logistics. The institute has strong ties with the School of Industrial and Systems Engineering at Georgia Tech and also has a strong relationship with the faculties of: engineering, science, computing and business at the NUS. The research agenda of this institute is to advance knowledge with the aim of applying it to: global logistics, information technology, industrial engineering and supply chain management.

[45] The programme offers an innovative and rigorous medical education programme with a distinctive focus on research aimed at building leaders and scholars in: medical, education, and patient care. It is post-baccalaureate medical education, in which students begin their medical studies after earning a bachelor's degree. Duke-NUS offer a potential to specialize in the fields of medicine and biomedical sciences and students who successfully complete the course of study are awarded a

Doctor of Medicine (M.D.) degree jointly by Duke University and the National University of Singapore.

[46] The institute aims to be a world-class centre in risk management through research, education and training. The institute was established as a university level research institute dedicated to the area in financial risk management research and education. It collaborates with Princeton University and the University of Waterloo.

[47] This involves: the NUS, Nanyang Technological University (NTU) and the Massachusetts Institute of Technology (MIT) and was initiated by the NUS in 1998 to promote global engineering education and research. SMA brings together the resources of three premiere academic institutions, whilst providing students with unlimited access to exceptional faculty expertise and superior research facilities. An important feature is the technologically advanced distance learning facilities.

[48] The institute was set up to engage in interdisciplinary scholarship relating to cultural and social change and to advance social science research knowledge in Asia. It networks with: the arts and social sciences, the school of design and environment and the schools of: business, public policy and law. It aims to provide a world-class focus and resource for research in the Asian region. At present the ARI is engaged in advancing knowledge on the geographies of: religion, cultural studies, migration, the family, science, technology and society and changing urban spaces in cities. The director, Professor Lily Kong, was awarded the Robert Stoddard Award by the Association of American Geographers in 2008 for her academic and research contribution stretching back 20 years, in relation to advancing knowledge on the geography of religion.

[49] GAI is a recent initiative of the NUS aimed at influencing the future of Asia, through the bringing to fruition its vision of it being a global university centred on that continent. In this regard, the rise of Asia in the world economy over the last decade has been associated with a multitude of societal challenges, such as: ageing and leisure, migration and cities, water, food and health security and safety around sustainable development. The GAI aims "to take the lead in research and scholarship directed at topics pivotal to Asia's future. Driven by the mission to provide in-depth insights to shape the nature of 21st Century Asia, the NUS Global Asia Institute will take a holistic approach to the fundamental issues confronting Asia and the world". The new institute will promote an interdisciplinary based methodology by focusing on integrative studies. In understanding challenges and designing solutions based on advancing knowledge "the work of the institute will go beyond public policies and also deal with matters of technological importance".

[50] APRU is a consortium of 42 leading research universities in the Pacific Rim. The consortium aims to foster: education, research and enterprise thereby contributing to the: economic, scientific and cultural advancement of the Pacific Rim.

[51] AUN is a network widely recognised as a vital mechanism for the building up of an active and renowned ASEAN community in higher education.

[52] Universitas 21 network's purpose is to facilitate collaboration and cooperation between the member universities and to create opportunities for them on a scale that none of them would be able to achieve operating independently or through traditional bilateral alliances.

[53] The IARU is an alliance of ten of the world's leading research universities: the Australian National University, ETH Zurich, the National University of Singapore, Peking University, the University of California, Berkeley, the University of Cambridge, the University of Copenhagen, the University of Oxford, the University of Tokyo and Yale University. It is a strategic drawing together of universities that share a similar vision and have a commitment to educating future leaders. Professor Tan Chorh Chuan, president of the National University of Singapore has been elected chair for the period 2009–2011.

[54] A recent report on 'The impact of the University of Cambridge on the UK Economy and Society' (prepared by Library House and chaired by Lord Simon, non-executive director of Uniliver and the Suez Group) refers to knowledge and technology transfer and commercialization of research via: licensing, faculty consulting, contract research and publications with economic impacts, as 'Third Stream' activities.

[55] Some of the data on the NUS patents and their comparison with private firms in Singapore is drawn from Wong et al. (2009).

[56] Professor Tan Chorh Chuan, 'Scaling New Heights in a Changing World', the State of the University Address, 30 October 2009, NUS, Singapore.

[57] Here institutional measures relate to the process of professionalization, which combines quality and excellence in teaching.

[58] Given the limitations of space and time, we could not explore this aspect and although it deserves a fuller and detailed exploration, we certainly are of the opinion that this factor has been a very important.

[59] However, such strategies and policies relating to university-industry relations or what has come to be known as "Triple Helix" partnerships need to be approached with caution, particularly with regard to universities in the developing countries.

[60] Attaining teaching and research excellence is an important step towards becoming relevant to innovation and training in entrepreneurship. In other words, only such universities will be in a better position to respond to private sector challenges and innovation, whilst at the same time sustaining standards of teaching and research excellence.

[61] The NUS has always placed a very high premium on quality, excellence and systematic peer evaluation in its recruitment and human resource policies and in so doing it has been a catalyst for nursing global talent for Singapore.

REFERENCES

Freeman, C. (1987). *Technology, policy and economic performanc: Lessons from JAPAN* (Vol. 290660). London: New York: Pinter Publishers.

Freeman, C. (1995). The national system of innovation in historical perspective. *Cambridge Journal of Economics, 19*(1), 5–24.

Gaillard, J. (2010). Measuring R&D in developing countries: Main characteristics and implications for the Frascati manual. *Science, Technology and Society, 15*(1).

Yeug, W.C. (2006). Innovating for global competition: Singapore's pathway to high-tech development. In Bengt-Ake Lundvall, P. Intarakumnerd and Jan Vang (Eds), *Asia's Innovation Systems in Transition.* Cheltenham, UK & Northampton, MA, USA: Edward Elgar.

Knight, J., & de Wit, H. (1997). *Internationalization of higher education in Asia Pacific countries.* Amsterdam: European Association for International Education.

Kong, L. (2000). *Science and education in an Asian tiger: Talk delivered as Vice-Provost (Education).* Singapore: National University of Singapore.

Krishna, V. V. (1997). A portrait of the scientific community in India: Historical growth and contemporary problems. In J. Gaillard, V. V. Krishna, & R. Waast (Eds.), *Scientific communities in the developing world.* Thousand Oaks, CA: Sage Publications.

Krishna, V. V. (2009). *Emerging singapore science community: Seminar series.* Singapore: Asia Research Institute, National University of Singapore.

Lee, K. Y. (2000). *From third world to first : The Singapore story, 1965–2000.* New York: HarperCollins Publishers.

Library House. (2006). *The impact of the University of Cambridge on the UK economy and society.* Cambridge: Library House.

NSF. (2006). *Science and engineering indicators 2006.* Virginia, VA: National Science Foundation.

NSF. (2008). Science and technology: Public attitudes and understanding. In *Science and engineering indicators 2008.* Virginia, VA: National Science Foundation.

Parayil, G. (2005). From "Silicon Island" to "Biopolis of Asia": Innovation policy and shifting competitive strategy in Singapore. *California Management Review, 47*(2), 50–73.

Philips, S.A.M. & Yeung, W.C. (2003). A place for R&D? The Singapore science park. *Urban Studies, 40*(4), 707–732.

Ramakrishna, S., & Ng, D. (forthcoming). *Changing face of innovation: Is it shifting to Asia?* Singapore: World Scientific Publishing.

Schott, T. (1991). The world scientific community: Globality and globalisation. *Minerva, 29*(4), 440–462.

Turpin, T., & Krishna, V. V. (2007). *Science, technology policy and the diffusion of knowledge: Understanding the dynamics of innovation systems in the Asia pacific.* Cheltenham, England: Edward Elgar.

Wong, P. (2007). Commercializing biomedical science in a rapidly changing "Triple-Helix" Nexus: The experience of the national university of Singapore. *The Journal of Technology Transfer, 32*(4), 367–395.

Wong, P. K., Ho, Y. P., & Singh, A. (2009). *Towards a "Global Knowledge Enterprise": The entrepreneurial university model of the NUS.* Singapore: National University of Singapore.

Yeoh, B. S. A., Huang, S., & Willis, K. (2000). Global cities, transnational flows and gender dimensions, the view from Singapore. *Tijdschrift Voor Economische En Sociale Geografie, 91*(2), 147–158.

Yue, C. S. (2005). *The Singapore model of industrial policy: Past evolution and current thinking.* Paper presented at the LAEBA second annual meeting.

Seeram Ramakrishna
The National University of Singapore, Singapore

Venni Venkata Krishna
Asia Research Institute
The National University of Singapore, Singapore
Jawaharlal Nehru University, India

COLIN B. GRANT

12. STRATEGY FOR IMPACT

The University Global Partnership Network

University of Surrey[1] - North Carolina State University -
Universidade de São Paulo - Seoul National University -
University of Cape Town

OVERVIEW

This paper presents the University Global Partnership Network as a case study in a new approach to international university strategy based on tight multilateralism. It begins with a description of various types of multilateralism in higher education, placing emphasis on *tight multilateralism*. It then introduces the University of Surrey, Guildford (United Kingdom) as a key player in the Global Partnership Network. This is followed by a discussion of international benchmarking for research and the rather more challenging areas of teaching, curriculum innovation and student and faculty mobility. The next section explores implications for performance management and human resources strategy and argues for a shift in culture and attitude to an acknowledgement of the role of overseas activity as an integral part of the responsibilities of faculty, students and staff. Such an holistic enterprise as a global partnership network cannot emerge *ex nihilo* and there is therefore a need to articulate the values that inform and sustain it. The paper then proceeds to a presentation of the principles and operational practices of the Global Partnership Network (GPN) - a new network that comprises research-led universities across five continents: the University of Surrey, North Carolina State University (NCSU), the Universidade de São Paulo (USP), Seoul National University (SNU) and the University of Cape Town (UCT). Research excellence is central to the self-understanding of each of the partners and therefore also to the GPN itself. The third section of the paper is therefore devoted to a presentation of the salient research themes in which the various GPN members are engaged. The final section sets out to argue that the approach embodied by the GPN is best equipped to offer long-term, sustainable practice (not merely the rhetoric) in internationalization.

THE SHIFT TO MULTILATERALISM

Multilateralism is not new: in military and commercial sectors it has been pursued as a means of securing greater legitimacy and distributed risk (consider the various

N.C. Liu et al., (eds.), Paths to a World-Class University: Lessons from Practices and Experiences, 237–246.

coalitions of forces in the Iraq and Afghanistan wars) and also as a means by which to enlarge presence and reduce costs (consider the various airline alliances such as Star Alliance). The chronology of the development of multilateral consortia, coalitions or alliances is worthy of mention: Star Alliance was set up in 1997, Oneworld in 1999 and SkyTeam in 2000. Major military coalitions, such as ISAF, the coalitions in both Iraq wars and NATO-led forces in Bosnia experienced significant growth in the period that can be broadly described at the post-Cold War era. In higher education, consortia emerged in the same period, with ASEA-Uninet being established in 1994, Universitas in 1997, the World Universities Network in 2000 and AC21 in 2002. Whereas commercial and military alliances and coalitions, unavoidably, are predicated on shared command structures for code-sharing and other forms of shared infrastructure, university consortia to date, have, unsurprisingly, rested on looser formations. As a rough heuristic, there are two dominant types of multilateralism: loose multilateralism and tight multilateralism. *Loose multilateralism* implies mobility agreements (e.g. mostly bilateral student exchange accords) amongst independent entities, whilst *tight multilateralism* implies institutional commitment to concerted action, shared resources, dual or even multiple awards, networked research and networked placement activity. Tight multilateralism is the preferred option of the new alliance - the Global Partnership Network, established in 2008. Moreover, tight multilateralism does presuppose that self-interest will come second to the collective interest - an interesting position for our turbulent times, perhaps, but equally in keeping with a new spirit of global solidarity.

THE UNIVERSITY OF SURREY

The University of Surrey is one of a range of research-intensive universities established in the UK in the 1960s and these include such well-known universities as Essex, York, Bath, Warwick, Sussex and Reading, amongst others. Many of them, including the University of Surrey, belong to one of three dominant university associations in the UK: the 1994 Group of research intensive universities[2], the Russell Group[3] of established and mostly large, research-intensive universities and the Million+ Group[4] of new universities, with a strong teaching mission and some niche research quality. Surrey is ranked in the top quartile of the extremely competitive UK university sector and it is located 40 minutes from London in Guildford, a city in one of the most economically developed regions of Europe. With for many years the best employment record in England for its graduates and the safest campus in England, the University of Surrey is a world-class research university in a range of disciplines:
- Satellite technology (with collaborations with KAIST, CAST, JPL);
- Electronic engineering (mobile communications and signal processing) - top ten in the UK's Research Assessment Exercise;
- General engineering - rated amongst the top ten in the UK's Research Assessment Exercise;
- Nanotechnology;

- Subjects Allied to Health (rated amongst the top ten in the UK in the Research Assessment Exercise in 2008) - chronobiology, circadian rhythms, zoonotic disease, systems biology;
- Tourism and Hospitality (the leading school in Europe); and
- Sociology (social simulation, methodology, lifecycle, gender) - rated amongst the top ten.

Although the university has a reputation for excellence in engineering, physical and natural sciences, it also has a unique history in the performing arts, with the oldest Ph.D. programme in Dance Studies in the UK, the world-renowned Tonmeister Music programme and composers and musicologists of world repute. It also boasts one of the world's foremost linguistic morphology research groups, the Surrey Morphology Group. The university also has one of the oldest research parks in the UK university sector and its expertise is sought by governments and international organizations across the world, for advice on developing research and technology parks.[5] The Surrey Research Park is of vital importance to the regional economy and to incubating new business. However, it is also of enormous strategic value to the university by virtue of its role in supporting its core investments. The Surrey Clinical Research Centre provides an important interface between the Faculty of Health and Medical Sciences and commercial trials. This unit has over 30 years of psychopharmacological profiles with investigations in anaesthetics, analgesics, antidepressants, nootropics, social substances and herbal products.

In another dimension, Surrey has started to develop a multi-faith centre in recognition of the role played by faith for the 100+ cultures we accommodate on campus. Further, its Sports Park, inaugurated officially in April 2010, is recognized as one of the very best in Europe. It combines a commitment to sports for all (with a world-class swimming pool for people of all abilities and ages), elite sports (e.g. rugby, netball, Olympic sports) and community engagement. Commitment to sports for the disabled is a particularly important part of the Sports Park's mission.[6]

Despite its size (Surrey is a medium-sized university by UK standards, with 15,000 students), the university is particularly proud to boast a full range of disciplines in four faculties:

- Health and Medical Sciences (Health and Social Care, Biochemistry, Chemistry, Biology, Nutrition, Toxicology, Postgraduate Medicine);
- Arts and Human Sciences (Dance, Theatre, Music, Film, Literature, Linguistics, Translation, Politics, Economics, Sociology, Psychology);
- Engineering and Physical Sciences (Electronic, Materials, Medical and Aerospace Engineering, Chemical, Environmental and Satellite Engineering, Physics, Mathematics, Computing, Advanced Technology); and
- Management and Law (Tourism and Hospitality, Healthcare Management, Information Systems, Retail, Marketing, Environmental, Property and IP, EU and International Law).

All research-intensive universities have similar or different strengths and many can justifiably claim international excellence. This creates a need for differentiation from other UK universities and also from those in other parts of the world. This in turn calls for a new type of international strategy. The uniqueness of the University of Surrey approach lies in its commitment to translational strategy. This means insisting on the need to translate strategic vision into concrete action in a holistic manner and there is no alternative to holism since internationalization either embraces the entire institution or it is an appendage, an irrelevant exercise in rhetoric.

TRANSLATING VISION: TIGHT MULTILATERALISM

Surrey launched its new International Strategy in 2008 after much internal discussion. One important demarcation internally was the insistence on the distinction to be made between international recruitment and international relations. This demarcation has proved helpful in creating a genuine international relations strategy, under the responsibility of a separate office. Moreover, the strategy recognized from the outset the existence of high-value bilateral relationships at individual faculty level and avowedly set out to support these as contributors to the university's reputation in their own right. These *bilateral accords* are often restricted in scale but they usually are of long standing. Management of these relationships tends to be located at faculty level, in accordance with the principle of subsidiarity (where decisions are taken at the most relevant level of impact) and it is important to the university strategy that such accords be sustained as meaningful and valuable to faculty colleagues. Thus, the International Relations Office works closely with individual academics and especially the Associate Deans (International) to support these vibrant micro-networks.

The next level of international engagement is known as the strategic partnership level, with these partnerships typically involving more than one academic faculty or school and often being emergent and innovative. Management of these strategic partnerships (e.g. in management disciplines or in a range of natural sciences) follows a matrix model involving Executive Board-level and also senior faculty-level decision-making.

The flagship of the new International Strategy is the University Global Partnership Network (GPN) and in keeping with the need for differentiation, impact and innovation it strives to meet a range of key criteria.

– The GPN must be global in reach. This global reach needs to differentiate members from existing networks or consortia. This principle implies inter-continental membership, as evidenced by the fact that the five member institutions represent four continents.
– The GPN invests in linguistic and intercultural competence for faculty, admini-strators and students.
– The GPN is a partnership of universities and non-academic organizations.
– The GPN is research-led. Research is critically important to our position as creators and challengers of knowledge across the disciplines.
– The GPN strongly supports mobility. Mobility is the concrete manifestation of international activity and extends from student mobility on either academic or professional programmes, to faculty mobility in either teaching or research activity.
– The GPN is intensive, not extensive. Unlike the prevailing models of consortia, it seeks a small membership in order to guarantee depth of activity. This is the best means by which to secure sustainability, tangible activity and trust.

Like any other economic activity, higher education is not immune to recessionary pressures and the impending cutbacks in public sector expenditure. Although government practices vary across member institutions (e.g. no fees are currently levied at public universities in Brazil whereas the government cap on fees is the subject of intense debate in the UK[7]), there is acute pressure on public organizations to provide value for money, efficiency and impact. In the challenging environment of budget deficits, the strong tendency is that there will expectations of more diversified support for universities. The GPN recognizes this pressure and therefore sets out to extend partnership to a range of organizations from outside higher education, which can be commercial foundations, philanthropic or charitable entities, enterprises or banks. The GPN has already registered success in attracting such non-conventional support in support of specific activities that are strongly aligned with the principles set out above - notably pump-priming of research activity that is scalable (i.e. multi-lateral) and support for student mobility. It is important that commercial partners in the GPN see value in joining, which could be expressed in terms of access to world-class science, access to markets, students and so on.

Almost inevitably, the virtuous multiple environments of the GPN (and strategic and bilateral partnerships) will induce centripetal effects, drawing the member institutions together in developing innovation in the curriculum. In time, a strong multilateral network will seek shared, transferable activity (or "economies of scale", in a different discourse), in the form of teaching programmes that offer articulations, transferable credits and exit awards. It is possible that we will move beyond dual awards to multiple awards for Ph.D. programmes, for example. That is, a desirable outcome would be a multilateral GPN Ph.D. programme, for example in veterinary science, in which students could take credits in research at any member institution of the GPN. Similarly, and this is particularly true of the English-speaking world, there is a need to recognize the fundamental importance of credit-bearing linguistic training in ensuring that faculty and students make the most of their international experience. The University of Surrey has pioneered a scheme known as the Global Graduate Award in which students at undergraduate level may take credit-bearing qualifications in addition to their core academic programmes, as discussed below. This kind of initiative requires university resources and recognition across all units that an investment in such an activity represents good strategic sense.

INTERNATIONAL BENCHMARKING IN RESEARCH AND TEACHING

As noted above, the GPN is a research-led, tight multilateral network. However, although research is central to its conception, this must be complemented by an equally strong commitment to teaching. A number of research themes has arisen from the first year of partnership network activities and in general terms, they map onto the following disciplines:
- Cardiovascular Health;
- Veterinary Science;
- Computing;
- Sleep Research;

- Public Health;
- Systems Biology;
- Energy Research;
- Chemical Science;
- Social Science;
- Mathematics;
- Sports;
- Arts; and
- Intervention and Development.

Specific sub-themes under these general headings are worthy of further elaboration. For instance, the cardiovascular health initiative focuses on atherosclerosis, but also examines how natural products or micro-organisms, including toxins, can be used in the treatment of serious illness. Moreover, public health focuses on such issues as ageing populations, tele-medicine and nursing ethics, whilst in terms of bioscience research zoonotic disease has been identified as a key area for further multilateral research. Further areas undergoing development include the bioscientific applications of nanotechnology. Energy research extends across a range of disciplines, including law (environmental regulation), water technology (reverse osmosis) and economics. Social science research has identified global tourism, identity, neuroscience and international politics (intervention and development). In addition, crisis management across several social science disciplines is being investigated.

Activities to support these initiatives include research seminars, such as the Surrey-NCSU Zoonoses Workshop, held at Surrey in spring 2009. Zoonotic diseases threaten our health, food safety and our livestock industry and also have global consequences impacting upon trade, economics and security, which makes multi-disciplinary studies at the interface between human and veterinary medicine important and timely. A follow-up NCSU-Surrey-USP seminar was held in Raleigh, North Carolina in November 2009 and it covered topics including metabolonomics/bacterial systems, genetics, high throughput NMR projects, virology/transcriptional biology and enterics and also human/animal genomics. A further example of research activity concerns the tripartite social science research seminar scheduled for Seoul National University and involving academics from SNU and Surrey and Nanjing Universities.

PERFORMANCE AND HUMAN RESOURCES

From the experience of the University of Surrey, it is essential to recognize that concrete implementation of a deep international strategy requires leadership at the Executive Board level. As Surrey emerged from the tired, orthodox vision of international strategy as a proxy for recruitment from big overseas markets (especially China), it invested in an inchoate International Relations Office. Although initially this office did not include a senior academic executive, in 2007 the university confirmed the appointment of a Dean of International Relations, which was subsequently consolidated to Pro Vice Chancellor (International Relations) in 2009, in recognition of the vital strategic importance of the role. Without direct representation at Executive Board level the international strategy would be misunderstood and considered to be an appendage rather than a core component of the University's identity.

A myth has persisted in universities that there is a choice between "hard" recruitment activities (with tangible outcomes in the form of student numbers) and "soft" diplomacy (with intangible, indirect benefits in the long run, if one takes a charitable view). An international strategy based on partnership and networking is far removed from such a simplistic caricature, but it does require an understanding that gestation takes time. The challenge for a multilateral international strategy is not that it might eschew tangible benefits, because achieving an impact in this dimension is as important as it is in research strategy. Rather, the challenge is to devise a series of key performance indicators (KPIs) that are more than blunt instruments. The criteria for performance or success are subtle, extensive and interconnected and they can include:

- Dual and joint degree awards - development, demand and throughput;
- Competitive government funding for programme development;
- Bids for large-scale research;
- Student exchange volumes at undergraduate, graduate and Ph.D. levels;
- Extending partnership to non-academic actors;
- Faculty and staff exchange volumes and quality; and
- Curricular innovation in core and additional disciplines.

Whilst combinations of the above are encountered in British universities, the model adopted by Surrey is radically different. Here, performance management has been a central component of the work of the Dean's function and subsequently that of the Pro Vice Chancellor for a significant period of time, resulting in successive restructurings until an appropriately qualified group of colleagues was recruited. Unquestionable requirements for such roles include diplomacy, drive, an understanding that international relations occupy a position between faculties and individual academics on the one hand and central functions, such as registry and finance, on the other.

An immediate challenge relates to faculty willingness to spend time overseas, particularly where teaching commitments might be concerned. Incentivization has too often been almost entirely financial (the award of an honorarium, for example) and there has been little investment in embedding international activity as part of the standard expectations of academic or indeed administrative faculty. There is a paradox in this state of affairs. It is not true that academics are reluctant travellers: the vast majority will travel for the purposes of research conferences including such conferences outside the US or EU. However, such visits are frequently limited to a few days whereas teaching activities overseas tend to require longer commitments of greater intensity (with teaching, feedback and quality assurance). Management schools tend to have significant experience in overseas delivery that can be shared with other disciplines in which such activity is frequently remote or time-restricted research. Mobility of faculty for reasons other than simply research conferences is a priority.

THE ETHOS OF PARTNERSHIP NETWORKS

One of the greatest cultural challenges facing the GPN arises directly from its multilateral character. Unlike existing consortia, where there are multiple bilateral relationships, the commitment to multilateralism in the GPN actually implies "institutional disinterestedness". This means that benefits to the whole - or indeed to parts of the whole that might not directly favour one institution's interests - are of greater value than bilateral or unilateral benefits. This commitment, which eschews the Darwinism of much of international university politics, has already been translated into action in the building of the South East - India Partnership Network (SE-IPNet) of six UK universities, where there is a commitment to even distribution of benefits across the six members, even when levels of engagement vary. It is also visible in the support of Banco Santander for the university's special relationship with the Universidade de São Paulo. Here, there are specific funding streams for five USP Ph.D. students, every year, for three years. Future corporate partnerships in the GPN will be sought where multilateral interests are supported - for example, in student and faculty exchange. The same multilateral commitment guides the GPN's engagement with philanthropic donors, for whilst there are doubtless institutional and political pressures to adopt a financially unilateral approach, it engages specifically with a view to securing support for its members as a whole.

BUILDING A CULTURE OF INTERNATIONAL QUALITY

For most research faculty there has long been an understanding that the only quality benchmarks of any significance are international. While it is certainly true that this understanding of the need to be world-leading in research greatly assists in winning hearts and minds, the picture is rather more challenging regarding other university functions. With respect to this, there is a reluctance to innovate at the curriculum level and to reflect on what an internationalized curriculum, assuming that it is desirable, might look like. There is certainly scope for empirical innovation, with case studies and data sets across a range of academic disciplines and much remains to be done in this relatively unproblematic area. Theoretical innovation outside the field of intercultural pragmatics, for example, is more challenging, because often access to the theoretical work of the non-English-speaking world is more difficult, particularly when it is a question of non-European languages.

The UGPN at the University of Surrey has moved forward with a scheme of providing additional credit for study relevant to the global environment, known as the Global Graduate Award. Three pathways are envisaged: the first is a language pathway (including English as a foreign language for non-native speakers); a pathway in international politics is being designed, whilst a third pathway in global environments is undergoing exploratory planning. The Global Graduate Award confers credit on students who complete such a pathway outside their main academic discipline. Thus, a student of mechanical engineering can take additional credit in Chinese language whilst a student of economics might take an additional credit in global environments. These additional awards are clearly directly relevant to employment in a globalized world. However, they also provide grounding for an extended knowledge base and invaluable preparation for an exchange programme at a partner university in a different region of the world.

Indeed, even where a commitment amongst research faculty can be taken for granted, all too often it is the case that Anglo-Saxon researchers tend to concentrate on Anglo-Saxon or EU collaborators. There are naturally exceptions to this observation, but faculty retains a cautious attitude towards partners from less conventional regions, particularly where there might be linguistic barriers or perceived linguistic barriers. With these challenges in mind, national activity is rewarded. In research, such reward can take the form of peer esteem (for the only esteem indicator in research is intrinsically international) or "big research" bids. In student mobility, reward can take the form of the inherent value of the international experience per se or also credit transfer or dual and even multiple awards.

THE NEW SUSTAINABILITY

Although just beginning the phase of consolidation, the UGPN has developed a strong sense of multilateralism that upholds a series of key principles and translates these into tangible actions. Whereas individual academics have long defined themselves in international terms, through their research collaborators worldwide, universities as institutions have often faced significant challenges in acting strategically in the international arena, whilst maintaining the trust of faculty. The GPN is designed to provide a sustainable approach to tight multilateralism that seeks to address a number of challenges in the following way:

Scalability

Membership of the GPN is intentionally limited, with the optimum requiring one further university in Europe in this first phase, as such a scale gives it a relative advantage in developing responsiveness and concerted action.

Mobility

The UGPN is committed strongly to mobility for students and faculty at all levels. This mobility requires resource and unconventional funding from external sources or strategic investment from internal sources.

Excellence

The UGPN adopts international excellence as its benchmark in research and teaching, learning and professional placements.

Innovation

The UGPN seeks to develop innovation in multilateral research (e.g. systems biology, crisis management, water, transformational impact of the arts, health and well-being) and also teaching (credit transferability, multiple awards, Global Graduate Award streams).

Trust

GPN members operate in close co-operation, sharing opportunities and intelligence, often including commercially sensitive areas in recognition of the value of global education:

> This new world demands a special brand of leadership... global leadership. We need new vision, bold action, powerful partnerships for enduring peace and prosperity. That is why I call for a new multilateralism. (UN Secretary General, Ban Ki-Moon, 21 May 2009)

NOTES

[1] Whereas the Global Partnership Network is the university's flagship international initiative, the university has a range of other relationships categorised in two ways. There are two key strategic partnerships of a narrower disciplinary scope: 1. Dongbei University of Finance and Economics in Dalian, PR China in a joint venture known as the Surrey International Institute (SII) and 2: the Indian Institute of Science Education and Research (IISER) Pune where the University of Surrey is the lead institution in a consortium of six UK universities (Southampton, Kent, Queen Mary, Sussex and Royal Holloway).

[2] For reference, please see: 1994group.ac.uk.

[3] The Russell Group includes the universities of Oxford, Edinburgh and Southampton. For reference, please see: russellgroup.ac.uk.

[4] The Million+ Group includes amongst its members City University, Oxford Brookes and Manchester Metropolitan University. For reference, please see: millionplus.ac.uk.

[5] See http://www.surrey-research-park.com.

[6] The Surrey Sports Park is now the official home of Harlequins Rugby Football Club (one of the leading premiership teams in England) and Surrey Storm (England's leading netball team). See surreysportspark.co.uk.

[7] The university fees regime is currently being reviewed for the government by Lord Browne. It will report after the general election on 6 May, with a strong expectation that it will raise the limit ('cap') on university fees to home and EU students. It is interesting to note that fees for a private secondary school in London can reach as much as £25,000 per annum, whilst fees for an undergraduate programme at any UK university are capped at £3,280.

Colin Grant
University of Surrey, UK

HAROLD M. MAURER AND JIALIN C. ZHENG

13. BECOMING A WORLD-RENOWNED HEALTH SCIENCES CENTRE IN THE ERA OF THE GLOBAL MARKET

Institutional Effort and Policies for the Promotion of Academic Talent

INTRODUCTION

The University of Nebraska Medical Center (UNMC) is the only public academic health sciences centre in the State of Nebraska (USA) and its educational programmes are responsible for training more health professionals that practise in Nebraska than any other institution. Through its commitment to education, research, patient care and outreach, the UNMC and its hospital partner, the Nebraska Medical Center (NMC), deliver state-of-the-art healthcare, prepare the best-educated health professionals and scientists and rank among the leading research centres. Moreover, the UNMC seeks to advance its historic commitment to community health, embrace the richness of diversity to build unity and create economic growth in Nebraska.

On 1 December 1998, at a time when the main focus of the medical centre was education and patient care for Nebraska, the newly appointed chancellor Harold M. Maurer vowed to bring research to the forefront of the UNMC's vision, making it his top priority. He articulated a new vision and strategic plan to become a world-renowned health sciences centre, repositioning the UNMC from a regional to a national centre of excellence in the 21st century. For more than ten years, while aiming to improve the educational performance of students, fostering state-of-the-art patient care, targeting community health and embracing diversity, the UNMC has also placed major emphasis on becoming a ranking health sciences research centre to fuel both its educational and clinical programmes. Moreover, it has emphasized the importance of research as a new economic driver for the state.

Today, with over 13,000 employees, the UNMC has established itself as one of the country's leading centres in transplantation biology, bioterrorism preparedness, genetics, biomedical technology, ophthalmology and the treatment of cancer, neurodegenerative diseases and cardiovascular diseases. UNMC's physician practice group, UNMC Physicians, includes 513 physicians in fifty specialties and subspecialties, who practise primarily at the NMC. Construction has recently been completed on the ten-storey Durham Research Center and Durham Research Center II, the Michael F. Sorrell Center for Health Science Education, the four-storey Hixson-Lied Center for Clinical Excellence, a 1,500 stall employee parking garage and a new utility

N.C. Liu et al., (eds.), Paths to a World-Class University: Lessons from Practices and Experiences, 247–261.

plant, among other projects. Plans are also underway or have been completed for a Good Manufacturing Process facility for cellular transplants and vaccine research, the Home Instead Center for Successful Aging, the Center for College of Nursing Sciences and the Harold M. and Beverly Maurer Center for Public Health, among other facilities.

In 1999, the UNMC's research funding was $31 million. Since then, under the new chancellor's leadership, it has grown to more than $100 million and continues to rise. This has resulted in the creation of more than 2,400 highly skilled jobs in the state. This article briefly introduces the UNMC's vision of being a world-class institution, summarizes each year's strategic efforts towards this vision and provides data for the significant accomplishments it has made in education, patient care and research. Moreover, we would like to take this opportunity to discuss the UNMC's strategies and efforts made for these proposed objectives, share our experiences and invite feedback from colleagues from around the world. We also briefly summarize our recent efforts in international collaborations, especially in the Asia-Pacific regions, and focus on the benefits of sustained long-term collaboration when utilizing the strengths of each partner toward a common goal: meeting the healthcare needs of a whole population given the constraints of our current global economy. We will expand upon the nature of partnerships, successes and challenges as we extend our vision of medicine and research beyond Nebraska, and the future efforts being made to amplify the global impact of these collaborations.

THE STATUS OF THE UNMC IN THE 1990S, PREVIOUS MISSION AND CHALLENGES FACED BY THE NEW CHANCELLOR IN 1998

In the early 1990s, the UNMC focused on patient care and medical education, predominantly for the community and the surrounding states. It was primarily a community-oriented medical school with professional schools for nursing, dentistry, and pharmacy, among other related medical fields. Its mission was essentially caring for the health of and providing education for Nebraskans and the importance of research in the academic centre was then minimal. It was in 1993, after becoming Dean of the UNMC College of Medicine, that Maurer inquired of the then President of the University of Nebraska system and the then Chancellor of UNMC why research was not an important focus for the medical school and medical centre?

In 1997, Maurer led negotiations to merge Clarkson and University Hospitals to form the Nebraska Health System (NHS), which is now known as the NMC, the clinical teaching facility for the UNMC. On 1 December 1998, when he assumed the position of UNMC Chancellor, the total amount of annual research funding at the medical centre was less than $31 million, below the average for most regional medical centres across the U.S. In many ways, this was a golden opportunity, much like an open book for him to write his own story and build his legacy at the UNMC, beginning with his own words:

To build a renowned research infrastructure and a world-class institution in the Midwest.

The chancellor firmly believes "vision" is more compelling than "mission". He presented his ideas to the Board of Regents of the university, who were fully supportive. However, he began to face many challenges.

Support from the community, especially philanthropy, was needed for the chancellor's ideas. It was imperative that he presented effectively his exciting vision and build a supporter base towards that vision. The chancellor needed to be both persistent and consistent in continually projecting the message of his vision to faculty and community so as to receive their continuous support. Remaining extremely focused, not diffusing his vision, was vital. He needed to build trust with both the community and faculty in order to align them with his ideas. He believed that the UNMC could successfully realize goals and get to where it wanted to be. He needed to make sure that what he initiated would generate a true and great outcome. He believed that true leaders do not predict the future, but make it.

With these ideas in mind, the chancellor formed a powerful cabinet, appointing six important local community leaders. He concentrated on raising community funds to build a strong infrastructure, which would attract the best and brightest scientists to power new growth for the medical centre. Thus, under his leadership and with strong support of community and faculty, the medical centre began to move forward. Furthermore, he initiated new strategic efforts each year towards his vision and to this day continues to do so, with the UNMC achieving significant accomplishments in education, patient care and research.

THE UNMC NEW VISION, MISSION AND VALUES

Vision is the guiding principle that has and will continue to sustain UNMC's performance in an economy shaped by a multi-generational workforce, techno-logical advances, and economic slowdown. The chancellor articulated this new vision and strategic plan to become a world-renowned health sciences centre several years ago. Being world-class includes having the commitment as well as the capabilities to be world-class and having the ability to communicate these goals to the world. He believes that the UNMC would not be fulfilling its mission, if it chose not to become world-class. To become a world-renowned health sciences centre, it must accomplish the following:
- Deliver state-of-the-art healthcare. To be world-class in the clinical area, the UNMC must be the premier cardiac centre in Nebraska, develop a comprehensive cancer centre and adapt and utilize the new disciplines of biotechnology and personalized medicine.
- Prepare the best-educated health professionals and scientists. To be world-class in education, the UNMC must be focused on quality care, curriculum renewal/ education and research, public health and international health.
- Rank among the leading research centres. To be world-class in the research arena, the UNMC must be focused on issues such as regenerative medicine, informatics, and further developing its intellectual property.
- Advance an historic commitment to community health.
- Embrace the richness of diversity.
- Create economic growth in Nebraska.

With the accomplishment of the above, the UNMC would fulfil its mission, which is to improve the health of Nebraskans through leading educational programmes, innovative research, the highest quality patient care, and outreach to under-served populations. To achievement this will require the dedicated efforts of faculty, staff, and students to:

- Emphasize quality and perform at the highest level;
- Pursue excellence in an ethical manner;
- Foster an environment of learning and communication;
- Respect individuals for their cultures, contributions and points of view;
- Support the mission and vision of the UNMC in the best interests of our customers; and
- Promote individual accountability for organizational success.

STRATEGIC PLANNING RETREATS AND TIMELY EXECUTION OF THE PLAN

For the past seven years, with the goal of becoming a world-renowned health sciences centre, the UNMC's leaders have pursued excellence via strategies discussed at the Chancellor's Annual Strategic Planning Retreat, a day designed to outline the campus's direction for the next three years. The retreat serves to re-validate the strength of the current vision to become world-class, while challenging the centre to take the medical centre to even greater heights in service to the state and nation. The planning retreat also plays an essential role in shaping the medical centre's future and in making sure everyone is working toward the same goals each term. Although competing goals and distractions will appear throughout each year, as the chancellor stresses, everyone must be prepared, but remain focused on the strategic plan. All ideas are refined during the retreat so they can be used to help the UNMC progress. However, strategic plans are not static documents, and each quarter a report is published, marking the progress and recommendations on that specific year's goals. The following is a brief list of the goals set for each year and an assessment of progress toward these goals, carried out three years after the original plan was initiated:

2009 - Chancellor's Strategic Planning Retreat

Personalized medicine was one of two foci of the most recent retreat. It is believed that this could allow healthcare professionals to tailor treatment to individuals based on biomarkers, such as genetics and other factors, and that it is the responsibility of healthcare professionals to make this happen. As the UNMC considers a move into the world of personalized medicine, it was suggested by Dr. Gordon Mills, M.D., Ph.D., Ransom Horne Professor in Cancer Research and chairman in the department of molecular therapeutics at the University of Texas, M. D. Anderson Cancer Centre, an invited speaker for the annual planning retreat and a world-renowned expert in personalized medicine, that the medical centre develop solid leadership in this area and play to its strengths. In this regard, he mentioned the UNMC's outstanding programmes in pancreatic cancer and lymphoma treatment as possible entry points for personalized medicine investigations.

Another area of emphasis developed during the retreat was the formation of an academy of teaching scholars, which would serve as a body that would reward and support faculty members who view themselves primarily as teachers. The academy would help such faculty members conduct and publish education-related research, which, in turn, would assist these faculty members in receiving promotions and achieving tenure. Some of the challenges that the UNMC might face in developing such a programme include:
- Fostering departmental cultures that place value on academic scholarship;
- Building a critical mass of educators interested in academic scholarship;
- Installing sustained and committed leadership of such an academy; and
- Assembling a small pool of funding for academic scholarship.

The formation of such an academy would be a strong demonstration of the UNMC's commitment to quality education and furthermore, institutions that emphasize teaching by forming such academies often have a high rate of student satisfaction.

The UNMC continues to be positioned among the nation's top programmes in U.S. In this regard, in the News and World Report's rankings of the country's graduate schools, five graduate programmes are currently ranked among the best in the nation, with the College of Medicine's rural health medicine programme being tied for 15th, and the College of Medicine tied for 17th in the U.S. News's listing of top schools of medicine in terms of primary care. Academic health centres are affected by these tough economic times, struggling to maintain programmes and keep their strength whilst at the same time, being cost conscious and as a result, some have had to cut programmes. The UNMC has made a strategic decision that it will not abandon its core programmes and its commitment to rural communities and primary care; these rankings affirm that our programmes remain among the best in the country[1].

A more scientifically literate populace is another goal in the UNMC's strategic plan, and a 17 member team comprising UNMC faculty and staff, as well as Omaha area community leaders, is addressing the issue. This is a direct result of a report released earlier this year by the U.S. Department of Education, showing science literacy levels among American students to be lower than they are among students in many other countries. A public armed with facts and understanding of science is better able to appreciate and apply scientific advances and to vote knowledgeably on ballot issues and initiatives related to science, and as the state's academic health sciences centre, it is natural for the UNMC to be among the leading proponents for science literacy in Nebraska[2]. The team has met since the summer and identified three areas of focus:
- Providing assistance and resources to the state's elementary and secondary school science teachers;
- Establishing public education programmes to increase interest in science among young adults; and
- Creating a mobile science laboratory that serves as an educational resource for students around the state. One way the group aims to do this is by hosting "Science Cafes," which are informal science discussions at local coffeehouses and bars that feature healthcare experts and they are part of an effort by the UNMC and other groups to increase the population's science literacy.

2008 - Chancellor's Strategic Planning Retreat

This year's retreat was highlighted by presentations on regenerative medicine and biomedical informatics by international experts in those fields. The Chancellor's Council believes these are vital areas that the UNMC must excel in to achieve its goal of becoming a world-class academic health sciences centre. The chancellor specifically believes these areas represent the future of biomedical research.

If the UNMC wishes to thrive in the world of biomedical research, it must form a regenerative medicine centre, albeit facing challenges as developments in the field come fast and competition for top scientists is fierce. Moreover, it should create a physical structure to house the centre, being an educational resource that provides objective information on regenerative medicine, and garner the significant philanthropic support needed to attract the quality scientists needed to do the work[3]. The world of regenerative medicine is: exciting, fast paced, and highly competitive and requires strong leadership and commitment from all angles. However, a regenerative medicine focus should not only be on a global level, but also at the local level, as it serves Nebraskans. Furthermore, it is important for the UNMC to educate the public about the great promise that regenerative medicine holds, in terms of saving and improving lives[4].

Bioinformatics research is also believed to be a key element for the future success of any medical centre. To improve this specific research at the UNMC, it must create policies and procedures for data sharing that researchers in different colleges, departments and disciplines can utilize, creating a common language and increased cooperation across disciplines[5]. Furthermore, improving bioinformatics infrastructure is required if the UNMC wishes to receive major grants including a Clinical and Translational Science Award from the National Institute of Health (NIH)[6]. Simply put, the UNMC must improve its bioinformatics research so as to achieve world-class status.

In addition to regenerative medicine and biomedical informatics, other ideas or focus areas for the retreat included curriculum renewal, employee loyalty and wellness, promotion of science literacy, technology transfer, health disparities, healthcare workforce and clinical research organization.

2007 - Chancellor's Strategic Planning Retreat and Follow-up

To be a world-class academic health sciences centre, the UNMC must be strong in biomedical research; and outstanding education and patient care are associated with strong research programmes. Thus, the two main foci of the 2007 Chancellor's Strategic Planning Retreat were making healthcare quality a focal point of medical education and improving the UNMC's clinical/translational research.

To be successful in the implementation of these two goals, while keeping up with developments and with funding, UNMC researchers must adjust by taking a more collaborative approach to their work, across disciplines and with other institutions. Furthermore, more clinical space must be acquired, research processes will need to be more transparent, and clinical research training programmes must grow.

The retreat also featured several breakout sessions on topics related to the main panel discussions, during which participants determined areas that the UNMC should focus on during the next year. During the final breakout sessions, the 2007–2010 UNMC Strategic Plan was created by matching suggested goals and actions from the earlier sessions against the medical centre's critical success factors for: education, research, community partnerships, cultural competence, economic growth and employee loyalty.

Following the retreat, the UNMC leaders discussed two new strategic initiatives, one being the Center for Healthy Aging, which addresses projections that there will be more living parents than children and that those who reach age 60 will have at least one chronic illness. The other new strategic initiative is the Center for Translational Research (CCTR), which would take research from the bench to the bedside and into industry. This centre would allow the UNMC to evaluate the clinical and translational research resources it has and how or whether they need to be improved; consolidate those resources and establish a clear path of access so they are more transparent to investigators across the campus; improve communication with and between scientists about clinical and translational resources, research opportunities and potential collaborators who can enhance the development of new interdisciplinary teams; and develop new educational programmes for students, staff and faculty to enhance their clinical and translational research capabilities.

Later in 2007, the leadership team for a fully functional CCTR was formed and finalized. Other efforts have included both newly designed and renovated CCTR facilities and consolidating existing databases into a meta-database. Moreover, some new NIH-funded investigators have been recruited and are now in place, and grant applications for clinical and translational research have been submitted.

2006 - Chancellor's Strategic Planning Retreat and its Outcomes Today

The UNMC is strongly committed to providing the best possible patient care, education and research, while embracing community outreach and diversity, and, as an economic engine for the state and region, it must blend economic development in all of its activities and embed it into its mission and vision as a natural extension.

Panel members representing the Nebraska Department of Economic Development, Greater Omaha Chamber of Commerce and McCarthy Group Inc., discussed why economic development is a critical role for academic health science centres, as well as how effective the UNMC is in promoting this. Participants also engaged in breakout sessions that addressed economic development issues, including the UNMC's top priorities in relation to this in the areas of education, research, community partnerships, cultural competence, technology development and employee loyalty. Rather than undertaking the traditional strategic update, more time was taken to explore new ideas along with introducing the notion of economic development and how it permeates all of the UNMC's activities, which resulted in a number of innovative ideas[7].

- Groups explored five initiatives introduced in 2005 by the Chancellor's Council as "BIG IDEAS", that span UNMC's critical success factors: Establishing a College of Public Health and its benefits to Nebraska;
- Enhancing the UNMC's role in global health education, research, and patient care and improving the coordination of global health activities;
- Creating a centre for interdisciplinary education and the possible outcomes; and
- Expanding the UNMC's clinical research-rural focus and its benefits to Nebraska; and utilizing emerging communication technologies, such as blogging and pod-casting to convey its message to the public.

The means by which the UNMC can tell the world about itself are expanding rapidly, so technologies specialists have been hired in the Public Affairs department, whose expertise will help maximize resources, in terms of communicating its message internally and externally[8].

The aforementioned merger with the NMC has been very successful. The College of Public Health was officially formed in 2008, and it remains the only such college within 1000 kilometres in the Midwest region. Moreover, the construction of the college's new home, the Harold M. and Beverly Maurer Center for Public Health, was started a few months ago. The following additional construction projects are evidence of success in accomplishing goals set in 2006: the completion of the Hixson-Lied Clinical Centre of Excellence, a new outpatient clinical cancer centre in West Omaha, the Michael F. Sorrell Centre for Health Science Education, The Durham Research Centre I and II, and the Good Manufacturing Practices (GMP) Transplant Production Facility. Further, completion of a new medical centre in Bellevue, NE is just months away. All of this has been achieved while facing challenges of manpower shortages, skyrocketing healthcare costs, cuts in national research funding, campus space constraints, and the ongoing cultural evolution between the UNMC and the NMC.

2005 - Chancellor's Strategic Planning Retreat and its Outcomes

The top priority in 2005 was increasing faculty and staff salaries, among other new goals, such as becoming the best place to do biomedical research in the country, leading the state in reducing or controlling healthcare costs through prevention strategies, SimplyWell (a workplace wellness programme), utilizing electronic medical records, and being learning-centred in education.

Two separate panels explored ways to improve the UNMC's entrepreneurial effectiveness and stay competitive in the global healthcare market. Subsequent sessions focused on each of the UNMC's strategic goals: education (transitioning to learning-centred education), university/hospital partnership (communicating its strength), cultural competency (moving from diversity projects to a welcoming attitude), healthcare (controlling costs through prevention strategies), research (advancing biomedical research), community engagement (boosting our state-wide impact), employee loyalty (valuing employees), and entrepreneurship and new technologies (moving ideas into the marketplace).

In an effort to become learning-centred in education, the UNMC has been evaluating and expanding integrated, outcomes-focused, learning-centred experiences for each programme and rewarding outstanding teachers who foster this new style of education. Furthermore, it has already developed faculty education programmes to enhance understanding and skills related to learning-centred education. For example, the College of Nursing has presented several retreats using a consultant in the "appreciative inquiry" method, which is a learning-centred approach.

Working toward becoming the best place in the country to do biomedical research, the Durham Research Centre II's design and construction was approved by the Board of Regents and was completed and dedicated in May 2009. The Durham Research Centre I opened in 2003. A combined total of 215 labs and more than 550,000 square feet of space dedicated to research allows for nearly 400 research projects being underway at the UNMC today, in bench science labs, translational research centres and clinical trials.

Furthermore, the UNMC serves as an advisor to state government officials and participates in its key planning activity of establishing an Electronic Health Record for Nebraska. Regarding the SimplyWell workplace wellness programme, created in 2003, employees are vested in their own care and are given the tools to measure, achieve and maintain their health. In this regard, as a major employer and as a health sciences centre, the UNMC ought to be an exemplary employer, in terms of the opportunities it offers employees to identify and manage their own risk factors and healthy lifestyle needs[9]. Further, preventative medical maintenance strategies continue to progress in this special programme.

The goal of developing selected new technologies to advance health education, science and clinical programmes promoting economic growth in Nebraska has led to the identification and advancement of commercializing and licensing of UNMC technologies. For example, it has secured venture capital for start-up companies; developed collaboration with a European research organization regarding technology development and commercialization; and established consultation and assessment agreements with the University of Nebraska, Omaha's (UNO) College of Business, based on commercializing UNMC technology. Furthermore, in an effort to develop advanced biotechnology in software development and devices, the Center for Advanced Surgical Technology (CAST) was formed in 2005, with a key focus on improving surgical technologies related to computer-assisted surgery, computer enhanced surgery, image-guided surgery, minimally invasive surgery and robotic surgery and it will involve individuals from the UNMC, the University of Nebraska-Lincoln and the UNO, as well as Creighton University.

2004 - Chancellor's Strategic Planning Retreat and its Outcomes

A year of progress towards becoming a future world-class health sciences centre included plans for a university-wide mentoring programme for students, each of the UNMC's colleges ranking in the top half of NIH research funding, a new health sciences education building for students, a second Durham Research Center tower, research funding increasing to $100 million per year, entrepreneurial initiatives pursued, strengthening the future of the NMC and practice plans, attracting higher levels of philanthropy, and achieving operational efficiencies.

The UNMC and NMC developed the 2004 Partnership Strategy, with the goal of becoming a world-renowned, academic health sciences centre. The strategy highlights a commitment to moving ahead together, with dedication, creativity and hard work to become world-renowned in education, patient care, research and outreach.

The UNMC's goals are to:
– Enhance and expand the educational environment;
– Increase its prominence as a research health sciences centre;
– Advance community/campus partnerships for health;
– Create a culturally competent organization;
– Develop selected new technologies to advance health education, science and the Nebraska economy; and
– Create a culture that builds employee loyalty and satisfaction.

The NMC, meanwhile, is focused on gaining financial strength by being the market leader in a set of clinical services, building regional and national recognition through excellence in research, education, best practice and reputation, and creating responsive infrastructure that exceeds patient, physician and staff expectations.

Symbolizing this working relationship is the new Clinical Center for Excellence, which would connect University Towers with Clarkson Towers. In 2005, this centre was established and formally called the Hixson-Lied Center for Clinical Excellence, which consolidates many of the NMC's services into one building, leading to more efficient care. It houses emergency, radiology, cardiology, surgery and the newborn intensive care unit.

The partnership between the UNMC and NMC was formed in 1997, when Clarkson Regional Health Services and the UNMC merged their respective hospitals and clinical operations to form a non-profit corporation, the NMC. Today, that partnership yields a number of clinical, research and educational benefits, which range from UNMC physicians practising medicine at Clarkson and University Towers, to clinical research trials which bring patients to campus for cutting-edge medical care.

One of the partnership benefits is the Clinical Trials Office, which offers support for services for investigators conducting industry-sponsored clinical trials. This office receives internal and external inquiries about clinical research studies and directs information and connects callers with the appropriate campus research resources. Other research resources include the Clinical Research Center, for investigator-initiated or NIH-funded trials, the Minority Health Education and Research Office for minority-focused studies, as well as the Institutional Review Board and Sponsored Programmes Administration. Another aspect of the partnership is the 2003 formation of a new residency programme in emergency medicine, which benefits the emergency care of citizens across Nebraska and the region, with the first six physicians beginning their three year residencies in 2004.

In 2005, the residents began practising in one of the largest emergency departments in the region, its home being in the Hixson-Lied Center for Clinical Excellence,

The new emergency department, which combines those at Clarkson and University Towers, has 20,000 square feet, 33 beds including 13 critical care rooms, 16 exam rooms, eight observation rooms and four trauma beds in one large suite. It also has four paediatric rooms and four fast-track rooms, as well as pharmacy and radiology services. In addition to the new facility, it will be a very secure environment staffed by 13 physicians, who are board certified in emergency medicine, as well as experienced emergency department nurses. In fact, among the physicians, there will be over 150 years of ER experience.

Recently, research funding at the UNMC soared 22% to more than $100 million during the previous fiscal year and more than $76 million of that funding came from federal sources. Rising above the $100 million mark in extramural support is a major milestone for the UNMC research initiative[10]. In 1998, the chancellor challenged UNMC's researchers to double funding in five years and triple it in ten and thus they have exceeded both goals, increasing funding by 322% in that time period, despite major challenges. Most of the growth in research funding in the past ten years has been for basic laboratory research and about half of the UNMC's research funding has historically been for cancer. However, new areas of translational research in infectious diseases and neurodegenerative diseases are now rapidly growing. It is the momentum from these developing initiatives that will send the UNMC soaring towards the next benchmark, $200 million[11].

GLOBAL STRATEGIES AND EFFORT: BECOMING A WORLD-CLASS INSTITUTION REQUIRES WORLD-CLASS PARTNERS

A global economy is a dominant feature of the 21st century and the key to successful economic growth in each nation is collaboration, especially in education. To achieve our goal of building a world-class institution, collaboration in medical education and research with world-class partners has been an important objective for the last few years. Out of five major initiatives first introduced in 2005 by the Chancellor's Council as "BIG IDEAS" that span the UNMC's critical success factors, "enhancing the UNMC's role in global health education, research, and patient care and improving the coordination of global health activities" was a prominent one. Clinically, with the effort of the Office of International Healthcare Services, collaborative partnerships have been formed with 34 prominent medical institutions in 17 countries. Coordinated and supported by our office of international studies and programmes, our medical and nursing students have gone to South America and other countries for clinical rotations and medical missions, which have contributed greatly to the UNMC building world-class partners in patient care, education and research. Regarding the UNMC's international collaborations, it has, and continues to, put forth strategies, focusing on the benefits of sustained long-term collaboration, further developing partnerships and increasing efficiency, as the UNMC goes global.

During the last few decades, sustained and significant economic growth in the Asia Pacific region, especially in China, India, Russia and Japan, has made this area an attractive area for the UNMC to expand collaborations. In this report, we have chosen to focus on China, one of the major players in the current global economy, and its needs for education, medicine, and research. Through joint effort with Chinese governmental agencies and institutions, the UNMC has developed solid partnerships with three prominent Chinese institutions: Shanghai Jiao Tong University School of Medicine (SJTUSM) and the Chinese Academy of Sciences (CAS), since 2004, and Xi'an Jiao Tong University Health Science Center (XJTUHSC), since 2007. Each partnership reveals strengths that have enhanced one another's programmes. For example, the collaboration between the UNMC and SJTUSM, one of the leading higher education institutions in China and a first-class medical university, presents complementary strengths, as the two institutions have differing educational backgrounds and research environments. Furthermore, the Chinese Academy of Sciences (CAS), being the highest rated research institute in China and its graduate school, the Graduate University of CAS (GUCAS), being among the best graduate schools in China, both have long and productive histories of collaboration within the international academic and research communities. Moreover, CAS and the UNMC have common interests in graduate student training and in various biomedical-related areas, such as cancer biology, genetics, development, neuroscience and immunology.

To promote the growth of these important partnerships between SJTUSM, CAS, and XJTUHSC, and other institutions in China, the UNMC established the Asia Pacific Rim Development Program (APRDP) in 2005. We have seven global market objectives, three of which are to increase UNMC's international visibility/reputation and strive to help with its mission to build a world-class institution in the 21st century, to establish solid working relationships with scientific/medical programmes in Asia including China, India, Russia, Japan, and other countries; and to support the State of Nebraska's economic relations with Asian and Pacific countries. As Nebraska offers certain unparalleled advantages for transportation, warehousing and logistics, it plays a major role in bringing in products from Asia and distributing them throughout North America, and its exports to China have more than doubled in recent years.

These global market objectives through the following means of collaboration:
– Establishing global friendships and connections have been met through the exchange of medical, graduate and nursing students,
– Making a global impact through visionary programmes, and
– Helping to increase efficiency in the global health workforce.

Our efforts in the past few years have led to significant collaboration in research and medical education, through a vigorous exchange of medical, nursing, graduate students, postdoctoral fellows, faculty members and administrators between the UNMC and these institutions. The UNMC's APRDP coordinates the education, training, clinical/medical observations, and rotations for these exchanges, through a variety of programmes with very specific global market objectives, as follow:

A) The medical and nursing student exchange programme helps establish global friendships and connection. Chinese medical students complete three months of clinical medical observations/rotations, and nursing students spend one month on clinical observation. In exchange, medical and nursing students from the UNMC complete one month of clinical medical observations/rotations at Chinese university partners, while UNMC faculty members perform teaching and give seminars and lecture series there. This meets the fourth global market objective of increasing the diversity of the student body, gaining high-quality international students and securing more opportunities for current UNMC students.

B) The UNMC is making a global impact through visionary programmes, such as the establishment of a family medicine training centre in China: joint Ph.D. and M.D./Ph.D. programmes with China; training Chinese administrators in global methodology and procedure; and expanding this administrator training programme by establishing a joint Ph.D. in public health administration and a joint Masters in health services administration/M.D. or one in public health (MPH)/M.D.

Aware of the lack of a family medicine system in China, the UNMC, with a nationally and internationally renowned family medicine programme, responded by helping establish the "Sino-U.S. Training Center for General Practitioners" in Xi'an, China, designed to provide continuing medical education for general practitioners and medical students, training for teachers, and research for general medicine in China. The first Family Medicine Training Course was held in October 2008, where over 300 general practitioners attended and this joint centre was formally established in April 2009.

The UNMC has established joint Ph.D. and MD/Ph.D. programmes to provide training to future biomedical research and translational research leaders. Chinese graduate students may obtain research training through the UNMC-CSC programme (working with the China Scholarship Council) for from 24 to 48 months or obtain a Ph.D. at the UNMC through the Degree-Seeking programme. The UNMC's PSGTP (Physician Scientist Graduate Training Programme) is a unique joint M.D./Ph.D. programme with training in both clinical medicine and scientific research for the future physician-scientists of China. This meets a fifth global market objective to establish joint education programmes, such as joint degrees in nursing and the M.D./Ph.D. programme in biomedical research, which has not yet been offered by any other US university. This joint programme will help meet the needs of improved Chinese medical care, higher quality healthcare workers, and better medical products for the people of China in this new century.

In another unique aspect of our collaboration, the UNMC has established a special short-term training programme designed to expose administrators selected from our Chinese partners to the methods used in American academic health sciences centre. In this programme, Chinese administrators receive 3 to 6 months of education and training in administrative methods and procedures at the UNMC. These administrators are being groomed in order to help their institutions move aggressively toward adapting some of the westernized curriculum and administration methods for their educational and administrative systems, so as to provide best efficiency and quality in research and education. This kind of collaboration in training middle level administrators helps promote future collaboration between institutions. In addition, we are in the process of expanding this administrator training programme, by establishing a joint Ph.D. degree in public health administration, with a joint Masters degree in health services administration/M.D. or one in public health MPH/M.D., based on our experience of forming a joint M.D.-Ph.D.

programme with SJTUSM. It is through these new initiatives and visionary programmes that the future leaders of biomedical research, hospital and leaders in China are being trained.

C) Collaboration in research helps to increase efficiency in the global health workforce. Stemming from the partnership the UNMC has with the most highly regarded research institution in China, CAS, the China-U.S. Joint Research Center for Life Science was founded between Beijing Life Science Institute of CAS and the UNMC. This newly established centre supports joint research projects and provides opportunity for symposiums involving other top institutions, such as the National Institutes of Health (NIH) in the US, promoting extensive collaboration beyond the current partnerships. In October 2008, symposiums in the areas of Neuroscience and Immunology were held at the newly established China-U.S. Joint Research Center for Life Science. Similar symposia with various topics, such as heart related diseases, neurological and neurodegenerative disorders and neurodevelopmental related problems and diseases were also held at Shanghai Jiao Tong University School of Medicine in 2006, 2007 and 2008. In September 2009, the UNMC will host the next Joint Research Symposium on topics, such as Cancer, Genetics, Immunology and Therapy. This helps us meet our sixth global market objective: to increase research scope and efficiency (in the areas of cancer, development, neuro-science, transplantation, and cardiovascular diseases) through collaboration.

Our seventh global market objective is for our successful programmes and partnerships to be utilized as models for collaboration in other areas. The experiences gained and friendships established between these institutions and the UNMC will help facilitate increased opportunities for other cultural, educational, scientific, and business partnerships between the greater communities of China, India, Russia, Japan and Nebraska, ultimately bringing more economic growth and furthering opportunities for a remarkable global health impact.

Overall, this chapter has discussed our strategies and efforts made towards the UNMC becoming world-class in this decade. For such a daunting goal, and not without great challenge, we have built the concept of being world-class, made a commitment to being world-class, increased our capacity to be world-class and enhanced our ability to communicate this to the world, by collaborating closely with prominent partners. Moreover, we've expanded our vision beyond providing education and patient care to include research, which is now a significant and invaluable aspect of our vision to deliver excellence to every Nebraskan and beyond. Each year, we review current and create new strategies and efforts, and achieve our goals with vision, promise, effort and dedication. In addition, the centre has strengthened its efforts internationally, especially in the Asia Pacific regions. UNMC has followed up on its proposed objectives and focuses on the benefits of sustained long-term collaboration when utilizing the strengths of each partner toward a common goal: meeting the healthcare needs of a whole population. The centre will expand upon the nature of its partnerships, as its vision of medicine and research is extended beyond Nebraska, with future efforts to amplify the global impact of these collaborations and eventually build an excellent world-class healthcare, educational and biomedical research institution in the heart of America, Nebraska.

ACKNOWLEDGEMENTS

We kindly thank Ms Mary Cavell and Dr Terry D. Hexum for their valuable comments and suggestions about the manuscript. Special thanks also go to Ms Emilie Scoggins, Staff Associate and Dr Kai Fu, Associate Director of the UNMC Asia Pacific Rim Development Programme, and UNMC Vice Chancellors Tom Rosenquist, Don Leuenberger and Rubens Pamies, without whose help the success of this undertaking could not have been realized.

NOTES

[1]   Rubens Pamies, M.D., Vice Chancellor for Academic Affairs.
[2]   James Turpen, Ph.D., Professor, Dept. of Genetics, Cell Biology & Anatomy, and the leader of the science literacy team.
[3]   Paul Simmons, Ph.D., Director of the Centre for Stem Cell Biology at the University of Texas Health Scences Centre in Houston - a world-renowned expert on regenerative medicine.
[4]   Richard Holland, Omaha community leader.
[5]   Simon Sherman, Ph.D., Director of the Bioinformatics Shared Resources at UNMC.
[6]   Jennifer Larsen, M.D., Associate Dean for Clinical Research in the College of Medicine, and member of the 2008 Chancellor's Strategic Planning Retreat panel.
[7]   John Adams, Assistant Vice Chancellor for Budget and Strategic Planning at UNMC.
[8]   Robert D. Bartee, Vice Chancellor for External Affairs.
[9]   Donald Leuenberger, Vice Chancellor for Business and Finance.
[10]   Thomas Rosenquist, Ph.D., Vice Chancellor for Research.
[11]   Thomas Rosenquist, Ph.D., Vice Chancellor for Research.

Harold M. Maurer and Jialin C. Zheng
University of Nebraska Medical Center, USA

JACQUES LANARÈS

14. DEVELOPING A QUALITY CULTURE TO BECOME A WORLD-CLASS UNIVERSITY

INTRODUCTION

The pursuit of excellence is undoubtedly an essential feature of any world-class university and to make progress in that direction, quality systems certainly play a critical role. Due to several influences, Higher Education Institutions (HEIs) have developed their internal quality systems over the past decades. In this regard, the development of institutional autonomy has increased pressure for accountability in many regions and countries. Moreover, the growth of a higher education market has raised expectations among the "clients" of HEIs (students, employers, other stakeholders). Obviously, globalization of higher education with mobility of students and graduates in the job market has also become an important factor. For instance, it is clear that in the Bologna process in Europe (currently involving 46 countries and intended to increase mobility) quality is a cornerstone of the transformation process.

Being a world-class university obviously has the supposition of international visibility and the ability to attract good foreign students and staff. Even though several of the rankings rely more in fact on research performance, quality of teaching is also crucial. Naturally, to attract Ph.D. candidates from all over the world quality of research is important, however, the quality of doctoral programmes and other support measures is also an influential choice criterion. Indeed, quality affects all aspects of the HEI, which accords with the fact that becoming a world-class university requires developments in different areas (Niland, 2007). In other words, world-class universities must take into account the same demands as other HEIs, but to a higher standard. That is, to achieve excellence means to go beyond basic mechanisms of quality assurance as the indicators normally used in the rankings are only a partial view of these requirements. Excellence can be likened to an iceberg, where the indicators used are the visible part and the quality system is somehow the hidden part. Much as "treating the symptoms" does not guarantee eradication of the illness, indicators that are not based on a "robust" quality system are fragile and can fluctuate widely. The author's conviction is, therefore, that to remain or to become a world-class university, as far as quality is concerned, institutions face real challenges. The goal is not only to create and operate a quality system in line with international standards, but also to develop a coherent system for fostering creativity and innovation, and to create ownership of the system. In other words, it is critical that everyone in the university should see the relevance of

N.C. Liu et al., (eds.), Paths to a World-Class University: Lessons from Practices and Experiences, 263–274.

the various quality processes and be actively involved in their realization, which for the author defines the establishment of a Quality Culture.

In this chapter views about these issues and how they have been addressed in a specific university, the University of Lausanne, are presented. Three questions are addressed: Why should the HEI develop a Quality Culture? What does it mean to an institution? How can development of the culture be monitored? Before addressing these questions, the institutional context is clarified.

THE UNIVERSITY OF LAUSANNE IN CONTEXT

Founded in 1537, the University of Lausanne (UNIL) has recently undergone a reconfiguration and is now composed of seven faculties. From the beginning of the 21st century, the university has been involved in an ambitious project aiming at greater cooperation and development amongst the French speaking universities of Switzerland and in particular with the Federal Polytechnical School of Lausanne (EPFL), situated on the same campus. In this regard, in 2003 two new faculties were founded concentrating on life and human sciences: the Faculty of Biology and Medicine; and the Faculty of Geosciences and Environment. The Faculty of Biology and Medicine is now composed of all those disciplines which have to do with life in all its manifestations and mystery including, for example, the origins of life, its fundamental mechanisms, the evolutionary process and the protection of life. The study skills taught range from basic research techniques to the daily practice of medicine with hospital patients. The Faculty of Geosciences and Environment focuses on human geography, physics and geology, in order to respond to the need of society to understand more clearly the role played by humans in the environment. The goal is to create a dynamic scientific interaction, through the exploration of new fields of research and teaching, particularly those at the interface of two or more disciplines.

By having the aim of grouping together disciplines concerned with the study of mankind and living organisms in their natural and social environment, the UNIL has created an unprecedented break-through in the Swiss university scene. For this cooperation means now there is interdependence of these institutions, with, for instance UNIL giving Chemistry, Physics and Mathematics to EPFL, whilst still needing these fields for other programmes (like medical studies or forensic sciences). On the other hand, EPFL includes roughly 10% of humanities and social sciences in its curriculums and these are mainly offered by UNIL. All together approximately 7,000 teaching hours are exchanged between these two institutions.

These transformations have given an attractive profile to UNIL which has enabled UNIL to secure important national projects. In fact, there are more than 130 research units currently at work in a wide variety of disciplines, ranging from Greek Numismatics to Cyber-marketing and Developmental Biology. Moreover, within the institutes and laboratories, 2000 researchers, 500 of whom are professors, work daily on research projects of national or international importance. Working on the principle that knowledge transcends boundaries, collaboration between disciplines is now a priority, in order to explore new fields of research to provide more pertinent answers to the questions posed by society and many collaborations of such a nature are at present under way. Interdisciplinary and inter-institutional cooperation are priorities also for teaching and within many joint degrees. Currently 12,000 students are among them doctoral candidates.

The University of Lausanne has been subject to new legislation since 2005 and as is often the case, nowadays, this gives much more autonomy to the university, with regard to its finance, human resources, programmes on offer, and organization. Its relation with the regional state authority, which covers roughly 50% of expenses, is based on a five-year strategic plan negotiated between the university and the politicians. One of the seven main strategic objectives contained within this plan is the development of a Quality Culture and regarding the quality processes entailed within this process, the right to public funding (at the national and regional levels) depends on a quality audit. In this regard, each university can develop its own internal quality system, as long as it conforms to seven standards which are very similar to the European Standards and Guidelines, Part 1. Every four years the internal quality system of the university is audited by the National Accreditation Agency with the help of external experts. In December 2008, the Federal Secretariat for Education and Research (SER) published the four yearly audit report on the Quality of Swiss Universities, produced by the Centre of Accreditation and Quality Assurance of the Swiss Universities (OAQ). It concluded

> The quality management system (of the UNIL) is excellent and forms a coherent and integrated whole. Changes undertaken have encouraged the implementation of a Quality Culture at all levels of the university. In conclusion the experts consider that the university conforms fully to the required standards.

THE NEED TO DEVELOP A QUALITY CULTURE

The development of quality assurance (QA) mechanisms in higher education is an integral component of the Bologna process and has become a high priority in many European institutions. Two main issues following from this desire to include quality on the agenda of the construction of the European Higher Education Area: one is to create or adapt a quality system compatible or in line with international standards and the other is to integrate the system into the HEI concerned.

Thanks to national and international standards (e.g. European Standards and Guidelines), institutions have frameworks by which they can create methodologically sound quality systems. However, analysis of the literature shows that this first condition is not necessarily enough to improve quality. Several investigations have suggested, indeed, that some quality processes have had no real effect on the quality of teaching, research or other activities, at least not on par with expectations (e.g. Gosling and D'Andrea, 2001; Newton, 2002). In particular, standard certification procedures do not always result in improved services (e.g. Staines, 2007). Moreover, there have been frequent calls for QA to involve greater adhesion with institutions (e.g. Jones and Darshi de Saram, 2005; Goodlad, 1995, Harvey 2002).

To overcome this lack of quality integration in institutions, the concept of Quality Culture has emerged, which has been promoted in a consistent manner by the European University Association (EUA), the term being:

> chosen to convey a notion of quality as a shared value and collective responsibility of all members of an institution, including students and administrative staff. Quality Culture signals the need to ensure a grass-roots acceptance, to develop a compact within the academic community through effective community building, as well as changes in values, attitude and behaviour within an institution (EUA, 2006).

THE CONCEPT OF QUALITY CULTURE

The concept of Quality Culture, which was formulated as a reaction to bureaucratic approaches to quality, is usually given a relatively warm welcome, with the expression, nowadays, being quite fashionable and it can be found in numerous publications and even some regulations. It is appealing because it would appear to give a human touch to a word ("quality") now associated with cold notions, such as control, assurance and industrial processes. Indeed, the development of a Quality Culture is an extremely relevant alternative to overtly normative approaches, not only because it favours real change, but also because it can take into account the diversity of contexts and leave space for creativity, thereby offering opportunities to create new ways of giving concrete expression to quality.

> Quality Culture refers to an organisational culture that aims to enhance quality permanently and is characterized by two distinct elements: on the one hand, a cultural/psychological element of shared values, beliefs, expectations and commitment towards quality; and on the other a structural/managerial element with defined processes that enhances quality and seeks to coordinate individual efforts. (EUA, 2006, p.10).

In the author's understanding (Lanarès 2008), the expression Quality Culture can have two meanings. The first of these implies that quality is an organizational priority and it is one of the values of the organizational culture. However, quality as a value has to be defined and there has been a long debate about its definition, with it now considered to be a multidimensional concept and a polysemic word. Moreover, there seems to be general agreement that there can be no consensus on a unique definition of quality (Harvey, 2006). The term Quality Culture itself, therefore, remains quite unspecific, because it is tied to implicit or explicit definitions of quality. That is, in reality, quality as a value incorporates and integrates other qualities or values, such as reflexivity, communication or participation (EUA, 2006), depending on the definition of quality chosen by the institution (e.g. transformation, fitness for purpose, etc). With regards to the second understanding, Quality Culture is seen as a subculture of the organizational culture, where, whatever the approach chosen, quality is always associated with espoused values that form a sub-culture of the institution's own organizational culture.

There is no universally accepted definition of organizational culture, but as a short definition Brennan and Shah (2000) underline three dimensions generally agreed among researchers: "Culture embraces values, attitudes and behaviours" (ibid. p. 341). Since attitudes and behaviours are based on values (Bontis 2006, Hofstede 2001, Klenke 2005, Kowalkiewicz 2007, Schein 1990, Sundrum 2004), we like to see the values as the basic foundations, the heart of the culture. Quality Culture, as a sub-culture, can include several different values, and a different set of values will lead to different Quality Cultures. They will differ by what is more valued: control or development? Specialization of some people involved in quality or ownership by the greatest number of people? Conformity or adaptation? For instance, in some HEIs, quality processes are managed by quality specialists who try to control the conformity of processes, whereas in others, ownership by the largest majority and creativity, are stressed. Both kinds of institutions have a Quality Culture, but these are not the same, for the first is rather normative in nature, whereas the second could be defined as being more developmental (Kowalkiewicz, 2007; Harvey and Stensaker, 2008).

Quality processes should support HEIs in their pursuit of excellence, in particular with regards to creativity and innovation, so as to strengthen their capacity to face new challenges. From this perspective, there are strong links to the notion of the learning organization and drawing on works on the latter and creativity is useful for identifying certain key conditions for reinforcing the development process. In a broader sense, what kind of Quality Culture should be favoured to support develop-ment, creativity and innovation in the HEI? Taken as a whole, literature on learning organizations, cultural change and Quality Culture projects (e.g. Birdi, 2007; EUA, 2006; EUA, 2007; McKenna, 1994; Senge, 1999; Short, 2007; Strydom, Zulu and Murray, 2004; West, 1997), shows interesting convergences and underlines certain core values which merit emphasis (in no particular order of importance):

- Raising responsibility - empowerment;
- Reflective process;
- Participation - cooperation;
- Communication;
- Systems thinking; and
- Balance (between stability and flexibility; top-down and bottom up; risk-taking and conformity).

THE DEVELOPMENT OF A QUALITY CULTURE

Therefore, developing a Quality Culture implies cultural change, in order to reach a broad convergence of ways of thinking and acting about quality and associated values. It means a new way of doing things, but also a new understanding of these actions. The first step is, thus, the identification of core values and the creation of an adhesion to them. Since values are beliefs, in the sense that it is difficult to demonstrate their superiority, changing the prevailing culture implies conviction-building, the goal being to increase the sense of identification with the adopted values (Kotter and Cohen, 2002). The next step is making sure that the values are translated in both the concept and the practice of the quality system. However, there is not always a perfect match between declared values and the other latent values, which really influence behaviour and decisions (Hofstede, 2001). Therefore, a critical question that should be asked, even if it appears naïve, is how do we prove to others and to ourselves that these values are a priority for us? On which basis are people from both inside and outside the organization able to identify these values as priorities? Of course, as mentioned earlier, several decisions and actions can be based on a single value.

The critical role of leadership in developing a world-class university has been underlined (Hsuan, 2007; Hennard, 2009) and is also crucial to the development of a Quality Culture, in particular in guaranteeing coherence and creating adhesion. To illustrate with an example, at the University of Lausanne an important quality process takes places every four years. This is the self evaluation of the seven faculties, which under the authority of each dean, involves all the staff and all activities in each faculty. Apart from this big effort, there are other ongoing measures, such as the evaluation of teaching by students, recruitment policies, evaluation of dossiers for renewal of contracts, training of teaching staff, and pedagogical innovation awards. These measures are intended, on the one hand, to be coherent with the university's values for Quality Culture, and on the other hand to provide some data for use in the periodic self-evaluation of each faculty.

The main values underlying these first steps in quality processes and which the university wants to maintain are summarized below, with some examples of how these were operationalized.

- Fitness for purpose: In practice this priority is made evident through the self-evaluation methodology, which contains four basic questions intended to explore this aspect (what are the objectives and the priorities of the faculty? How does the faculty know that its objectives are being met? What evaluation has taken place? What are the next steps for improvement?). Another example is the yearly follow-up process through an action plan;
- Responsibility: Examples could be that the faculty is involved in the definition of priorities and of the rules for constructive feedback (for experts, leadership, etc.);
- Participation: The main quality process (self evaluation of the seven faculties) is overseen by a committee, including representatives from all university bodies. The faculty under evaluation organizes a participative self evaluation committee and relevant working groups;
- Reflective approach: The basic process, either at staff or faculty level, is based on open and reflective questions; and
- Balance between autonomy and accountability: This value is made concrete in several ways, one of them being that total access to all data is limited to members of the faculty, and synthetic information is unrestricted.

In summary, a system that promotes the development of a Quality Culture is an entire set of measures which are coherent at different levels, as shown in Figure 1. The starting point is a set of values (1) which are given substance in the principles and modalities of the quality concept (2). These principles and modalities are then implemented in individual and collective practices (3).

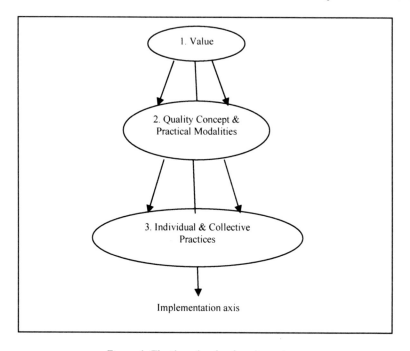

Figure 1. The three levels of quality culture.

OBSERVING OR MEASURING THE DEVELOPMENT OF A QUALITY CULTURE

As with any cultural change, the development of a Quality Culture is a long-term process, which is the result of various interactions (Schein, 1990) and of a combined effect of top-down and bottom-up processes. In order to strengthen and support this evolutionary process, it is necessary to observe and in some way monitor the establishment of the Quality Culture, in order to help to evaluate the path covered and determine which specific effort is required for further development.

DESCRIPTION OF THE PROCESS

From the author's point of view, the development of the Quality Culture can be seen in two dimensions, resembling the development of waves when a stone is thrown into water. At the surface level, it requires observing how people, who are further and further from leadership positions or who are highly motivated, agree with the values and are involved in quality. At the deep level, it concerns the change of behaviours associated with adhesion at the surface level, where the deeper these are the greater the spontaneity of their being integrated into praxis. So, it is a two-fold process that we need to observe the increased number of people who adhere to the culture and the extent to which this agreement is translated into actions, as illustrated in Figure 2.

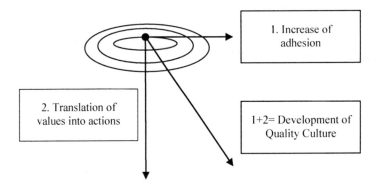

Figure 2. Schematic development of a quality culture in two dimensions.

Since cultural change is a long term and somewhat implicit process, it is necessary to find ways to track the development of the Quality Culture. However, very few papers have been devoted to identifying the relevant measures to observe this development or have described such evolution. Since this is a critical issue for each institution, it be interesting and useful to develop tools to track the establishment of the Quality Culture and because it can be considered as being an organizational subculture, one option is to explore more widely how organizational culture is measured in practice. However, if it is efficacious to observe the development of a Quality Culture, it must be acknowledged that this cannot be a straightforward process, for it involves a complex process in the sense that several interactive variables are involved, making it difficult to identify clear causal relations in quality matters (Stensaker, 2008; Newton, 2002). Moreover, choices of measures are determined by definitions of quality, approaches to organizational culture and other considerations (Scott, 2003). In other words, one must be clear about the fact that there is no absolute measure or definitive observation of a Quality Culture, but an observation grid can provide good food for thought.

Analysis of the literature reveals that most studies rely on what people say about their values or actions (e.g. Cook and Lafferty, 1989/2003; Koslowsky and Stashevsky, 2005; Koufteros et al., 2007; Kowalkiewicz, 2007; Meglino et al., 1989; Waldman et al., 2006; Javidan et al., 2006) and generally espoused values can be good measures of organizational cultures (Javidan et al., 2006). At the behavioural level, several studies show the link between values and choices (Javidan et al., 2006; Koufteros, 2007; Waldman et al., 2006), thus demonstrating that decisions could be good indicators of the culture. In particular, innovations represent a specific case of decision and action and seem to be related to cultures (Jaskyte, 2004). In short, three main categories of measures are used: what people say about their values and beliefs, what people say about what they do, and what people do or the results of their actions.

Most studies rely on what people say and in this regard since culture is about adhesion to values, what people say is useful but not sufficient considering that there are discrepancies between values and practices (Javidan et al., 2006; Waldman et al., 2006). Moreover, agreement on values does not imply satisfaction as far as concretization of values is concerned (Telford and Masson, 2005) and therefore it is necessary to include observations about what people actually do. Based on our review of the literature and our experience at the University of Lausanne we propose a grid (see Table 1) for creating a tool to observe the "grass rooting" of a Quality Culture within an HEI. We use this framework to observe the development of the Quality Culture in our university and by way of illustrating a sample of the indicators we employ is described in Table 1:

Table 1. Draft grid for creating an observation framework

	What people say	*What people do*
Individual Level Leadership Staff Students	- Commentaries about quality processes - Percentage of people who adhere to the institutional quality approach and values	- Involvement in quality processes. - Spontaneous evaluation of teaching - Responses to teaching evaluation
Collective Level Institution Faculty Unit	- Quality concept of UNIL - Evolution of quality regulations	- Annual innovations in relation to quality - Application of regulations - Research Policy

Depending on the measure chosen, the analysis will rely either on one-off events (like new regulations) or the evolution of quantitative data (such as the number of spontaneous evaluations of teaching).

AN ILLUSTRATIVE CASE

We have started to use this grid to observe the development of Quality Culture in our university and have identified some of the measures we employ as indicators of this in the four segments of Table 1, examples of which are described below.

1. What people say at the individual level:
- Answers to questions set by external experts during the governmental quality audit (for example, the experts' report underlines that whilst people found self-evaluation quite demanding, they all said that it was interesting and useful).
- Discussions in specific committees: minutes of participative committees involved in quality processes at university or faculty level contain comments about their relevance, the evolution of practices, the involvement of various types of actors in the discussions and the development of ownership of quality issues.

2. What is said at the collective level:
- Quality concept of the university: there is a public and fully developed document about quality policies and processes at all levels of the university (university, faculty, central units, staff, etc.).
- Evolution of regulations: several regulations, for instance those dealing with faculties' contracts renewal, have been modified to be in line with the values of the Quality Culture.
- Appointment of a vice rector in charge of quality, which has been a clear sign of the importance given to quality issues.

3. What people do at the individual level:
- How students answer teaching evaluation questionnaires (qualitative analysis of comments which shows mainly constructive comments).
- Whether teachers complete their reports spontaneously (evolution of their reflexive involvement in writing their reports for renewal of their contracts).
- Involvement in self-evaluation of faculties (participation level, etc.).
- Involvement in teaching evaluation (answering rate, number of answers to open questions).

4. What is done at the collective level:
- The "rules of the game" of the quality process are in line with the values of the Quality Culture.
- Modifications of the action plan of the faculty following self-evaluation, indicating that quality processes are not bureaucratic activities but are used in daily governance.
- Communication about self-evaluation (for instance, self-evaluation that reflects on the academic year).

CONCLUSION

To promote excellence in order to contribute to the establishment of a world-class university, the HEI must not only have a good internal quality system but must also develop a Quality Culture, so that everyone in the institution sees the relevance of quality processes and is actively involved in their realization. Moreover, the author considers that the Quality Culture is a subculture of the organizational culture, underpinned by generally espoused values. A key issue in creating or developing it is to make explicit these values and priorities, so that they are infused into the organization, thus influencing collective and individual practices. The development of a Quality Culture is a long-term process, requiring the means to track its development and to assess whether there is real ownership by the participants. Regarding the latter, evaluation of ownership has to be based on what people say and do, because both aspects are important for "grass rooting" a Quality Culture.

A grid has been proposed to assist in the development of practical tools for tracking the establishment of such a culture and, although it still needs clearer definition, it certainly has proved useful at the University of Lausanne. Further, it has taken time to see the emergence of a Quality Culture at our university, but thanks to this grid we have been able to observe the beginnings of desirable concepts and attractive behaviours (e.g. increase in student satisfaction, peda-gogical innovation, more research projects, more money from external funds for research, etc.).

We have no ambition to promote undeniable truths or to tout undisputable measures for the development of a Quality Culture, but rather we seek to find some relevant indicators that are commensurate with achieving such a goal and that can provide useful information on progress towards this end. Of course, if these indicators are, in theory, to be applied to other settings, they will probably need to be contextualized. The metaphor of an iceberg could be applied to the concept of Quality Culture, in that it is not a completely transparent phenomenon, because for the most part it is submerged within an HEI. That is, the relation between values and behaviours, which is at the heart of the notion, is a complex issue involving hidden links that can therefore often lead to unpredicted outcomes with regard to the progress that is achieved. Moreover, extending the iceberg analogy, Quality Culture can be seen as having a number of different interpretations, depending on the angle from which it is surveyed.

Given the complexity of creating a Quality Culture, in this chapter we have provided an assessment of the intermediate steps that need to be undertaken if such an outcome is to be realized. It is only by identifying and addressing the obstacles to increasing the quality of research, teaching and services, which are the ultimate goal of QA processes, that an institution will be able to claim the accolade of being a world-class university.

REFERENCES

Birdi, K. (2007). Learning organizations. In S. Rogelberg (Ed.), *Encyclopedia of industrial and organizational psychology* (Vol. 1). Thousand Oaks, CA: Sage Publications.

Bontis. (2006). Ethical values and leadership: A study of business school deans in Canada. *International Journal of Business Governance and Ethics, 2*(3/4), 217–236.

Brennan, J., & Shah, T. (2000). Quality assessment and institutional change: Experience from 14 countries. *Higher Education, 40*, 331–349.

Cooke, R. A., & Lafferty, J. C. (1989, 2003). *Organizational culture inventory, human synergistics.* Plymouth, MI.

EUA. (2006). *Quality culture in European Universities: A bottom-up approach.* Brussels: EUA.

EUA. (2007). *Creativity in higher education.* Brussels: EUA.

Goodlad, S. (1995). *The quest for quality.* Buckingham: SRHE and Open University Press.

Gosling, D., & D'Andrea, M. (2001). Quality development: A new concept for higher education. *Quality in Higher Education, 7*(1), 7–17.

Harvey, L. (2002). The end of quality? *Quality in Higher Education, 8*(1), 5–22.

Harvey, L. (2006). Understanding quality. In E. Froment, J. Kohler, L. Purser, & L. Wilson (Eds.), *EUA Bologna handbook.* Article B.4.1-1, Berlin: Raabe Verlag.

Harvey, L., & Stensaker, B. (2008). Quality culture: Understandings, boundaries and linkages. *European Journal of Education, 43*(4), 427–442.

Henard, F. (2009). Soutenir la qualité de l'enseignement dans le supérieur: possible, utile ? Paper presented at the Qualita Conference, March18-20, 2003, Besançon , France.

Hofstede, G. (2001). *Culture's consequences.* Thousands Oaks, CA: Sage Publications.

Hsuan Feng Victor, D. (2007). World universities rankings: Generic and intangible features of world-class universities. In J. Sadlak & N. C. Liu (Eds.), *The world-class university and ranking: Aiming beyond status.* Bucharest: Unesco-Cepes, Presa Universitaria Clujeana.

Jaskyte, K. (2004). Transformational leadership, organizational culture, innovativeness in nonprofit organizations. *Nonprofit Management and Leadership, 15*(2), 153–168.

Javidan, M., House, R., Dorfman, P., Hanges, P., & Sully de Luque, M. (2006). Conceptualizing and measuring cultures and their consequences: A comparative review of GLOBE's and fofstede's approaches. *Journal of International Business Studies, 37,* 897–914.

Jones, J., & Darshi de Saram, D. (2005). Academic staff views of quality systems for teaching and learning: A Hong Kong case study. *Quality in Higher Education, 11*(1), 47–58.

Klenke, K. (2005). Corporate values as multi-level, multi-domain antecedents of leader behaviours. *International Journal of Manpower, 26*(1), 50–66.

Koslowsky, M., & Stashevsky, S. (2005). Organizational values and social power. *International Journal of Manpower, 26*(1), 23–34.

Kotter, J., & Cohen, D. (2002). *The heart of change,* Boston: Harvard Business School Press.

Koufteros, X., Nahm, A., Cheng, T., & Lai, K. (2007). An empirical assessment of a nomological network of organizational design constructs: From culture to structure to pull production to performance. *International Journal Production Economics, 106,* 468–492.

Kowalkiewicz, A. (2007). The impact of quality culture on quality of teaching- a case of business higher education in Poland. In *Embedding Quality Culture in higher Education.* Brussels: EUA.

Lanarès, J. (2008). Developing a quality culture. In E. Froment, J. Kohler, L. Purser, & L. Wilson (Eds.), *EUA Bologna handbook.* Article C.2.1-1. Berlin: Raabe Verlag.

McKenna E. (1994). *Business psychology and organizational behaviour.* Hove, UK: Lawrence Erlbaum Associates.

Meglino, B., Ravlin, E., & Adkin, C. (1989). A work values approach to corporate culture: A field test of the value congruence process and its relationship to individual outcomes. *Journal of Applied Psychology, 74*(3), 424–432.

Newton, J. (2002). Views from below: Academics coping with quality. *Quality in Higher Education, 8*(1), 39–61.

Niland, J. (2007). The challenge of building world-class universites. In J. Sadlak, & N. C. Liu (Eds.), *The world-class university and ranking: Aiming beyond status.* Bucharest: Unesco-Cepes, Presa Universitaria Clujeana.

Schein, E. (1990). Organizational culture. *American Psychologist, 45*(2), 109–119.

Scott, T. (2003). The Quantitative measurement of organizational culture in health care: a review of the available instruments. *Health Service Research, 38*(3), 1-37.

Senge, P. (1999). *La Danse du changement.* Paris: First.

Short, A. (2007). Bureaucracy: The enemy of a quality culture. In E. Froment, J. Kohler, L. Purser, & L. Wilson (Eds.), *EUA Bologna handbook,* Article B 4.5-1. Berlin: Raabe Verlag.

Staines, A. (2007). *Linking quality improvement programs and clinical results: From conception to implementation.* Unpublished, Ph.D. Thesis, Université Lyon 3, France.

Stensaker, B., (2008). Outcomes of quality assurance: A discussion of knowledge, methodology and validity. *Quality in Higher Education,* 14, 3-13.

Strydom, J., Zulu, N., & Murray, L. (2004). Quality, culture and change. *Quality in Higher Education, 10*(3), 207–217.

Sundrum, E. (2004). Moving beyond compliance and control: Building a values-based corporate governance culture supportive of a culture of mutual accountability. *International Journal of Business Governance and Ethics, 1*(2/3), 192–209.

Waldman, D., Sully de Luque, M., Washburn, N., & House, R. (2006). Cultural and leadership predictors of orporate social responsibility values of top management: A globe study of 15 countries. *Journal of International Business Studies, 37,* 823–837.

West, M. (1997). *Developing creativity in organizations.* Leicester: British Psychological Society.

Jacques Lanarès
University of Lausanne, Switzerland

OSAMA S. TAYEB AND ZOHEIR A. DAMANHOURI

15. TRANSFORMATION TOWARDS A WORLD-CLASS UNIVERSITY

Action and Prospects in the Case of King Abdulaziz University

INTRODUCTION

According to UNESCO, higher education has given ample proof of its viability over the centuries and of its ability to change and to induce change and progress in society. Society has become increasingly knowledge-based so that higher learning and research now act as essential components in the cultural, socio-economic and environmentally sustainable development of individuals, communities and nations. Higher education itself is confronted therefore with formidable challenges and must achieve radical change and renewal in the future (UNESCO, 2010).

In the era of knowledge, information and communication technologies (ICTs), prolific developments, globalization, and a focus on total quality, it has become imperative that traditional universities have to face transformation, become more responsive, and accentuate their capacities if they are to meet the increasing expectations with regards to their roles in knowledge societies. Universities are the homeland of knowledge, the main engines for its development and enhancement in all areas of scientific creativity and innovation, and the agents of societal development and progress. Accordingly, universities cannot become static or indolent organizations and to the contrary, they should always endeavour to adopt development initiatives and seek to achieve continuous improvements in the quality of their internal and external efficiencies. Moreover, to succeed in their missions they need to have clear visions in terms of their goals and strategies.

This chapter illustrates the experience of building a world-class university from an Arabic country's perspective, by considering the experience of King Abdulaziz University (KAU) and its envisaged hybrid identity.

KING ABDULAZIZ UNIVERSITY (KAU)

KAU is named after the founder of the Kingdom of Saudi Arabia and it is currently a dynamic and expanding higher education institution that is aspiring to be a more active agent of change, a value adding institution, a committed citizen to better serve society, a beacon of knowledge through its educational and innovative research activities and a quality higher education institution oriented towards being competitive and international. In 1964 the idea of establishing the university was initiated by a group of dedicated citizens and in 1967 the aim was fulfilled when

N.C. Liu et al., (eds.), Paths to a World-Class University: Lessons from Practices and Experiences, 275–281.

it was founded as a private higher education institution. Finally, in 1973 KAU became a public institution owing to its need for expansion and to attract funding from the state. Presently, it is the largest university in Saudi Arabia with approximately 50,000 full-time students , 4,500 teaching and 15,000 administrative and technical staff. Moreover, it has hundreds of departments and programmes of tertiary education in various disciplines (KAU, 2006 and 2010).

STRATEGIC PLANNING

Five years ago, KAU began its challenge of changing its old practices, by developing a new identity, recalibrating its roles, building capacities, reversing the pattern of wastage and underachievement, following effective management techniques, meeting quality standards, and adapting identified best practices. To fulfill this goal it charted its first strategic plan, which set out the dramatic functional, structural and cultural institutional changes that would be required (Damanhouri, 2007; Tayeb and Damanhouri, 2008). In particular, this came in response to a number of exploratory studies and workshops that had investigated KAU outputs, from which it had become abundantly clear that its educational system, quality, and ability to innovate were inadequate for meeting the challenges that it face if it were in the future to become an internationally ranked world-class university delivering high quality. Subsequently, members of KAU faculty drew on the experiences and practices of highly reputed universities through a series of visits, searches of the Internet, and reviewing appropriate publications. However, although we undertook the endeavour of investigating other institutions' practices from all corners of the globe, we are of the opinion that what best suits other universities would not necessarily fit KAU, because of its unique culture and assets and there we need customize our development in accordance with this.

As a consequence, it has been decided that KAU should re-focus its vision and mission so as to become a multi-faceted hybrid university. In this regard, its traditional identity as a comprehensive large university will be maintained, whilst a new emphasis will be placed on facets such as electronics, research, thinking and entrepreneurship. In accordance with these proposed future changes a wave of initiatives has been launched (Damanhouri, 2007; Tayeb and Damanhouri, 2008) and in particular a post of Vice-Presidency for Development (VPD) has been created so as to strengthen the university's capability and thereby match the international standards of quality in the advanced world.

HUMAN RESOURCE DEVELOPMENT

At KAU we have abstracted and absorbed the lessons of best practice and have reached the conclusion that long lasting performance in HE rests in high quality human resources. As a consequence, our human resource development (HRD) strategy is aimed at substantial improvement in all staff categories: teaching, research, administrative and technical. However, as students are our most valued output, we have kept their needs at the top of the list. In sum, we believe that maintaining an effective balance between all these entities by having sufficient and efficient HRD activities will form a solid platform for quality university education and synergistic performance.

HR represents the main pillar for any nation's progress in terms of its real wealth. In particular, at the university level it is the resource of highest value in terms of the achievement of its objectives of improved performance and competitiveness. Moreover, by adopting the human intellectual capital (IC) perspective, the intention is to pursue the goal of creating elite human resources with excellent intellectual skills, abilities, and experiences that will thus allow them to contribute intellectually in all milieux and perform at the highest levels. Furthermore, continuous development needs to be seen as a priority at both the micro and macro levels and in the modern university environment internal and external considerations must be incorporated in to HRD strategies. With regard to the internal environment, this refers to academic staff, administrative and technical staff, and students, whereas the external environment partially relates to students undertaking distance learning programmes as well as the administrative and academic support networks for these. In other words, each category should be provided with an effective agenda in terms of its future developmental activities.

In sum, HRD lies at the core of providing dynamic solutions that will enhance educators' competencies towards producing world-class education. Moreover, imaginative forward looking programmes should be devised on a continual basis so that teaching staff keep their knowledge up to date and abreast of best practice, both internally and externally. By so doing, we can ensure that our students' learning experiences are of the highest value, creativity and innovativeness across the university curriculum. As a result, when our students leave KAU they will be equipped to play a full part as modern citizens by taking up opportunities which will allow them to substantially contribute to the nation's social and economic success.

To serve such developments, universities rely on a number of key actors to optimize their operational capacity, most important of which are their faculty members. We at KAU concur strongly with this perspective and have set in train a range of staff development measures for our teaching staff. In this regard, training programmes are organized all the year around under the aegis of the Center for Teaching and Learning Development (CTLD). At the external level, an "Initiative for Innovation and Excellence Development Programmes" was launched by the Ministry of Higher Education which is now in its third year of delivery.

ICT DEVELOPMENT AND ITS APPLICATIONS IN KAU MANAGEMENT

KAU is embarking on open and distance learning based mainly on multimedia-rich e-learning, with the goal of reaching across Saudi Arabia. It will provide high quality education, training and development, from a lifelong learning perspective. Moreover, in the near future the system will be backed up by a satellite interactive TV channel. With regards to face-to-face learning on campus, steps are being taken to enrich the teaching process by supplementing these experiences with blended learning. Furthermore, there are plans to utilize e-learning to provide distance learning graduate studies programmes, for which a recent pilot study has indicated that there is substantial demand.

In addition, KAU is utilizing the concepts of electronic management with regards to all of its administrative, service, and information dissemination functions. With respect to this, ICT has been embedded throughout the university in terms of the administrative, teaching and learning structures and is a core element of staff and students' day to day practice. Nearly all university classes have been equipped with multimedia technology and a big initiative in relation to a comprehensive electronic course portfolio is near to completion and this will provide both staff and students at KAU a valuable tool able to deliver interactive teaching and learning. By adopting a two-pronged approach of on the one hand developing a positive and viable organizational culture through extensive staff development, and on the other aligning this with effective implementation of ICT infrastructure, the university is in the process of greatly enriching the experience for both staff and students.

KAU can expect a continuing rapid pace of development in information technology instruction, as the incoming students will increasingly be more techno-logically literate and therefore demand more sophisticated applications of technology when undertaking university courses. This inevitably will require us to maintain ongoing improvement in our ICT infrastructure and continual updating of the skills of the users. That is, with regards to the latter point, rolling training programmes will need to become an embedded feature of the institution for any individual crossing its threshold. Moreover, these programmes will need to be delivered on an external basis so as to facilitate the distance learning programmes across the nation, as discussed above. To date, our ICT system has gained KAU rewards and benefits which have resulted in our rank of excellence and our being cited as the leading university among all Saudi universities.

OTHER STRATEGIES AND ROUTES FOR TRANSFORMING KAU

Benchmarking Exercise

One important concern related to the implementation of the ICT strategy at KAU has been the need to enhance the quality of the university's data handling, information, and metrics so as to make decision-making more effective. Recently, in a quality drive, key performance indicators (KPI) have been put into place, but as yet these are only in the early application stage. In the longer run, the plan is to use these indicators for benchmarking KAU's year-on-year performance. More-over, the aim is to use the data collected in these exercises to compile online insti-tutional repositories and data warehouses, as KAU is committed to ensuring that this data is sensitively handled as well as being correctly stored, on a long term basis.

Building University Culture

KAU views every student as an internal customer of great potential value to his/her university and country. Being committed to each student's learning and subsequent academic success, the university is dedicated to having a positive and a strongly grounded culture, providing the appropriate learning conditions and having a balanced environment that stimulates the student to achieve their highest potential. Moreover, through creating such a learning environment the intention is to instil in the student high levels of motivation, clear purpose and effective communication, critical thinking and problem solving skills, so that they get the best possible experience during their course of study. Furthermore, the aim is to foster in the student the development of virtues of a mature, self-aware and responsible citizen, thereby enabling him/her to be a worthy member of society capable of great achievements.

KAU has been mobilizing its strengths in terms of its resources to maximize its capabilities and performance across all sectors. In this regard, one of the main routes has been an initiative in the sphere of teaching with regards to critical thinking, encouraging creativity and ideas generation, all of which being aimed at transforming KAU into a thinking university able to have an impact in the 21st century. Moreover, plans are afoot to develop curricula based on ideas generation coupled with student thinking clubs which will involve staff members having to take onboard new techniques that will provide them with the necessary skills for them to act as catalysts in the promotion of ideas and initiatives. With respect to this, one of the main strategies to be employed is the establishment of Think Tank Groups (TTGs) that will soon be expanded across the KAU campus and beyond. These TTGs are expected to generate plans to operationalize the results of thinking in the form of ideas produced by staff members of both an academic and administrative hue. In other words, maximum efforts are being placed on galvanizing the human intellectual capital inherent in the faculty and other employees of KAU.

One further goal of KAU at this present time is to imbue the notion of being an entrepreneurship university across the institution. The two main aspects regarding this endeavour are educational and business entrepreneurship. Regarding the former, curricula throughout the university need to be updated so as to highlight this prerogative and there is also a need to ensure that these are continually modified from now on, in accordance with practice gleaned from both the national and international levels. By so doing this will help to foster students' business orientations and consequently lead to their being able to make a valuable contribution to the private sector. In relation to business entrepreneurship, KAU has recently established incubator enterprises of both a business and scientific nature.

Accreditation and Quality

Another major route in our strategic development is the focus on accreditation and quality, where we are heading towards full academic accreditation of our programmes within the next five years. In this regard, at present 36 programmes have got international accreditation and institutional accreditation is to start this academic year, both through local and international accrediting bodies. Non academic accreditation has been gained for both the Blood Bank and recently, the 800 bed Hospital in the Medical Centre. In relation to the importance of the quality of KAU's administration, as discussed above, approximately 25 quality certificates of ISO 9001–2000 have been granted to the different units across the campus. In sum, the route of accreditation and quality at the university is a continuously improving story of success.

International Dimension

KAU values the efforts that have been made towards promoting and expanding its international presence and overseas cooperation. A number of strategies have been employed to this end, which include exchange visits, cooperation and twinning agreements, joint research, and the establishment of the International Advisory Board of KAU.

Focusing on Research Capacity

One further essential route being followed by the university relates to its becoming recognized as a research university. Given this is an enormous undertaking, we briefly summarize here our current achievements and areas for further development, these being: increasing the amount of public funds allocated for research; soliciting endowed scientific research chairs; endowment funds for research; establishing six research centres of excellence; promoting the conduct of research and its publication; investing in laboratory and research capabilities; winning research prizes; and establishing a research science park.

From the above it can be seen that improving research capacity is at the heart of KAU's current strategic mission and although to date some success has been achieved, this endeavour necessitates increased capacity, operational balance and continual maintenance. Further, it is not just a matter of creating research laboratories and other infrastructure, but it also involves the availability of capable human resources, sufficient funding, a responsive and tolerant culture and effective administration. In this regard, we are working to increase the numbers of research assistants, the numbers of Ph.D. research students, and the levels of research funding and therefore, we expect to achieve some significant research breakthroughs in the coming few years.

Finally, we are striving to be more consistent and focused in our efforts to foster and nurture public engagement by encouraging our faculty and students to bring their knowledge and skills to bear on pressing contemporary problems and, through communication, to encourage widespread public understanding and subsequent civil society involvement in our institution's future.

CONCLUSION AND LESSONS TO SHARE

By meeting the objectives in terms of building a strategic planning culture, set out in the First Five Year Strategic Plan, we believe that we have established a solid platform to proceed in setting our Second Five Year Strategic Plan (2010–2014) which is at present being carefully crafted. That is, KAU's achievements under the first plan have reassured us that we are moving in the right direction. However, there is some way to go before sufficient transformation will have taken place for KAU to become a world-class university. Nevertheless, we trust that our collaborative efforts during the Second Five Year Strategic Plan will ensure the veracity of our current motto, that being "KAU Takes-Off".

To conclude this chapter, we share a summary of the lessons learnt from KAU's experience. First, in the endeavour to follow a successful route of university capacity building resulting in the transformation into a world-class university, a viable culture and appropriate values need to be institutionalized at its inception. Second, to make the transformation to being a world-class university, it is necessary to develop human capacities in balanced and conscientious manner across the institution for all types of staff so as to take advantage of all potential intellectual human capital. Third, good management practices should be followed in the transformation process, in terms of, for instance quality assurance, strategic planning, and business process re-engineering (BPR). Fourth, a good starting point for the world-class university journey is to review best practice of current world-class universities and that of professional associations and organizations relating to higher education. Fifth, priority should be given to implementing fit-for-purpose ICT strategies across all areas of the institution, including administration, faculty, students and other stakeholders and ensuring that all those involved are kept abreast of new developments as well as continually buying in equipment of the highest standard. Sixth, during the transformation process, the university should seek to build a community involving the bringing together of all stakeholders who can then apply their thinking capabilities and creativity to achieve the vision set by the university leaders. Seventh, and last but certainly not least, through focusing on the ongoing enhancement of research capacity, university ranking status will be enhanced and the ultimate goal of becoming a world-class university will be that much nearer.

REFERENCES

Damanhouri, Z. A. (2007). *Transformation prospective into modern universities in the age of knowledge: The case of King Abdulaziz University (in Arabic)*. Paper presented at the First Arab Conference on "Arab Universities: Challenges and Future Horizons", Al-Rabat, Morroco.

King Abdulaziz University. (2006). *KAU: Steps towards progress*. Jeddah: King Abdulaziz University.

King Abdulaziz University. (2010). *The second KAU strategic plan (2010–2014)*. Unpublished Document, KAU.

Tayab, O. S., & Damanhouri, Z. A. (2008). *The transformation of university roles in human development in the Era of knowledge and ICTs: King Abdulaziz University*. Paper presented at the 4th International Barcelona Conference on Higher Education, Global University Network for Innovation, Barcelona, Spain.

UNESCO. (2010). *Reforming higher education*. Retrieved from http://www.unesco.org/en/highereducation/reform

Osama S. Tayeb and Zoheir A. Damanhouri
King Abdulaziz University, Saudi Arabia

ABOUT THE AUTHORS

Paul Şerban Agachi is President of the Academic Council of Babeş-Bolyai University (BBU), Cluj-Napoca, Romania; Professor of Process Control at the Department of Chemical Engineering of the same university; and member of the Academy of Technical Sciences of Romania. He has been involved in academic management at BBU since 1996, and occupied various positions such as Chancellor and Vice-Rector for Research. His responsibilities were related to design and implemention of the university strategies regarding reform, academic management and research. He was involved in the PHARE programme for the reform of higher education in Romania, and was a member of the National Council for Higher Education Reform (1998–2000). He has worked as a visiting associate at the California Institute of Technology, guest professor at Eötvös Lorand University, Budapest, and as a UNESCO higher education consultant in the "Oil for Food" programme in Iraq. In 2008, he was been involved as a senior HE expert in different strategic programs at national level aiming to evaluate the RDI system and to reform the research schools and doctoral programs.

Etienne Zé Amvela is a Full Professor of English Language and Linguistics. Etienne Zé Amvela holds a BA degree from State University of New York; an MS degree from Georgetown University, Washington, D.C.; and a Ph.D. degree in Applied Linguistics from the University of Leeds in England. Former Deputy Director General of Buea University Centre, former Director of the Advanced School of Translators and Interpreters, University of Buea; former Director of Academic Affairs and Cooperation, and former technical advisor to the Rector, University of Douala; Professor Zé Amvela is the former Vice-Rector in charge of inspection, and currently vice-rector in charge of internal control and evaluation at University of Yaounde I (UYI). Professor Zé Amvela is heading a research team on English in higher education in Cameroon; he is the coordinator of an international research project on French-English Bilingualism; he is also involved in four individual research projects. He has supervised numerous theses and has published widely on English language and linguistics. Professor Zé Amvela is member of several learned societies. He has been elevated to supreme dignitary for life by his native Ndong Clan in South Cameroon. Among other titles, he is an Officer of the National Order of Valour in Cameroon.

John T. Casteen III is President of University of Virginia. John Casteen has served as President of the University of Virginia since August 1990. During Professor Casteen's presidency, the University has been recognized for its leadership in educating minority students, for the quality of its undergraduate teaching and faculty research, and for its success in refinancing itself and restructuring its relationship with the state following historic reductions in state tax support. Professor Casteen was designated as the Outstanding Virginian in 1993. He was awarded the Gold Medal of the National Institute of Social Sciences in 1998, and the Virginia AIA's Architecture Medal for Virginia Service in 2004. He was inducted as a fellow of the American Academy of Arts and Sciences in October 2009. Professor Casteen is active in government, in business, and in all of the national organizations that represent academic interests. He served as two-time chair of the Association of American Universities. Professor Casteen stepped down in August 2010, after serving as the University of Virginia's president for 20 years.

Ying Cheng is a lecturer and the Executive Director of Center for World-Class Universities at Graduate School of Education, Shanghai Jiao Tong University (SJTU). He entered SJTU in 1996. There he obtained his Bachelor degree in Polymer Science and Engineering (2000) and his doctoral degree in S&T and Education Management (2007). From 2007 to 2008, Dr. Cheng went to Paris as a postdoctoral fellow attached to Ecole des Hautes Etudes en Sciences Sociales (EHESS) but conducted his studies at the Observatoire des Sciences et des Techniques (OST). He has worked full time at Office of Planning and Graduate School of Education (formerly Institute of Higher Education) of SJTU since 2000. His current research interests include the benchmarking, evaluation and ranking of universities, and the use, analysis and design of scientometric indicators and methods for supporting decision-making. He is responsible for the annual update and new development of the Academic Ranking of World Universities.

Romana Emilia Cucuruzan is an Assistant Professor at the Faculty of European Studies, Babeş Bolyai University, holding an MA degree in Human Resources Management and a Ph.D. degree in Economics and International Affairs (field of expertise: mobility and migration in EU). She has been collaborating for various projects with the Centre for University Development, Babeş Bolyai University. She is currently involved, as junior expert, in strategic projects for the HE system in Romania.

Adrian Curaj is President of the National Authority for Scientific Research, Bucharest, Romania, Professor of Innovation Management at Polytechnical University, Bucharest, and director of the Centre for Strategic Management and Quality Assurance in Higher Education. He occupied several strategic positions at national level such as Vice President of the National Council for Research Ethics, Executive Secretary of the National Council for Scientific Research in Higher Education, state counsellor for e-government, IT and scientific research. He was World Bank consultant for higher education and innovation, UNESCO consultant for science and technology, UNIDO consultant for foresight in science and techno-logy and evaluator for EU FP6, member of the external advisory board - PEOPLE, EU FP7.

Zoheir Damanhouri is Vice-President for Development at King Abdulaziz University (KAU) in Saudi Arabia, and an Associate Professor of Pharmacology in the Faculty of Medicine at KAU. He obtained his BSc degree from the University of Lancaster in the United Kingdom in 1982, and his master's degree from the University of Wales in 1983 and his Ph.D. degree from the same University in 1988.

Dr. Damanhouri started his academic career in the Department of Pharmacology in the Faculty of Medicine at KAU. He held various posts in the university as Deputy-Director of King Fahad Medicine Research Centre (1989–1990), Vice-Dean of the Faculty of Medicine (1990-1998), Chairman of the Pharmacology Department (1998–2002), Assistant Cultural Attache in the Royal Embassy of Saudi Arabia in Canada (2002–2004), Dean of Graduate Studies in the University (2005–2007) and later as Vice-President for Development in 2007 till present. He is a member of the Executive University Council since 2007, and headed many academic and administrative committees at KAU. He was a Visiting Professor at the University of Ottawa in Canada from 2003–2004. Dr. Damanhouri headed the Team that proposed the Strategic Plan (2005–2025) for Postgraduate Studies for Saudi Universities. He had over 25 publications in his speciality in pharmaceutical sciences as well as in strategic planning and postgraduate studies.

Michael Gallagher was Director of Policy and Planning at the Australian National University, prior to his appointment in May 2007 as Executive Director of the Go8. He was responsible for Commomwealth administration of higher education from 1990–1994 and again from 2000–2002. Between 1994 and 1996 he was head of Department of Employment Education and Training Corporate Services. From 2002 to 2003 he was head of Australian Education International within the Department of Education, Science and Training. He has a long history in the education industry including as a teacher and lecturer at secondary and tertiary level and as a member of the Wran Committee on Higher Education Financing in 1987. Michael has worked overseas for the World Bank and also continues to undertake work for the OECD on higher education issues.

Colin B. Grant was born in Edinburgh in 1966. He obtained his BA degree (First Class, Honours with Distinction) in Modern Languages from Heriot Watt University Edinburgh 1988 (one of the UK's leading Modern Languages Departments), and his Ph.D. Degree in Contemporary Literature from University of Bath, 1993. He was a Post-doctoral Fellow, at University of Siegen, Germany, in 1996 and 1997 (collaboration with Siegfried J. Schmidt). He has been Head of Department (2005), Dean of Faculty (2005–7), Dean of International Relations (2007–9), Pro Vice Chancellor, International Relations (2009–) at University of Surrey. Professor Grant has been invited to address audiences in Brazil, Korea, China, France, Germany, USA, and Finland. He has published nine books and over 50 articles and chapters, book series editor, research council assessor. A special issue of the Siegener Peridoicum zur Internationalen Empirischen Literaturwissenschaft was recently devoted to his work. Professor Grant is a native speaker of English and has native competence in German, Portuguese and French. He is a Mandarin learner. His details have been covered by Who's Who in the World since 2009.

V.V. Krishna is currently a Visiting Senior Research Fellow (2008–2010) at Asia Research Institute, NUS. He is a Professor in Science Policy, Centre for Studies in Science Policy, School of Social Sciences, Jawaharlal Nehru University (JNU),

New Delhi; and Visiting Professor, United Nations University - Institute of Advanced Study, Japan (2009–2012).

Jacques Lanarès is Vice Rector of the University of Lausanne, Switzerland. He is in charge of the Development of Teaching, Quality and Interface between science and society. He has created and developed the Teaching Support Unit of the University of Lausanne and was also in charge of the development of the Quality Project in this University. Beyond his institutional responsibilities he is involved in Quality matters at national and international level. He is the Chairman of the Quality Network for Swiss Higher Education Institutions. It is the board of vice presidents in charge of quality and of quality executives from all Swiss universities. This board is the body of reference for the Conference of Swiss University Rectors (CRUS) for Quality matters and the interlocutor of the Swiss Rectors to the Swiss Quality and Accreditation agency (OAQ). He is expert for Quality issues in Higher Education for several bodies such as the European University Association (EUA), the French agency for Quality in Higher Education (AERES), the Irish Universities Quality Board (IUQB) and the World Bank. He has published several papers dealing with Quality issues. He obtained a Ph.D. in Neuropsychology and Genetic Psychology at the University of Geneva and worked as researcher and clinician in that field. Thereafter, He narrowed the focus on Memory, Learning and Adult Education. His current teaching is in the field of Teaching and Learning in Higher Education and Adult Education.

Nian Cai Liu took his undergraduate studies in chemistry at Lanzhou University of China. He obtained his master's and Ph.D. degrees in polymer science and engineering from Queen's University at Kingston, Canada. Professor Liu worked as an associate and full professor at the School of Chemistry and Chemical Engineering of Shanghai Jiao Tong University from 1993 to 1998. He moved to the field of higher education research in 1999. He is now the Dean of Graduate School of Education and the Director of Center for World-Class Universities, Shanghai Jiao Tong University. His current research interests include world-class universities, science policy, and strategic planning of universities. He has published extensively in both Chinese and English journals. The Academic Ranking of World Universities, an online publication of his group, has attracted attentions from all over the world. He is on the advisory boards of Scientometrics, Research Evaluation, Journal of Engineering Education and Higher Education of Europe.

Harold M. Maurer, M.D., Chancellor of the University of Nebraska Medical Center since December 1998, and a pediatric hematologist and oncologist, served as Dean of the College of Medicine in the prior five years. Dr. Maurer has been recognized widely for his expertise in rhabdomyosarcoma. The Children's Oncology Group awarded Dr. Maurer with the Lifetime Achievement Award. His achievements at UNMC include merging of University Hospital and Clarkson Hospital to form the Nebraska Medical Center, leading the institution to new heights of excellence in education, research and clinical care, including the construction of many new facilities, including the Maurer Center for Public Health. Among the honours and awards received, he was named as the Midlander of the Year, King of Ak-Sar-Ben, Omaha Press Club awardee, given the "Men of Honour" award, and was inducted into the Omaha Business Hall of Fame.

Simon Marginson is a Professor of Higher Education in the Centre for the Study of Higher Education at the University of Melbourne, Australia. The Centre is located in the Melbourne Graduate School of Education. Simon began academic life in 1993 as a specialist on national higher education policy. In recent years he has worked primarily on globalization, comparative and international higher education, and creativity in knowledge economies. He has completed policy papers for the OECD, the European Commission and governments in Australia, New Zealand, Malaysia, Hong Kong and Vietnam. Active as a scholar in Asia, Europe and the Americas, he sits on the editorial boards of among others Educational Researcher, Higher Education, Journal of Higher Education, Higher Education Policy, and Thesis Eleven. His books include The Enterprise University (with Mark Considine, 2000), Prospects of Higher Education (2007), Global Creation: Space, Mobility and Synchrony in the Age of the Knowledge Economy (with Peter Murphy and Michael Peters, 2010), International Student Security (with Chris Nyland, Erlenawati Sawir and Helen Forbes-Mewett, 2010), and Higher Education in the Asia-Pacific: Strategic Responses to Globalization (with Sarjit Kaur and Erlenawati Sawir, forthcoming).

Chris Marlin has been Pro-Vice-Chancellor (International) at the University of Sussex in the United Kingdom since late 2009. Previously, at Flinders University in Australia, he was Head of Computer Science from 1992–1998, Pro-Vice-Chancellor (Research) from 1998–2004 and Deputy Vice-Chancellor (Research) from 2004–2009. Prior to joining Flinders University, he held academic positions in Computer Science at the University of Iowa in the United States and at the University of Adelaide in Australia. From 2003–2009, Professor Marlin was the inaugural Chair of South Australia's Information Economy Advisory Board, advising the Minister for Science and Information Economy in the South Australian government on all matters relating to information technology, including broadband infrastructure, workforce planning and industry development. He was also a member of the Premier's Science and Research Council in South Australia over an extended period. From 2003 to 2005, he was the inaugural Chair of the Research Group for Innovative Research Universities Australia, a group consisting of six Australian universities. He was Chair of the National Committee of the Deputy and Pro Vice-Chancellors (Research) for Australia in 2000. A Fellow of the Australian Institute of Company Directors, he has been a director of a number of companies.

Camelia Moraru is an Assistant Professor at the Faculty of European Studies and expert at the Centre for University Development at Babeş-Bolyai University (BBU), Cluj-Napoca, Romania. She is the co-editor of the Babeş-Bolyai University's Journal of University Development and Academic Management. She has been working since 1998 with various educational institutions and with several NGOs from Romania, Hungary or UK that implemented different types of educational projects. She is conducting research on higher education system change, institutional evaluation and development, and the evaluation of students' research competencies in a multidisciplinary team and published several articles on Romanian universities classification and rankings together with Paul Șerban Agachi and Panaite Nica.

Seeram Ramakrishna is Research Strategy Vice-President of the National University of Singapore (NUS). He is a Professor of Mechanical Engineering and former Dean of NUS Faculty of Engineering from 2003 to 2008. He is an International Fellow of UK Royal Academy of Engineering and a Fellow of American Association for the Advancement of Science. He is a recipient of Changjiang Professorship of China, ASEAN Outstanding Engineering Award, NUS Outstanding Researcher Award, Lee Kuan Yew Fellowship, and Cambridge Nehru Scholarship.

Natalia Ruiz Rodgers is Academic Vice-Rector of National University of Colombia. In this position, she provides leadership in relation to the new academic process. Furthermore, she has worked to place the National University to the higher international level. Prior to taking up this position, Professor Ruiz Rodgers held the Chair as a Vice Rector for Research; Campus Vice Rector; Academic Director, Executive Dean and Vice Dean of the Faculty of Sciences. Her previous research and teaching positions were at Institute of Natural Sciences of Colombia, Royal Botanical Garden of Madrid, and Jacob Blaustein Institute for Desert Research of Israel. In addition as a biologist and doctor of ecology, she has been professor for almost twenty years in several Colombian universities. Professor Ruiz Rodgers' research interests are concerned with the study of plant systemology and ecology, but lately her contributions have ranged from basic research into the development of research systems and research groups; as well as research doctorates, and strategic lines. She has produced several scientific journal articles, book chapters, technical reports and conference papers, and served as Peer Evaluator for the National Ministry of Education of Colombia. She has also supervised the research theses of many master's and doctoral students.

Jamil Salmi, a Moroccan education economist, is the World Bank's tertiary education coordinator and was the Bank's official representative at the UNESCO World Conference on Higher Education (WCHE, Paris, October 1998) and at the WCHE + 5 Conference in June 2003. Dr. Salmi was a member of the Board of the African Virtual University in 2003 and 2004. He is currently a member of the International Advisory Network of the UK Leadership Foundation for Higher Education, OECD's expert group on Assessing Higher Education Learning Outcomes, the Editorial Committee of OECD's Journal of Higher Education Management and Policy, and the International Rankings Expert Group. Dr. Salmi in the principal author of the Bank's new Tertiary Education Strategy entitled "Constructing Knowledge Societies: New Challenges for Tertiary Education". He was also responsible for the preparation of the World Bank's first Policy Paper on Higher Education, published in July 1994 under the title "Higher Education: Lessons of Experience". In the past thirteen years, Dr. Salmi has provided policy and technical advice on tertiary education reform to the governments of more than 40 countries. Dr. Salmi has also guided the strategic planning efforts of several public and private universities in Colombia, Kenya, Madagascar, Mexico and Peru. Prior to joining the World Bank in December 1986, Dr. Salmi was a professor of education economics at the National Institute of Education Planning in Rabat, Morocco. He also worked as a consultant to various ministries, national professional associations, and international organizations. Dr. Salmi is a graduate of the French Grande Ecole ESSEC. He holds a master's degree in Public and International Affairs from the University of Pittsburgh (USA) and a Ph.D. in Development Studies from the University of Sussex (UK). He also completed an Executive Development Program at Harvard Business School. Dr. Salmi is the author of five books and numerous articles on education and development issues. Over the past thirteen years, he has written extensively on tertiary education reform issues.

Osama Tayeb is President of King Abdulaziz University (KAU) from 2003 till present, and a professor of Pharmacology in the Faculty of Medicine at KAU. He obtained his BPharm Degree in Pharmaceutical Sciences in 1976, and his Ph.D. from Vanderbilt University in Nashville, Tennessee in the USA in 1981. He started his academic career as Assistant Professor in the Dept of Pharmacology at KAU, then promoted to Associate Professor in 1986 and to a full Professor in 1991. Prof Tayeb held various academic/administrative and leading posts at KAU as Vice-Dean for postgraduate Studies and Research in the Faculty of Medicine (1983–1987), Dean of the Faculty of Medicine and Allied Medical Sciences (1990–1995), Vice-President of KAU University (1995–2001) and currently the President of KAU from 2003 till present. He is a member of large number of governmental/ministerial committees in Saudi Arabia both in government and the private sector. He has more than 60 publications in various areas of pharmaceutical sciences and member of the American Pharmacology and Experimental Therapy Society and the American Academy for Clinical Toxicology.

Qi Wang is a lecturer at the Graduate School of Education (GSE), Shanghai Jiao Tong University (SJTU). She completed her MA and Ph.D. studies in the Department of Education, University of Bath, UK, from September 2002 to November 2008. She joined SJTU in May 2009 and works in the Centre for World-Class Universities. Her research interests include building world-class universities, employability building and skill training, and educational sociology.

Marijk van der Wende is a Professor of Higher Education at the Vrije University Amsterdam and a Visiting Professor at the Centre for Higher Education Policy Studies (CHEPS) at the University of Twente. She is the founding Dean of Amsterdam University College, an international liberal arts and science college being established jointly by the Vrije University Amsterdam and the Universiteit van Amsterdam. She chairs the Honours programme and the Internationalization Board of the Vrije Universiteit Amsterdam. She is the President of the Governing Board of the Programme on Institutional Management in Higher Education (IMHE) of the OECD, member of the Governing Board of Nuffic, member of the Scientific Board of the Dutch Military Academy, and member of various national and international advisory committees and editorial boards. Her research focuses on innovation in higher education, the impact of globalization on higher education and related processes of internationalization and Europeanization. She published widely on how these processes affect higher education systems, their structure and governance, institutional strategies, curriculum design, quality assurance methods. She holds a master's and Ph.D. degree in educational sciences (from the University of Amsterdam and the University of Utrecht respectively).

Akiyoshi Yonezawa is an Associate Professor at the Center for the Advancement of Higher Education (CAHE) in Tohoku University. With sociological background, he is mainly researching on the comparative higher education policies, especially focusing on world-class universities, quality assurance of higher education, and public-private relationship of higher education. Before moving to Tohoku University in April 2007, he has worked at National Institution for Academic Degrees and University Evaluation (NIAD-UE), Hiroshima University, OECD and Tokyo University.

Jialin C. Zheng is currently a Professor of Pharmacology/Experimental Neuroscience and Pathology/Microbiology at the University of Nebraska Medical Center (UNMC). He also serves as the Associate Dean for Graduate Studies-International Affairs and the Director of Asia Pacific Rim Development Program at UNMC. Dr. Zheng is the principal investigator on two R01 grants, one R21 grant and one project within a program project grant and a grant that is part of the Centers of Biomedical Research Excellence from the National Institutes of Health.

GLOBAL PERSPECTIVES ON HIGHER EDUCATION

Volume 1
WOMEN'S UNIVERSITIES AND COLLEGES
An International Handbook
Francesca B. Purcell, Robin Matross Helms, and Laura Rumbley (Eds.)
ISBN 978-90-77874-58-5 hardback
ISBN 978-90-77874-02-8 paperback

Volume 2
PRIVATE HIGHER EDUCATION
A Global Revolution
Philip G. Altbach and D. C. Levy (Eds.)
ISBN 978-90-77874-59-2 hardback
ISBN 978-90-77874-08-0 paperback

Volume 3
FINANCING HIGHER EDUCATION
Cost-Sharing in International perspective
D. Bruce Johnstone
ISBN 978-90-8790-016-8 hardback
ISBN 978-90-8790-015-1 paperback

Volume 4
UNIVERSITY COLLABORATION FOR INNOVATION
Lessons from the Cambridge-MIT Institute
David Good, Suzanne Greenwald, Roy Cox, and Megan Goldman (Eds.)
ISBN 978-90-8790-040-3 hardback
ISBN 978-90-8790-039-7 paperback

Volume 5
HIGHER EDUCATION
A Worldwide Inventory of Centers and Programs
Philip G. Altbach, Leslie A. Bozeman, Natia Janashia, and Laura E. Rumbley
ISBN 978-90-8790-052-6 hardback
ISBN 978-90-8790-049-6 paperback

Volume 6
FUTURE OF THE AMERICAN PUBLIC RESEARCH UNIVERSITY
R. L. Geiger, C. L. Colbeck, R. L. Williams, and C. K. Anderson (Eds.)
ISBN 978-90-8790-048-9 hardback
ISBN 978-90-8790-047-2 paperback

Volume 13
HIGHER EDUCATION IN TURMOIL: THE CHANGING WORLD OF
INTERNATIONALIZATION
Jane Knight
ISBN 978-90-8790-521-7 hardback
ISBN 978-90-8790-520-0 paperback

Volume 14
UNIVERSITY AND DEVELOPMENT IN LATIN AMERICA: SUCCESSFUL
EXPERIENCES OF RESEARCH CENTERS
Simon Schwartzman (Ed.)
ISBN 978-90-8790-524-8 hardback
ISBN 978-90-8790-523-1 paperback

Volume 15
BUYING YOUR WAY INTO HEAVEN: EDUCATION AND CORRUPTION IN
INTERNATIONAL PERSPECTIVE
Stephen P. Heyneman (Ed.)
ISBN 978-90-8790-728-0 hardback
ISBN 978-90-8790-727-3 paperback

Volume 16
HIGHER EDUCATION AND THE WORLD OF WORK
Ulrich Teichler
ISBN 978-90-8790-755-6 hardback
ISBN 978-90-8790-754-9 paperback

Volume 17
FINANCING ACCESS AND EQUITY IN HIGHER EDUCATION
Jane Knight (Ed.)
ISBN 978-90-8790-767-9 hardback
ISBN 978-90-8790-766-2 paperback

Volume 18
UNIVERSITY RANKINGS, DIVERSITY, AND THE NEW LANDSCAPE OF
HIGHER EDUCATION
Barbara M. Kehm and Bjørn Stensaker (Eds.)
ISBN 978-90-8790-815-7 hardback
ISBN 978-90-8790-814-0 paperback

Volume 19
HIGHER EDUCATION IN EAST ASIA: NEOLIBERALISM AND THE
PROFESSORIATE
Gregory S. Poole and Ya-chen Chen (Eds.)
ISBN 978-94-6091-127-9 hardback
ISBN 978-94-6091-126-2 paperback

Volume 20
ACCESS AND EQUITY: COMPARATIVE PERSPECTIVES
Heather Eggins (Ed.)
ISBN 978-94-6091-185-9 hardback
ISBN 978-94-6091-184-2 paperback

Volume 21
UNDERSTANDING INEQUALITIES IN AND BY HIGHER EDUCATION
Gaële Goastellec (Ed.)
ISBN 978-94-6091-307-5 hardback
ISBN 978-94-6091-306-8 paperback

Volume 22
TRENDS IN GLOBAL HIGHER EDUCATION: TRACKING AN ACADEMIC
REVOLUTION
Philip G. Altbach, Liz Reisberg and Laura E. Rumbley
ISBN 978-94-6091-338-9 hardback
ISBN 978-94-6091-339-6 paperback

Volume 23
PATHS TO A WORLD-CLASS UNIVERSITY: LESSONS FROM PRACTICES
AND EXPERIENCES
Nian Cai Liu, Qi Wang and Ying Cheng
ISBN 978-94-6091-354-9 hardback
ISBN 978-94-6091-353-2 paperback

Lightning Source UK Ltd.
Milton Keynes UK
14 January 2011

165708UK00001B/19/P